Lecture Notes in Computer Science　　10074

Commenced Publication in 1973
Founding and Former Series Editors:
Gerhard Goos, Juris Hartmanis, and Jan van Leeuwen

More information about this series at http://www.springer.com/series/7410

Lidong Chen · David McGrew
Chris Mitchell (Eds.)

Security
Standardisation
Research

Third International Conference, SSR 2016
Gaithersburg, MD, USA, December 5–6, 2016
Proceedings

 Springer

Editors
Lidong Chen
Computer Security Division
NIST
Gaithersburg, MD
USA

David McGrew
Cisco Systems Inc.
San Jose
USA

Chris Mitchell
University of London
Egham
UK

ISSN 0302-9743   ISSN 1611-3349 (electronic)
Lecture Notes in Computer Science
ISBN 978-3-319-49099-1   ISBN 978-3-319-49100-4 (eBook)
DOI 10.1007/978-3-319-49100-4

Library of Congress Control Number: 2016955996

LNCS Sublibrary: SL4 – Security and Cryptology

Printed on acid-free paper

This Springer imprint is published by Springer Nature
The registered company is Springer International Publishing AG
The registered company address is: Gewerbestrasse 11, 6330 Cham, Switzerland

Preface

The Third International Conference on Research in Security Standardization was held at the National Institute for Standards and Technology (NIST), in Gaithersburg, MD, USA, during December 5–6, 2016. This event was the third in what is now an established series of conferences focusing on the theory, technology, and applications of security standards.

SSR 2016 built on the successful SSR 2014 and SSR 2015 conferences, held near London, UK, in December 2014 and in Tokyo, Japan, during December 2015. The proceedings of the 2014 and 2015 conferences were published in volumes 8893 and 9497 of the *Lecture Notes in Computer Science*.

The conference program consisted of two invited talks, 12 contributed papers, and a panel session. We would like to express our special thanks to the distinguished keynote speakers, John Kelsey (NIST, USA) and William Whyte (Security Innovation, USA), who gave very enjoyable and enlightening talks. Special thanks are also due to Salvatore Francomacaro (NIST, USA) who organized the panel session on "Can Security Standards Be Ahead of the Game?," and to the panel members, who included: Liqun Chen, Eric Hibbard, Russ Housley, and David McGrew.

Out of 18 submissions with authors from nine countries, 12 papers were selected, presented at the conference, and included in these proceedings. The accepted papers cover a range of topics in the field of security standardization research, including hash-based signatures, algorithm agility, secure protocols, access control, secure APIs, payment security, and key distribution.

The success of this event depended critically on the help and hard work of many people, whose help we gratefully acknowledge. First, we heartily thank the Program Committee and the additional reviewers, listed on the following pages, for their careful and thorough reviews. Each paper was reviewed by at least three people, and on average by almost four. A significant time was spent discussing the papers. Thanks must also go to an (anonymous) hard-working shepherd for guidance and helpful advice on improving one of the papers. We also thank the general chair for her excellent organization of the conference, as well as Sara Kerman from NIST for her expert and dedicated assistance in ensuring the success of the conference.

We must also sincerely thank the authors of all submitted papers. We further thank all the authors of papers in this volume for revising their papers in accordance with the various referee suggestions and for returning the source files in good time. The revised versions were not checked by the Program Committee, and so authors bear final responsibility for their contents.

Thanks are due to the staff at Springer for their help with producing the proceedings. We must further thank the developers and maintainers of the EasyChair software, which greatly helped simplify the submission and review processes, as well as the production of these proceedings.

December 2016

David McGrew
Chris Mitchell

Organization

Security Standardization Research 2016
NIST, Gaithersburg, MD, USA
December 5–6, 2016

General Chair

Lidong Chen   NIST, USA

Program Chairs

David McGrew   Cisco, USA
Chris Mitchell   Royal Holloway, University of London, UK

Steering Committee

Liqun Chen   Hewlett-Packard Labs, UK
Shin'ichiro Matsuo   MagicCube Inc., USA
Chris Mitchell   Royal Holloway, University of London, UK
Bart Preneel   Katholieke Universiteit Leuven, Belgium
Sihan Qing   Peking University, China

Program Committee

Colin Boyd   NTNU, Norway
Nancy Cam-Winget   Cisco Systems, USA
Liqun Chen   Hewlett Packard Labs, UK
Takeshi Chikazawa   IPA, Japan
Cas Cremers   University of Oxford, UK
Riaal Domingues   DDSI ISD, South Africa
Scott Fluhrer   Cisco Systems, USA
Aline Gouget   Gemalto, France
Feng Hao   Newcastle University, UK
Jens Hermans   KU Leuven - ESAT/COSIC and iMinds, Belgium
Deukjo Hong   Chonbuk National University, Republic of Korea
Dirk Kuhlmann   HP Enterprise Labs, UK
Xuejia Lai   Shanghai Jiaotong University, China
Pil Joong Lee   Postech, Republic of Korea
Peter Lipp   Graz University of Technology, Austria
Joseph Liu   Monash University, Australia
Javier Lopez   University of Malaga, Spain
Shin'ichiro Matsuo   MagicCube Inc., USA

Catherine Meadows	NRL, USA
Jinghua Min	China Electronic Cyberspace Great Wall Co., Ltd., China
Atsuko Miyaji	School of Information Science, Japan Advanced Institute of Science and Technology, Japan
Valtteri Niemi	University of Turku, Finland
Pascal Paillier	CryptoExperts, France
Kenneth Paterson	Royal Holloway, University of London, UK
Sihan Qing	School of Software and Microelectronics, Peking University, China
Kai Rannenberg	Goethe University Frankfurt, Germany
Matt Robshaw	Impinj, USA
Christoph Ruland	University of Siegen, Germany
Mark Ryan	University of Birmingham, UK
Kazue Sako	NEC, Japan
Ben Smyth	Huawei, France
Jacques Traore	Orange Labs, France
Claire Vishik	Intel Corporation, UK
Debby Wallner	National Security Agency, USA
Michael Ward	MasterCard, UK
Yanjiang Yang	Huawei Singapore Research Center, Singapore
Jianying Zhou	Institute for Infocomm Research, Singapore

Additional Reviewers

Eom, Sungwook
Lee, Eunsung
Long, Yu
Mori, Kengo
Omote, Kazumasa

Schmitz, Christopher
Szepieniec, Alan
Tesfay, Welderufael
Tran, Thao

Contents

Analyzing and Fixing the QACCE Security of QUIC

Hideki Sakurada[1(✉)], Kazuki Yoneyama[2], Yoshikazu Hanatani[3],
and Maki Yoshida[4]

[1] NTT Communication Science Laboratories, NTT Corporation, Kanagawa, Japan
`sakurada.hideki@lab.ntt.co.jp`
[2] Ibaraki University, Ibaraki, Japan
`kazuki.yoneyama.sec@vc.ibaraki.ac.jp`
[3] Corporate Research & Development Center, Toshiba Corporation,
Kanagawa, Japan
`yoshikazu.hanatani@toshiba.co.jp`
[4] Network Security Research Institute, National Institute of Information and
Communications Technology (NICT), Tokyo, Japan
`maki-yos@nict.go.jp`

Abstract. QUIC is a secure transport protocol developed by Google. Lychev et al. proposed a security model (QACCE model) to capture the security of QUIC. However, the QACCE model is very complicated, and it is not clear if security requirements for QUIC are appropriately defined. In this paper, we show the first formal analysis result of QUIC using automated security verification tool ProVerif. Our symbolic model formalizes the QACCE model and the specification of QUIC. As the result of the verification, we find three attacks against QUIC in the QACCE model. It means that the Lychev et al.'s security proofs are not correct. We discuss why such attacks occur, and clarify there are unnecessarily strong points in the QACCE model. Finally, we give a way to improve the QACCE model to exactly address the appropriate security requirements.

Keywords: QUIC · QACCE model · Automated verification · ProVerif

1 Introduction

1.1 Backgrounds

As mobile Internet devices (smartphones, tablet computers, wearable computers, etc.) are growing explosively, various web applications are used in our daily life. Devices and servers of applications frequently execute transport protocols to communicate via the Internet. Hence, to reduce latency of transport protocols is an important issue.

TLS (Transport Layer Security) [1] is the most widely used secure transport protocol. However, latency of TLS on establishing a connection between a device and a server is not low, and it may be a bottleneck of web applications

© Springer International Publishing AG 2016
L. Chen et al. (Eds.): SSR 2016, LNCS 10074, pp. 1–31, 2016.
DOI: 10.1007/978-3-319-49100-4_1

in restricted bandwidth networks. Thus, several transport protocols [2–5] have been studied to achieve both low latency and sufficient security. QUIC (Quick UDP Internet Connection) [5] is one of the most promising candidates of such protocols.

QUIC was developed by Google and implemented as a secure transport protocol of Google Chrome in 2013. TLS is the protocol on TCP (Transmission Control Protocol), and relies on the packet retransmission mechanism of TCP. On the other hand, QUIC is the protocol on UDP (User Datagram Protocol), and has a specific packet retransmission mechanism to reduce latency. Also, the number of rounds for key exchange is smaller than that of TLS. QUIC is widely implemented in Google's servers, and Google Chrome is now the most popular browser (it takes 60.5 % of worldwide desktop browser usage in April 16, 2016) [6]. Therefore, to clarify the security of QUIC is very important in practice. However, no formal security discussion is given in Google's documents.

There are some previous studies to formally define the security requirements for QUIC and to prove the security under appropriate assumptions of building blocks. Fischlin and Günther [7] proposed a security model for multi-stage key exchange protocols based on the Bellare-Rogaway model [8], and prove the key exchange part of QUIC satisfies their security definition. Their work is only for the key exchange part, and it still not clear if the entire protocol of QUIC is secure. Lychev et al. [9] proposed a new security model for Quick Connections (QC) protocols, called Quick Authenticated and Confidential Channel Establishment (QACCE) model. QC protocols represent an abstraction of transport protocols including QUIC and TLS1.3 [10]. The QACCE model captures the security of the entire transport protocol as well as the key exchange part. In the QACCE model, three security requirements are formulated: the server impersonation resistance, the channel corruption resistance, and the IP spoofing resistance. The server impersonation resistance guarantees that any adversary cannot impersonates an honest server. The channel corruption resistance guarantees that any adversary cannot reveal information about groups of messages exchanged between a client and a server without corrupting the server before or during the session. The IP spoofing resistance guarantees that any adversary cannot make the server accept a connection request on behalf of a client who did not request the connection to the server. These security requirements seem reasonable for QC protocols. They further proved the security of QUIC in the QACCE model. However, actually, the QACCE model is very complicated; and thus, it is hard to understand if the model captures requirements just enough.

1.2 Our Contribution

We show the first automated security verification of QUIC based on the QACCE model. We use verification tool ProVerif [11–14] because ProVerif can generically deal with subtle security definitions like the QACCE model.

First, we formalize a symbolic model for QUIC and the QACCE model. Though the specification of QUIC contains updates of state and time synchronizations, ProVerif cannot directly support state and time. Hence, we reformulate the protocol of QUIC to avoid the direct management of state and time. Three security requirements of the QACCE model are exactly formalized as verification queries of ProVerif.

Next, we verify QUIC based on our symbolic formalization. If Lychev et al.'s security proofs were correct, ProVerif would be also expected to decide "secure". However, ProVerif finds concrete attacks against all three security requirements. These attacks break the matching between a client and a server by modifying protocol flows. It causes that the client and the server believe distinct sessions as the matching session. Therefore, Lychev et al.'s security proofs are actually not correct.

Finally, we discuss the reasons why attacks occur. We conclude that there is no practical impact to the security of QUIC. The reason of attacks is that the QACCE model contains unnecessary strong definitions against desirable security requirements. Actually, by appropriately weakening the model, these attacks are easily prevented. We show how to weaken the QACCE model to capture the security of QUIC just enough.

2   Definition of QC Protocol

In this section we quote the definition of a *Quick Connections (QC)* protocol in [9], which is a communication protocol between a client and a server (the latter holds a public key and the corresponding secret key). The parties first agree on an initial session key, which can be used to exchange data until the final key is set. After the final key is set, it is used for further data exchange.

The protocol is associated with the security parameter λ, a server key generation protocol Kg that on input λ returns public and secret keys, an authenticated encryption with associated data scheme $\text{AEAD} = (\mathcal{E}, \mathcal{D})$ with key space $\{0,1\}^{\lambda}$, header space $\{0,1\}^*$, message space $\{0,1\}^*$, an IV-extraction function get_iv that takes a key and a header and outputs an IV $\in \{0,1\}^n$ for each message to be encrypted or decrypted via the associated AEAD, and a scfg_gen function that the server can use to update part of its global state scfg. The server can maintain global state other than its scfg. All global state is initially set to ε. A protocol's execution is associated with the universal notion of time, which is divided into discrete periods $\tau_1, \tau_2, \ldots$. The keys are generated via $(pk, sk) \leftarrow_R \mathsf{Kg}(\lambda)$. The input of each party (representing what parties know at the beginning) consists of the public key of the server pk and the list of messages $M^{send} = M_1, \ldots, M_m$ for some $m \in \mathbb{N}$ and where each $M_i \in \{0,1\}^*$, that a party needs to send securely (M^{send} can also be ε). The server has an additional input: the secret key. All parties can keep global state. We suppose that the client and server are given vectors of messages as input.

A QC protocol consists of four phases. Each message exchanged by the parties must belong to some unique stage, but the second and third stages may overlap:

Stage 1: Initial Key Agreement. At the end of this stage, each party sets the initial key variable $ik = (ik_c, ik_s, iaux)$, where $iaux \in \{0,1\}^*$ (initially set to ε) is any additional information used for encryption and decryption.

Stage 2: Initial Data Exchange. In this stage, messages from the input data list can be transmitted using the associated AEAD scheme and the key ik. The server uses ik_c to encrypt and ik_s to decrypt, whereas the client uses ik_s to encrypt and ik_c to decrypt. At the end of this stage, each party outputs the list of messages $M^{iget} = M_1, \ldots, M_{m'}$ for some $m' \in \mathbb{N}$ and where each $M_i \in \{0,1\}^*$, (M^{iget} can also be ε), representing the messages the party received in the initial data exchange phase.

Stage 3: Key Agreement. At the end of this stage, each party sets the session key variable $k = (k_c, k_s, aux)$, where $aux \in \{0,1\}^*$ (initially set to ε) is any additional information used for encryption and decryption.

Stage 4: Data Exchange. In this stage, messages from the input data list can be sent using the associated AEAD scheme and the key k. The server uses k_c to encrypt and k_s to decrypt, whereas the client uses k_s to encrypt and k_c to decrypt. At the end of this stage, each party outputs the list of messages $M^{get} = M_1, \ldots, M_{m''}$ for some $m'' \in \mathbb{N}$ and where each $M_i \in \{0,1\}^*$, (M^{get} can also be ε), representing the messages the party received in the final stage.

We say that a party rejects a packet if it outputs $\perp$, and accepts it otherwise.

When a client (or server) party sets ik in Stage 1 corresponding to a particular QC protocol execution instance, we say that client (or server) party *sets* that ik with a particular server (or client) party if every sent and received packet by that client (or server) party in Stage 1 of that QC protocol execution instance belongs to that client (or server) party's connection with that server (or client) party. We can define an analogous notion for setting k with respect to Stage 3. We will refer to parties that set ik's in Stage 1 with each other as each other's *peers*. The *correctness* of the protocol requires that the input data of one party's M^{send} be equal to outputs of the other party's M^{iget}, M^{get}. In other words, the protocol is correct if it allows the parties to exchange the data that they intended to exchange with their corresponding communication partners in the protocol, while preserving the order of the messages.

3   QACCE Model, Revisited

In this section, we quote the QACCE model. However, the QACCE model in [9] has several errors regardless of our verification result. We show a corrected version of the QACCE model.

Security Experiment. Fix the security parameter λ and a QC protocol Π with associated server key generation protocol Kg, scfg_gen, an authenticated encryption with associated data scheme $\mathrm{AEAD} = (\mathcal{E}, \mathcal{D})$ with key space $\{0,1\}^\lambda$ and additional authenticated data (which we will denote by H) space $\{0,1\}^*$.

The experiment $\mathrm{Exp}_\Pi^{\mathrm{QACCE}}(A)$ associated with the adversary A is defined as follows: We consider two sets of parties, clients and servers, $C = \{C_1, \ldots, C_\ell\}$ and $S = \{S_1, \ldots, S_\ell\}$, for parameter $\ell \in \mathbb{N}$ denoting the maximum possible number of servers or clients. The experiment first generates server key pairs

$(pk_i, sk_i) \leftarrow_R \mathsf{Kg}(\lambda)$, $k_{stk} \leftarrow_R \{0,1\}^{128}$, and $\mathsf{scfg}_i^t \leftarrow_R \mathsf{scfg\_gen}(sk_i, \tau_t, \lambda)$, for all time periods, for all $i \in [\ell]$.

To capture several sequential and parallel executions of the protocol we follow the standard approach and associate each party $P_i \in C \cup S$ with a set of stateful oracles $\pi_{p,i}^1, \ldots, \pi_{p,i}^d$, for parameter $d \in \mathbb{N}$ and $p \in \{c, s\}$, where each oracle $\pi_{p,i}^{r \in [d]}$ represents a process that executes one single instance of the protocol at party P_i and p indicates whether the party in question is a client or server. Intuitively, each oracle $\pi_{p,i}^q$ of some party $P_i \in C \cup S$ models that party's IP address and a unique port number. The experiment flips a bit $b_{p,i}^q \leftarrow_R \{0,1\}$ for each oracle $\pi_{p,i}^q$.

Each server oracle gets the corresponding scfg_i^t at the beginning of each time period. We assume that at each point of the protocol's execution each party (adversary included) can tell what time period it is. We also assume that every server oracle is aware what protocol stage it is in for every client oracle that it is and/or has been exchanging messages with. With this assumption we are not required to keep track of the stages in the simulations. Even though the server keeps local state and knows which stage it is in, it may have inaccurate view of the stage of the protocol because it is not guaranteed to know the correct identity of the party it is talking with. We refer to oracles that set ik with each other as *peers*.

The adversary A is given the public keys of all servers $pk_1, \ldots, pk_\ell$ and can interact with all oracles of all parties by issuing queries. The values in parentheses are supplied by A. If the parameter in parentheses is an oracle, e.g. $\pi_{p,i}^q$, this means that A needs to supply the indices p, i, q specifying the oracle.

- connect$(\pi_{c,i}^q, \pi_{s,j}^r)$, for $i, j \in [\ell]$, $q, r \in [d]$.
  As a result, $\pi_{c,i}^q$ outputs the initial connection request packet (first connection for that client party for that particular time period) that it would send specifically to oracle $\pi_{s,j}^r$ according to the protocol. The output of this query is not delivered to the recipient oracle, but is just given to A. This query allows the adversary to ask a client oracle to start communicating with a particular server party for the first time between those parties for a particular time period.

- resume$(\pi_{c,i}^q, \pi_{s,j}^r)$, for $i, j \in [\ell]$, $q, r \in [d]$.
  This query returns $\perp$ if ik corresponding to oracle $\pi_{c,i}^q$ is not set. Otherwise, $\pi_{c,i}^q$ outputs the 0-RTT connection request packet that it would send to an oracle $\pi_{s,j}^r$ according to the protocol. The output is given to A, who can deliver it to the destination oracle, modify it, or drop it. This query allows the adversary to ask a particular client oracle to request a 0-RTT connection with a particular server party, if the client party corresponding to that oracle has communicated before with that server in a particular time period. Recall that every server party is aware of its communication status with respect to every client oracle that may contact it.

- send$(\pi_{p,j}^r, m)$, for $p \in \{c, s\}$, $j \in [\ell]$, $r \in [d]$ and $m \in \{0,1\}^*$.
  As a result, m is sent to $\pi_{p,j}^r$, which will respond with $\perp$ if the oracle is in data exchange phase. Otherwise, A gets the response, which is defined according to the protocol. This query allows the adversary to send a specified packet m to

a specified destination oracle. Note that the attacker must provide a header for the packet that specifies the source and destination IP addresses and port numbers as well as packet sequence numbers of its choice. The destination oracle can check this information. The adversary gets control of the resulting packet and can choose to modify, drop, or deliver it to an oracle.

- revealik($\pi_{p,i}^q$), for $p \in \{c,s\}$, $i \in [\ell]$, $q \in [d]$.

  As a result, A receives the contents of variable ik for oracle $\pi_{p,i}^q$. This query allows the adversary to learn the initial key set by the oracle of its choice.

- revealk($\pi_{p,i}^q$), for $p \in \{c,s\}$, $i \in [\ell]$, $q \in [d]$.

  As a result, A receives the contents of variable k for oracle $\pi_{p,i}^q$. This query allows the adversary to learn the final key set by the oracle of its choice.

- corrupt(S_i), for $i \in [\ell]$.

  A gets back sk_i and the current scfg_i^t and any other state of S_i. This query allows the adversary to corrupt the server of its choice and learn its long-term secrets including scfg_i^t for the current time period.

- encrypt($\pi_{p,j}^r, m_0, m_1, H, \mathsf{init}$), for $p \in \{c,s\}$, $j \in [\ell]$, $r \in [d]$, $m_0, m_1, H \in \{0,1\}^*$, and $\mathsf{init} \in \{0,1\}$:

  It returns $\perp$ if $|m_0| \neq |m_1|$. When $\mathsf{init} = 1$, it returns $\perp$ if $\pi_{p,j}^r$ is not in the initial data exchange stage, or $IV \leftarrow get\_iv(ik, H)$ was used; otherwise, it returns $(H, \mathcal{E}(ik_{p'}, IV, H, m_{b_{p,j}^r}))$. When $\mathsf{init} = 0$, it returns $\perp$ if $\pi_{p,j}^r$ is not in the data exchange stage, or $IV \leftarrow get\_iv(k, H)$ was used; otherwise, it returns $(H, \mathcal{E}(k_{p'}, IV, H, m_{b_{p,j}^r}))$. This query, unlike the previous ones, deals with the initial and final data exchange phases[1] (flag init specifies which), while the previous ones concerned the initial and final key exchange phases. It is designed to follow the standard approach of capturing message privacy under chosen message attack. It allows the adversary to obtain a randomly chosen ciphertext out of the two messages provided by the adversary. Just like in the security definition for AEAD, the attacker can select the header H. For QUIC it means that the adversary can specify the source and destination IP addresses and port numbers as well as packet sequence numbers of its choice. Unlike the AEAD security model, however, we do not let the adversary select the IV because in QUIC the IV depends on the secrets of a party and is not under the attacker's control. get_iv is the function that we require to produce initialization vectors used for encryption and appropriate headers. The initialization vector is not given to the adversary. The adversary is restricted to providing H whose destination IP address and port number correspond to $\pi_{p,j}^r$ and whose source IP address and port number correspond to an oracle $\pi_{p',i}^q$ in the experiment, for $p' \in \{c,s\}\setminus\{p\}$.

- decrypt($\pi_{p,j}^r, C, H, \mathsf{init}$), for $p \in \{c,s\}$, $j \in [\ell]$, $r \in [d]$, $C, H \in \{0,1\}^*$, and $\mathsf{init} \in \{0,1\}$:

---

[1] In the original model, this query returns the encryption of $m_{b_{p,j}^q}$. However, since p in $m_{b_{p,j}^q}$ is equal to p in $\pi_{p,j}^r$, $m_{b_{p,j}^q}$ must be changed to $m_{b_{p,j}^r}$.

It returns $\perp$ if $(H, \mathcal{C})$ was output before by $\mathsf{encrypt}(\pi^q_{p',i}, *, *, *, \mathsf{init})$.[2]

When $\mathsf{init} = 1$, it returns $\perp$ if $\pi^r_{p,i}$ is not in the initial data exchange phase, or $\mathcal{D}(ik_p, \mathrm{IV}, H, \mathcal{C}) = \perp$, where $\mathrm{IV} \leftarrow get\_iv(ik, H)$; otherwise it returns $b^r_{p,j}$. When $\mathsf{init} = 0$, it returns $\perp$ if $\pi^r_{p,i}$ is not in the data exchange phase, or $\mathcal{D}(k_p, \mathrm{IV}, H, \mathcal{C}) = \perp$, where $\mathrm{IV} \leftarrow get\_iv(k, H)$; otherwise it returns $b^r_{p,j}$. This query also concerns the initial and final data exchange phases. It follows the standard approach to capture authenticity for AEAD schemes. The adversary's goal is to create a "new" valid ciphertext. If it succeeds, it is given the challenge bit and thus can win.

- $\mathsf{connprivate}(\pi^q_{c,i}, \pi^r_{s,j})$, for $i, j \in [\ell]$, $q, r \in [d]$.
  As a result, the initial connection request is sent to $\pi^r_{s,j}$. The response, which is defined according to the protocol, is sent to $\pi^q_{c,i}$ and not shown to A. Any following response of $\pi^q_{c,i}$ is not shown to A. It models IP spoofing attacks.

After the adversary is done with queries it may output a tuple (p, i, q, b), for $p \in \{c, s\}$.

Matching Conversation. For $p \in \{c, s\}$, $p' \in \{c, s\}\setminus\{p\}$, $i, j \in [\ell]$, $q, r \in [d]$, we denote with $R^q_{p,i}$ the sequence of all messages used for establishing keys (during stages 1 and 3) sent and received by $\pi^q_{p,i}$ in chronological order, and we call $R^q_{p,i}$ the message record at $\pi^q_{p,i}$. With respect to two message records $R^q_{p,i}$ and $R^r_{p',j}$, we say that $R^q_{p,i}$ is a prefix of $R^r_{p',j}$, if $R^q_{p,i}$ contains at least one message, and the messages in $R^q_{p,i}$ are identical to and in the same order as the first $|R^q_{p,i}|$ messages of $R^r_{p',j}$. We say that $\pi^q_{p,i}$ has a *matching conversation* with $\pi^r_{p',j}$, if either $R^r_{p',j}$ is a prefix of $R^q_{p,i}$ and $\pi^q_{p,i}$ has sent the last message(s), or $R^q_{p,i}$ is a prefix of $R^r_{p',j}$ and $\pi^r_{p',j}$ has sent the last message(s).

Note that the notion of a matching conversation is not sufficient to define peers because, unlike in TLS, communicating parties in QUIC may set initial keys without having a matching conversation. This is why throughout our analysis the notion of peers is instead equivalent to the notion of one party *setting a key with* another party.

Security Requirements.

- The *server impersonation advantage* of A $\mathbf{Adv}^{\mathsf{s-imp}}_{\Pi}(A)$ is the probability that there exists an oracle $\pi^q_{c,i}$ such that k of this oracle is set and there is no oracle $\pi^r_{s,j}$ corresponding to a server party S_j such that $\pi^q_{c,i}$ has a matching conversation to $\pi^r_{s,j}$, no reveal_{ik} contained ik possibly set in the optional initial key agreement stage between $\pi^q_{c,i}$ and $\pi^r_{s,j}$, and S_j was not corrupted.

The above captures the attack when the adversary impersonates an honest server and makes a client think it sets a key shared with the server, but the adversary may have the shared key instead.

---

[2] In the original model, $\mathsf{encrypt}$ query for $\pi^r_{p,j}$ is prohibited. However, $\mathsf{encrypt}(\pi^r_{p,j}, *, *, *, \mathsf{init})$ returns the ciphertext generated by p, and it is not reasonable. In this definition, the ciphertext of generated by p' should be prohibited. Thus, $\pi^r_{p,j}$ must be changed to $\pi^q_{p',i}$.

- The *channel-corruption* *advantage* of A $\mathbf{Adv}_{\Pi}^{\mathsf{ch-corr}}(A)$ is $2\Pr[b = b_{p,i}^q] - 1$, where if $p = s$, then it must be the case that $\pi_{s,i}^q$ has a matching conversation with some client oracle $\pi_{p',j}^r = \pi_{c,j}^r$ satisfying the conditions below, and if $p = c$, then the peer server oracle $\pi_{p',j}^r$ of $\pi_{c,i}^q$ must satisfy the same conditions. Let S be the server in this session.

  1. no $\mathsf{encrypt}(\pi_{p,i}^q, *, *, *, 1)$ and $\mathsf{encrypt}(\pi_{p',j}^r, *, *, *, 1)$ queries were made for any $*$ after or during the same time period τ_t that S was corrupted,
  2. no $\mathsf{encrypt}(\pi_{p,i}^q, *, *, *, *)$ and $\mathsf{encrypt}(\pi_{p',j}^r, *, *, *, *)$ queries were made for any $*$ after S was corrupted, and
  3. no $\mathsf{revealik}(\pi_{p,i}^q)$ and $\mathsf{revealik}(\pi_{p',j}^r)$ or $\mathsf{revealk}(\pi_{p,i}^q)$ and $\mathsf{revealk}(\pi_{p',j}^r)$ queries returned the key used to answer any $\mathsf{encrypt}(\pi_{p,i}^q, *, *, *, *)$ and $\mathsf{encrypt}(\pi_{p',j}^r, *, *, *, *)$ queries for any $*$ respectively.

The above captures the attacks in which information about groups of messages exchanged between the client and the server is leaked without the adversary corrupting the server party (1) before or (2) during the same time period as attempting the breach as well as without (3) revealing the initial and session keys *ik* and *k*. Thus, we capture a slightly weaker notion of forward secrecy by restricting the adversary to corrupt the appropriate server only after the time period when the adversary attempts the breach.

- The *IP spoofing* of A $\mathbf{Adv}_{\Pi}^{\mathsf{ips}}(A)$ is the probability that there exist oracles $\pi_{c,i}^q$ and $\pi_{s,j}^r$ such that at some time period τ_t A makes a $\mathsf{send}(\pi_{s,j}^r, m')$ query, $\pi_{s,j}^r$ does not reject this query, S_j was not corrupted, m' is not an output resulting from any previous connection request query (done via $\mathsf{connect}$ or resume queries), and the only other query A is allowed to make concerning $\pi_{c,i}^q$ during τ_t is the $\mathsf{connprivate}(\pi_{c,i}^q, \pi_{s,j}^r)$ query.

This goal captures attacks in which the adversary wins if it succeeds in having the server accept a connection request on behalf of a client who either did not request connection to that server or previously requested only an initial connection but did not request any further connections in the same time period. The adversary issues a connection query hoping it gets accepted by the server, possibly preceded by the only other allowed query in that time period: connection request ($\mathsf{connprivate}$) whose output it cannot see.

Security Definition. We say that a QC protocol Π is QACCE-secure if its advantage $\mathbf{Adv}_{\Pi}^{\mathsf{QACCE}}(A)$, defined as $\mathbf{Adv}_{\Pi}^{\mathsf{s-imp}}(A) + \mathbf{Adv}_{\Pi}^{\mathsf{ips}}(A) + \mathbf{Adv}_{\Pi}^{\mathsf{ch-corr}}(A)$, is negligible (in λ) for any polynomial-time adversary A.

4   Specifications of QUIC

We recall the specification of QUIC. Due to the page limitation, we cannot give the entire specification here. Please see [9] for the details. QUIC has the 1-RTT and 0-RTT protocols. Let $\mathcal{SS} = (\mathsf{Kg}_s, \mathsf{Sign}, \mathsf{Ver})$ be a digital signature scheme.

We assume that each server has generated a key pair $(pk_S, sk_S) \leftarrow_R \mathsf{Kg}_s(\lambda)$ and distributed the verification key pk_S using PKI. The 1-RTT protocol proceeds as follows (more detailed protocol flow is shown in Table 1 in Appendix A).

Stage 1: Initial Key Agreement. The client and the server run Diffie-Hellman (DH) key exchange as follows. The client sends a message m_1, which we call the initial connection request message of this session, containing a randomly generated connection id cid. The server responds with a message m_2 containing a part $\mathsf{scfg}^t_{\mathrm{pub}}$ of the server's global state scfg^t and the source-address token stk of the client. The part $\mathsf{scfg}^t_{\mathrm{pub}}$ contains the server's static DH public value signed with sk_S. The token stk contains the client's IP address encrypted using AEAD with the key k_{stk} generated by the server. Then, the client sends a message m_3 containing the stk and the client's DH public value. The server rejects this if stk is expired or does not contain the client's IP address. Finally, they compute the key ik by DH and a key derivation function xtrct_xpnd.

Stage 2: Initial Data Exchange. The client and the server sends messages m_4 and m_5 (and more, if any) encrypted by AEAD with the key and nonces extracted from ik.

Stage 3: Key Agreement. The server sends a message m_6 containing an ephemeral DH public value encrypted by AEAD with the key and nonces extracted from ik. The client and the server computes the key k using the server's new public value.

Stage 4: Data Exchange. The client and the server sends messages m_7 and m_8 (and more, if any) encrypted by AEAD with the key and nonces extracted from k.

The 0-RTT protocol omits the messages m_1 and m_2 above, assuming that the client have received $\mathsf{scfg}^t_{\mathrm{pub}}$ and stk in a 1-RTT session. In a 0-RTT session, the message m_3 is called the 0-RTT connection request message of this session. The server's global state scfg^t and the token stk are eventually expired, in which case the 1-RTT protocol is used.

5 Protocol Languages and Informal Semantics

We use the ProVerif tool [11–14] for our analysis. ProVerif is a tool for automatically analyze various security properties of security protocols. ProVerif adopts a dialect of the applied pi calculus as a protocol language, which we can extend with functions symbols and equational rules. ProVerif can efficiently analyze protocols for an unbounded number of sessions by using abstraction based of Horn clauses.

We introduce ProVerif's languages for specifying protocols and security properties. Due to space limitation, we present only fragments of the languages and their informal semantics that are used in our analysis. We further omit *types* of terms in the presentations below for brevity. Please refer to [11] for more complete explanation and details.

Variables, Terms, and Equations. We assume that there is an infinite number of *variables* $x, y, z, n, \ldots$. A *term* is constructed from variables by applying a number of *function symbols*, which are declared by users. Function symbols that take no argument are called *constants*. Along with function symbols, *equations* involving them are also defined. Terms are rewritten by using the equations as axioms. Some function symbols are declared as *destructors*. When a destructor is used in a protocol execution, it must be immediately rewritten by an equation; otherwise the execution halts. Function symbols and the equations for cryptographic primitives in QUIC are shown in Appendix B.

Processes. A protocol is described as a *process*, which typically consists of some subprocesses. The syntax for processes are given as follows.

$$P, Q :: = 0 \mid \; !P \mid P \| Q \mid \text{in}(c, \; x); P \mid \text{out}(c, \; t); P \mid \text{new} \; x; P \mid$$
$$\text{if} \; cond \; \text{then} \, P \mid \text{let} \; x{=}t \; \text{in} \, P \mid \text{event} \; ev(t_1, \ldots, t_n); P \mid$$
$$\text{insert} \; tab(t); P \mid \text{get} \; tab({=}t); P \mid$$

The process 0 is an inactive process and is usually omitted when it is a subprocess of other process. $!P$ is an unbounded number of copies of a process P running in parallel. $P \| Q$ is a parallel execution of processes P and Q. Processes running in parallel may communicate each other over channels using commands $\text{in}(c, x)$ and $\text{out}(c, t)$, which stores the received term in a variable x and sends a term t through the channel c, respectively. A fresh random data such as keys and nonces are generated and stored on a variable x by $\text{new} \, x$. A condition *cond* is checked by $\text{if} \; cond \; \text{then}$, where *cond* is an equation $t{=}t'$ or an inequation $t{<}{>}t'$; if *cond* is not true, the process halts. A term t is assigned on a variable x by $\text{let} \; x{=}t \; \text{in}$. An event is issued by $\text{event} \; ev(t_1, \ldots, t_n)$, where ev is a function symbol for events. Events do not affect the protocol execution but are referred to in the security definitions. A table *tab* is extended with an entry t by $\text{insert} \; tab(t)$, and the existence of an entry t is checked by $\text{get} \; tab({=}t)$; if t is not on *tab*, the process halts.

We actually use a little larger fragment of this language that has pattern-matching. For example, a process $\text{let} \; (x, \; {=}s){=}t \; \text{in} \, P$ deconstructs t as a pair $(t_1, t_2) = t$, assigns t_1 on the variable x, and checks if $s = t_2$ as in $\text{if} \; s{=}t_2 \; \text{then} \, P$.

Security Properties. Among various security properties that ProVerif can analyze, we use correspondence assertions and observational equivalence. A *correspondence assertion* is described as follows:

$$\text{query} \; x_1, \ldots, \; x_n;$$
$$\text{event}(ev(x_1, \ldots, x_n)) \; ==> \; \text{event}(ev_1(\tilde{x}^{(1)})) \; \| \cdots \| \; \text{event}(ev_k(\tilde{x}^{(k)}))$$

where $\tilde{x}^{(j)} \subseteq \{x_1, \ldots, x_n\}$, i.e., $\tilde{x}^{(j)} = x_{i_1^{(j)}}, \ldots x_{i_l^{(j)}}$ for some indices $i_1^{(j)}, \ldots, i_l^{(j)}$. This assertion means that, for all values of variables $x_1, \ldots, x_n$, if the event $ev(x_1, \ldots, x_n)$ occurs in an execution of a process, then at least one of the events $ev_1(\tilde{x}^{(1)}), \cdots, ev_k(\tilde{x}^{(k)})$ must occur in this execution.

An *observational equivalence* property is specified by using a special function symbol `choice` in the protocol. Intuitively, if a term `choice[msg0,msg1]` is used in a process, either `msg0` or `msg1` is chosen as the value of the term, and ProVerif checks if the adversary may know which one is chosen.

6   Formalization of the QUIC Protocol

While a protocol is modeled as a collection of stateful oracles in the QACCE model, ProVerif has a limited support for dealing with state and time. We therefore reformulate QUIC without using explicit updates of local states (variables) and assume that server configurations and source-address tokens are never expired. The latter allows us to capture more attacks than [9], which assumes no two server configurations of a server are valid at the same time period. On the other hand, this also may allow false attacks that are impossible in reality.

We model QUIC as processes for servers and clients defined in Figs. 1 and 2, respectively. The whole ProVerif script for our analysis is given in Appendix D. They are invoked unbounded number of times from the main process (shown in Appendix C) and are given some parameters such as IP addresses and keys for digital signatures. They receive messages from the public channel and send the responses to the channel following the protocol definition. The adversary may also send messages to the processes and receive the responses. This models send queries in the QUIC protocol model.

A client process starts with arguments such as IP addresses and port numbers of the client and the peer server, which are received from the adversary in the main process. After receiving m_2, it executes the subsequent part of the protocol unbounded number of times, which is indicated by "!." The first and the other executions correspond to a 1-RTT session and 0-RTT sessions, respectively. In this way the adversary controls timings and parameters of client processes as it does with connect and resume queries in the QUIC protocol model. Similarly, server processes also repeat the execution after sending m_2 unbounded number of times.

After the initial and final key agreement phase, each process invokes two subprocesses `Oenc` and `Odec`, which models encrypt and decrypt queries, that encrypts and decrypts messages received from the adversary. `Oenc` is defined to receive a plaintext from the adversary. We later consider a variation of `Oenc`, which receives two plaintexts. Each server and client process also invokes other subprocesses `Ocorrupt` and `Oreveal`, which models corrupt and reveal queries, that leaks the server's long-term secrets and the session keys, respectively, when queried by the adversary. Queries to these subprocesses are recorded as events, which is referred to in the security definitions. The definitions of these subprocesses are shown in Appendix C.

For modeling matching conversations, messages that have sent and received at each step of the initial and final key agreement phases are recorded on a table called `conversations`. A conversation that should be matched is given

```
let server(pk_s: bitstring, sk_s: bitstring, k_stk: bitstring,
      current_time_s: bitstring, scfg_t_pub: bitstring, sec_s: exponent,
      IP_s: bitstring, port_s: bitstring) =
   let (scid: bitstring, pub_s: bitstring, expy: bitstring, prof: bitstring)
      = scfg_t_pub in
   Ocorrupt(pk_s, (sk_s, k_stk, sec_s)) |
   (* Initial Key Agreement *)
   in(c, m1: bitstring);
   let (IP_c: bitstring, =IP_s, port_c: bitstring, =port_s, cid: bitstring,
      =seqno(phase_initial_key_agreement)) = m1 in
   new iv_stk: bitstring;
   let stk = (iv_stk, E(k_stk, iv_stk, (IP_c, current_time_s), null)) in
   let m2 = (IP_s, IP_c, port_s, port_c, cid, seqno(phase_initial_key_agreement),
            scfg_t_pub, stk) in
   out(cp, m2);
   insert conversations((role_server, m1, m2));
   Ocorrupt(pk_s, (sk_s, k_stk, sec_s, iv_stk)) |
   ! in(c, m3: bitstring);
      insert conversations((role_server, m1, m2, m3));
      let (pkt_info: bitstring, =cid, =seqno(phase_initial_key_agreement),
   stk': bitstring, =scid, nonc: bitstring, pub_c: bitstring) = m3 in
      let (=IP_c, =IP_s, =port_c, =port_s) = pkt_info in
      let (iv_stk': bitstring, tk: bitstring) = stk' in
      let (=IP_c, current_time_s': bitstring) = D(k_stk, iv_stk', null, tk) in
      event server_accept_m3(pk_s, tk, m3);
      let (=g, =q, y_c: G) = pub_c in
      let (ipms: G) = expS(y_c, sec_s) in
      let ik = xtrct_xpnd(ipms, nonc, cid, m3, n1) in
      (Oreveal(cid, phase_initial_data_exchange, role_client, k_s_of(ik)) |
       Oreveal(cid, phase_initial_data_exchange, role_server, k_c_of(ik)) |
       (* Initial Data Exchange *)
       (! Oenc((role_client, m1, m2, m3), k_c_of(ik), iv_c_of(ik), cid,
       phase_initial_data_exchange, role_server)) |
       (! Odec((role_client, m1, m2, m3), pk_s, k_s_of(ik), iv_s_of(ik), cid,
       phase_initial_data_exchange, role_client)) |
       (* Key Agreement *)
       new x_s': exponent;
       Ocorrupt(pk_s, (sk_s, k_stk, sec_s, iv_stk, x_s')) |
       let y_s' = exp(g, x_s') in
       let pub_s' = (g, q, y_s') in
       let sqn = seqno(phase_key_agreement) in
       let e = E(k_c_of(ik), (iv_c_of(ik), sqn), (scfg_t_pub, pub_s', stk'),
       (cid, sqn)) in
       let m6 = (IP_s, IP_c, port_s, port_c, ((cid, sqn), e)) in
       let pms = expS(y_c, x_s') in
       event server_k_set((role_server, m1, m2, m3, m6), cid);
       out(c, m6);
       insert conversations((role_server, m1, m2, m3, m6));
       let k = xtrct_xpnd(pms, nonc, cid, m6, n0) in
       (Oreveal(cid, phase_data_exchange, role_client, k_s_of(k)) |
        Oreveal(cid, phase_data_exchange, role_server, k_c_of(k)) |
        (* Data Exchange *)
        (! Oenc((role_client, m1, m2, m3, m6),
        k_c_of(k), iv_c_of(k), cid, phase_data_exchange, role_server)) |
        (! Odec((role_client, m1, m2, m3, m6), pk_s,
        k_s_of(k), iv_s_of(k), cid, phase_data_exchange, role_client)))).
```

Fig. 1. Descripton of the server process

```
let client(pk_s: bitstring, IP_c: bitstring, IP_s: bitstring,
           port_c: bitstring, port_s: bitstring) =
  (* Initial Key Agreement *)
  new cid: bitstring;
  let m1 = (IP_c, IP_s, port_c, port_s, cid, seqno(phase_initial_key_agreement)) in
  out(c, m1);
  in(cp, m2: bitstring);
  insert conversations((role_client, m1, m2));
  let (=IP_s, =IP_c, =port_s, =port_c, =cid, =seqno(phase_initial_key_agreement),
       scfg_t_pub: bitstring, stk: bitstring) = m2 in
  ! in(c, (current_time_c: bitstring, cid': bitstring));    (*Input from adversary*)
    let (scid: bitstring, pub_s: bitstring, expy: bitstring, prof: bitstring)
        = scfg_t_pub in
    if Ver(pk_s, (str_qscfg, n0, scid, pub_s, expy), prof) = true then
    new r: bitstring;
    let nonc = (current_time_c, r) in
    new x_c: exponent;
    let y_c = exp(g, x_c) in
    let pub_c = (g, q, y_c) in
    let pkt_info = (IP_c, IP_s, port_c, port_s) in
    let (iv_stk: bitstring, tk: bitstring) = stk in
    let m3 = (pkt_info, cid', seqno(phase_initial_key_agreement), stk, scid, nonc,
              pub_c) in
    event client_send_m3(m3);
    out(c, m3);
    insert conversations((role_client, m1, m2, m3));
    let (=g, =q, y_s: G) = pub_s in
    let ipms = exp(y_s, x_c) in
    let ik = xtrct_xpnd(ipms, nonc, cid', m3, n1) in
    (Oreveal(cid', phase_initial_data_exchange, role_client, k_s_of(ik)) |
     Oreveal(cid', phase_initial_data_exchange, role_server, k_c_of(ik)) |
     (* Initial Data Exchange *)
     (! Oenc((role_server, m1, m2, m3), k_s_of(ik), iv_s_of(ik), cid',
             phase_initial_data_exchange, role_client)) |
     (! Odec((role_server, m1, m2, m3), pk_s, k_c_of(ik), iv_c_of(ik), cid',
             phase_initial_data_exchange, role_server)) |
     (* Key Agreement *)
     in(c, m6: bitstring);
       (* k := get_key_c(m6, sqn_s) *)
     let sqn = seqno(phase_key_agreement) in
     let (=IP_s, =IP_c, =port_c, =port_s, ((=cid', =sqn), e: bitstring)) = m6 in
     let (=scfg_t_pub, pub_s': bitstring, =stk)
         = D(k_c_of(ik), (iv_c_of(ik), sqn), (cid', sqn), e) in
     let (=g, =q, y_s': G) = pub_s' in
     let pms = exp(y_s', x_c) in
     let k = xtrct_xpnd(pms, nonc, cid', m6, n0) in
     event client_k_set((role_server, m1, m2, m3, m6), cid', pk_s);
     (Oreveal(cid', phase_data_exchange, role_client, k_s_of(k)) |
      Oreveal(cid', phase_data_exchange, role_server, k_c_of(k)) |
      (* Data Exchange *)
      (! Oenc((role_server, m1, m2, m3, m6),
              k_s_of(k), iv_s_of(k), cid', phase_data_exchange, role_client)) |
      (! Odec((role_server, m1, m2, m3, m6), pk_s,
              k_c_of(k), iv_c_of(k), cid', phase_data_exchange, role_server)))).
```

Fig. 2. Descripton of the client process

as arguments when subprocesses Oenc and Odec are invoked, and these subprocesses check if the conversation is on the table, i.e., there is a peer that has
the conversation.

7 Formalization of the QACCE Security

The QACCE security is formalized as follows, as security properties against the
server impersonation, channel corruption, and IP spoofing attacks.

Server Impersonation. The security against the server-impersonation attack is
formalized by the following query:

```
query conv: bitstring, cid: bitstring, S: bitstring;
  event(client_k_set(conv, cid, S)) ==>
  event(server_k_set(conv, cid))
  || event(revealed(cid, phase_initial_data_exchange, role_server))
  || event(corrupted(S)).
```

Intuitively, this query means that if a client sets a key during a conversation
conv with a session identified by cid with a server S, one of the following cases
must be true:

- There is a server that sets a key during this (matching) conversation in this
  session, indicated by the server_k_set event.
- The key (ik_c) for encrypting messages to the client in the initial data exchange
  and the key agreement phases of this session is revealed, indicated by the
  revealed event.
- The server is corrupted, indicated by the corrupted event.

Channel Corruption. The channel-corruption attack succeeds if a decrypt query
succeeds, returning the secret bit $b_{p,j}^r$, or the adversary successfully guesses the
bit. We separately formalize these two cases as a correspondence assertion and
as observational equivalence. We call the security properties for these cases as
authenticity and *secrecy*.

Similarly to the case of server-impersonation, authenticity is formalized as
follows:

```
query S: bitstring, cid: bitstring, ph: bitstring,
      sender_role: bitstring, C: bitstring, H: bitstring;
  event(decrypt(S, cid, ph, sender_role, C, H)) ==>
  event(encrypt(cid, ph, sender_role, C, H))
  || event(revealed(cid, ph, sender_role))
  || event(corrupted(S)).
```

This means that if a decryption query with a ciphertext C with a header H
succeeds, the ciphertext must have been made an encryption query within this
session, unless the server is corrupted or the session secret has been revealed.

While the original security definition allows corruption of the server S of this session as long as encrypt query is not issued after that, our formalization does not allow to corrupt the server because ProVerif does not precisely model time as in "after that."

Secrecy is formalized as observational equivalence between two variations of the protocol. In these variations, Oenc is modified to receive a pair of plaintexts msg0 and msg1 and encrypt choice[msg0, msg1], which is msg0 and msg1 in the first and the second variations, respectively. This is defined as Oenc2 in Appendix C. Since ProVerif does not allow us to use events and observational equivalence at the same time, we disable Ocorrupt and Oreveal in the analysis of secrecy.

IP Spoofing. We assume that initial connection requests (m_1) to servers are sent only by connprivate queries because otherwise the IP spoofing attack trivially succeeds. Equivalently, instead of prohibiting initial connection requests and implementing connprivate queries, we define the success condition of the IP spoofing attack so that the attack succeeds only if the response to the initial connection request is not received. We also let the IP spoofing attack succeed only if m_3 is accepted by a server. The security against the IP spoofing attack is formalized by the following query:

```
query S: bitstring, m2: bitstring, m3: bitstring;
  event(server_accept_m3(S, m2, m3)) ==>
  event(client_send_m3(m3)) || event(capture_m2(m2))
  || event(corrupted(S)).
```

Intuitively, this query means that if a server S who has sent m2 accepts m3, a client has sent m3, unless m2 is has been captured or the server S has been corrupted.

8   Results of the Analysis

ProVerif reports attacks shown below, on all the properties formalized in previous section. These attacks exploit the following facts:

(I) Server accepts a valid source-address token (stk) even though it is distinct from the one generated in the current session.

(II) The same keys are used in the initial data exchange and the final key agreement phases of a session, and in the QACCE model headers, which contain sequence numbers, in encrypt and decrypt queries are arbitrarily chosen by the adversary and are not checked by the oracles.

Server Impersonation. The first attack exploits the above fact I. A man-in-the-middle-adversary has a source-address token stk' that is issued in the previous session and is not yet expired. It replaces the new source-address token stk sent from the server with stk'. Since this causes parties to have distinct conversations, in which the tokens are distinct, although the same key is set, this attack meets the definition of the (successful) server impersonation attack.

This attack is excluded from the server impersonation attacks if we modify the definition of matching conversations so that it remarks only m_3 and m_6. i.e., the argument conv of the events client_k_set and server_k_set may contain those messages. However, another attack that exploits the fact II is reported in this case: in the key agreement phase of a session, a man-in-the-middle adversary forges m_6 using an encrypt query in which the plaintext is $(\mathrm{scfg}^t_{\mathrm{pub}}, \mathrm{pub}'_s, \mathrm{stk})$ with an arbitrary $\tilde{\mathrm{pub}}'_s$, and the sequence number in the header is the one for m_6. It then replaces the m_6 from the server with the forged version. This causes the parties to fail to have matching conversations.

Channel Corruption. Attacks similar to the above second attack are reported for authenticity and secrecy.

In the attack on authenticity, a man-in-the-middle adversary captures m_6 sent from the server and sends it as a message in the initial data exchange phase, i.e., issues a query $\mathrm{decrypt}(\pi^r_{c,j}, m_6, H, \mathrm{init})$ to the client $\pi^r_{c,j}$ where $H = (\mathrm{cid}, \mathrm{sqn})$ is a pair of the connection id and the sequence number. Since the client is still in the initial data exchange phase and has a matching conversation of the server, and the messages is not output of an encryption query, this attack meets the definition of the channel-corruption attack.

In the attack on secrecy, a man-in-the-middle attacker issues a query $\mathrm{encrypt}(\pi^r_{s,j}, m, m', H, \mathrm{init})$ in the data exchange phase so that it succeeds to obtain the ciphertext e' of m_6 with probability $1/2$; m is a random plaintext and m' is the triplet $(\mathrm{scfg}^t_{\mathrm{pub}}, \mathrm{pub}'_s, \mathrm{stk})$ with an arbitrary $\tilde{\mathrm{pub}}'_s$, and the sequence number in H is the one for m_6. The adversary then sends the $(\mathrm{IP}_s, \mathrm{IP}_c, \mathrm{port}_s, \mathrm{port}_c, H, e')$ to the client in the key agreement phase. If $b^r_{s,j} = 1$, the client proceeds to the data exchange phase; otherwise, the client halts because the message is not a valid m_6.

IP Spoofing. This attack exploits the fact I. A man-in-the-middle attacker captures a valid source-address token sent in the previous session. In the current session started using a connprivate query, it makes a c_hello message using the token and sends it by a send query to the server. This message is accepted by the server, and thus this IP spoofing attack succeeds.

9   Fixing the QACCE Security

In this section, we suggest some fixes for the security definitions. ProVerif reports that QUIC is secure for the fixed definitions suggested below.

In our first server-impersonation attack, the source-address tokens are not agreed by the server and the client, although the tokens have the same IP address. This is not harmful if we assume that tokens are only for avoiding IP-spoofing attacks. It is therefore reasonable to exclude this attack from the definition of the server-impersonation attacks, modifying the definition of matching conversations so that it takes care of only m_3 and m_6 messages.

Our second server-impersonation attack and channel-corruption attacks relies on the fact that in the QACCE model the headers in encrypt and decrypt queries are arbitraryly chosen by the adversary and are not checked by the oracles. However, in reality, headers are not arbitrary: at least sequence numbers contained in the headers must be incremented in each encryption and checked by the recipient. We therefore suggest to fix the QACCE model so that headers in encrypt and decrypt queries are defined and checked according to the (QUIC) protocol, respectively.

In the IP-spoofing security, the adversary cannot see messages containing the source-address token (stk) issued in the current sessions. However, our attacks use a stk in the previous session that is still valid. We therefore suggest to fix the definition of the IP-spoofing security to assume that the adversary does not see any valid stk that can be used in the current session.

10 Conclusion

In this paper, we have automatically analyzed the QUIC protocol based on the QACCE model, using the ProVerif protocol analyzer. The main technical contribution is that we have given symbolic formalization of QUIC and the QACCE security for automatic analysis. Since the QACCE model is a general model for QC protocols, our formalization can be used for analyzing other QC protocols such as TLS. Our analysis have found some attacks, which show that the definition of QACCE security is unnecessarily strong and that analysis in [9] is not correct, alghouth these attacks have no practical impact on QUIC. We have further suggested fixes for the QACCE security and analyzed QUIC with the fixed security definitions.

Our results can be seen as a case study on how formal automatic analysis complements cryptoraphic analysis by hands of experts on cryptorgaphy. Since security analysis plays an important role in recent development of security protocols, believing an incorrect analysis result may lead the development to a wrong direction. It is therefore important to refine existing analysis results by automatic analysis.

A Protocol Flow of QUIC

The 1-RTT protocol of QUIC is shown in Table 1. The 0-RTT protocol simply omits m_1 and m_2 from the 1-RTT protocol and renumber the sequence number, which starts from 1.

The client has following information.

- pk_S: a verification key of a server which is obtained from PKI
- τ_t: current time period

Table 1. The 1-RTT connection establishment

Client		Server
(1) Initial Key Agreement		
$\text{cid} \leftarrow_R \{0,1\}^{64}$ $m_1 \leftarrow (\text{IP}_c, \text{IP}_s, \text{port}_c, \text{port}_s, \text{cid}, 1)$	$\xrightarrow{m_1}$	$\text{iv}_{\text{stk}} \leftarrow_R \{0,1\}^{96}$ $e \leftarrow \mathcal{E}(k_{\text{stk}}, \text{iv}_{\text{stk}}, \epsilon, (\text{IP}_c, \text{current\_time}_s))$ $\text{stk} \leftarrow (\text{iv}_{\text{stk}}, e)$ $m_2 \leftarrow (\text{IP}_s, \text{IP}_c, \text{port}_s, \text{port}_c, \text{cid}, 1, \text{scfg}^t_{\text{pub}}, \text{stk})$
abort if $\text{expy} \leq \tau_t$ or $\text{Ver}(pk_S, (\text{str}, 0, \text{scid}, \text{pub}_s, \text{expy}), \text{prof}) \neq 1$, where $\text{str} \leftarrow$ "QUIC server config signature" $r \leftarrow_R \{0,1\}^{160}$ $\text{nonc} \leftarrow (\text{current\_time}_c, r)$ $x_c \leftarrow \mathbb{Z}_{q-1}, y_c \leftarrow g^{x_c}, \text{pub}_c \leftarrow (g, q, y_c)$ $\text{pkt\_info} \leftarrow (\text{IP}_c, \text{IP}_s, \text{port}_c, \text{port}_s)$ $m_3 \leftarrow (\text{pkt\_info}, \text{cid}, 2, \text{stk}, \text{scid}, \text{nonc}, \text{pub}_c)$	$\xleftarrow{m_2}$ $\xrightarrow{m_3}$	$(\text{iv}_{\text{stk}}, tk) \leftarrow \text{stk}$ $\text{dec} \leftarrow \mathcal{D}(k_{\text{stk}}, \text{iv}_{\text{stk}}, \epsilon, tk)$ abort if either $\text{dec} = \perp$, or first 4 bytes of $\text{dec} \neq \text{IP}_c$, or last 4 bytes correspond to a time stamp outside allowed time, or $r \in \text{strike}$, or $\tau_t \notin \text{strike}_{rng}$, or scid is unknown or corresponds to an expired $\text{scfg}^{t' < t}_{\text{pub}}$ or g, q of pub_c are not the same as g, q of pub_s
$ik \leftarrow \text{xtrct\_xpnd}(y_s^{x_c}, \text{nonc}, \text{cid}, m_3, 40, 1)$		$ik \leftarrow \text{xtrct\_xpnd}(y_c^{x_s}, \text{nonc}, \text{cid}, m_3, 40, 1)$
(2) Initial Data Exchange		
for each $\alpha \in [i]$: $\text{sqn}_c \in \alpha + 2; m_4^\alpha \leftarrow \text{pak}(ik, \text{sqn}_c, M_c^\alpha)$ $m_4 \leftarrow (m_4^1, \ldots, m_4^i); \text{process\_packets}(ik, m_5)$	$\xrightarrow{m_4}$ $\xleftarrow{m_5}$	for each $\beta \in [j]$: $\text{sqn}_s \in \beta + 1; m_5^\beta \leftarrow \text{pak}(ik, \text{sqn}_s, M_s^\beta)$ $m_5 \leftarrow (m_5^1, \ldots, m_5^j); \text{process\_packets}(ik, m_4)$
(3) Key Agreement		
		$\text{sqn}_s \leftarrow 2 + j$ $(ik_c, ik_s, \text{iv}_c, \text{iv}_s) \leftarrow ik$ $\tilde{x}_s \leftarrow_R \mathbb{Z}_{q-1}, \tilde{y}_s \leftarrow g^{\tilde{x}_s}, \tilde{\text{pub}}_s \leftarrow (g, q, \tilde{y}_s)$ $H \leftarrow (\text{cid}, \text{sqn})$ $e \leftarrow \mathcal{E}(ik_c, (\text{iv}_c, \text{sqn}_s), H, (\text{scfg}^t_{\text{pub}}, \tilde{\text{pub}}_s, \text{stk}))$ $m_6 \leftarrow (\text{IP}_s, \text{IP}_c, \text{port}_s, \text{port}_c, H, e)$
$(\text{IP}_s, \text{IP}_c, \text{port}_s, \text{port}_c, H, e) \leftarrow m_6$ abort if $\mathcal{D}(ik_c, (\text{iv}_c, \text{sqn}_s), (\text{cid}, \text{sqn}_s), e) = \perp$ $k \leftarrow \text{xtrct\_xpnd}(\tilde{y}_s^{x_c}, \text{nonc}, \text{cid}, m_6, 40, 0)$	$\xleftarrow{m_6}$	$k \leftarrow \text{xtrct\_xpnd}(y_c^{\tilde{x}_s}, \text{nonc}, \text{cid}, m_6, 40, 0)$
(4) Data Exchange		
for each $\alpha \in \{i+1, \ldots, u\}$: $\text{sqn}_c \in \alpha + 2; m_7^\alpha \leftarrow \text{pak}(ik, \text{sqn}_c, M_c^\alpha)$ $m_7 \leftarrow (m_7^{i+1}, \ldots, m_7^u); \text{process\_packets}(k, m_8)$	$\xrightarrow{m_7}$ $\xleftarrow{m_8}$	for each $\beta \in \{j+1, \ldots, w\}$: $\text{sqn}_s \in \beta + 2; m_8^\beta \leftarrow \text{pak}(ik, \text{sqn}_s, M_s^\beta)$ $m_8 \leftarrow (m_8^{j+1}, \ldots, m_8^w); \text{process\_packets}(k, m_7)$

The server has following information.

- pk_S: a verification key
- sk_S: a signing key corresponding with pk_S
- k_{stk}: a server secret key where $k_{\text{stk}} \leftarrow_R \{0,1\}^{128}$
- $Y' = g^{y'}$ where $y' \leftarrow_R \#\langle g \rangle$ (ServerConfiguration for 0-RTT)
- τ_t: current time period
- scfg^t: a part of global state of server in the time period τ_t
- stk: source-address token stk

- xtrct_xpnd: key derivation function for QUIC
- strike: set of used nonce
- strike$_{rng}$: arrowed time period
- pak: packet generate function for QUIC
- process_packets: packet process function for QUIC

We assume that the server's scfg is refreshed every time period τ_t using the scfg_gen function as follows.

$scfg\_gen(sk, \tau_t, \lambda)$:

$q \leftarrow_R \{$primes of size $\lambda\}$, $g \leftarrow_R \{$generators of $\mathbb{Z}_q\}$, $x_s \leftarrow_R \mathbb{Z}_{q-1}$, $y_s \leftarrow g^{x_s}$, $\text{pub}_s \leftarrow (g, q, y_s)$, $\text{sec}_s \leftarrow x_s$, $\text{expy} \leftarrow \tau_{t+1}$, $\text{scid} \leftarrow \mathcal{H}(\text{pub}_s, \text{expy})$, $\text{str} \leftarrow$ "QUIC server config signature", $\text{prof} \leftarrow \text{Sign}(sk, (\text{str}, 0x00, \text{scid}, \text{pub}_s, \text{expy}))$, $\text{scfg}^t_{\text{pub}} \leftarrow (\text{scid}, \text{pub}_s, \text{expy}, \text{prof})$, $\text{scfg} \leftarrow (\text{scfg}^t_{\text{pub}}, \text{sec}_s)$.

B   Formalization of Cryptographic Primitives

The cryptographic primitives used in QUIC are authenticated encryption with associated data (AEAD), Diffie-Hellman key agreement, digital signatures, the hash function ($\mathcal{H}$), and the key derivation function (xtrct_xpnd). Diffie-Hellman key agreement and digital signatures are formalized in the same way as in [11]. The hash function and the key derivation function are formalized merely as function symbols Hash and xtrct_xpnd that have no equation, respectively. Additionally, we use some function symbols for representing extraction of keys such as k_s and k_c from k output by the key derivation function.

AEAD is formalized by first introducing a function symbol E for encryption. A term E(k, iv, m, h) represents encryption of the plaintext m with additional authenticated data h encrypted with key k and nonce iv. We also introduce destructor function symbol D, extract_nonce, extract_AD and equations

$$D(k, \text{ iv, h, E}(k, \text{ iv, m, h})) = m$$

$$\text{extract\_nonce}(E(k, \text{ iv, m, h})) = \text{nonce}$$

$$\text{extrac\_AD}(E(k, \text{ iv, m, h})) = h.$$

The first equation means that a ciphertexts is decrypted and verified by using the valid key and the nonce. Note that since D is a destructor, if decryption fails in a process, e.g., due to incorrect nonce or key, the process halts. The other equations enables the adversary to obtain the nonce and the associated data from a ciphertext.

C   Definitions of Some Processes

The "main" processes that invokes clients and servers is shown in Fig. 3. It receives some parameters from the adversary through the public channel c. Figure 4 shows the processes that replies to encrypt, decrypt, reveal, and corrupt

```
process
  (! new rg: bitstring;
    (! new k_stk: bitstring;
       out(c, pk(rg));
       ! in(c, IP_s: bitstring);
         in(c, port_s: bitstring);
       ! in(c, current_time_s: bitstring);
         let y_s = exp(g, x_s(rg, current_time_s)) in
         let sec_s = x_s(rg, current_time_s) in
         let pub_s = (g, q, y_s) in
         let str = str_qscfg in
         let expy: bitstring = s(current_time_s) in
         let scid = Hash((pub_s, expy)) in
         new r: nonce_t;
         let prof = Sign(sk(rg), (str_qscfg, n0, scid, pub_s, expy), r) in
         let scfg_t_pub = (scid, pub_s, expy, prof) in
         server(pk(rg), sk(rg), k_stk, current_time_s, scfg_t_pub, sec_s,
                IP_s, port_s))
    | (! in(c, IP_c: bitstring);
         in(c, IP_s: bitstring);
         in(c, port_c: bitstring);
         in(c, port_s: bitstring);
         client(pk(rg), IP_c, IP_s, port_c, port_s))
    | tap_m2)
```

Fig. 3. Descripton of the main process

queries and the process tap_m2 that serves as a secret channel that securely transmits m_2 from the server to the client when a connprivate query is issued.

In the formalization of secrecy, Oenc2 instead of Oenc is used. We must prohibit the adversary to send a plaintext twice in the encrypt query, e.g., $(msg0, msg1)$ and $(msg0, msg1')$, because otherwise the adversary trivially knows the secret bit by comparing the two ciphertexts. However, this restriction cannot be directly modeled in ProVerif. We therefore use another function symbol Ef instead of E in Oenc2 for producing distinct ciphertext on each query, even if the adversary sends a plaintext more than once. This makes it useless to compare ciphertexts received by Oenc2.

D   ProVerif Script

```
#ifdef SELFUN
set selFun = SELFUN.
#elif SECRECY
set selFun = Nounifset.
#endif

(* types *)
type nonce_t.
type G. (* DH *)
type exponent. (* DH *)
type nat.
```

```
(* Encryption *)
let Oenc(matching_conversation: bitstring,
        key: bitstring, iv: bitstring,
        sess: bitstring, ph: bitstring, sender_role: bitstring) =
  in(c, (msg: bitstring, H: bitstring));
  let (cid: bitstring, sqn: bitstring) = H in
  let C = E(key, (iv, sqn), msg, H) in
  event encrypt(sess, ph, sender_role, C, H);
  out(c, (H, C)).

(* Encryption, for analyzing secrecy *)
let Oenc2(matching_conversation: bitstring,
        key: bitstring, iv: bitstring,
        sess: bitstring, ph: bitstring, sender_role: bitstring) =
  in(c, (msg0: bitstring, msg1: bitstring, H: bitstring));
  let msg = choice[msg0, msg1] in
  let (cid: bitstring, sqn: bitstring) = H in
  new r: bitstring;
  let C = Ef(key, (iv, sqn), msg, H, r) in
  get conversations(=matching_conversation) in
  out(c, (H, C)).

(* Decryption *)
let Odec(matching_conversation: bitstring, S: bitstring,
        key: bitstring, iv: bitstring,
        sess: bitstring, ph: bitstring, sender_role: bitstring) =
  in(c, (C: bitstring, H: bitstring));
  let (cid': bitstring, sqn: bitstring) = H in
  let nonce = (iv, sqn) in
  let msg = D(key, nonce, H, C) in
  get conversations(=matching_conversation) in
  event decrypt(S, sess, ph, sender_role, C, H).

(* Reveal *)
let Oreveal(sess: bitstring, ph: bitstring, sender_role: bitstring, k: bitstring) =
  (in(c, =q_reveal); event revealed(sess, ph, sender_role); out(c, k)).

(* Corruption *)
let Ocorrupt(S: bitstring, s: bitstring) =
  in(c, =q_corrupt);
  event corrupted(S);
  out(c, s).

(* Tap m2 *)
let tap_m2 =
  ((! in(cp, m2: bitstring);                              (* capture m2 *)
      let (IP_s: bitstring, IP_c: bitstring, port_s: bitstring, port_c: bitstring,
          cid: bitstring, n: bitstring, scfg_t_pub: bitstring, stk: bitstring)
          = m2 in
      let (iv_stk: bitstring, tk: bitstring) = stk in
      event capture_m2(m2);
      out(cp, m2))
  |(! in(c, m2: bitstring); out(cp, m2))).              (* inject m2 *)
```

Fig. 4. Descripton of other processes that reply to queries from the adversary

```
(* constants *)
const bot: bitstring.
const n0: bitstring. (* 0x00 *)
const n1: bitstring. (* 1 *)
const str_qscfg: bitstring. (*"QUIC server config signature" *)
const null: bitstring. (* the null bitstring *)

const q_reveal: bitstring.
const q_corrupt: bitstring.

const phase_initial_data_exchange: bitstring.
const phase_initial_key_agreement: bitstring.
const phase_data_exchange: bitstring.
const phase_key_agreement: bitstring.
const role_server: bitstring.
const role_client: bitstring.

(* packet numbers *)
fun seqno(bitstring): bitstring.

(* time *)
fun s(bitstring): bitstring.   (* successor (+1) function *)

(* AEAD *)
fun E(bitstring, bitstring, bitstring, bitstring): bitstring.
fun Ef(bitstring, bitstring, bitstring, bitstring, bitstring):
bitstring.
reduc
forall k: bitstring, iv: bitstring, h: bitstring, m: bitstring;
D(k, iv, h, E(k, iv, m, h)) = m;
forall k: bitstring, iv: bitstring, h: bitstring, m: bitstring,
r: bitstring;
D(k, iv, h, Ef(k, iv, m, h, r)) = m.
reduc
forall m: bitstring, nonce: bitstring, k: bitstring, h: bitstring;
extract_nonce(E(k, nonce, m, h)) = nonce;
forall m: bitstring, nonce: bitstring, k: bitstring, h: bitstring,
r: bitstring;
extract_nonce(Ef(k, nonce, m, h, r)) = nonce.
reduc
forall m: bitstring, nonce: bitstring, k: bitstring, h: bitstring;
extract_AD(E(k, nonce, m, h)) = h;
forall m: bitstring, nonce: bitstring, k: bitstring, h: bitstring,
r: bitstring;
extract_AD(Ef(k, nonce, m, h, r)) = h.
```

```
(* Signature *)
fun pk(bitstring): bitstring.
fun sk(bitstring): bitstring.
fun Sign(bitstring, bitstring, nonce_t): bitstring.
fun Ver(bitstring, bitstring, bitstring): bool
reduc
forall rg: bitstring, m: bitstring, rs: nonce_t;
Ver(pk(rg), m, Sign(sk(rg), m, rs)) = true.

(* Diffie-Hellman *)
const q: nat. (* used just as a spaceholder *)
const g: G.
fun exp(G, exponent): G.
nounif x: exponent; attacker(exp(g, x)). (* for speedup *)
#ifdef NO_DH_COMM     /* define NO_DH_COMM if you want speedup */
reduc
forall x: exponent, y: exponent;
expS(exp(g, y), x) = exp(exp(g, x), y).
#else
equation forall x: exponent, y: exponent;
exp(exp(g, x), y) = exp(exp(g, y), x).
#define expS exp
#endif

(* Hash *)
fun Hash(bitstring): bitstring.

(* Generaiton of server's secret (for every time period) *)
fun x_s(bitstring, bitstring): exponent [private].

(* xtrct_xpnd  *)
fun xtrct_xpnd(G, bitstring, bitstring, bitstring, bitstring):
bitstring.
fun k_c_of(bitstring): bitstring.
fun k_s_of(bitstring): bitstring.
fun iv_c_of(bitstring): bitstring.
fun iv_s_of(bitstring): bitstring.

free c: channel.
#ifdef IP_SPOOFING
free cp: channel [private]. (* for security against IP spoofing*)
#else
#define cp c
#endif
free secret: bitstring [private]. (* for sanity check *)
```

```
(* table *)
table conversations(bitstring).
table clientIKAtable(bitstring).
table serverIKAtable(bitstring).

(* events and queries *)
event revealed(bitstring, bitstring, bitstring).
event corrupted(bitstring).

event encrypt(bitstring, bitstring, bitstring, bitstring, bitstring).
event decrypt(bitstring, bitstring, bitstring, bitstring, bitstring,
bitstring).
event client_k_set(bitstring, bitstring, bitstring).
event server_k_set(bitstring, bitstring).

event serverKeyAgreementFinished(bitstring, bitstring, bitstring,
bitstring, bitstring, bitstring, bitstring, G).

event capture_m2(bitstring).
event client_send_m3(bitstring).
event server_accept_m3(bitstring, bitstring, bitstring).

(*
query attacker(secret).
out(c, secret);
*)

#if SERVER_IMPERSONATION
(* Security against the server impersonation attack *)
query conv: bitstring, sess: bitstring, S: bitstring;
event(client_k_set(conv, sess, S)) ==>
event(server_k_set(conv, sess))
|| event(revealed(sess, phase_initial_data_exchange, role_server))
|| event(corrupted(S)).
#elif AUTHENTICITY
(* Message authenticity of security
against the channel-corruption attack *)
query S: bitstring, sess: bitstring, ph: bitstring, sender_role:
bitstring,
C: bitstring, H: bitstring;
event(decrypt(S, sess, ph, sender_role, C, H)) ==>
event(encrypt(sess, ph, sender_role, C, H))
|| event(revealed(sess, ph, sender_role))
|| event(corrupted(S)).
#elif IP_SPOOFING
(* Security against IP spoofing attack *)
#ifdef FIXED
query S: bitstring, tk: bitstring, m3: bitstring;
event(server_accept_m3(S, tk, m3)) ==>
event(client_send_m3(tk))
```

```
|| event(capture_m2(tk))
|| event(corrupted(S)).
#else
query S: bitstring, m2: bitstring, m3: bitstring;
event(server_accept_m3(S, m2, m3)) ==>
event(client_send_m3(m3))
|| event(capture_m2(m2))
|| event(corrupted(S)).
#endif /* FIXED */
#elif SECRECY
#define DISABLE_REVEAL 1
#define DISABLE_CORRUPT 1
#else
#error "You must define one of the options SERVER_IMPERSONATION,
AUTHENTICITY, SECRECY, and IP_SPOOFING!"
#endif

(* PROCESSES *)

(* Encryption / Decription oracle *)
let Oenc(matching_conversation: bitstring,
key: bitstring, iv: bitstring,
sess: bitstring, ph: bitstring, sender_role: bitstring) =
#ifdef SECRECY
in(c, (msg0: bitstring, msg1: bitstring, H: bitstring));
let msg = choice[msg0, msg1] in
let (cid: bitstring, sqn: bitstring) = H in
new r: bitstring;
let C = Ef(key, (iv, sqn), msg, H, r) in
get conversations(=matching_conversation) in
#else /* SECRECY */
in(c, (msg: bitstring, H: bitstring));
let (cid: bitstring, sqn: bitstring) = H in
let C = E(key, (iv, sqn), msg, H) in
event encrypt(sess, ph, sender_role, C, H);
#endif /* SECRECY */
#if FIXED && (SECRECY || SERVER_IMPERSONATION)
if sqn = seqno(ph) then
#endif /* FIXED && (SECRECY || SERVER_IMPERSONATION) */
out(c, (H, C)).

let Odec(matching_conversation: bitstring, S: bitstring,
key: bitstring, iv: bitstring,
sess: bitstring, ph: bitstring, sender_role: bitstring) =
#ifdef SECRECY
0.
#else /* SECRECY */
in(c, (C: bitstring, H: bitstring));
let (cid': bitstring, sqn: bitstring) = H in
let nonce = (iv, sqn) in
```

```
let msg = D(key, nonce, H, C) in
#if FIXED && AUTHENTICITY
if sqn = seqno(ph) then
#endif /* FIXED && AUTHENTICITY */
get conversations(=matching_conversation) in
event decrypt(S, sess, ph, sender_role, C, H).
#endif /* SECRECY */

(* Responding reveal queries *)
let Oreveal(sess: bitstring, ph: bitstring, sender_role: bitstring,
k: bitstring) =
#ifdef DISABLE_REVEAL
0.
#else
(in(c, =q_reveal); event revealed(sess, ph, sender_role); out(c, k)).
#endif /* DISABLE_REVEAL */

(* corruption *)
let Ocorrupt(S: bitstring, s: bitstring) =
#ifdef DISABLE_CORRUPT
0.
#else
in(c, =q_corrupt);
event corrupted(S);
out(c, s).
#endif /* DISABLE_CORRUPT */

(* Client process *)
let client(pk_s: bitstring, IP_c: bitstring, IP_s: bitstring,
port_c: bitstring, port_s: bitstring) =
(* Initial Key Agreement *)
(* m1 := c_i_hello(pk_s) *)
new cid: bitstring;
let m1 = (IP_c, IP_s, port_c, port_s, cid,
seqno(phase_initial_key_agreement)) in
out(c, m1);
(* m2 *)
in(cp, m2: bitstring);
insert conversations((role_client, m1, m2));
(* m3 := c_hello(m2) *)
let (=IP_s, =IP_c, =port_s, =port_c, =cid,
=seqno(phase_initial_key_agreement),
scfg_t_pub: bitstring, stk: bitstring) = m2 in
! in(c, (current_time_c: bitstring, cid': bitstring));
(* m3 := c_hello(m2) *)
let (scid: bitstring, pub_s: bitstring, expy: bitstring, prof: bitstring)
= scfg_t_pub in
if Ver(pk_s, (str_qscfg, n0, scid, pub_s, expy), prof) = true then
new r: bitstring;
let nonc = (current_time_c, r) in
```

```
new x_c: exponent;
let y_c = exp(g, x_c) in
let pub_c = (g, q, y_c) in
let pkt_info = (IP_c, IP_s, port_c, port_s) in
let (iv_stk: bitstring, tk: bitstring) = stk in
let m3 = (pkt_info, cid', seqno(phase_initial_key_agreement), stk, scid,
nonc, pub_c) in
#if FIXED && IP_SPOOFING
event client_send_m3(tk);
#else
event client_send_m3(m3);
#endif /* FIXED && IP_SPOOFING */
out(c, m3);
insert conversations((role_client, m1, m2, m3));
(* ik := get_i_key_c(m3) *)
let (=g, =q, y_s: G) = pub_s in
let ipms = exp(y_s, x_c) in
let ik = xtrct_xpnd(ipms, nonc, cid', m3, n1) in
((* reveal *)
Oreveal(cid', phase_initial_data_exchange, role_client, k_s_of(ik)) |
Oreveal(cid', phase_initial_data_exchange, role_server, k_c_of(ik)) |
(* Initial Data Exchange *)
(! Oenc((role_server, m1, m2, m3),
k_s_of(ik), iv_s_of(ik), cid', phase_initial_data_exchange, role_client))|
(! Odec((role_server, m1, m2, m3), pk_s,
k_c_of(ik), iv_c_of(ik), cid', phase_initial_data_exchange, role_server))|
(* Key Agreement *)
(* m6 *)
in(c, m6: bitstring);
(* k := get_key_c(m6, sqn_s) *)
let sqn = seqno(phase_key_agreement) in
let (=IP_s, =IP_c, =port_s, =port_c, ((=cid', =sqn), e: bitstring)) = m6
  in
let (=scfg_t_pub, pub_s': bitstring, =stk) = D(k_c_of(ik), (iv_c_of(ik),
  sqn),
(cid', sqn), e) in
let (=g, =q, y_s': G) = pub_s' in
let pms = exp(y_s', x_c) in
let k = xtrct_xpnd(pms, nonc, cid', m6, n0) in
#if FIXED && SERVER_IMPERSONATION
event client_k_set((role_server, m3, m6), cid', pk_s);
#else
event client_k_set((role_server, m1, m2, m3, m6), cid', pk_s);
#endif /* FIXED && SERVER_IMPERSONATION */
((* reveal queries *)
Oreveal(cid', phase_data_exchange, role_client, k_s_of(k)) |
Oreveal(cid', phase_data_exchange, role_server, k_c_of(k)) |
(* Data Exchange *)
(! Oenc((role_server, m1, m2, m3, m6),
k_s_of(k), iv_s_of(k), cid', phase_data_exchange, role_client)) |
```

```
(! Odec((role_server, m1, m2, m3, m6), pk_s,
k_c_of(k), iv_c_of(k), cid', phase_data_exchange, role_server)))).

(* Server *)
let server(pk_s: bitstring, sk_s: bitstring, k_stk: bitstring,
current_time_s: bitstring,
scfg_t_pub: bitstring, sec_s: exponent,
IP_s: bitstring, port_s: bitstring) =
let (scid: bitstring, pub_s: bitstring, expy: bitstring, prof: bitstring)
= scfg_t_pub in
(* corruption *) Ocorrupt(pk_s, (sk_s, k_stk, sec_s)) |
(* Initial Key Agreement *)
(* m1 *)
in(c, m1: bitstring);
(* m2 = s_reject(m1) *)
let (IP_c: bitstring, =IP_s, port_c: bitstring, =port_s, cid: bitstring,
=seqno(phase_initial_key_agreement)) = m1 in
new iv_stk: bitstring;
let stk = (iv_stk, E(k_stk, iv_stk, (IP_c, current_time_s), null)) in
let m2 = (IP_s, IP_c, port_s, port_c, cid,
seqno(phase_initial_key_agreement), scfg_t_pub, stk) in
out(cp, m2);
insert conversations((role_server, m1, m2));
(* corruption *) Ocorrupt(pk_s, (sk_s, k_stk, sec_s, iv_stk)) |
(* m3 *)
! in(c, m3: bitstring);
insert conversations((role_server, m1, m2, m3));
(* ik := get_i_key_s(m3) *)
let (pkt_info: bitstring, =cid, =seqno(phase_initial_key_agreement),
stk': bitstring, =scid, nonc: bitstring, pub_c: bitstring) = m3 in
let (=IP_c, =IP_s, =port_c, =port_s) = pkt_info in
let (iv_stk': bitstring, tk: bitstring) = stk' in
let (=IP_c, current_time_s': bitstring) = D(k_stk, iv_stk', null, tk) in
#if FIXED && IP_SPOOFING
event server_accept_m3(pk_s, tk, m3);
#else
event server_accept_m3(pk_s, tk, m3);
#endif /* FIXED && IP_SPOOFING */
let (=g, =q, y_c: G) = pub_c in
let (ipms: G) = expS(y_c, sec_s) in
let ik = xtrct_xpnd(ipms, nonc, cid, m3, n1) in
((* reveal *)
Oreveal(cid, phase_initial_data_exchange, role_client, k_s_of(ik)) |
Oreveal(cid, phase_initial_data_exchange, role_server, k_c_of(ik)) |
(* Initial Data Exchange *)
(! Oenc((role_client, m1, m2, m3),
k_c_of(ik), iv_c_of(ik), cid, phase_initial_data_exchange, role_server))|
(! Odec((role_client, m1, m2, m3), pk_s,
k_s_of(ik), iv_s_of(ik), cid, phase_initial_data_exchange, role_client))|
(* Key Agreement *)
```

```
(* m6 := s_hello(m3, ik, sqn_s) *)
new x_s': exponent;
(* corruption *) Ocorrupt(pk_s, (sk_s, k_stk, sec_s, iv_stk, x_s')) |
let y_s' = exp(g, x_s') in
let pub_s' = (g, q, y_s') in
let sqn = seqno(phase_key_agreement) in
let e = E(k_c_of(ik), (iv_c_of(ik), sqn), (scfg_t_pub, pub_s', stk'),
(cid, sqn)) in
let m6 = (IP_s, IP_c, port_s, port_c, ((cid, sqn), e)) in  '
let pms = expS(y_c, x_s') in
#if FIXED && SERVER_IMPERSONATION
event server_k_set((role_server, m3, m6), cid);
#else
event server_k_set((role_server, m1, m2, m3, m6), cid);
#endif /* FIXED && SERVER_IMPERSONATION */
out(c, m6);
insert conversations((role_server, m1, m2, m3, m6));
(* k   := get_key_s(m6) *)
let k = xtrct_xpnd(pms, nonc, cid, m6, n0) in
((* reveal *)
Oreveal(cid, phase_data_exchange, role_client, k_s_of(k)) |
Oreveal(cid, phase_data_exchange, role_server, k_c_of(k)) |
(* Data Exchange *)
(! Oenc((role_client, m1, m2, m3, m6),
k_c_of(k), iv_c_of(k), cid, phase_data_exchange, role_server)) |
(! Odec((role_client, m1, m2, m3, m6), pk_s,
k_s_of(k), iv_s_of(k), cid, phase_data_exchange, role_client)))).

(* tap m2 and m3 *)
let tap_m2 =
((! in(cp, m2: bitstring);                              (* capture m2 *)
let (IP_s: bitstring, IP_c: bitstring, port_s: bitstring,
port_c: bitstring, cid: bitstring, n: bitstring,
scfg_t_pub: bitstring, stk: bitstring) = m2 in
let (iv_stk: bitstring, tk: bitstring) = stk in
#if FIXED && IP_SPOOFING
event capture_m2(tk);
#else
event capture_m2(m2);
#endif /*  FIXED && IP_SPOOFING */
out(cp, m2))
|(! in(c, m2: bitstring); out(cp, m2))).         (* inject m2 *)

(* *)
process
(! new rg: bitstring;
(! new k_stk: bitstring;
out(c, pk(rg));
(**)
! in(c, IP_s: bitstring);
```

```
in(c, port_s: bitstring);
(* The following line allows the attacker to make a server use
scfg_t_pub many times. *)
! in(c, current_time_s: bitstring);
(* scfg_gen *)
let y_s = exp(g, x_s(rg, current_time_s)) in
let sec_s = x_s(rg, current_time_s) in
let pub_s = (g, q, y_s) in
let str = str_qscfg in
let expy: bitstring = s(current_time_s) in
let scid = Hash((pub_s, expy)) in
new r: nonce_t;
let prof = Sign(sk(rg), (str_qscfg, n0, scid, pub_s, expy), r) in
let scfg_t_pub = (scid, pub_s, expy, prof) in
server(pk(rg), sk(rg), k_stk, current_time_s, scfg_t_pub, sec_s,
IP_s, port_s))
| (! in(c, IP_c: bitstring);
in(c, IP_s: bitstring);
in(c, port_c: bitstring);
in(c, port_s: bitstring);
client(pk(rg), IP_c, IP_s, port_c, port_s))
| tap_m2)
```

References

1. Dierks, T., Allen, C.: The TLS protocol version 1.0. In: RFC 2246 (Proposed Standard), Internet Engineering Task Force (1999)
2. Ford, B.: Structured streams: a new transport abstraction. In: SIGCOMM 2007, pp. 361–372 (2007)
3. Stewart, R.: Stream control transmission protocol. In: RFC 4960 (Proposed Standard), Internet Engineering Task Force (2007)
4. Erman, J., Gopalakrishnan, V., Jana, R., Ramakrishnan, K.K.: Towards a SPDY'ier mobile web? In: CoNEXT 2013, pp. 303–314 (2013)
5. Roskind, J.: QUIC (Quick UDP Internet Connections): Multiplexed Stream Transport Over UDP (2013). https://docs.google.com/document/d/1RNHkx_VvKWyWg6Lr8SZ-saqsQx7rFV-ev2jRFUoVD34/
6. StatCounter: StatConter Global Stats: Top. 5 Desktop Browsers from to Apr 2016 (2016). http://gs.statcounter.com/#desktop-browser-ww-monthly-201504-201604
7. Fischlin, M., Günther, F.: Multi-stage key exchange and the case of Google's QUIC protocol. In: ACM Conference on Computer and Communications Security 2014, pp. 1193–1204 (2014)
8. Bellare, M., Rogaway, P.: Entity authentication and key distribution. In: Stinson, D.R. (ed.) CRYPTO 1993. LNCS, vol. 773, pp. 232–249. Springer, Heidelberg (1994). doi:10.1007/3-540-48329-2_21
9. Lychev, R., Jero, S., Boldyreva, A., Nita-Rotaru, C.: How secure and quick is QUIC? Provable security and performance analyses. In: 2015 IEEE Symposium on Security and Privacy, pp. 214–231 (2015)
10. Rescorla, E.: The Transport Layer Security (TLS) Protocol Version 1.3. Internet-Draft draft-ietf-tls-tls13-13 (2016)

11. ProVerif: Cryptographic protocol verifier in the formal model. http://prosecco.gforge.inria.fr/personal/bblanche/proverif/
12. Blanchet, B.: Automatic verification of correspondences for security protocols. J. Comput. Secur. **17**(4), 363–434 (2009)
13. Blanchet, B., Abadi, M., Fournet, C.: Automated verification of selected equivalences for security protocols. J. Logic Algebraic Program. **75**(1), 3–51 (2008). Algebraic Process Calculi. The First Twenty Five Years and Beyond. III
14. Cheval, V., Blanchet, B.: Proving more observational equivalences with ProVerif. In: Basin, D., Mitchell, J.C. (eds.) POST 2013. LNCS, vol. 7796, pp. 226–246. Springer, Heidelberg (2013). doi:10.1007/978-3-642-36830-1_12

Cross-Tool Semantics for Protocol Security Goals

Joshua D. Guttman[⊠], John D. Ramsdell, and Paul D. Rowe

The MITRE Corporation, Bedford, USA
{guttman,ramsdell,prowe}@mitre.org

Abstract. Formal protocol analysis tools provide objective evidence that a protocol under standardization meets security goals, as well as counterexamples to goals it does not meet ("attacks"). Different tools are however based on different execution semantics and adversary models. If different tools are applied to alternative protocols under standardization, can formal evidence offer a yardstick to compare the results?

We propose a family of languages within first order predicate logic to formalize protocol safety goals (rather than indistinguishability). Although they were originally designed for the strand space formalism that supports the tool CPSA, we show how to translate them to goals for the applied π calculus that supports the tool ProVerif. We give a criterion for protocols expressed in the two formalisms to correspond, and prove that if a protocol in the strand space formalism satisfies a goal, then a corresponding applied π process satisfies the translation of that goal. We show that the converse also holds for a class of goal formulas, and conjecture a broader equivalence. We also describe a compiler that, from any protocol in the strand space formalism, constructs a corresponding applied π process and the relevant goal translation.

1 Introduction

Automated tools for analyzing cryptographic protocols have proven quite effective at finding flaws and verifying that proposed mitigations satisfy desirable properties. Recent efforts to apply these tools to protocols approved by standards bodies has led Basin et al. [5] to stress the importance of publishing the underlying threat models and desired security goals as part of the standard. This advice is in line with the ISO standard, ISO/IEC 29128 "Verification of Cryptographic Protocols," [23] which codifies a framework for certifying the design of cryptographic protocols. There are three key aspects to this framework (described in [26]). It calls for explicit (semi-)formal descriptions of the protocol, adversary model, and security properties to be achieved. One final aspect is the production of self-assessment evidence that the protocol achieves the stated goals with respect to the stated adversary model. This fourth aspect is critical. It increases transparency by allowing practitioners the ability to independently inspect and verify the evidence. So, for example, if the evidence is the input/output of some analysis tool, the results could be replicated by re-running the tool.

© Springer International Publishing AG 2016
L. Chen et al. (Eds.): SSR 2016, LNCS 10074, pp. 32–61, 2016.
DOI: 10.1007/978-3-319-49100-4_2

Sometimes, however, two different tools are used to evaluate the same protocol. For example, in 1999, Meadows [28] found weaknesses in the Internet Key Exchange (IKE) protocol using the NRL Protocol Analyzer [27], while in 2011 Cremers [17] found additional flaws using Scyther [16]. In such situations it can be quite difficult to determine exactly what the cause of the difference is. Small differences in any of the first three aspects of the framework could result in important differences in the conclusions drawn. This has the potential to undermine some of the transparency gained by including the self-assessment evidence to begin with.

Ideally the first three aspects of the assessment framework (i.e. protocol description, adversary model, and protocol goals) could be described rigorously in a manner that is independent of the tool or underlying formalism used to verify them. For example, many tools assume a so-called Dolev-Yao adversary model. Although some details vary depending on which cryptographic primitives are being considered, there is generally a common understanding of what is involved in this adversary model. However, this is typically not the case for the other aspects. The particular syntax for describing a protocol is closely tied to the underlying semantics which is entirely tool-dependent. Similarly, security goals are frequently expressed in a stylized manner that is tightly coupled to the tool or underlying formalism. We focus on this last point in this paper, by providing a consistent interpretation of a particular language of security goals in two chosen tools, CPSA and ProVerif [7,32].

We adopt a security goal language $\mathcal{GL}$ for safety properties. It was first introduced in the strand space context [22]. $\mathcal{GL}$ contains both protocol-specific and -independent vocabulary, so each protocol $\mathbb{P}$ determines the protocol-specific language $\mathcal{GL}(\mathbb{P})$ with its protocol-specific vocabulary. Security goals take the so-called "geometric" form:

$$\forall \overline{x} . \; \Phi \Longrightarrow \Psi$$

where Φ, Ψ are built from atomic formulas using conjunction, disjunction, and existential quantification. $\mathcal{GL}(\mathbb{P})$ was designed with limited expressivity in order to capture security goals that are preserved by a class of protocol transformations. The limited expressivity is advantageous for the current work because $\mathcal{GL}$ talks only about events, message parameters and the relevant relations among them. While some tools may represent more types of events than others, there is a common core set of events such as message transmission and reception that every tool must reason about. As a consequence, all statements of security goals related to this core set of events and parameters are independent from the particular formalism that might be used to verify them. Indeed, this core set suffices to express the security properties that protocols aim to achieve.

In this paper we aim to demonstrate how to cross-validate results between the two tools CPSA [32] and ProVerif [7]. We will interpret goal formulas *consistently* relative to the underlying formalisms used by both tools, in this case strand spaces and the applied π calculus respectively. Figure 1 diagrammatically depicts the consistency we demonstrate for such cross-tool semantics.

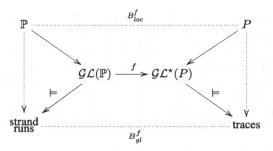

Fig. 1. Consistency of cross-tool semantics

We draw the reader's attention to several aspects of this diagram. First, the two triangles represent standalone logical semantics for the goal language $\mathcal{GL}$ with respect to each of the execution semantics of the two tools. In Sect. 3 we describe the left triangle: the strand space semantics for CPSA of $\mathcal{GL}(\mathbb{P})$ relative to a notion of executions we call "strand runs." We cover the right triangle in Sect. 4 by giving the semantics of $\mathcal{GL}^\star(P)$ relative to a trace execution semantics of the applied π calculus for ProVerif.

Figure 1 includes two different logical languages $\mathcal{GL}(\mathbb{P})$ and $\mathcal{GL}^\star(P)$, because applied π processes P can represent strictly more events than strand spaces. In particular, P may represent *internal* events required to parse received messages. Thus we will offer an embedding $f : \mathcal{GL}(\mathbb{P}) \to \mathcal{GL}^\star(P)$ on the goal language. We can therefore only hope to get consistent answers from CPSA and ProVerif on goals expressible in $\mathcal{GL}(\mathbb{P})$, or equivalently, its f-image, $f(\mathcal{GL}(\mathbb{P})) \subseteq \mathcal{GL}^\star(P)$.

Of course, if the corresponding predicates of $\mathcal{GL}(\mathbb{P})$ and $\mathcal{GL}^\star(P)$ refer to essentially different things, we cannot expect consistent results. In Sect. 5, Definition 4, we present a relation—P *represents* $\mathbb{P}$ *under* f—that characterizes when a protocol $\mathbb{P}$ and process term P "can only do the same things." The idea is to ensure that the corresponding formulations of each of the roles are locally bisimilar. The *represents* relation thus expresses a correctness criterion for translating protocols from one formalism to the other. Since again the applied π calculus is more expressive than strand spaces, we focus on an embedding from strands into applied π. We describe a *compiler* that transforms a strand space protocol $\mathbb{P}$ into a bisimilar process term P; the *represents* relation defines compiler correctness for it.

Finally, in Sect. 6 we demonstrate how *represents* relation on protocols lifts to a global bisimulation B^f on the configurations in the operational semantics of the two sides. We then show that this bisimulation respects security goals in the sense that any goal satisfied on the left by a strand run is also satisfied on the right by a corresponding trace. The converse cannot be true for all goals because applied π traces are totally ordered whereas strand runs may be only partially ordered. However, we conjecture that for any goal that is insensitive to the *inessential* orderings of a trace, if a trace satisfies the goal then so does a corresponding strand run.

Related Work. We have described above how this paper connects to the protocol verification framework described by Matsuo et al. [26] and standardized in the ISO in [23]. Although the use of formal logics to express protocol security goals is not new [10,18], our focus on using such a logic to connect distinct verification formalisms seems to be new. There was a lot of work in the early 2000s detailing the connections between the various protocol analysis formalisms being developed at the time [6,11,15,31]. This work tended to focus on connecting the underlying execution semantics of the various formalisms without explicit reference to formal security goals. Thus, in reference to Fig. 1, only the outside edges were described. By filling in the details of the internal connections, explicitly relating the execution semantics to a security goal language, it is easier for a practitioner to understand how the two sides relate. More recently Kremer and Künnemann [24] provided a similar translation between a stateful applied π calculus and that of the tamarin tool's [29] multiset rewriting formalism. They show their translation correct with respect to a first-order logic of security goals very similar to our own. However, rather than relating the results of different tools performing analysis in different formalisms, they rely on this translation to justify the use of tamarin as a back-end utility for the stateful applied π front-end.

There have been several related projects that unite a variety of protocol validation tools into a single tool suite. Most notably, the AVISPA [3] and AVANTSSAR [4] projects provide a unified interface to several back-end tools. The available toolset seems to be limited to bounded verification, whereas in this paper we connect two formalisms capable of unbounded verification. Their protocol description language, ASLan++, however does serve as a formalism-independent protocol description format for the available analysis tools. Similarly, Almousa et al. [2] define translations from Alice-and-Bob protocol descriptions into various formal models and implementations. They prove the correctness of these translations with respect to a simple yet general (local) semantics. Such correctness seems to be related to our semantic correctness criterion discussed in Sect. 5. Perhaps it would be possible to prove that any pair of translations from their high-level description language into both strand spaces and the applied π calculus that respect their semantics would satisfy our correctness criterion.

Many tools have also embarked on establishing indistinguishability properties of protocols, also sometimes called privacy-type properties. In this area, logical languages to express goals are less developed. However, we consider this an important area to pursue the present cross-tool logical program also.

2   A Simple Example

In this section we introduce an example protocol, and mention the goals that it achieves. We then show how to formalize the goals it achieves in a first order language introduced for the strand space formalism [22,33].

A Simple Example Protocol. As a minimal example, consider the Simple Example Protocol (SEP) used by Blanchet [8] and many others [14]. In this protocol, an initiator A chooses a session key s, which it signs and then encrypts using the public encryption key of an intended peer B. It then waits to receive in exchange a sensitive payload d, delivered encrypted with s.

$$A \rightarrow B : \{\![\,[\![s]\!]_{\mathsf{sk}(A)}\,]\!\}_{\mathsf{pk}(B)}$$
$$B \rightarrow A : \{\![d]\!\}_s$$

One is traditionally interested in whether confidentiality is assured for d, and whether A authenticates B as the origin of d or B authenticates A as the origin of s. Actually, SEP already indicates why this way of expressing the goals is too crude. In Fig. 2(a), we show the assumptions needed for a conclusion, from A's point of view, and the conclusion that B behaved according to expectations. That is, the protocol is successful from A's point of view. However, the story is different from B's point of view, as shown in Fig. 2(b). Although B certainly can't know whether A receives the final message, the fact that A's intended peer is some C who may differ from B is troublesome. If C's private decryption key is compromised, then the adversary can recover s and A's signature, repackaging them for B, and using s to recover the intended secret d.

If A has a run of the protocol apparently with B;	**If** B has a run of the protocol apparently with A;
and B's private decryption key $\mathsf{pk}(B)^{-1}$ is uncompromised;	**and** B's private decryption key $\mathsf{pk}(B)^{-1}$ and A's signature key $\mathsf{sk}(A)$ are both uncompromised;
and the session key s is freshly chosen,	**and** the session key s and payload d are freshly chosen,
then B transmitted d with matching parameters,	**then** A took the first step of an initiator session, originating the key s, with some intended peer C.
and d remains confidential.	
(a)	(b)

Fig. 2. Main goal achieved by SEP from the points of view of each role

The Goal Language. We wish to express protocol security goals, such as those in Fig. 2, in a language that is independent of the underlying formalism used to verify the goals. We adopt a first order goal language developed in the context of the strand space formalism. It was originally designed by Guttman [22] to limit expressiveness in order to ensure goals in the language are preserved under a certain class of protocol transformations. The limited expressivity was leveraged by Rowe et al. [33] to measure and compare the strength of "related" protocols. We believe the limited expressivity makes it possible for the formal statement of security goals to be independent of any underlying verification methodology or formalism. Although the goal language was originally developed for the strand space formalism and incorporated into CPSA, the main purpose of this paper is to provide a semantics of the language for the applied π calculus that is consistent with the strand space semantics so that it might be used also by ProVerif.

As suggested by the informal goal statements of Fig. 2, the language needs predicates to express how far a principal progressed in a role, the value of parameters used in messages, the freshness of values, and the non-compromise of keys. We explain each of these in turn.

The progress made in a role is expressed with *role position predicates*. For example, predicates of the form $\mathtt{InitDone}(n)$ or $\mathtt{RespStart}(m)$ say that an initiator has completed its last step, or that a responder has completed its first step. Each role position predicate is a one-place predicate that says what kind of event its argument n, m refers to.

At each point in a role, the agent will have bound some of its local parameters to concrete values. The *parameter predicates* are two place predicates that express this binding. For example, if n refers to an initiator's event, we would use $\mathtt{Self}(n, a)$ to express that the initiator's local value for their own identity is a. Similarly, $\mathtt{SessKey}(m, s)$ would say that the value bound to the local session key parameter is referred to by s.

The role position predicates and the parameters predicates are *protocol-dependent* in that the length of roles and the parameter bindings at various points depend on the details of the protocol.

The goal language also contains *protocol-independent* predicates that apply to any protocol. These predicates appear in Table 1. They help to express the structural properties of protocol executions. $\mathtt{Preceq}(m, n)$ asserts that either m and n represent the same event, or else m occurs before n; $\mathtt{Coll}(m, n)$ says that they are both events of the same local session. $m = n$ is satisfied when m and n are equal.

The remaining predicates are used to express that values are fresh or uncompromised. This way of expressing freshness and non-compromise comes from the strand space formalism, but it is possible to make sense of them in any formalism. The idea is to characterize the effects of local choices as they manifest in executions. Randomly chosen values cannot be guessed by the adversary or other participants, so they may only "originate" from the local session in which it is chosen, if at all. We will make the meaning of "origination" more precise for each of the formalisms, but the intuition is that $\mathtt{Unq}(v)$ says that v is a randomly chosen value, $\mathtt{UnqAt}(n, v)$ specifies the node at which it originates, and $\mathtt{Non}(v)$ says that v is never learned by the adversary. Within this language we can formally express the two goals of Fig. 2 as we have done in Fig. 3 for the second goal.

A formal semantics for this language has already been given with respect to the execution model of strand spaces [22]. Our main contribution is to provide a consistent semantics for this language with respect to the execution model of the applied π calculus. To simplify this task we assume that messages have the same representation in both formalisms. We now provide the necessary details of the underlying term algebra for modeling messages.

Table 1. Protocol-independent vocabulary of languages $\mathcal{GL}(\Pi)$

Functions:	$\text{pk}(a)$	$\text{sk}(a)$	$\text{inv}(k)$
	$\text{ltk}(a,b)$		
Relations:	$\text{Preceq}(m,n)$	$\text{Coll}(m,n)$	$=$
	$\text{Unq}(v)$	$\text{UnqAt}(n,v)$	$\text{Non}(v)$

Term Algebra. We will use an order-sorted term algebra to represent the values exchanged in protocols. There is a partial order of *sorts* S ordered by $<$. We assume the existence of a top sort $\top$ that is above all other sorts. We build terms from sorted names and variables. We call $<$-minimal sorts *basic sorts* and terms of those sorts are called *basic values*. The set of names is the disjoint union of names for each basic sort: $\mathcal{N} = \uplus_{\mathsf{s}\in\mathsf{S}}\mathcal{N}_\mathsf{s}$, where $\mathcal{N}_\mathsf{s} = \mathcal{N}_\mathsf{s}^0 \uplus \mathcal{N}_\mathsf{s}^\nu$ is the disjoint union of two sets. We also consider two disjoint sets of variables $\mathcal{X} = \uplus_{\mathsf{s}\in\mathsf{S}}\mathcal{X}_\mathsf{s}$ and $\mathcal{W} = \uplus_{\mathsf{s}\in\mathsf{S}}\mathcal{W}_\mathsf{s}$. Variables in $\mathcal{X}$ will be bound to parts of messages received by protocol participants, while variables in $\mathcal{W}$ will be used by the intruder.

We write $\mathcal{T}(\Sigma, A)$ to denote the set of terms built from set A using signature Σ in the usual way. A term is *ground* if it contains no variables. An *environment* is a map from $\mathcal{N} \cup \mathcal{X} \cup \mathcal{W}$ that maps names to names and variables to terms. The result of applying an environment σ to a term u is denoted $\sigma(u)$. We only consider sort-respecting environments in that for every term $u : \mathsf{s}$, $\sigma(u) : \mathsf{s}'$ with $\mathsf{s}' \leq \mathsf{s}$. Environments also respect the difference between $\mathcal{N}_\mathsf{s}^0$ and $\mathcal{N}_\mathsf{s}^\nu$. Environments can be updated so that, for example, $\sigma[x \mapsto v]$ is the environment that maps x to v and otherwise acts like σ. We identify a subset of terms called *messages* by partitioning Σ into constructor symbols and destructor symbols, $\Sigma_c \uplus \Sigma_d$, and letting $\mathsf{MSG} = \mathcal{T}(\Sigma_c, \mathcal{N} \cup \mathcal{X})$. These are the terms that are sent and received by protocols. For concreteness assume $\Sigma_c = \{\{\!|\cdot|\!\}^\mathsf{s}, \{\!|\cdot|\!\}^\mathsf{a}, [\![\cdot]\!]., \cdot\hat{\ }\cdot, \mathsf{pk}, \mathsf{sk}, \mathsf{ltk}, (\cdot)^{-1}\}$, and that $\Sigma_d = \{\mathsf{dec}^\mathsf{s}, \mathsf{dec}^\mathsf{a}, \mathsf{ver}, \mathsf{fst}, \mathsf{snd}\}$.

We say that t_0 is an *ingredient* of t, written $t_0 \sqsubseteq t$, iff either (i) $t_0 = t$; or (ii) $t = t_1 \hat{\ } t_2$ and $t_0 \sqsubseteq t_1$ or $t_0 \sqsubseteq t_2$; or (iii) $t = \{\!|t_1|\!\}_{t_2}^*$ for $* \in \{\mathsf{s}, \mathsf{a}\}$ and $t_0 \sqsubseteq t_1$; or (iv) $t = [\![t_1]\!]_{t_2}$ and $t_0 \sqsubseteq t_1$. The key of a cryptographic operation does not contribute to the ingredients of the result; only the plaintext does.

The adversary's ability to derive messages is represented in two ways. In the first method, we partition Σ into $\Sigma_{\mathsf{pub}} \uplus \Sigma_{\mathsf{priv}}$ and consider a convergent rewrite system with rules $\mathsf{g}(t_1, \ldots, t_n) \to t$ for $\mathsf{g} \in \Sigma_d$. Since the system is convergent, every term t has a normal form denoted $t\!\downarrow$. The set of messages derivable from

$$\forall n, b, a, s, d \,.\, \mathsf{RespDone}(n) \wedge \mathsf{Self}(n,b) \wedge \qquad\qquad \exists m, c \,.\, \mathsf{InitStart}(m) \wedge \mathsf{Self}(m,a) \wedge$$
$$\mathsf{Peer}(n,a) \wedge \mathsf{SessKey}(n,s) \wedge \mathsf{Datum}(n,d) \wedge \;\Rightarrow\; \mathsf{Peer}(m,c) \wedge \mathsf{SessKey}(m,s) \wedge$$
$$\mathsf{Non}(\mathsf{sk}(b)) \wedge \mathsf{Non}(\mathsf{sk}(a)) \wedge \mathsf{Unq}(s) \qquad\qquad \mathsf{UnqAt}(m,s) \wedge \mathsf{Preceq}(m,n)$$

Fig. 3. Formalized goal achieved by SEP from the responder point of view

some set X is thus $nf(\mathcal{T}(\Sigma_{\mathsf{pub}}, X)) \cap \mathsf{MSG}$, where $nf(T)$ produces the set of normal forms of the set of terms T. In the second method, the adversary uses derivability rules of the form $\{t_1, \ldots, t_n\} \vdash t$. The set of messages derivable from some set X is the smallest set containing X and closed under $\vdash$. When each rewrite rule $\mathbf{g}(t_1, \ldots, t_n) \rightarrow t$ corresponds to a derivation rule $\{t_1, \ldots, t_n\} \vdash t$ and vice versa, the two notions of derivability coincide on a large class of protocols. The two notions of derivability are equivalent when standard best practices are used that prevent principals from inadvertently applying a constructor to a term in Σ_d whose normal form is not in MSG [25, 30].

3   Strand Spaces

In this section we present the syntax and execution semantics of strand spaces and we discuss how the executions furnish semantic models for the formulas of the goal language $\mathcal{GL}(\mathbb{P})$.

Strands. A *strand* is a sequence of transmission and reception events, each of which we will call a *node*. We use strands to represent the behavior of a single principal in a single local protocol session. By convention, we draw strands with double-arrows connecting the successive nodes $\bullet \Rightarrow \bullet$. We use single arrows $\bullet \rightarrow \bullet$ to denote the type of node (transmission vs. reception).

We write $+t$ for a node transmitting the term t and $-t$ for a node receiving t, and we write $\mathsf{msg}(n)$ for t if n is a node $\pm t$. We write $\mathsf{dmsg}(n)$ for the pair $\pm \mathsf{msg}(n)$, i.e. the message together with its direction, $+$ or $-$.

If s is a strand, we write $|s|$ for its length, i.e. the number of nodes on s. We use 1-based indexing for strands, writing $s@i$ for its ith node. Thus, the sequence of nodes along s is $\langle s@1, \ldots, s@|s| \rangle$. A message t *originates* at a node $n = s@j$ iff (i) n is a transmission node; (ii) $t \sqsubseteq \mathsf{msg}(n)$; and (iii) t is not an ingredient of any earlier $\mathsf{msg}(m)$ where $m = s@k$ and $k < j$.

Protocols. A *protocol* $\mathbb{P}$ is a finite sequence of strands, called the *roles* of $\mathbb{P}$, together with possibly some auxiliary assumptions (detailed below) about fresh values. Regarding $\mathbb{P}$ as a sequence instead of a set will be convenient in Sect. 5.

The messages sent and received on these strands contain *parameters*, which are the names, nonces, keys, and other data occurring in the messages. The parameters account for the variability between different instances of the roles. More formally, a $\mathbb{P}$-*instance* is a triple consisting of a role $\rho \in \mathbb{P}$, a natural number $h \leq |\rho|$, and an environment σ that assigns messages to precisely those variables and names in ρ that occur in its first h nodes. If $\iota = (\rho, h, \sigma)$ is an instance, then the *nodes* of ι are $\mathsf{nodes}(\iota) = \{(\iota, j) \colon 1 \leq j \leq h\}$. The transmission and reception

Fig. 4. The SEP protocol.

nodes of ι are denoted $\mathsf{nodes}^+(\iota)$ and $\mathsf{nodes}^-(\iota)$ respectively. The message of a node is $\mathsf{msg}((\rho, h, \sigma), j) = \sigma(\mathsf{msg}(\rho@j))$. The idea is that the nodes are the part that has already happened. When $h = 0$, then $\mathsf{nodes}(\iota) = \emptyset$.

Each $\mathbb{P}$-instance $\iota = (\rho, h, \sigma)$ corresponds to a *regular strand* s of $\mathbb{P}$ by applying σ to ρ up to height h. That is $\mathsf{dmsg}(s@i) = \sigma(\mathsf{dmsg}(\rho@i))$ for each $i \leq h$ and $|s| = h$. An interesting subtlety arises when two roles have a common instance. That is (ρ, h, σ) and (ρ', h, σ') may satisfy $\sigma(\mathsf{dmsg}(\rho@i)) = \sigma'(\mathsf{dmsg}(\rho'@i))$ for each $1 \leq i \leq h$. This can represent a branching role that has a fixed trunk and alternate continuations. In the present paper we restrict our attention to non-branching protocols in the sense that no two roles share a common instance. This eases our connection to the applied π semantics later. We leave for future work the consideration of how to relate results for branching protocols.

$\mathbb{P}$ may make *role origination assumptions* rlunique, stipulating that certain expressions involving the parameters originate at most once. These assumptions apply to *all* instances of the role. Formally, rlunique is a function of the roles of $\mathbb{P}$ and a height, returning a finite set of expressions: $\mathsf{rlunique} \colon \mathbb{P} \times \mathbb{N} \to \mathcal{P}(\mathsf{MSG})$. The set $\mathsf{rlunique}(\rho, i)$ gives ρ its unique origination assumptions for height i. We require that the image of rlunique consist only of terms in $\mathcal{N}_\mathsf{s}^\nu$ for the appropriate sort s, and that all other names in roles are chosen from the sets $\mathcal{N}_\mathsf{s}^0$.

We will assume that each protocol $\mathbb{P}$ contains the *listener role*, which consists of a single reception node $\xrightarrow{x}\bullet$. Each instance witnesses for the fact that the message instantiating x has been observed unprotected on the network. Thus, we use the listener role to express confidentiality failures. We also include a kind of dual to the listener role called a *blab role* that discloses a basic term to the adversary for it to use in deriving messages for reception. A blab strand witnesses for the fact that the adversary has managed to guess a value.

The two roles in Fig. 4 make up a strand-style definition of the SEP protocol (in which the listener and blab roles have been omitted). In the right-hand role ρ_2 we assume d to be uniquely originating, i.e. $\mathsf{rlunique}(\rho_2, 2) = \{d\}$. We make no such assumption about the value s in the left-hand role. This is a subtle point that is discussed at the end of Sect. 4.

Candidate Strand Runs. For the purposes of this paper, we slightly alter the notion of execution used for strand spaces. We argue below that this new notion preserves the semantics of $\mathcal{GL}(\mathbb{P})$. The notion of execution we consider, called a *candidate strand run*, or frequently, just a *candidate*, is a pair $\mathcal{I} = (I, \preceq)$ where $I = \langle \iota_1, \ldots, \iota_k \rangle$ is a finite sequence of $\mathbb{P}$-instances, and $\preceq$ is a partial order extending the strand succession orderings of $\mathsf{nodes}(\iota_i)$. We further require that $\mathcal{I}$ respect the rlunique assumptions of the roles. More formally, if $\iota_i = (\rho, h, \sigma)$ and $i \leq h$, then if $a \in \mathsf{rlunique}(\rho, i)$, then $\sigma(a)$ originates at most once in $\mathcal{I}$. The nodes of $\mathcal{I}$ are $\mathsf{nodes}(\mathcal{I}) = \{(i, n) \colon 1 \leq i \leq k \wedge n \in \mathsf{nodes}(\iota_i)\}$.

A reception node of $\mathcal{I}$ is *realized* if the adversary is in fact able to deliver $\mathsf{msg}(n)$ in time for each reception node n. This means that $\mathsf{msg}(n)$ should be derivable from previously transmitted messages. More formally, if $\mathcal{I} = (I, \preceq)$ is a candidate and $n \in \mathsf{nodes}^-(I)$, then n is *realized in* $\mathcal{I}$ iff

$$\{\mathsf{msg}(m) \in \mathsf{nodes}^+(I) \colon m \prec n\} \vdash \mathsf{msg}(n).$$

A candidate $\mathcal{I} = (I, \preceq)$ is a *strand run*, or just a *run*, iff, for every $n \in \mathsf{nodes}^-(I)$, n is realized in $\mathcal{I}$. We write $\mathsf{Runs}(\mathbb{P})$ for the set of strand runs of $\mathbb{P}$.

Operational Semantics. The operational semantics of strand runs is obtained by defining an immediate successor relation on candidates and restricting it to runs. We first rely, however, on a localized notion of successor for instances.

If $\iota = (\rho, h, \sigma)$ and $\iota' = (\rho', h', \sigma')$ are instances, then ι' is *an immediate successor* of ι iff (i) $\rho = \rho'$; (ii) $h + 1 = h'$; and (iii) σ' restricted to the domain of σ agrees with σ. If ι' is an immediate successor of ι, then it extends σ to choose values for any new parameters that occur in $\mathsf{msg}(\rho @ h + 1)$, but not in $\mathsf{nodes}(\iota)$. This local successor relation lifts to a global successor relation on candidates.

One candidate $\mathcal{I}' = (I', \preceq')$ is an *immediate successor* of another candidate $\mathcal{I} = (I, \preceq)$ when there is one new node n in $\mathcal{I}'$, and the only change to the order is that some old nodes may precede n. More formally, $\mathcal{I}' = (I', \preceq')$ is an *immediate successor* of $\mathcal{I} = (I, \preceq)$ iff, letting $I = \langle \iota_1, \ldots, \iota_k \rangle$,

1. $\mathsf{nodes}(I') = \mathsf{nodes}(I) \cup \{n\}$, for a single $n \notin \mathsf{nodes}(I)$, i.e. either
   (a) $\mathsf{dom}(I') = \mathsf{dom}(I)$ and there is a $j \in \mathsf{dom}(I)$ s.t. $I'(j)$ is an immediate successor of ι_j, and for all $k \in \mathsf{dom}(I)$, if $k \neq j$ then $I'(k) = \iota_k$; or else
   (b) $I' = \langle \iota_1, \ldots, \iota_k, \iota'_{k+1} \rangle$, and ι'_{k+1} has height $h = 1$; and
2. There is a set of nodes $M \subseteq \mathsf{nodes}(I)$ such that $\preceq' = \preceq \cup \{(m, n) \colon m \in M\}$.

The empty candidate $\mathsf{NullRun} = (\langle \rangle, \emptyset)$ is a strand run, since it has no unrealized nodes. We regard it as the initial state in a transition relation, which is simply the "immediate successor" relation restricted to realized strand runs. We will write $S_{\mathbb{P}}$ for the immediate successor relation restricted to strand runs of $\mathbb{P}$, i.e. $S_{\mathbb{P}}(\mathcal{I}, \mathcal{I}')$ iff $\mathcal{I}, \mathcal{I}'$ are runs of $\mathbb{P}$ and $\mathcal{I}'$ is an immediate successor of $\mathcal{I}$.

Definition 1. *Let $\mathbb{P}$ be a protocol. The operational semantics of $\mathbb{P}$ is the state machine $M_{\mathbb{P}} = (\mathsf{Runs}(\mathbb{P}), \mathsf{NullRun}, S_{\mathbb{P}})$ where the set of states is $\mathsf{Runs}(\mathbb{P})$, the initial state is $\mathsf{NullRun}$, and the transition relation is $S_{\mathbb{P}}$.*

A sequence of runs $\langle R_1, \ldots, R_i \rangle$ is an $M_{\mathbb{P}}$-history iff $R_1 = \mathsf{NullRun}$ and, for every j such that $1 \leq j < i$, $S_{\mathbb{P}}(R_j, R_{j+1})$.

A run R is $\mathbb{P}$-accessible iff for some $M_{\mathbb{P}}$-history $\langle R_1, \ldots, R_i \rangle$, $R = R_i$. ///

By induction on the well-founded partial orders $\preceq_R$, we have:

Lemma 1. *Every $\mathbb{P}$ run is $\mathbb{P}$-accessible.* ///

Syntax and Semantics of $\mathcal{GL}(\mathbb{P})$. $\mathcal{GL}(\mathbb{P})$'s protocol-dependent vocabulary contains one role position predicate $P_i^\rho(\cdot)$ for each role node $\rho @ i$ of $\mathbb{P}$, and a collection of role parameter predicates $P_p^\rho(\cdot, \cdot)$, one for each parameter p in role ρ.

Candidates furnish models for the language $\mathcal{GL}(\mathbb{P})$ for security goals [22,33]. Candidates that are actually runs are the most important: They determine whether a protocol $\mathbb{P}$ *achieves* a formula $\Gamma \in \mathcal{GL}(\mathbb{P})$. In particular,

$\mathbb{P}$ *achieves* Γ iff, for every *realized* run R and assignment η of objects in R to free variables in Γ, R satisfies Γ under η, typically written $R, \eta \models \Gamma$. The details of the semantics, using a slightly different notion of execution than the one used here, are in [22]. We now show that the semantics for runs is equivalent.

Equivalence of Two Strand Space Semantics. The new operational semantics presented above is only inessentially different from the usual strand space semantics in terms of realized skeletons. In order to demonstrate this, we now present the usual notion of execution for strand spaces, and demonstrate the equivalence of the two semantics.

A *skeleton* $\mathbb{A}$ for $\mathbb{P}$ is a structure that provides partial information about a set of executions of $\mathbb{P}$. It consists of (i) a finite sequence of regular strands (or equivalently, instances) of $\mathbb{P}$; (ii) a partial ordering $\preceq_{\mathbb{A}}$ on the nodes of $\mathbb{A}$ extending the strand succession orderings; and (iii) two sets of terms $\mathsf{unique}_{\mathbb{A}}$ and $\mathsf{non}_{\mathbb{A}}$ representing terms that may originate on at most one node and terms that must not originate respectively. We assume that $\mathbb{A}$ inherits the origination assumptions from the roles of the protocol in that the set $\mathsf{unique}_{\mathbb{A}} \supseteq \sigma(\mathsf{rlunique}(\rho, i))$ for every instance $\iota = (\rho, h, \sigma)$ of $\mathbb{A}$ and every $i \le h$.

A skeleton $\mathbb{A}$ is *realized* iff, for every reception node $n \in \mathsf{nodes}^-(\mathbb{A})$, $\mathsf{msg}(n)$ is derivable from previously transmitted messages and guessable values. More formally, $T \cup (B \setminus X) \vdash \mathsf{msg}(n)$ where $T = \{\mathsf{msg}(m) \mid m \in \mathsf{nodes}^+(\mathbb{A}) \wedge m \prec_{\mathbb{A}} n\}$, B is the set of basic values, and $X = \mathsf{unique}_{\mathbb{A}} \cup \mathsf{non}_{\mathbb{A}}$ is the set of all non-guessable basic values.

We can correlate the realized skeletons of any protocol $\mathbb{P}$ (that excluded blab roles) with the $\mathbb{P}'$-accessible runs, where $\mathbb{P}' = \mathbb{P} \cup \{blabs\}$. The idea is to add blab nodes for all the basic values the adversary is allowed to guess. More formally, let

$$B_{\mathbb{A}} = \{b \mid \exists n \in \mathsf{nodes}(\mathbb{A}) . \ b \text{ is a subterm of } \mathsf{msg}(n) \wedge b \text{ is a basic value}\}$$

and let B' be a set of blab nodes, one for each element of $B_{\mathbb{A}} \setminus (\mathsf{unique}_{\mathbb{A}} \cup \mathsf{non}_{\mathbb{A}})$. We say that a realized skeleton $\mathbb{A}$ and a run R are *related* iff $\mathsf{nodes}(R) = \mathsf{nodes}(\mathbb{A}) \cup B'$, and $\preceq_{\mathbb{A}} = \preceq_R \cap (\mathsf{nodes}(\mathbb{A}) \times \mathsf{nodes}(\mathbb{A}))$.

Lemma 2. *Let* $\mathbb{P}' = \mathbb{P} \cup \{blabs\}$. *Every realized* $\mathbb{P}$-*skeleton* $\mathbb{A}$ *has a related* $\mathbb{P}'$ *run* R. *Every* $\mathbb{P}'$ *run* R *has a related realized* $\mathbb{P}$-*skeleton* $\mathbb{A}$.   ///

Lemma 3. *Let* $\mathbb{P}' = \mathbb{P} \cup \{blabs\}$, *and let* $\mathbb{A}$ *be a realized* $\mathbb{P}$-*skeleton, and* R *a related* $\mathbb{P}'$ *run. Then for any atomic formula* ϕ *and any variable assignment* η *of variables to nodes and terms in* $\mathbb{A}$, $\mathbb{A}, \eta \models \phi$ *iff* $R, \eta \models \phi$.   ///

Lemma 3 in fact lifts to goal formulas Γ as a natural corollary. The set of goals achieved by $\mathbb{P}'$ is essentially the same as that achieved by $\mathbb{P}$. In particular, any goal Γ true of a skeleton $\mathbb{A}$ is also true of some related run R. Similarly, as long as the Γ does not express anything explicitly about the blab nodes, if the formula is true of R it is also true of $\mathbb{A}$. It is therefore no danger to use the operational semantics of runs instead of the skeleton semantics when forming a connection to the applied π semantics.

4   The Labeled Applied π Calculus

In this section we describe the triangle on the right side of Fig. 1. We introduce a version of the applied π calculus [1]; we define a trace-based execution semantics; and we show how to extract $\mathcal{GL}^\star(P)$ from a protocol P, giving it a semantics with respect to the traces. Our process calculus is adapted from the one used by ProVerif [9]. It differs in several inconsequential ways by adopting a few changes inspired by Cortier et al. [13]. It also includes a couple new features designed to aid the connection with strand spaces.

Applied π Calculus Syntax. Protocols are modeled as processes built on an infinite set of channel names Ch, using the following grammar.

$$P, Q = 0 \qquad | \; \text{in}(c, x) . \; P \qquad | \; \text{out}^\ell(c, u) . \; P \qquad | \; \text{let } x : \text{s} = v \text{ in } P \text{ else } Q$$
$$| \; (P \mid Q) \qquad | \; \text{new } n : \text{s} . \; P \qquad | \; \text{sum } n' : \text{s} . \; P \qquad | \; !\text{new } tid . \, \text{out}(c, tid) . \; P$$
$$| \; \ell . \; P$$

Here $c, tid \in Ch$, $x \in \mathcal{X}$, $n \in \mathcal{N}_s^\nu$, and $n' \in \mathcal{N}_s^0$. We assume $u \in \mathsf{MSG}$ is a constructor term; $v \in \mathcal{T}(\Sigma, \mathcal{N} \cup \mathcal{X})$ can be any term.

The free variables, free names, and free channels of P are denoted $fv(P)$, $fn(P)$, and $fc(P)$ respectively. P is a *basic process* iff P contains no parallel or replication operators, and all else branches in P are 0.

We now discuss the main differences from the standard calculus used in ProVerif. Readers familiar with that calculus will notice we have omitted an if-then-else construction. As discussed in [13], this is without loss of expressivity as long as the rewrite theory contains a reduction of the form $\mathsf{eq}(x, x) \rightarrow \mathsf{ok}$ in which $\mathsf{eq} \in \Sigma_d$. The if-then-else process can then be replaced by let $x = \mathsf{eq}(u, v)$ in P else Q, and the operational semantics will ensure P cannot proceed if $\mathsf{eq}(u, v){\downarrow}$ is not in MSG, that is, if $u \neq v$.

This grammar also ties replication to channel restriction new tid. Since the new channel is always immediately made public, the adversary has no restrictions on its use. That is, any message that could be sent or received over the public channel c could also be sent or received over the new channel tid.

Labels ℓ appear in two ways. As standalone prefixes, they implement the *begin-end events* in ProVerif and many other approaches, e.g. [20,34]. They signal the occurrence of steps mentioned in security goals such as authentication properties. In ProVerif these begin-end events come equipped with explicit arguments representing some subset of values seen so far. This is then used to express protocol goals in a tool-dependent manner. Since we will be able to infer the full set of values seen so far, we omit the explicit arguments to these labels. The labels also decorate transmissions $\mathsf{out}^\ell(c, u)$. The operational semantics reduces the label and the transmission simultaneously. As we will see below, this is designed to ensure the goal language semantics of origination is sensible on the applied π side.

Finally, the most notable difference is in our inclusion of the operator sum $n' : \text{s}$. This is essentially an infinite, non-deterministic choice operator (see e.g. [21]).

Whereas $P + Q$ represents a (non-deterministic) choice between processes P and Q, sum $n' : \mathsf{s} \cdot P$ acts by choosing a binding $[n' \mapsto n_i]$ for any $n_i \in \mathcal{N}_\mathsf{s}^0$ and continuing as P using this binding. This choice does not preclude another process from choosing the same value at another time. Such choices arise frequently in protocols. For example, a role that may be run by any agent might start by choosing the name of the agent that is inhabiting the role in the current local session. It might also be used to represent non-random data that two peers of a protocol must agree on such as the name or price of a product in an e-commerce protocol, or when we do not want to assume *every* agent has access to a good source of randomness.

The inclusion of this operator is important for our purposes. In later sections when we describe a bisimulation between strands and processes, we need to ensure that for any $\mathbb{P}$-instance that can occur there is also some corresponding local trace of a process that can occur. Without the sum operator the π calculus has no way of accessing the infinitude of the carrier sets for the various sorts. In practice, this can be approximated by pre-pending the protocol with some finite number of new-bound names, sending them to the adversary if they are not meant to remain secret. This is the typical style of modeling protocols in ProVerif. Indeed, since any counterexample to a security goal only uses finitely many values, then given a particular attack there is some number of values that one could create at the beginning of the protocol that will suffice to find the attack. Even more promising is the existence of results such as Comon and Cortier's [12] which establishes an a priori finite bound on the number of agents necessary to discover an attack if there is one. Thus, although ProVerif's input language does not contain a sum operator, we will continue to use it in this paper with the understanding that there may be principled ways of using ProVerif to verify finite approximations to our translations.

Modeling Protocols. The roles of protocols are formalized as replicated processes !new $tid \cdot \mathsf{out}(c, tid) \cdot P$ where P is a basic process. It is no restriction to assume that every role uses the *same* channel tid since each replicated session will instantiate tid with a distinct fresh channel. Any parameters $p : \mathsf{s}$ assumed to be freshly chosen during *every* local session of a role will be bound new $p : \mathsf{s}$ in P. Other parameters of the local session will be bound sum $p : \mathsf{s}$ in P.

$$
\begin{aligned}
A :=\ & \mathsf{sum}\ a : \mathsf{agt}.\ \mathsf{sum}\ b : \mathsf{agt}.\ \mathsf{sum}\ s : \mathsf{skey}.\ \mathsf{out}^{\mathtt{InitStart}}(tid, \{\!| [\![s]\!]_{\mathsf{sk}(a)} |\!\}^{\mathsf{a}}_{\mathsf{pk}(b)})\ . \\
& \mathsf{in}(tid, z)\ .\ \mathsf{let}\ d : \mathsf{data} = \mathsf{dec}^{\mathsf{s}}(z, s)\ \mathsf{in}\ \mathtt{InitDone}\ .\ 0 \\
B :=\ & \mathsf{sum}\ a : \mathsf{agt}.\ \mathsf{sum}\ b : \mathsf{agt}.\ \mathsf{in}(tid, z)\ .\ \mathsf{let}\ x : \top = \mathsf{dec}^{\mathsf{a}}(z, \mathsf{sk}(b))\ \mathsf{in} \\
& \mathsf{let}\ s : \mathsf{skey} = \mathsf{ver}(x, \mathsf{pk}(a))\ \mathsf{in}\ \mathtt{RespStart}\ .\ \mathsf{new}\ d : \mathsf{data}\ . \\
& \mathsf{out}^{\mathtt{RespDone}}(tid, \{\!| d |\!\}^{\mathsf{s}}_{s})\ .\ 0 \\
P :=\ & !\mathsf{new}\ tid\ .\ \mathsf{out}(c, tid)\ .\ A\ |\!|\mathsf{new}\ tid\ .\ \mathsf{out}(c, tid)\ .\ B\ | \\
& !\mathsf{new}\ tid\ .\ \mathsf{out}(c, tid)\ .\ \mathsf{sum}\ v : \mathsf{s}.\ \mathsf{out}^{\mathtt{Blabs}}(tid, v)\ .\ 0\ |\ \ldots
\end{aligned}
$$

Fig. 5. Applied π representation of SEP.

The effects of this choice between new and sum bindings is discussed in more detail at the end of this section.

Each protocol includes *blab* roles, namely replicated processes !new *tid* . sum v : s . out$^{\text{Blab}_s}(tid, v)$. We must also include versions that send $f(v)$ for each $f \in \Sigma_{\text{priv}}$. The representation of SEP is shown in Fig. 5, where the remaining blab processes are elided.

Operational Semantics. Our operational semantics includes traces, namely sequences of *events*, i.e. triples $(\ell, \mathsf{a}, \mathcal{E})$ consisting of the label ℓ being reduced, the network action a (i.e. in(c, x) or out(c, u)) being reduced, and the environment $\mathcal{E}$ that results from the reduction. Not every prefix in the grammar above contributes to the trace when it is reduced. Only labels and message transmissions/receptions do. We denote the absence of a label or network action by the symbol $\perp$ in the appropriate position. The trace joins together the begin-end events that the ProVerif semantics use with the message events in other semantics such as Cortier et al.'s [13]. The labels help to provide semantics for role position predicates and parameter predicates, much as ProVerif etc. express authentication properties. Transmission and reception events reconstruct the semantics of origination.

The operational semantics acts on *configurations* $\mathcal{C}$, which are triples:

$\mathcal{S}$ is a *trace*, namely a sequence of triples of a label, a network action, and an environment. It records the successive prefixes that have undergone reduction, and the environment in force when each reduction had occurred.

$\mathcal{PE}$ is a multiset of pairs $(P, \mathcal{E})$ of a process and an environment. Each process is a subexpression of the original process expression, and represents possible future behavior. The environment records the bindings in force for its names and variables. We use it to remember the association of these values with the names and variables occurring in the original expression.

The multiset operator is essentially the parallel operator, which obeys the usual associative-commutative structural rules, with unit 0.

ϕ is a *frame*. It associates variables $w \in \mathcal{W}$ to transmitted messages. It indicates which messages from the regular participants the adversary is acting on.

The operational semantics (see Fig. 6) is a transition relation $\longrightarrow$ on configurations. In the IN rule, we do not substitute the new binding into the process expression, but simply accumulate it in the environment. An analogous environment update occurs in the rules for SESS, NEW, SUM, and LET. In the OUT rule, the environment is consulted, producing the same effect the substitution would have had. Notice also that while NEW ensures the environment is updated with a *fresh* value, the SUM rule has no such restriction. To avoid the SUM rule binding to a previously chosen random number, we choose the values from different sets ($\mathcal{N}_s^\nu$ vs. $\mathcal{N}_s^0$). As usual, we assume that $!P$ is structurally equivalent to $P \mid !P$.

The rules IN, OUT, and LB also append $(\ell, \mathsf{a}, \mathcal{E})$ to the end of the trace. By recording the environment $\mathcal{E}$ we retain the particular value to which a variable or name is bound when each prefix is reduced. The role parameter predicates

$$\text{IN}: \qquad\qquad\qquad \mathcal{S}; \, (\mathsf{in}(c, x : \top).P, \mathcal{E}) \uplus \mathcal{PE}; \, \phi \longrightarrow \quad \mathcal{S}.(\bot, \mathsf{in}(c, x : \top), \mathcal{E}');$$
$$(P, \mathcal{E}') \uplus \mathcal{PE}; \, \phi$$

$$\text{OUT}: \qquad\qquad\qquad \mathcal{S}; \, (\mathsf{out}^\ell(c, u).P, \mathcal{E}) \uplus \mathcal{PE}; \, \phi \longrightarrow \quad \mathcal{S}.(\ell, \mathsf{out}(c, u), \mathcal{E});$$
$$(P, \mathcal{E}) \uplus \mathcal{PE}; \, \phi[w \mapsto \mathcal{E}(u)]$$

$$\text{LB}: \qquad\qquad\qquad\qquad \mathcal{S}; \, (\ell.P, \mathcal{E}) \uplus \mathcal{PE}; \, \phi \longrightarrow \quad \mathcal{S}.(\ell, \bot, \mathcal{E}); \, (P, \mathcal{E}) \uplus \mathcal{PE}; \, \phi$$

$$\text{SESS}: \qquad \mathcal{S}; \, (!\mathsf{new} \; tid \, .\mathsf{out}(c, tid).P, \mathcal{E}) \uplus \mathcal{PE}; \, \phi \longrightarrow \quad \mathcal{S}; \, (P, \mathcal{E}') \uplus \mathcal{PE}; \, \phi$$

$$\text{NEW}: \qquad\qquad\qquad \mathcal{S}; (\mathsf{new} \; n : \mathsf{s}.P, \mathcal{E}) \uplus \mathcal{PE}; \phi \longrightarrow \quad \mathcal{S}; (P, \mathcal{E}') \uplus \mathcal{PE}; \phi$$

$$\text{SUM}: \qquad\qquad\qquad \mathcal{S}; (\mathsf{sum} \; n : \mathsf{s}.P, \mathcal{E}) \uplus \mathcal{PE}; \phi \longrightarrow \quad \mathcal{S}; (P, \mathcal{E}') \uplus \mathcal{PE}; \phi$$

$$\text{LET}: \qquad \mathcal{S}; (\mathsf{let} \; x : \mathsf{s} = v \; \mathsf{in} \; P \; \mathsf{else} \; Q, \mathcal{E}) \uplus \mathcal{PE}; \phi \longrightarrow \quad \mathcal{S}; (P, \mathcal{E}') \uplus \mathcal{PE}; \phi$$

$$\text{LET-FAIL}: \quad \mathcal{S}; (\mathsf{let} \; x : \mathsf{s} = v \; \mathsf{in} \; P \; \mathsf{else} \; Q, \mathcal{E}) \uplus \mathcal{PE}; \phi \longrightarrow \quad \mathcal{S}; (Q, \mathcal{E}) \uplus \mathcal{PE}; \phi$$

$$\text{NULL}: \qquad\qquad\qquad\qquad\qquad \mathcal{S}; (0, \mathcal{E}) \uplus \mathcal{PE}; \phi \longrightarrow \quad \mathcal{S}; \mathcal{PE}; \phi$$

$$\text{PAR}: \qquad\qquad\qquad\qquad \mathcal{S}; (P \mid Q, \mathcal{E}) \uplus \mathcal{PE}; \phi \longrightarrow \quad \mathcal{S}; (P, \mathcal{E}) \uplus (Q, \mathcal{E}) \uplus \mathcal{PE}; \phi$$

where, in
- IN: $\mathcal{E}' = \mathcal{E}[x \mapsto \phi(R)\!\downarrow]$ for some $R \in \mathcal{T}(\Sigma_{\mathsf{pub}}, \mathcal{W})$;
- OUT: $w \in \mathcal{W}$ is fresh;
- SESS: $\mathcal{E}' = \mathcal{E}[tid \mapsto ch]$ where $ch \in \mathcal{C}h$ is fresh
- NEW: $\mathcal{E}' = \mathcal{E}[n \mapsto n']$ where $n' \in \mathcal{N}_{\mathsf{s}}^\nu$ is fresh
- SUM: $\mathcal{E}' = \mathcal{E}[n \mapsto n']$ with $n' \in \mathcal{N}_{\mathsf{s}}^0$
- LET: $\mathcal{E}' = \mathcal{E}[x \mapsto v\!\downarrow]$ with $v\!\downarrow: \mathsf{s} \in \mathcal{M}_\Sigma$
- LET-FAIL: $v\!\downarrow \notin \mathcal{M}_\Sigma$ or $\neg v\!\downarrow: \mathsf{s}$

Fig. 6. Reduction rules

get their semantics from the bindings in $\mathcal{E}$, and the role position predicates get theirs from the label ℓ. The origination predicates get their semantics from the information contained in the network actions a.

Goal Language Syntax. The goal language $\mathcal{GL}^\star(P)$ for a process P contains the same *protocol-independent* vocabulary as shown in Table 1. Its *protocol-dependent* vocabulary consists of *event predicates*, which are like role-position predicates of $\mathcal{GL}(\mathbb{P})$, and *environment predicates*, which are akin to parameter predicates.

Event predicates are one-place predicates. For each non-$\bot$ label ℓ occurring in P, $\ell(\cdot)$ will be a (one-place) event predicate; it holds true of index i in trace $\mathcal{S}$ if the event $\mathcal{S}(i) = e$ is of the form $(\ell, \mathsf{a}, \mathcal{E})$ for some a and $\mathcal{E}$. The value a may be $\bot$ here; we will write $(\ell, \bullet, \mathcal{E})$ where $\bullet$ indicates that the existentially quantified value may be $\bot$ as well as a normal value.

The environment predicates are two-place predicates. For each name or variable u occurring in P, $u(\cdot, \cdot)$ will be a (two-place) environment predicate. It will be true of pairs i, v when e is an event $(\ell, \mathsf{a}, \mathcal{E})$ at index i in the trace, v is a message in normal form, and $\mathcal{E}(u) = t$ maps the name or variable u to t. When u is not bound in $\mathcal{E}$, $u(\cdot, \cdot)$ is false for i and every t.

Goal Language Semantics. Suppose that $\langle\rangle; P; \emptyset \longrightarrow^* \mathcal{S}; Q; \phi$, so that $\mathcal{S}$ is a trace of P. The semantics of the atomic predicates of $\mathcal{GL}^\star(P)$ is presented in Fig. 7. The clauses are particularly simple, because we arranged for $\mathcal{S}$ to hold just the information needed to express them. In particular, retaining the

$$\mathcal{S}, \eta \models \ell(m) \qquad \text{iff} \qquad \mathcal{S}(\eta(m)) = (\ell, \bullet, \mathcal{E})$$

$$\mathcal{S}, \eta \models u(m, v) \qquad \text{iff} \qquad \mathcal{S}(\eta(m)) = (\bullet, \bullet, \mathcal{E}) \text{ and } \mathcal{E}(u) = \eta(v)$$

$$\mathcal{S}, \eta \models v = v' \qquad \text{iff} \qquad \eta(v) = \eta(v')$$

$$\mathcal{S}, \eta \models \texttt{Preceq}(m, n) \qquad \text{iff} \qquad \eta(m) \leq \eta(n)$$

$$\mathcal{S}, \eta \models \texttt{Coll}(m, n) \qquad \text{iff} \qquad \mathcal{S}(\eta(m)) = (\bullet, \bullet, \mathcal{E}_m), \mathcal{S}(\eta(n)) = (\bullet, \bullet, \mathcal{E}_n) \text{ and}$$
$$\mathcal{E}_m(tid) = \mathcal{E}_n(tid)$$

$$\mathcal{S}, \eta \models \texttt{Unq}(v) \qquad \text{iff} \qquad \eta(v) \text{ uniquely originates in } \mathcal{S}$$

$$\mathcal{S}, \eta \models \texttt{UnqAt}(m, v) \qquad \text{iff} \qquad \eta(v) \text{ uniquely originates at } \mathcal{S}(\eta(m))$$

$$\mathcal{S}, \eta \models \texttt{Non}(v) \qquad \text{iff} \qquad \eta(v) \text{ does not originate in } \mathcal{S}$$

Fig. 7. Formal semantics of $\mathcal{GL}^*(P)$, when $\langle\rangle; P; \emptyset \longrightarrow^* \mathcal{S}; Q; \phi$. In the first clause, label $\ell \neq \bot$.

environments $\mathcal{E}$ in $\mathcal{S}$ makes the semantics of the environment predicates very easy.

The predicate $\texttt{Coll}(\cdot, \cdot)$ says that two events belong to the same instance ("session") of a role. By tying process replication to channel restriction, we ensure that $\mathcal{E}(tid)$ identifies the session that an event belongs to.

The final three predicates $\texttt{Unq}(\cdot)$, $\texttt{UnqAt}(\cdot, \cdot)$, and $\texttt{Non}(\cdot)$ rely on *origination*, which thus must be determined by $\mathcal{S}$. This is why we include network actions a as elements of events in our traces.

Message t *originates* at $\mathcal{S}(i) = (\ell, \mathsf{a}, \mathcal{E})$ if $\mathsf{a} = \mathsf{out}(tid, u)$, $t \sqsubseteq \mathcal{E}(u)$ and for all $j < i$, if $\mathcal{S}(j) = (\ell', \mathsf{a}', \mathcal{E}')$ with $\mathcal{E}'(tid) = \mathcal{E}(tid)$ and $\mathsf{a}' = \mathsf{out}(tid, u')$ or $\mathsf{a}' = \mathsf{in}(tid, u')$ then $t \not\sqsubseteq \mathcal{E}'(u')$. A message t *uniquely originates* at $\mathcal{S}(i)$ if t originates at $\mathcal{S}(i)$ and for all $j \neq i$, t does not originate at $\mathcal{S}(j)$. Similarly, we say t originates uniquely in $\mathcal{S}$ if it originates at $\mathcal{S}(i)$ for some unique i.

Name Restriction vs. Unique Origination. Before proceeding we briefly discuss a subtle point about how freshness is modeled in the two formalisms. The typical way of modeling a random choice in the applied π calculus is to use a new binding to create a fresh random name. When this occurs in a replicated role then the result is that *every* instance of that role will generate a fresh random number at that point. This guarantees that when the value is later transmitted by $\mathsf{out}^{\mathsf{evt}}(tid, u)$, then it will be uniquely originating in the trace at the event resulting from reducing that transmission. That is, the protocol will satisfy the following formula:

$$\mathsf{evt}(m) \wedge \texttt{Nonce}(m, v) \Rightarrow \texttt{UnqAt}(m, v)$$

The same effect can be achieved in strand spaces by equipping the role with a rlunique unique origination assumption for the value.

Interestingly, most protocols do not rely on *every* instance of a role making random choices. The SEP protocol provides a nice example. From the initiator's perspective, the secrecy of d relies on the initiator choosing a fresh random key, but it does not rely on other initiators (who are not involved in this session) choosing fresh random keys. Omitting the rlunique assumption does not preclude us from assuming that the relevant value is uniquely originating for a particular, chosen session. The unaltered applied π calculus does not have this same flexibility. Our introduction of the sum operator together with the semantics of origination for traces equips the applied π calculus with the flexibility necessary to ensure goals are faithfully preserved when we translate from strand spaces to applied π.

5   Compiling Strand Protocols to the Applied π Calculus

The previous two sections described the left and right triangles of Fig. 1. Each triangle makes sense in isolation: given a security goal and a protocol description, we can choose to use either formalism to validate that the protocol achieves the goal. However, we want goals verified in one formalism to hold in the other also. We thus expect to receive the same answer when evaluating the same protocol in either formalism. This of course requires a useful notion of *sameness* for descriptions of protocols in the two formalisms. However, a syntactic criterion for this would be difficult.

Instead, in this section we will briefly summarize a compiler (written in Prolog) that translates strand protocols $\mathbb{P} = \langle \rho_1, \ldots, \rho_k \rangle$ to processes P in the applied π calculus. Details of the compiler can be found in Appendix A. We designed it to correlate the goal languages $\mathcal{GL}(\mathbb{P})$ and $\mathcal{GL}^\star(P)$ smoothly, when P is an output from input $\mathbb{P}$.

$$!\text{new } tid \ . \ \text{out}(c, tid).$$
$$\text{out}^{(2,1)}(tid, \{\!|\, [\![s]\!]_{\text{sk}(a)} \,|\!\}^{\text{a}}_{\text{pk}(b)}).$$
$$\text{in}(tid, x_1). \, \text{let } x_2 : \mathsf{T} = \text{dec}^{\text{s}}(x_1, s) \, \text{in let } d : \mathsf{D} = x_2 \, \text{in } (2,2). \, 0$$

Fig. 8. Translation of SEP initiator

We implement labels ℓ by pairs of natural numbers (i, j), and also use each label ℓ as a one place role position predicate $\ell(x)$ in $\mathcal{GL}^\star(P)$. The compiler associates each label used in the output with a node by constructing an injective function $\Lambda \colon \text{Labs}(P) \to \text{nodes}(\mathbb{P})$ where $\Lambda(i, j) = \rho_i @ j$. The action of the function $f \colon \mathcal{GL}(\mathbb{P}) \to \mathcal{GL}^\star(P)$ on role position predicates (see Fig. 1) is inverse to Λ. More precisely,

$$\Lambda(f(\tau_r(\rho_i @ j))) = \rho_i @ j, \tag{1}$$

for all roles ρ_i and nodes $\rho_i @ j$ on it. We have written τ_r here for the map from role nodes to role position predicates, which partly determines the function $\mathbb{P} \to \mathcal{GL}(\mathbb{P})$. Thus, Λ is essentially inverse to $f \circ \tau_r$.

The compiler also translates each parameter u of ρ_i, which may be either a name or a variable, to the same name or variable u in its target output. We use u as a two-place parameter predicate in $\mathcal{GL}^\star(P)$, where in this case f must satisfy:

$$f(\tau_p(\rho_i, u)) = u, \tag{2}$$

where we write τ_p for the map from roles ρ_i and parameters u to parameter predicates in $\mathcal{GL}(\mathbb{P})$. The function f is the identity function on protocol-independent vocabulary, so Eqs. 1–2 characterize the translation f. There will also be other names and variables used in the process output by the compiler, which is why the map $f \colon \mathcal{GL}(\mathbb{P}) \to \mathcal{GL}^\star(P)$ is an embedding in this direction.

For simplicity, our compiler makes an assumption: It is designed to compile protocols whose roles are disjoint, in the sense that there are no strands that are common instances of distinct roles. Roles with overlapping instances are used to represent branching protocols, in which choices are made by principals or determined by the messages they receive. We have not refined our compiler to emit corresponding if-then-else expressions in the target π calculus. Throughout the remainder of this paper, we will assume that each strand-based protocol $\mathbb{P}$ has disjoint roles.

Compiler Sketch. If the compiler translates the tail $n_{j+1} \Rightarrow \ldots \Rightarrow n_k$ of role ρ_i to a process P, then it prepends some code to P to translate $n_j \Rightarrow n_{j+1} \Rightarrow \ldots \Rightarrow n_k$. In particular, if $\mathsf{dmsg}(n_j) = +t$, then it emits a labeled output as:

$$\mathsf{out}^{(i,j)}(c, t) . P.$$

If t has a parameter that is not previously bound by a reception, the compiler should wrap this parameter in a new-binding if the role declares it as uniquely originating. Otherwise it should be wrapped in a sum-binding. The current implementation of the compiler does not yet add these bindings.

If $\mathsf{dmsg}(n_j) = -t$, then the situation is more complicated. It must emit an input $\mathsf{in}(c, x)$ with a fresh variable x followed by a sequence of let bindings that destructure the received message. We insert the label (i, j) after this destructuring sequence. This is because its presence in a trace should imply that the expected message structure was present in the message bound to x. It also explains why message receptions do not carry their own label while message transmissions do. Message components that must equal known values will be checked, and previously unknown message components will be bound to fresh variables. When one of these components is represented by a parameter d in $-t$, the compiler re-uses d. Thus, parameters in ρ_i will also appear in its translation.

Having translated the content of a role ρ to a process P_0, the compiler wraps this and emits $!\mathsf{new}\,tid . \mathsf{out}(c, tid) . P_0$. The compiler does not rebind tid inside P_0, although it is convenient to use it as the public channel for input and output. As an example, the initiator role of SEP (left side of Fig. 4) yields the process expression shown in Fig. 8. The first line shows the wrapping; the second line, the label and output for the first node of the role (omitting the new and sum bindings since the compiler does not yet compute these); the third line, the input, destructuring, and label for the second node, and the null termination. The tricky part of the compiler is computing the sequence of destructurings and checks. For this we use a simple flow analysis to determine choices for the participant's initial knowledge, followed by a backtracking analysis to explore the feasible combinations of destructuring input components vs. building known terms and checking equality with input components. This backtracking made the compiler convenient to implement in Prolog.

In the output case, the code emitted by the compiler adds one entry to the trace when it is reduced. In the input case, the code emitted adds two entries to the trace for each single reception node of the source role ρ. Thus, we will correlate a single transmission node of ρ to a labeled output in the target process P, and we will correlate a single reception node of ρ to an input followed by a label (confirming that destructuring has succeeded) in the target process P.

We codify this in a transition relation on configurations $\mathcal{C}$. We say that a configuration $\mathcal{C}_2 = (\mathcal{S}_2; \mathcal{PE}_2; \phi_2)$ is an *immediate successor* of a configuration $\mathcal{C}_1 = (\mathcal{S}_1; \mathcal{PE}_1; \phi_1)$ iff $\mathcal{C}_1 \longrightarrow^+ \mathcal{C}_2$ and for some values of the remaining variables, either

$$\mathcal{S}_2 = \mathcal{S}_1.(\ell, \text{out}\,(c, u), \mathcal{E}) \quad \text{or else} \quad \mathcal{S}_2 = \mathcal{S}_1.(\bot, \text{in}\,(c, x), \mathcal{E}).(\ell, \bot, \mathcal{E}').$$

Semantic Correctness Criterion. Intuitively, a role ρ and a (replicated) process term P represent the "same" activity if they can produce corresponding sequences of observable events. This suggests a kind of local bisimulation between role instances ι and basic processes P. However, we will correlate nodes on the strand side with pairs on the process side, whether a label-out pair or a in-label pair. We use the map Λ from labels back to nodes to define the correspondence.

Now, because basic processes retain only their future events, whereas instances contain both their past and their potential future, we actually correlate ι with a basic process and its environment, together with the trace $\mathcal{S}$ which retains information about the past.

We begin by defining an auxiliary predicate B_0^{Λ}, parameterized by the function Λ above, which captures the notion that the instance and the process have the same past. This predicate uses only the labeled entries in the trace, and ignores the inputs and outputs that it also contains.

Definition 2. *1. If $\mathcal{S} = \langle(\ell_1, \mathsf{a}_1, \mathcal{E}_1), \ldots, (\ell_k, \mathsf{a}_k, \mathcal{E}_k)\rangle$, then let $\mathcal{S}\!\restriction_{tid}t$ be the subsequence of $\mathcal{S}$ which contains $(\ell_i, \mathsf{a}_i, \mathcal{E}_i)$ iff $\ell_i \neq \bot$ and $\mathcal{E}_i(tid) = t$.*
2. Let ι be an instance, and let $\mathcal{S}$ be a trace and $\mathcal{E}$ an environment. $B_0^{\Lambda}(\iota; \mathcal{S}, \mathcal{E})$ holds iff, letting $\iota = (\rho, h, \sigma)$ and $\mathcal{T} = \mathcal{S}\!\restriction_{tid}\mathcal{E}(tid)$,
   (a) $\mathcal{E}$ restricts to σ, i.e. $\mathsf{dom}(\sigma) \subseteq \mathsf{dom}(\mathcal{E})$, and $\mathcal{E}(x) = \sigma(x)$ for all $x \in \mathsf{dom}(\sigma)$; and
   (b) for all j such that $1 \leq j \leq h$, letting $\mathcal{T}(j) = (\ell_j, \mathsf{a}_j, \mathcal{E}_j)$,

$$\mathsf{dmsg}(\iota, j) = \mathcal{E}_j(\mathsf{dmsg}(\Lambda(\ell_j))). \qquad /\!/\!/$$

Condition (a) of Item 3 ensures that the parameters common to both formalizations have been bound in the same way by the two environments. Condition (b) ensures that if we apply Λ to the label of the jth event and then apply the environment in effect at that event, we get the same directed message as the jth node of the instance ι. Thus the successive messages sent and received in $\mathcal{S}$ that are attributable to tid match the messages that ι has sent and received so far.

Thus, given Λ, the input and output events in the trace are effectively redundant. We include them so that the $\mathcal{GL}^\star$ semantics of Sect. 4 may be defined using only the intrinsic content of P and its reduction sequences. We would not want the semantics to be well-defined only for processes in the range of the compiler.

Lemma 4. *Let $B_0^\Lambda(\iota; \mathcal{S}, \mathcal{E})$, $\mathcal{T} = \mathcal{S}\!\restriction_{tid}\mathcal{E}(tid)$, and θ be an order-preserving bijection between $\mathsf{nodes}(\iota)$ and events of $\mathcal{T}$. Then for any atomic formula ϕ with a role position predicate, or parameter predicate, $\iota, \eta \models \phi$ iff $\mathcal{S}, \theta \circ \eta \models \phi$.* ///

We next need to describe what it means for an instance and a process to have the same possible futures. We thus define B_1^Λ to be the largest bisimulation that respects B_0^Λ. We use the immediate successor relation on configurations by injecting $P, \mathcal{E}$ to the singleton multiset $P\mathcal{E} = \{P, \mathcal{E}\}$.

Definition 3. *Let B_1^Λ be the most inclusive relation such that $B_1^\Lambda(\iota; \mathcal{S}, P, \mathcal{E})$ implies $B_0^\Lambda(\iota; \mathcal{S}, \mathcal{E})$, and moreover:*

1. *for all ι' such that ι' is an immediate successor of ι with new node n, there exist $\mathcal{S}', P', \mathcal{E}', \phi, \phi'$ such that $\mathcal{S}'; \{P', \mathcal{E}'\}; \phi'$ is an immediate successor of $\mathcal{S}; \{P, \mathcal{E}\}; \phi$, and $B_1^\Lambda(\iota'; \mathcal{S}', P', \mathcal{E}')$.*
2. *for all $\mathcal{S}', P', \mathcal{E}', \phi, \phi'$, if $\mathcal{S}'; \{P', \mathcal{E}'\}; \phi'$ is an immediate successor of $\mathcal{S}; \{P, \mathcal{E}\}; \phi$, then there is an immediate successor ι' of ι and $B_1^\Lambda(\iota'; \mathcal{S}', P', \mathcal{E}')$.* ///

We can also lift the B_1^Λ relation from an individual instance and basic process to a relation between a protocol $\mathbb{P}$ and a fully replicated process expression. In particular, we will assume that the roles in $\mathbb{P}$ are ordered, so that we can correlate them with parts of a process expression.

Definition 4. *Let σ_0 be the empty environment; let $[tid \mapsto v]$ be the environment with domain $\{tid\}$ and range v; and let $\mathcal{S}_0 = \langle\rangle$ be the empty trace.*

Suppose that $\mathbb{P} = \langle \rho_1, \ldots, \rho_k \rangle$, and let P be of the form:

$$|_{j \in \{1, \ldots, k\}}\, !\mathsf{new}\, tid\,.\, \mathsf{out}(c, tid)\,.\, P_j.$$

Then P represents $\mathbb{P}$ via Λ iff, for each j such that $1 \leq j \leq k$, $B_1^\Lambda(\iota_j, \mathcal{S}_0, P_j, \mathcal{E}_j)$, where $\iota_j = (\rho_j, 0, \sigma_0)$, and $\mathcal{E}_j$ is of the form $[tid \mapsto v]$ for some v. ///

The above definition serves as a semantic correctness criterion for a compiler that takes a strand space protocol $\mathbb{P}$ and produces an applied π process P. We have not proved that our compiler meets this condition, although we believe that it does for role-disjoint $\mathbb{P}$. The hard part of writing the compiler is handling message receptions, which must be destructured by explicit operations in applied π to match the pattern matching in the source protocol $\mathbb{P}$. We then emit a label that corresponds to the role position predicate governing the source reception in $\mathbb{P}$. This suggests a proof strategy: We would argue by induction on source protocols. We say that one protocol $\mathbb{P}_1$ precedes $\mathbb{P}_2$, $\mathbb{P}_1 \leq \mathbb{P}_2$ if, for every role $\rho_1 \in \mathbb{P}_1$, there exists a role $\rho_2 \in \mathbb{P}_2$ such that either:

- ρ_1 is an initial segment of ρ_2; or
- ρ_1 and ρ_2 are identical up until their last node, which is a reception in both cases, and the pattern matching in ρ_2 refines the pattern matching in ρ_1.

In the latter case, the compiler emits code for ρ_2 that extends the code for ρ_1. If the code for ρ_1 is correct, then, by checking only that the additional destructuring code for ρ_2 will behave correctly, one can be sure that the latter will again be correct. The relation $\mathbb{P}_1 \leq \mathbb{P}_2$ is well-founded, so correctness would follow by induction.

The next section shows why Definition 4's *represents* is the right relation by lifting the local bisimulations to a global bisimulation and demonstrating that goal satisfaction is preserved when Definition 4 is met.

6   Bisimulation and Preserving Goals

Correctness: The Idea. Λ, as generated by the compiler, and $f : \mathcal{GL}(\mathbb{P}) \to \mathcal{GL}^\star(P)$ are closely related, as shown in Sect. 5 (Eqs. 1–2). Hence, the behavioral match between compiler input $\mathbb{P}$ and output P carries over to ensure that the goal formulas of $\mathcal{GL}(\mathbb{P})$ are preserved in $\mathcal{GL}^\star(P)$. We will not in fact prove that the compiler is correct—in the semantic sense of Def. 4—that its output P represents its input $\mathbb{P}$ via Λ, although we believe it. What we do prove is that *if* P represents $\mathbb{P}$, and the runs of $\mathbb{P}$ all achieve a security goal Γ, then the traces generated by P achieve $f(\Gamma)$.

The Bisimulation. To do so, we demonstrate a weak bisimulation between the strand space operational semantics and the applied π reduction semantics. The bisimulation is between run-protocol pairs $(R, \mathbb{P})$ on the one hand and trace-configuration pairs $(\mathcal{S}, \mathcal{PE})$ on the other.

The initial configuration of $|_{1 \leq j \leq k} P_j$ is $\langle \rangle, \{(P_1, \mathcal{E}_0), \ldots, (P_k, \mathcal{E}_0)\}, \emptyset$, and it evolves only to configurations $\mathcal{S}, \mathcal{PE}, \phi$ where $\mathcal{PE}$ splits into two parts:

$$\{(P_1, \mathcal{E}_0), \ldots, (P_k, \mathcal{E}_0)\} \uplus \{(BP_1, \mathcal{E}_1), \ldots, (BP_j, \mathcal{E}_j)\};$$

The latter is a multiset of pairs where each BP_i is a basic process. That is, the initially given replicated processes always remain unchanged, and all the additional processes can correspond to individual strand instances ι. We now formalize this correspondence via a bijection θ between labeled events and the nodes of these instances.

Definition 5. $B_\theta^\Lambda(R, \mathbb{P}; \mathcal{S}, \mathcal{P\mathcal{E}})$ *iff* θ *is an bijection between* $\mathsf{nodes}(R)$ *and labeled events* $(\ell, \mathsf{a}, \mathcal{E})$ *of* $\mathcal{S}$ *(i.e. where* $\ell \neq \bot$ *) that preserves the orderings of* R *such that the following both hold:*

1. θ *induces a bijection between* $\mathbb{P}$*-instances* ι *of* R *and basic processes* $P, \mathcal{E}$ *of* $\mathcal{P\mathcal{E}}$ *such that* $B_1^\Lambda(\iota; \mathcal{S}, P, \mathcal{E})$.
2. *There is a bijection* ζ *between roles* ρ *of* $\mathbb{P}$ *and replicated members of* $\mathcal{P\mathcal{E}}$ *such that, for some fresh channel* v, *letting* $\iota = (\rho, 0, \sigma_0)$, $B_1^\Lambda(\iota; \mathcal{S}_0, \zeta(\rho), [tid \mapsto v])$.

We write $B^\Lambda(R, \mathbb{P}; \mathcal{S}, \mathcal{P\mathcal{E}})$ *iff, for some* θ, $B_\theta^\Lambda(R, \mathbb{P}; \mathcal{S}, \mathcal{P\mathcal{E}})$.   ///

Lemma 5. *Suppose* $B^\Lambda(R, \mathbb{P}; \mathcal{S}, \mathcal{P\mathcal{E}})$, *and let* $R_{out} = \{\mathsf{msg}(m) : m \in \mathsf{nodes}^+(R)\}$ *and* $\mathcal{S}_{out} = \{\mathcal{E}(u) : \mathcal{S}(i) = (\ell, \mathsf{out}(tid, u), \mathcal{E})$ *for some* $i.\}$. *Then* $R_{out} \vdash t$ *iff* $\mathcal{S}_{out} \vdash t$.

Proof (Sketch). Being in the B^Λ relation ensures that $R_{out} = \mathcal{S}_{out}$.   □

Lemma 6. $B^\Lambda(R, \mathbb{P}; \mathcal{S}, \mathcal{P\mathcal{E}})$ *is a bisimulation.*

Proof. We begin by showing that $\mathcal{S}, \mathcal{P\mathcal{E}}$ simulates $R, \mathbb{P}$. By assumption, there is some θ that matches the instances ι of R to the unreplicated process environment pairs $P, \mathcal{E}$ of $\mathcal{P\mathcal{E}}$ so that $B_1^\Lambda(\iota; \mathcal{S}, P, \mathcal{E})$. Let $\phi = \phi(\mathcal{S})$ be the environment associated with trace $\mathcal{S}$. The run R can advance in one of two ways, (a) some current instance is extended to a successor instance, or (b) some new instance is created from a role of $\mathbb{P}$. In the first case, since $B_1^\Lambda(\iota; \mathcal{S}, P, \mathcal{E})$, the configuration $\mathcal{S}; \mathcal{P\mathcal{E}}; \phi$ can evolve similarly if either the new node in the extended instance is a transmission, or, in case it is a reception $-m$, if $\mathcal{S}_{out} \vdash m$. But since the run R could only have advanced with a reception if $R_{out} \vdash m$, Lemma 5 ensures that $\mathcal{S}_{out} \vdash m$, as required.

In the second case, we note that we can first silently create a new unreplicated basic process BP_{j+1} with environment $\mathcal{E}_{j+1} = [tid \mapsto v]$ for some fresh channel v by performing a *SESS* reduction. Condition 2 of Definition 5 ensures that $B_1^\Lambda(\iota'; \mathcal{S}, BP_{j+1}, \mathcal{E}_{j+1})$ where ι' is the 0-height prefix of the new instance ι. We can thus proceed to argue as in the first case above. The proof of the reverse simulation is similar.   □

Theorem 1. *Suppose that* $\mid_{1 \leq j \leq k} P_j$ *represents* $\mathbb{P}$ *via* Λ, *and let* θ *be the bijection with empty domain. Then* $B_\theta^\Lambda(\emptyset, \mathbb{P}; \langle\rangle, \{(P_1, \mathcal{E}_0), \ldots, (P_k, \mathcal{E}_0)\})$.

Proof. Condition 1 of Definition 5 is vacuously satisfied. Since $\mid_{1 \leq j \leq k} P_j$ represents $\mathbb{P}$ via Λ, Definition 4 applies which ensures Condition 2 holds.   □

Lemma 7. *Suppose that* $B_\theta^\Lambda(R, \mathbb{P}; \mathcal{S}, \mathcal{P\mathcal{E}})$, *where* $\theta: \mathsf{nodes}(R) \to \mathsf{Labs}(\mathcal{S})$. *Let* $\hat{\theta}$ *extend* θ *to* MSG *also by acting as the identity. Let* ϕ *be an atomic formula of* $\mathcal{GL}(\mathbb{P})$.

1. *If* $R, \eta \models \phi$, *then* $\mathcal{S}, \hat{\theta} \circ \eta \models f(\phi)$.
2. *If* ϕ *does not contain* `Preceq`, *then* $\mathcal{S}, \hat{\theta} \circ \eta \models f(\phi)$ *implies* $R, \eta \models \phi$.

Proof (Sketch). Lemma 4 takes care of the cases for role position predicates and parameter predicates. The bisimulation relation ensures that origination, message equality, and local session orderings are preserved. Since θ only preserves orders from R to $\mathcal{S}$, we must exclude Preceq for Condition 2.   □

Theorem 2. *If P represents $\mathbb{P}$ via Λ and $\mathbb{P}$ achieves $\forall \bar{x} . \Phi \implies \Psi$, where only $\vee, \wedge, \exists$ appear in Φ and Ψ, then P achieves $f(\forall \bar{x} . \Phi \implies \Psi)$.*   ///

The converse is false, since the execution model of P is linear, while the runs of $\mathbb{P}$ are partially ordered. In particular, the formula $\forall n, m . n \preceq m \vee m \preceq n$ holds of P, but need not hold of $\mathbb{P}$. However, we conjecture that $\mathbb{P}$ achieves a security goal $\forall \bar{x} . \Phi \implies \Psi$, where Φ, Ψ use only $\vee, \wedge, \exists$, if P satisfies $f(\forall \bar{x} . \Phi \implies \Psi)$ and either

1. $\preceq$ does not appear in Ψ; or else
2. $\vee$ does not appear in Ψ.

In the first case, we transport satisfying instances from traces of P back to corresponding runs of $\mathbb{P}$, as in Clause 2. The second appears to be true because if Ψ is $\vee$-free, its Preceq-containing atomic formulas are satisfied in all traces of P. Thus, they hold in all interleavings, whence they must be true in the corresponding partially ordered $\mathbb{P}$ run.

7   Conclusion

In this paper, we studied a particular case of the cross-tool security goal problem for protocol standardization. We showed how to correlate statements in a goal language for a strand space tool with statements in a related language for applied π. We proved that if a strand-based protocol achieves a security goal, then related protocols in applied π achieve the corresponding goal. We conjecture that the converse is true for a large set of security goals also. We provided a compiler to produce a related applied π protocol.

These technical contributions support the protocol verification framework codified in ISO/IEC 29128. A goal language that does not depend on the underlying verification tool allows for greater transparency for published standards: it allows practitioners to independently verify the same results using the tool of their choice.

We view this paper as a start on a program to which many hands may contribute, adapting the semantics of different tools to this or a comparable security goal language. Although the languages $\mathcal{GL}(\mathbb{P})$ express only safety properties, rather than indistinguishability properties also, it seems likely that a similar program could equally apply to indistinguishability properties.

Acknowledgments. We are grateful to Kelley Burgin, Dan Dougherty, and Moses Liskov. We also benefited from the comments of the anonymous referees.

A Compilation

In this section we describe our translation of a strand space role into a labeled applied π-calculus process term.

At a high level, the translation takes a transmission event $+m$ to $out(tid, m)$, and it takes a reception event $-m$ to $in(tid, z).P$ where P is a sequence of let bindings that attempt to parse the received term according to the structure of the expected term. The complexity of the latter translation is due to the use of pattern matching for receptions in strand spaces that is absent in processes. If we are to preserve the semantics of the goal language under this translation to the process calculus, we must ensure that receptions based on pattern matching succeed on a given message m if and only if the corresponding sequence of let bindings succeeds on the same message. This requires some care.

One issue is that there may be several sequences that can be used to verify the structure of a message. Since the parsing process binds some values and requires others already to be bound, some sequences are sensible with respect to some initial input and others are not.

We start with a strand space trace (a sequence of events) constructed from message terms derived from the order-sort signature in Fig. 9. We compute the relation between a strand space trace and a process calculus term two steps.

1. Perform a flow analysis to find a set of input basic values (See Fig. 10).
2. Translate the trace into a process calculus expression relative to a given set of inputs (See Fig. 13).

The algorithm has been simplified by ignoring role unique origination assumptions, but their processing is sketched near the end of this section. Most of the algorithm described here has been implemented in Prolog. The Prolog implementation operates on a many-sorted algebra isomorphic to the order-sorted algebra as described in [19, Sect. 4]. We leave that translation implicit in this document.

The signature in Fig. 9 is a simplification of the one used by CPSA. The Simple Example Protocol initiator role using this signature is:

$$init(a, b\colon N, s\colon S, d\colon D) = [+\{\!|\{\!|s|\!\}_{pk(a)^{-1}}|\!\}_{pk(b)}, -\{\!|d|\!\}_s]. \tag{3}$$

Sorts: T, D, S, A, N
Subsorts: $D < T, S < T, A < T, N < T$
Operations: $(\cdot, \cdot)$: $T \times T \to T$ Pairing
             $\{\!|\cdot|\!\}_{(\cdot)}$: $T \times S \to T$ Symmetric encryption
             $\{\!|\cdot|\!\}_{(\cdot)}$: $T \times A \to T$ Asymmetric encryption
             $(\cdot)^{-1}$: $A \to A$ Asymmetric key inverse
             pk : $N \to A$ Public key for name
Equation: $(x^{-1})^{-1} = x$ for $x : A$

Fig. 9. Simple crypto algebra signature

A.1   Flow Analysis

The aim of the flow analysis $C \triangleright I$ (see Fig. 11) is to find a set of basic values that allow a procedural interpretation of a trace, in particular, a procedural interpretation of the implied pattern matching that is part of a strand space reception event.

There are two ways to interpret the reception of a pair, either the left part is matched first or the right part. A decryption key might or might not become available based on this choice.

There are two ways to interpret the reception of an encryption. If its decryption key in known at the point of the match, the contents of the encryption can be extracted. Alternatively, if the encryption has been seen previously or can be constructed, then an equality check implements the match.

Figure 12 explores the various possibilities. The flow analysis for the initiator trace is:

$$I = \{\{pk(b), pk(a)^{-1}, s\}, \{d, pk(b), pk(a)^{-1}, s\}\}, \tag{4}$$

where $b, a : \mathsf{N}$, $s : \mathsf{S}$, and $d : \mathsf{D}$. Notice the second solution makes little sense. It assumes that the initiator's initial knowledge includes d, the data it is seeking from a responder. We rely on human intervention to choose sensible sets of input terms.

$$\frac{\emptyset, \emptyset, C \triangleright I, A}{C \triangleright I}$$

$$I, A, [\,] \triangleright I, A$$

$$\frac{I_1, A_1, M \triangleright^+ I_2, A_2 \qquad I_2, A_2, C \triangleright I_3, A_3}{I_1, A_1, +M :: C \triangleright I_3, A_3}$$

$$\frac{I_1, A_1, M \triangleright^- I_2, A_2 \qquad I_2, A_2, C \triangleright I_3, A_3}{I_1, A_1, -M :: C \triangleright I_3, A_3}$$

Fig. 10. Flow analysis

$$\frac{M \in A}{I, A, M \triangleright^+ I, A}$$

$$\frac{I_1, A_1, M \triangleright^+ I_2, A_2 \qquad I_2, A_2, N \triangleright^+ I_3, A_3}{I_1, A_1, \langle M, N \rangle \triangleright^+ I_3, A_3}$$

$$\frac{I_1, A_1, M \triangleright^+ I_2, A_2 \qquad I_2, A_2, N \triangleright^+ I_3, A_3}{I_1, A_1, \{\!|M|\!\}_N \triangleright^+ I_3, A_3}[N : \mathsf{S} \text{ or } N : \mathsf{A}]$$

$$\frac{M \text{ is a basic value and not in } A}{I, A, M \triangleright^+ \{M\} \cup I, \{M\} \cup A}$$

Fig. 11. Send flow analysis

$$\frac{I_1, A_1, M \vartriangleright^- I_2, A_2 \qquad I_2, A_2, N \vartriangleright^- I_3, A_3}{I_1, A_1, \langle M, N \rangle \vartriangleright^- I_3, A_3}$$

$$\frac{I_1, A_1, N \vartriangleright^- I_2, A_2 \qquad I_2, A_2, M \vartriangleright^- I_3, A_3}{I_1, A_1, \langle M, N \rangle \vartriangleright^- I_3, A_3}$$

$$\frac{I_1, \{\!| M |\!\}_N\} \cup A_1, N \vartriangleright^+ I_2, A_2 \qquad I_2, A_2, M \vartriangleright^- I_3, A_3}{I_1, A_1, \{\!| M |\!\}_N \vartriangleright^- I_3, A_3} [N : \mathsf{S} \text{ or } N : \mathsf{A}]$$

$$\frac{I_1, A_1, \{\!| M |\!\}_N \vartriangleright^+ I_2, A_2}{I_1, A_1, \{\!| M |\!\}_N \vartriangleright^- I_2, A_2}$$

$$\frac{M \text{ is a basic value}}{I, A, M \vartriangleright^- I, \{M\} \cup A}$$

Fig. 12. Receive flow analysis

A.2   Code Generation

Code generation has the form $C, E_1, N, \ell \gg P, E_2$, where C is a strand space trace, E_1 and E_2 are maps from strand space terms to process calculus terms, and we are translating the ℓth send or receive in the trace of the Nth role of the protocol.

An analysis begins with an environment E_0 mapping each input term computed by the flow analysis to itself. To compute the process calculus term P for a given strand space trace C and role number N, find P such that $C, E_0, N, 1 \gg P, E_2$ (See Figs. 13, 14, 15 and 16).

$$[\,], E_1, N, \ell \gg 0, E_2$$

$$\frac{T_1, E_1 \gg^+ T_2 \qquad C, E_1, N, \ell' \gg P, E_2}{+T_1 :: C, E_1, N_1, \ell \gg \mathsf{out}^{(N,\ell)}(c, T_2).P, E_2} [\ell' := \ell + 1]$$

$$\frac{x, T, (N, \ell).P_1, E_1 \gg^- P_2, E_2 \qquad C, E_2, N, \ell' \gg P_1, E_3}{-T :: C, E_1, N, \ell \gg \mathsf{in}(c, x).P_2, E_3} [x : \top \text{ fresh}, \ell' := \ell + 1]$$

Fig. 13. Code generation

$$\frac{(T, x) \in E}{T, E \gg^+ x}$$

$$\frac{T_1, E \gg^+ x_1 \qquad T_2, E \gg^+ x_2}{\langle T_1, T_2 \rangle, E \gg^+ \langle x_1, x_2 \rangle}$$

$$\frac{T_1, E \gg^+ x_1 \qquad T_2, E \gg^+ x_2}{\{\!| T_1 |\!\}_{T_2}, E \gg^+ \{\!| x_1 |\!\}_{x_2}} [T_2 : \mathsf{S} \text{ or } T_2 : \mathsf{A}]$$

Fig. 14. Send code generation

To handle role unique origination assumptions, the send code generator in Fig. 14 must prefix the code with a new form for each name that uniquely originates in the transmitted message.

A.3   Translation Relation

The relation $comp(N, C, P)$ relates a role number and the role's strand space trace with a process calculus term if

1. $C \triangleright I$,
2. E_0 is an environment generated from I, and
3. $C, E_0, N, 1 \gg P, E_2$.

Note that a translation is interesting only if I induces a sensible interpretation of C.

Blanchet Lnitiator Example. Assume the initiator is the second role in the protocol. The initiator trace C is defined in Eq. 3. The initial environment generated from the first input set in Eq. 4 is:

$$E_0 = \{(pk(b), pk(b)), (pk(a)^{-1}, pk(a)^{-1}), (s, s)\},$$

$$\frac{(T, y) \in E}{x, T, P, E \gg^{-} \operatorname{let} ok = eq(x, y) \operatorname{in} P, E}$$

$$\frac{y, T_1, P_1, E_1 \gg^{-} P_2, E_2 \qquad z, T_2, P_2, E_2 \gg^{-} P_3, E_3}{x, \langle T_1, T_2 \rangle, P_1, E_1 \gg \operatorname{let}\langle y, z \rangle = x \operatorname{in} P_3, E_3} \; [y, z : \top \text{ fresh}]$$

$$\frac{z, T_2, P_1, E_1 \gg^{-} P_2, E_2 \qquad y, T_1, P_2, E_2 \gg^{-} P_3, E_3}{x, \langle T_1, T_2 \rangle, P_1, E_1 \gg \operatorname{let}\langle y, z \rangle = x \operatorname{in} P_3, E_3} \; [y, z : \top \text{ fresh}]$$

$$\frac{(T_2, y) \in E_1 \qquad z, T_1, P_1, \{(\{\!|T_1|\!\}_{T_2}, x)\} \cup E_1 \gg P_2, E_1}{x, \{\!|T_1|\!\}_{T_2}, P_1, E_1 \gg \operatorname{let} z = dec(x, y) \operatorname{in} P_2, E_2} \; [z : \top \text{ fresh}, T_2 : \mathsf{S}]$$

$$\frac{E \vdash \{\!|T_1|\!\}_{T_2}}{x, \{\!|T_1|\!\}_{T_2}, P, E \gg \operatorname{let} ok = eq(x, \{\!|T_1|\!\}_{T_2}) \operatorname{in} P, \{(\{\!|T_1|\!\}_{T_2}, x)\} \cup E}$$

Analogous cases for asymmetric encryption omitted.

$$\frac{T : s \text{ is a variable}}{x, T, P, E \gg \operatorname{let} T : s = x \operatorname{in} P, \{(T, T)\} \cup E}$$

Fig. 15. Receive code generation

$$\frac{(T, x) \in E}{E \vdash T}$$

$$\frac{E \vdash T_1 \qquad E \vdash T_2}{E \vdash \langle T_1, T_2 \rangle}$$

$$\frac{E \vdash T_1 \qquad E \vdash T_2}{E \vdash \{\!|T_1|\!\}_{T_2}}$$

Fig. 16. Term synthesis

where $b, a : \mathsf{N}$ and $s : \mathsf{S}$.
The process term P that satisfies $C, E_0, 2, 1 \gg P, E_2$, is:

$$\mathsf{out}^{(2,1)}\left(c, \{\!| \{\!| s |\!\}_{pk(a)^{-1}} |\!\}_{pk(b)}\right).$$
$$\mathsf{in}(c, x_1).$$
$$\mathsf{let} x_2 : \mathsf{T} = dec(x_1, s) \mathsf{in}$$
$$\mathsf{let} d : \mathsf{D} = x_2 \mathsf{in} \ (2, 2). \ 0$$

Blanchet Responder Example. Assume the responder is the first role in the protocol. The responder trace is the one in Eq. 3 after interchanging sends and receives. A sensible set of input basic values is $\{d, pk(a), pk(b)^{-1}\}$. After inserting the new form by hand, the process term is:

$$\mathsf{in}(c, x_1).$$
$$\mathsf{let} x_2 : \mathsf{T} = dec(x_1, pk(b)^{-1}) \mathsf{in}$$
$$\mathsf{let} x_3 : \mathsf{T} = dec(x_2, pk(a)) \mathsf{in}$$
$$\mathsf{let} s : \mathsf{S} = x_3 \mathsf{in} \ (1, 1).$$
$$\mathsf{new} d : \mathsf{D}.$$
$$\mathsf{out}^{(1,2)}\left(c, \{\!| d |\!\}_s\right). \ 0$$

References

1. Abadi, M., Fournet, C.: Mobile values, new names, and secure communication. In: 28th ACM Symposium on Principles of Programming Languages (POPL 2001), pp. 104–115, January 2001
2. Almousa, O., Mödersheim, S., Viganò, L.: Alice and Bob: reconciling formal models and implementation. In: Bodei, C., Ferrari, G.-L., Priami, C. (eds.) Programming Languages with Applications to Biology and Security. LNCS, vol. 9465, pp. 66–85. Springer, Heidelberg (2015). doi:10.1007/978-3-319-25527-9_7
3. Armando, A., et al.: The AVISPA tool for the automated validation of internet security protocols and applications. In: Etessami, K., Rajamani, S.K. (eds.) CAV 2005. LNCS, vol. 3576, pp. 281–285. Springer, Heidelberg (2005). doi:10.1007/11513988_27
4. Armando, A., et al.: The AVANTSSAR platform for the automated validation of trust and security of service-oriented architectures. In: Flanagan, C., König, B. (eds.) TACAS 2012. LNCS, vol. 7214, pp. 267–282. Springer, Heidelberg (2012). doi:10.1007/978-3-642-28756-5_19
5. Basin, D.A., Cremers, C.J.F., Miyazaki, K., Radomirovic, S., Watanabe, D.: Improving the security of cryptographic protocol standards. IEEE Secur. Priv. **13**(3), 24–31 (2015)
6. Bistarelli, S., Cervesato, I., Lenzini, G., Martinelli, F.: Relating multiset rewriting and process algebras for security protocol analysis. J. Comput. Secur. **13**(1), 3–47 (2005)
7. Blanchet, B.: An efficient protocol verifier based on Prolog rules. In: 14th Computer Security Foundations Workshop, pp. 82–96. IEEE CS Press, June 2001
8. Blanchet, B.: Vérification automatique de protocoles cryptographiques: modèle formel et modèle calculatoire. Automatic verification of security protocols: formal model and computational model. Mémoire d'habilitation à diriger des recherches, Université Paris-Dauphine, November 2008

9. Blanchet, B., Smyth, B., Cheval, V.: ProVerif 1.93: Automatic Cryptographic Protocol Verifier. User Manual and Tutorial (2016)
10. Burrows, M., Abadi, M., Needham, R.: A logic of authentication. Proc. R. Soc. Ser. A **426**(1871), 233–271 (1989)
11. Cervesato, I., Durgin, N.A., Lincoln, P.: A comparison between strand spaces and multiset rewriting for security protocol analysis. J. Comput. Secur. **13**(2), 265–316 (2005)
12. Comon, H., Cortier, V.: Security properties: two agents are sufficient. Sci. Comput. Program. **50**(1–3), 51–71 (2004)
13. Cortier, V., Dallon, A., Delaune, S.: Bounding the number of agents, for equivalence too. In: Piessens, F., Viganò, L. (eds.) POST 2016. LNCS, vol. 9635, pp. 211–232. Springer, Heidelberg (2016). doi:10.1007/978-3-662-49635-0_11
14. Cortier, V., Kremer, S. (eds.): Formal Models and Techniques for Analyzing Security Protocols. Cryptology and Information Security Series. IOS Press (2011)
15. Crazzolara, F., Winskel, G.: Events in security protocols. In: Proceedings of the 8th ACM Conference on Computer and Communications Security, CCS 2001, 6–8 November 2001, Philadelphia, Pennsylvania, USA, pp. 96–105 (2001)
16. Cremers, C., Mauw, S.: Operational Semantics and Verification of Security Protocols. Springer, Heidelberg (2012)
17. Cremers, C.: Key exchange in IPsec revisited: formal analysis of IKEv1 and IKEv2. In: Atluri, V., Diaz, C. (eds.) ESORICS 2011. LNCS, vol. 6879, pp. 315–334. Springer, Heidelberg (2011). doi:10.1007/978-3-642-23822-2_18
18. Datta, A., Derek, A., Mitchell, J.C., Roy, A.: Protocol composition logic (PCL). Electron. Notes Theoret. Comput. Sci. **172**, 311–358 (2007)
19. Goguen, J.A., Meseguer, J.: Order-sorted algebra I: equational deduction for multiple inheritance, overloading, exceptions and partial operations. Theoret. Comput. Sci. **105**(2), 217–273 (1992)
20. Gordon, A.D., Jeffrey, A.: Types, effects for asymmetric cryptographic protocols. J. Comput. Secur. **12**(3–4), 435–484 (2004)
21. Groote, J.F., Mousavi, M.R.: Modeling and Analysis of Communicating Systems. MIT Press, Cambridge (2014)
22. Guttman, J.D.: Establishing and preserving protocol security goals. J. Comput. Secur. **22**(2), 201–267 (2014)
23. ISO/IEC 29128: Information Technology-Security techniques–Verification of Cryptographic Protocols (2011)
24. Kremer, S., Künnemann, R.: Automated analysis of security protocols with global state. In: 2014 IEEE Symposium on Security and Privacy, SP 2014, 18–21 May 2014, Berkeley, CA, USA, pp. 163–178 (2014)
25. Lynch, C., Meadows, C.A.: On the relative soundness of the free algebra model for public key encryption. Electron. Notes Theoret. Comput. Sci. **125**(1), 43–54 (2005)
26. Matsuo, S., Miyazaki, K., Otsuka, A., Basin, D.: How to evaluate the security of real-life cryptographic protocols? In: Sion, R., Curtmola, R., Dietrich, S., Kiayias, A., Miret, J.M., Sako, K., Sebé, F. (eds.) FC 2010. LNCS, vol. 6054, pp. 182–194. Springer, Heidelberg (2010). doi:10.1007/978-3-642-14992-4_16
27. Meadows, C.: The NRL protocol analyzer: an overview. J. Logic Program. **26**(2), 113–131 (1996)
28. Meadows, C: Analysis of the internet key exchange protocol using the NRL protocol analyzer. In: Proceedings of the 1999 IEEE Symposium on Security and Privacy. IEEE CS Press, May 1999

29. Meier, S., Schmidt, B., Cremers, C., Basin, D.: The TAMARIN prover for the symbolic analysis of security protocols. In: Sharygina, N., Veith, H. (eds.) CAV 2013. LNCS, vol. 8044, pp. 696–701. Springer, Heidelberg (2013). doi:10.1007/978-3-642-39799-8_48

30. Millen, J.K.: On the freedom of encryption. Inf. Process. Lett. **86**(6), 329–333 (2003)

31. Miller, D.: Encryption as an abstract data type. Electron. Notes Theoret. Comput. Sci. **84**, 18–29 (2003)

32. Ramsdell, J.D., Guttman, J.D.: CPSA: a cryptographic protocol shapes analyzer (2009). http://hackage.haskell.org/package/cpsa

33. Rowe, P.D., Guttman, J.D., Liskov, M.D.: Measuring protocol strength with security goals. International Journal of Information Security (Accepted, Forthcoming)

34. Woo, T.Y.C., Lam, S.S.: A lesson on authentication protocol design. Oper. Syst. Rev. **28**, 24–37 (1994)

Cryptanalysis of GlobalPlatform Secure Channel Protocols

Mohamed Sabt[1,2]([✉]) and Jacques Traoré[1]

[1] Orange Labs, 42 rue des coutures, 14066 Caen, France
{mohamed.sabt,jacques.traore}@orange.com
[2] Sorbonne universités, Université de technologie de Compiègne, Heudiasyc,
Centre de recherche Royallieu, 60203 Compiègne, France

Abstract. GlobalPlatform (GP) card specifications are the de facto standards for the industry of smart cards. Being highly sensitive, GP specifications were defined regarding stringent security requirements. In this paper, we analyze the cryptographic core of these requirements; i.e. the family of Secure Channel Protocols (SCP). Our main results are twofold. First, we demonstrate a theoretical attack against SCP02, which is the most popular protocol in the SCP family. We discuss the scope of our attack by presenting an actual scenario in which a malicious entity can exploit it in order to recover encrypted messages. Second, we investigate the security of SCP03 that was introduced as an amendment in 2009. We find that it provably satisfies strong notions of security. Of particular interest, we prove that SCP03 withstands algorithm substitution attacks (ASAs) defined by Bellare et al. that may lead to secret mass surveillance. Our findings highlight the great value of the paradigm of provable security for standards and certification, since unlike extensive evaluation, it formally guarantees the absence of security flaws.

Keywords: GlobalPlatform · Secure Channel Protocol · Provable security · Plaintext recovery · Stateful encryption

1 Introduction

Nowadays, smart cards are already playing an important role in the area of information technology. Considered to be tamper resistant, they are increasingly used to provide security services [38]. Smart cards do not only owe their tamper resistance for their success; programmability is a key issue for the wide adoption of this technology. Indeed, programmability made it possible to load new applications or remotely personalize existing ones during the cards life cycle [33]. However, this dynamicity did not come without price, as it has brought up security concerns about the novel system of content management. The absence of standards has motivated the creation of GlobalPlatform.

GlobalPlatform (GP) [21] is a cross-industry consortium that publishes specifications on how post-issuance management shall be carried out for smart cards. This includes the functionality to remotely manage cards content in a secure way.

© Springer International Publishing AG 2016
L. Chen et al. (Eds.): SSR 2016, LNCS 10074, pp. 62–91, 2016.
DOI: 10.1007/978-3-319-49100-4_3

The cryptographic heart of these mechanisms is the family of *Secure Channel Protocols* (SCPs) which protect the exchanged messages. Optimized for cards, the used encryption schemes in these protocols do not follow any standardized or provably secure construction.

Since its first publication, the GP card specifications have been the subject of diverse verifications. For instance, authors in [3] examine some aspects of these specifications and prove their soundness via the B method. Nevertheless, to the best of our knowledge, no rigorous analysis of the SCP encryption schemes has been provided before. Our goal is thus to study them through provable security, and hence to validate (or invalidate) the security guaranteed by GP.

1.1 Our Contribution

In this paper, we apply the methods of provable security on GP specifications. We start by analyzing the most popular GP SCP (i.e. SCP02). Much to our surprise, we find that SCP02 is vulnerable to a well-known security flaw caused by encrypting data using CBC mode with no random initialization vector (IV).

We illustrate this theoretical flaw by presenting a plaintext recovery attack where the adversary succeeds in getting some information about encrypted messages. To this end, we define an attack scenario in which several entities (e.g. service providers) communicate with the smart card via a trusted third party. Our attack allows a malicious entity to recover some encrypted messages belonging to another entity. In particular, messages including data with limited values and thus of low entropy, such as PINs, are the most exposed.

Then, we shift our analysis to the youngest member of the SCP family (i.e. SCP03). SCP03 encrypts messages using the "Encrypt-then-MAC" (EtM) method that is proved secure in [8]. In this paper, we provide a stronger result: SCP03 satisfies the security model defined by Bellare et al. in [6] which better models the particularity of SCP03. Indeed, SCP03 maintains a counter (i.e. state) for its decryption. One main advantage of this model is that, in addition to satisfying the existing notions of confidentiality [4] and integrity [7], it protects against replay and out-of-delivery attacks. More importantly, we prove that SCP03 defends against the recent threat of mass surveillance by algorithm-substitution attacks (ASAs) [9]. Typically closed-source, the industry of smart cards is concerned about ASAs, since no code scrutiny is possible to assert the absence of backdoors in the implemented protocols. This could damage the confidence in smart cards. Our proof guarantees that SCP03 cannot undetectably contain hidden backdoors allowing mass surveillance as it is outlined in [9].

Our work brings to light an interesting fact: security in well-established standards still does not withstand a simple cryptanalysis. We show, once again, that security by extensive verification or eminent authority is highly misleading. Indeed, being involved in sensitive services (e.g. payment), GP specifications have undergone rigorous verification and validation. This is why they are used in several systems achieving high assurance level in common criteria (CC) [36]. We emphasize that the presented vulnerability of SCP02 is well-known in the domain of cryptography [30]. Thus, our result raises serious concerns about CC certification. We encourage therefore further integration of *provable security* inside the enterprise of certification to improve the security of the certified protocols.

1.2 Related Work

Blockwise-Adaptive Attack. Formalized by Fouque et al. in [20], blockwise security has been firstly introduced in [29]. Its idea is simple: messages are not processed atomically in practice, so an adversary is able to get the ciphertext of a part of the message. Authors motivate this notion by attacking three encryption schemes proved to be secure against chosen plaintext attacks. We will focus solely on the case of CBC mode. The security proof of CBC in [4] holds only if all the calls to the underlying block cipher are independent from each other. This means that the $(i-1)$th block of ciphertext must not be known before choosing the ith block of plaintext, otherwise independence is lost and the proof fails. We note that using a predictable IV could be seen as a special case, since the first block of ciphertext, which is the IV, is known in advance before choosing the message.

Despite its popularity, Mitchell in [34] (and more recently Rogaway in [40]) concludes that the CBC mode involves so many security constraints that it would be better to abandon it for future designs. Indeed, a great number research effort has been dedicated to extend the weakness of CBC beyond theory. Some have adapted the vulnerability mentioned above in order to undermine the security of SSL3.0/TLS1.0 [2,14]. Both attacks were motivated by the fact that the SSL3.0/TLS1.0 standard mandates the use of CBC encryption with chained (IVs); i.e. subsequent IVs are the last block of the previous ciphertexts. The attack of [14], called BEAST, is so efficient that migration to TLS1.1 has been recommended by IETF. Independently from blockwise security, authors in [6], inspired from [12], outline a vulnerability in the secure shell protocol (SSH) caused by the same reason: CBC encryption with chained IVs. It is worth noting that all the attacks of [2,6,12,14] follow the same principle: some kind of plaintext recovery is possible when the attacker can both predict the next IV and control the first block of the message.

The presented attack against SCP02 follows a similar principle because constant IVs are always predictable. Despite similarity, we argue that the vulnerability presented in this paper is caused by the design of SCP02 that is quite delicate to secure. Indeed, it instructs the use of CBC encryption together with CBC-MAC for computing integrity tag. Such combination creates two contradictory requirements for security. Indeed, it is proved that a random IV is necessary for CBC encryption [4], while CBC-MAC must use constant IV [5].

Authenticated Encryption. Authenticated encryption (AE) is a symmetric encryption scheme that protects both data confidentiality and integrity (authenticity). The security notions of AE were formalized in the early 2000s in [7,31]. Generic composition [8] is the most popular approach for numerous security protocols, such as SSH, TLS and IPsec. This approach is about combining confidentiality-providing encryption together with a message authentication code

(MAC). Generally, three composition methods are considered: Encrypt-and-MAC, MAC-then-Encrypt and Encrypt-then-MAC.

The family of SCP protocols follows the paradigm of generic composition. On the one hand, SCP02 relies on the "Encrypt-and-MAC" (EaM) method. As pointed out in [8], this composition method is not generically secure, but we do not consider this result in our analysis for two reasons. First, chosen ciphertext attacks are not included in our threat model, since they are hardly applicable. Indeed, the decryption operation in SCP02 is only performed by smart cards that are unlikely to misbehave (due to their tamper-resistance and their controlled content management). Smart cards keep the decrypted messages and never output them outside, otherwise of course encryption would be of no use. Thus, attackers cannot obtain the result of the decryption operation. Second, the used cryptographic schemes for both encryption and authentication are not secure, hence simpler attacks exist. We provide further details in Sect. 3.

On the other hand, SCP03 utilizes the "Encrypt-then-MAC" (EtM) method which is proved to satisfy standard security notions: confidentiality (IND-CPA) and integrity of messages. We note that EtM is ill-suited to formalize all the power of SCP03. In this paper, we prove that SCP03 protects against a wider range of attacks, thanks to its stateful decryption. Of particular value, we prove that it withstands replay attacks and that any secret subversion of SCP03 for malicious goals can be detected. The latter is an important feature, since the absence of source code might cast doubts on the trustworthiness of smart cards.

1.3 Paper Outline

The rest of the paper is structured as follows: Sect. 2 gives background information on GlobalPlatform and reviews some classical definitions. In Sect. 3, we introduce the attack against SCP02 and demonstrate how it could be exploited in practice. Sections 4 and 5 presents our provable security results of SCP03. We end this paper by providing some discussion and specific recommendations related to the identified vulnerability.

2 Preliminaries

2.1 GlobalPlatform

GP card specification [23] refers to a number of technical standards that aim to develop flexible framework for smart cards. Within the GP architecture, the security domain (SD) controls applications on smart cards by supporting various cryptographic functions. For the purpose of this paper, we will be uniquely interested in secure communication, and we will be using the notion of SD as the component containing its private key that it uses to establish secure sessions.

SECURE CHANNEL PROTOCOL. The GP card specification defines secure channel protocols (SCPs) to provide secure communication. Mainly designed for content management, they are also used by applications for their sensitive operations.

Whenever a secure session is needed, the SCP executes three steps: (1) *initialization* that includes entities authentication and derivation of session keys; (2) *operation* in which exchanged data are protected; and (3) *termination* ending the session. Our target in this paper is the encryption schemes employed during the second step. In follows, we provide more details about the *operation* of SCP02 and SCP03. SCP01 is not discussed because of its deprecation. It is worth mentioning that all given details on SCPs come from the GP card specification version 2.3, which is the latest version at the time of writing this paper.

2.2 Definitions

NOTATION. A message is a string. A string is an element of $\{0, 1\}^*$. The concatenation of strings X and Y is denoted $X\|Y$ or simply XY. For a string X, its length is represented by $|X|$. For an integer $N \in \mathbb{N}$, N++ denotes the C-like ++ operator that returns the value N and then increases its value by 1. A *block cipher* is a function $E : \text{Key} \times \{0, 1\}^n \longrightarrow \{0, 1\}^n$, where Key is a finite nonempty set and $E_k(.) = E(k, .)$ is a permutation, hence invertible, on $\{0, 1\}^n$. The number n is called the *block length*. A *tweakable block cipher* (TBC) [32] extends the notion of block ciphers. A TBC $\widetilde{E} : \text{Key} \times \text{Tweak} \times \{0, 1\}^n \longrightarrow \{0, 1\}^n$ is a family of permutations parameterized by a pair (K, T), where K is a secret key and T is a public tweak. We define five finite nonempty sets of strings: Key, TWEAK, NONCE, MSG and CTXT. Let K be a key, T be a tweak, N be a nonce, M be a message and C be a ciphertext. Henceforth, unless stated otherwise, for all K, T, N, M and C, we have $\mathsf{K} \in \text{Key}$, $T \in \text{TWEAK}$, $N \in \text{NONCE}$, $M \in \text{MSG}$ and $C \in \text{CTXT}$. We use the notation $\mathbf{A}^{\mathcal{O}}$ to denote the fact that the algorithm $\mathbf{A}$ can make queries to the function $\mathcal{O}$. Hereafter, we say that the *adversary* $\mathbf{A}$ has access to the *oracle* $\mathcal{O}$. If f is a probabilistic (resp., deterministic) algorithm, then $y \xleftarrow{R} f(x)$ (resp., $y \leftarrow f(x)$) denotes the process of running f on input x and assigning the result to y. The notation $A \Rightarrow x$ means that the adversary $\mathbf{A}$ outputs the value x.

SYMMETRIC ENCRYPTION SCHEMES. A *symmetric encryption scheme* $\mathcal{SE}$ is defined by three algorithms $(\mathcal{K}, \mathcal{E}, \mathcal{D})$, where (1) the *key generation algorithm*, $\mathcal{K}$, takes a security parameter $k \in \mathbb{N}$ and returns a key K. We write $\mathsf{K} \xleftarrow{R} \mathcal{K}(k)$; (2) the *encryption algorithm*, $\mathcal{E}$, takes a key K and a plaintext M to produce a ciphertext C. We write $C \longleftarrow \mathcal{E}_k(M)$; and (3) the *decryption algorithm*, $\mathcal{D}$, takes a key K and a ciphertext C to return either the corresponding plaintext M or a special symbol $\perp$ to indicate that the ciphertext is invalid. We require that $\mathcal{D}_k(\mathcal{E}_k(M)) = M$ for all M and K.

THE CIPHER BLOCK CHAINING (CBC) MODE. Both SCP02 and SCP03 use symmetric encryption with the CBC mode. In CBC, each block of the plaintext is XORed with the previous ciphertext block before being encrypted. The first block of the plaintext is XORed with an initial value (IV). Here, we only consider the variant where the IV is explicitly given as input. We write $C \longleftarrow \mathcal{E}_k\text{-CBC}(iv, M)$ and $M \longleftarrow \mathcal{D}_k\text{-CBC}(iv, C)$.

NONCE-BASED SYMMETRIC ENCRYPTION. As defined by Rogaway in [39], a *nonce-based encryption* $n\mathcal{SE} = (n\mathcal{K}, n\mathcal{E}, n\mathcal{D})$ is a symmetric scheme where both the encryption and the decryption algorithms are deterministic and stateless. They take an extra input called the *nonce* N, which is a variable that takes a new value with every encryption. We write $C \longleftarrow n\mathcal{E}_k(N, M)$ and $M \longleftarrow n\mathcal{D}_k(N, C)$.

MESSAGE AUTHENTICATION SCHEMES. Conventionally, a *message authentication scheme* (MAC) $\mathcal{MA} = (\mathcal{K}, \mathcal{T}, \mathcal{V})$ consists of three algorithms. $\mathcal{K}$ is the probabilistic algorithm for key generation. The tagging algorithm, $\mathcal{T}_k$, takes a key K and a message M to return a tag τ. The verification algorithm, $\mathcal{V}_k$, takes a key K, a message M and a candidate tag τ' to return a bit. We require that $\mathcal{V}_k(M, \mathcal{T}_k(M)) = 1$ for all M and K.

TWEAKABLE FUNCTIONS. A *tweakable* function $\widetilde{F}(.,.)$ is a function where a 'tweak' is required for its computation. We write $y \longleftarrow \widetilde{F}(T, M)$.

STANDARD SECURITY NOTIONS. We associate to any adversary a number called its "advantage" that measures her success in breaking a given scheme. A scheme is said *secure* with respect to a given security notion if all related polynomial-time adversaries have a negligible advantage. We write $\mathbf{Adv}_{SC}^{SN}(A)$, where $\mathbf{A}$ is an adversary attacking the scheme SC regarding the security notion SN.

Definition 1 *(Indistinguishability of a Symmetric Encryption Scheme (IND)).* Given a symmetric encryption $\mathcal{SE} = (\mathcal{K}, \mathcal{E}, \mathcal{D})$ and a ciphertext of one of two plaintexts, no adversary can distinguish which one was encrypted. IND can be expressed as an experiment [4]. Let $\mathcal{E}_k(\mathcal{LR}(.,.,b))$ be a *left-or-right* oracle where $b \in \{0, 1\}$: the oracle takes two messages as input, m_0 and m_1, where $|m_0| = |m_1|$, and returns $C \leftarrow \mathcal{E}_k(m_b)$. The adversary submits queries of the form (m_0, m_1) to the oracle, and must guess the bit b, i.e. which message was encrypted. This security notion is often called *IND-CPA*, where *CPA* represents chosen-plaintext attacks. For an adversary $\mathbf{A}^{\mathcal{E}}$, the advantage is defined as $\mathbf{Adv}_{\mathcal{SE}}^{ind\text{-}cpa}(A) = \left| \Pr[A^{\mathcal{E}} \Rightarrow 1 \mid b = 1] - \Pr[A^{\mathcal{E}} \Rightarrow 1 \mid b = 0] \right|$. There is a stronger security notion associated to IND that is called IND-CCA (CCA stands for chosen-ciphertext attacks). In the IND-CCA experiment, besides the encryption oracle, the adversary has access to a decryption oracle $\mathsf{D}_k(.)$, so that she can choose any ciphertext and obtain its plaintext. There is one restriction for using $\mathsf{D}_k(.)$: the adversary cannot ask to decrypt ciphertexts that were previously generated by the encryption oracle, otherwise a trivial attack is possible.

Definition 2 *(Strong Unforgeability (SUF-CMA)).* This notion was adapted by Bellare et al. [5] from the definition of security of digital signatures. Given a message authentication scheme $\mathcal{MA} = (\mathcal{K}, \mathcal{T}, \mathcal{V})$, we consider a game in which the adversary makes arbitrary queries to a tagging oracle $\mathcal{T}_k$ as well as a verification oracle $\mathcal{V}_k$. The adversary $\mathbf{A}^{\mathcal{T},\mathcal{V}}$ wins (outputs 1) if she can find a pair (M, τ) such that $\mathcal{V}_k(M, \tau) = 1$, but τ was never returned by $\mathcal{T}_k$ as tag of M. The advantage of $\mathbf{A}$ is defined as $\mathbf{Adv}_{\mathcal{MA}}^{suf\text{-}cma}(A) = \Pr[A^{\mathcal{T},\mathcal{V}} \Rightarrow 1]$.

Definition 3 *(Integrity of Ciphertext (INT-CTXT))*. Defined in [8], this notion requires that no adversary be able to produce a valid ciphertext which the encryption oracle had never produced before. Given an encryption scheme $\mathcal{SE} = (\mathcal{K}, \mathcal{E}, \mathcal{D})$, we consider a game in which the adversary has access to an encryption oracle $\mathcal{E}_k(.)$ and to a decryption one $\mathcal{D}_k(.)$. The adversary $\mathbf{A}^{\mathcal{E}, \mathcal{D}}$ wins (outputs 1) if she can find a ciphertext C, such that (1) it was not produced by $\mathcal{E}_k(.)$ and (2) it does not decrypt to $\bot$. The advantage of $\mathbf{A}$ is defined as $\mathbf{Adv}_{\mathcal{SE}}^{int-ctxt}(A) = \Pr[A^{\mathcal{E}, \mathcal{D}} \Rightarrow 1]$.

Definition 4 *(Stateful Pseudorandom Function (sPRF))*. Let $F = \{F_k : \mathsf{K} \in \mathcal{K}(k)\}$ where F_k is a deterministic stateful function mapping l-bit strings to l'-bit strings for each $\mathsf{K} \in \mathcal{K}(k)$. Let $R_\mathcal{S}$ be a stateful random-bit oracle. This means that the output of $R_\mathcal{S}$ depends on its state. Indeed, given a message $M \in \{0,1\}^l$, $R_\mathcal{S}(M)$ returns two different l'-bit random strings for two subsequent calls. The goal is that no adversary $\mathbf{A}$ can distinguish whether she is interacting with a random instance of F or with its oracle $R_\mathcal{S}$. $\mathbf{A}$'s advantage is $\mathbf{Adv}_F^{sprf}(A) = \left| \Pr[A^F \Rightarrow 1] - \Pr[A^{R_\mathcal{S}} \Rightarrow 1] \right|$.

Definition 5 *(Indistinguishability from Tweakable Random Bits under CPA ($\widetilde{IND}$-CPA))*. Here, we present a variant of the distinguishing concept defined for tweakable functions and presented in [10]. We define $\widetilde{IND}$-CPA as follows. Let $\widetilde{F}$ be a tweakable function mapping pairs of (t, l)-bit strings for each $\mathsf{K} \in \mathcal{K}(k)$. Let $\widetilde{\mathcal{R}}$ be a tweakable random-bit oracle from $\{0,1\}^t \times \{0,1\}^l$ to $\{0,1\}^{l'}$. The goal is that no adversary $\mathbf{A}$ can distinguish whether she is interacting with a random instance of $\widetilde{F}$ or with its oracle $\widetilde{\mathcal{R}}$. The advantage of $\mathbf{A}$ is defined as $\mathbf{Adv}_{\widetilde{F}}^{ind-cpa}(A) = \left| \Pr[A^{\widetilde{F}} \Rightarrow 1] - \Pr[A^{\widetilde{\mathcal{R}}} \Rightarrow 1] \right|$.

3 Secure Channel Protocol '2'

3.1 Description

SCP02 is the recommended protocol in the GP specifications. It is built upon symmetric encryption based on block ciphers, hence the need of secret keys and padding data. Informally, it uses "Encrypt-and-MAC" construction, wherein the message is both encrypted and integrity protected (by using a MAC algorithm). The MAC value is appended to the encrypted message to produce the ciphertext.

In more detail, padding is first added to the message and a MAC tag is computed over the resulted data. Then, the payload is encrypted after stripping off the MAC padding to replace it by a payload one. Padding is done with binary zeroes started by 0x80. Figure 1 schematically shows the ciphertext format.

Concerning the schemes in use, SCP02 mandates to encrypt data using *triple DES* in CBC mode [26] with no IV, namely IV of binary zeroes (refer to Sect. E.4.6 in [23]). As for MAC computing, it uses a chained version of ISO9797-1 MAC algorithm 3, which includes a CBC-MAC processing with a simple DES and a Triple DES computation for the last block of the message. As a security

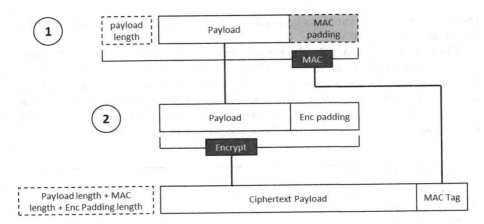

Fig. 1. Ciphertext Generation by SCP02. Grey boxes, i.e. 'MAC padding', are not included in the 'encrypt' operation.

enhancement, the last valid MAC tag is DES-encrypted before being applied to the calculation of the next MAC.

We note that both schemes are vulnerable. Indeed, authors in [19] perform a side-channel attack to defeat the ISO9797-1 MAC algorithm 3. Their attack allows one to recover the secret key used for the MAC computation. The consequences of such attack are limited for the reason that SCP02, like any SCP, generates the MAC tag using a temporary session key. Therefore, we do not consider this attack in the rest of the paper. In the sequel, we describe how an attacker might exploit the absence of random IVs to recover encrypted messages.

3.2 Try-and-Guess Attack

It is easy to see that for a fixed iv the CBC encryption $\mathcal{E}_k\text{-CBC}(iv, .)$ is a stateless deterministic function of the key K. Indeed, it always yields the same ciphertext when encrypting the same message multiple times (using the same key). This has both theoretical and practical consequences.

Theoretically, it violates the security goal IND-CPA. An adversary can tell which message was encrypted after only two queries: the first query contains the same plaintext M twice, while the second one includes M together with another plaintext. The adversary succeeds with a probability 1, since if M was encrypted, the encryption oracle would output the same result as for the first query. We note that the adversary succeeds due to the fact that the IND-CPA experiment does not constrain the adversary from submitting queries of the form (M, M) to the encryption oracle $\mathcal{E}_k(\mathcal{LR}(., ., b))$.

In practice, an eavesdropper observing the stream of ciphertexts is able to determine whether two ciphertexts come from the same message. Better yet, the eavesdropper can detect whether two messages share the same prefix. This could be useful to study the structure of the encrypted stream by recognizing the presence of the same data multiple times. Now, we turn the above scenario into a more serious attack.

Consider an adversary **A** who can mount a chosen-plaintext attack. **A** starts by observing a ciphertext C $(=\mathcal{E}_k\text{-SCP02}(M))$. Recall that the goal of **A** is to find M. **A** achieves her goal by repeatedly trying all possible values for M until the correct one is identified. For instance, if the adversary knows that M is one of N possible values, then she can determine the actual value of M after $N/2$ (on average) guesses. We describe the algorithm of **A** as follows.

Algorithm. $\mathbf{A}^{\mathcal{E}_k\text{-SCP02}(.)}$

1: Get C from eavesdropping
2: found $\longleftarrow$ false
3: repeat
4:     $M' \longleftarrow$ guess(C)
5:     $C' \longleftarrow \mathcal{E}_k\text{-SCP02}(M')$
6:     if C = C' then
7:         found $\longleftarrow$ true
8:     end if
9: until found = true
10: return M'

---

where guess is a function that takes a ciphertext C as input and returns one possible decryption of C for each call. We notice that the adversary keeps on making guesses until finding the message that encrypts to the eavesdropped ciphertext. Therefore, this theoretical attack is efficient against data with limited values and thus of low entropy, but it is worthless in case the exchanged data takes random values or their format is not known in advance.

We acknowledge that Try-and-Guess attack (TaGa) as outlined above has been previously suggested in other contexts (see [2,12,14]). Nevertheless, we believe that there is value in reiterating the discussion about this security flaw. The fact that the *de facto* standard of the sensitive industry of smart cards is still vulnerable to such attacks is of great interest. It indicates how the security community is divided between those designing theoretical cryptosystems and those implementing them in the real-world. We hope that our work would constitute a step towards bridging this gap.

In view of the ongoing popularity of SCP02, we believe that this vulnerability has not been identified yet. To the best of our knowledge, our work is the first one to apply TaGa in the context of GP specification for smart cards.

3.3 Plaintext Recovery Against Smart Cards

Here, we illustrate the fallout of TaGa by a theoretical, yet real-world, attack scenario. Our attack applies to smart cards following the GP model for content management.

Actors. We define four actors to describe the plot of the attack: (1) a *trusted service manager* (TSM) who owns a security domain on a smart card; (2) a *victim* who uses the said smart card to execute some critical services; (3) an *honest service provider* offering a sensitive service to the victim (e.g. payment); and (4) a *malicious service provider* that offers some service to the victim, but mainly aims to compromise the other services.

Threat Model. The intent of the attacker is to recover some sensitive data related to applications installed on smart cards.

For this purpose, we assume that the adversary is capable of installing an application on the targeted smart card. Any service provider does have this ability via a TSM. In addition, the application which the adversary is supposed to install includes no harmful behaviors. In particular, it does not attempt to attack the card system. Moreover, we assume that the adversary partially controls all communications with the card: she can drop and eavesdrop any exchanged message. Finally, we suppose that the adversary is targeting a well-protected card, and thus no direct attack is possible. This implies several assumptions. First, the card system shall contain no logical security flaw. Second, the card shall implement the appropriate countermeasures to withstand hardware attacks. Third, its security domains shall have been created and personalized with random keys. We emphasize that these assumptions are highly plausible for the smart card industry where products undergo extensive verification tests [36].

To sum up, in order to succeed her attack, the adversary should succeed in recovering the data while being transferred between the card and the TSM. This implies to break the encryption scheme implemented by the security domain. Being remote and software-only, our model represents a new kind of threat, since most related work involve some sophisticated hardware attacks [1,25]. Our model provides several advantages over those defined in the literature, since it concerns a large number of smart cards regardless of their manufacturers. Indeed, our attack solely involves details defined in the GP card specifications which are common to all GP compliant cards.

Attack Workflow. We suppose that the attacker has already convinced the TSM to install her application. The attack is structured into two phases.

During the first phase, the honest service provider needs to personalize her application with some secret data. She sends her query to the TSM that is responsible to carry out the secure communication to the smart card. The malicious provider detects this event and reacts accordingly. She starts by asking the TSM to send some dummy query to the smart card. Thus, the TSM shares the established secure session with the two service providers. Afterward, the attacker intercepts the encrypted messages, grabs that of the honest service provider, and drops hers (easily recognizable by, for instance, its header).

As for the second phase, the attacker makes some guess, asks the TSM to encrypt it, and then intercepts the produced ciphertext which she discards whenever the guess was wrong. The attacker repeats this until she succeeds.

One technical issue might rise by this scenario: SCP02 instructs to double-encrypt sensitive data by the TSM. Data are firstly encrypted by ECB (Electronic Code Book) mode before applying the encryption of the secure channel. We argue that this has no impact on our attack, since the overall encryption remains stateless and deterministic. Indeed, ECB is deterministic, and the composition of two deterministic functions is clearly deterministic.

3.4   Discussion About Theoretical Feasibility

Several conditions must be met before the attacker can successfully recover some sensitive data. Below, we present these conditions and discuss their relevance.

USING ONE COMMON SESSION. First and foremost, the attacker must encrypt her test cases with the same key that encrypts the data to be recovered. This supposes that the TSM shares a secure session between different service providers. Some might argue that this is not a trivial requirement, and therefore our attack scenario cannot be mounted in practice. However, we argue that session sharing is not uncommon for three reasons. First, there is no mention in the specifications that could be understood as it is *bad* practice to share sessions or even SD. Second, SCP02 generates its session keys by encrypting some constants concatenating to a 2-byte counter. Thus, the TSM must change its master key after only 2^{16} sessions, which makes the TSM very eager to optimize the opening of secure sessions. Third, being expensive, the TSM is also eager to reduce the number of its leased SDs. Thus, it might install several applications into the same SD for the service providers that are not willing to pay the cost of having their own SD.

SYNCHRONIZATION. The TSM accepts to continue sending the attacker queries without receiving any acknowledgment. As a matter of fact, this mode of asynchronous communication is often employed for optimization. Indeed, the transmission rate of smart cards is slow [38]. Therefore, the TSM usually pushes all the commands to the terminal. The terminal forwards them to the associated card, and then collects all the returned values to send them back to the TSM. Such method of communication helps improve not only the communication time, bu also the undetectability of the attack, since the attacker application needs not to secretly include a special mode to manage all the sent commands during a session of TaGa. The attacker just intercepts and drops them.

LOW-ENTROPY DATA. This requirement is essential to succeed the Try-and-Guess attack. Low-entropy data are not rare in the context of smart cards. First, applications on smart cards often process enumerated variables with limited choices. This includes variables representing numerical values (e.g. amount of money), since integers are generally coded by two bytes in smart cards (JavaCard v2 [11] only supports signed short as numerical type). In practice, 4-byte PIN codes ($\leq 10,000$ choices) are also considered as low-entropy data. Second, despite the length of plaintext, the format used for numerous card applications is quite predictable. Data, like those of GP commands [23] and the EMV standard [17], are often structured with ASN.1 BER-TLV [27]. Such a format contains at least two public bytes: the tag value and the data length which the adversary already knows. In addition, the padding in SCP02 is constant and public. We illustrate by an example. The attacker wants to know how much money the user has provisioned her payment application. If the payment application is GP compliant, the provisioning command will be the GP command `Store Data`. Thus, the plaintext to be recovered is of the form:

$$\texttt{Tag}(1 \text{ byte}) \,||\, \texttt{Length}(1 \text{ byte}) \,||\, \texttt{Value}(2 \text{ bytes}) \,||\, \texttt{Padding}(4 \text{ bytes})$$

Within these eight bytes, the only bytes to be guessed are those of the `Value`. Therefore, there are no more than $2^{15} = 32,768$ choices, due to the fact that money should always remain positive. In practice, much fewer queries are required, since specific amounts of money are often suggested for account recharge.

4   Secure Channel Protocol '3'

4.1   Description

SCP03, published as an amendment to card specification 2.2 [22], defines a new set of cryptographic methods based on AES. Similar to SCP02, it requires secret keys and padding, since it relies on block ciphers. SCP03 uses the "Encrypt-then-MAC" (EtM) method in which the ciphertext is produced by encrypting the message and then appending the result of applying the MAC scheme to the encrypted message. Refer to Construction 1 for more details about SCP03.

Construction 1 *(SCP03 Algorithms for Encryption and Decryption).* Let E_k be an l-block-cipher and let $\text{CBC}[E_k] = (\mathcal{K}\text{-CBC}, \mathcal{E}\text{-CBC}, \mathcal{D}\text{-CBC})$ be a CBC encryption scheme that explicitly takes the iv vector as input. Let $\mathcal{MA} = (\mathcal{K}', \mathcal{T}, \mathcal{V})$ be a message authentication scheme. Let `padding` be a stateless deterministic encoding scheme and let `Len` be a function returning the length of its input. For the sake of clarity, we do not include `padding` in the described algorithms. For $M \in \{0,1\}^{ln}$ with the variables `counter` and `chained` properly initialized, the scheme SCP03-EtM $= (\mathcal{K}, \mathcal{E}, \mathcal{D})$ is defined as follows:

Encryption $\mathcal{E}_k(M)$

1: $iv \longleftarrow E_{k1}(\texttt{counter++})$
2: $C \longleftarrow \mathcal{E}_{k1}\text{-CBC}(iv, M)$
3: $C' \longleftarrow \text{Len}(C) \,||\, C$
4: $\tau_1 || \tau_2 \longleftarrow \mathcal{T}_{k2}(\texttt{chained} \,||\, C')$
5: `chained` $\longleftarrow \tau_1 || \tau_2$
6: **return** $C' \,||\, \tau_1$

Decryption $\mathcal{D}_k(C)$

1: Parse C as $\text{Len}(C') \,||\, C' \,||\, \tau$
2: **if** cannot parse **then return** $\bot$
3: $C'' \longleftarrow \texttt{chained} \,||\, \text{Len}(C') \,||\, C'$
4: $\tau_1 || \tau_2 \longleftarrow \mathcal{T}_{k2}(C'')$
5: **if** $\tau_1 \neq \tau$ **then**
6:      **return** $\bot$ **and** halt
7: **end if**
8: `chained` $\longleftarrow \tau_1 || \tau_2$
9: $iv \longleftarrow E_{k1}(\texttt{counter++})$
10: **return** $\mathcal{D}_{k1}\text{-CBC}(iv, C')$

We highlight four points in the construction above. First, SCP03 ensures that all the message inputs to $\mathcal{T}_k$ and $\mathcal{V}_k$ are encoded. The encoding consists of appending the length of the input (i.e. C). Such encoding makes the set of inputs 'prefix-free', which means that no input can be the prefix of another one. This is an important requirement, since many MAC schemes, like CBC-MAC [5], are secure only for prefix-free set of inputs. Second, we notice that SCP03 ends the opened secure session when a decryption fails. This approach of "halting state" makes SCP03 vulnerable to denial-of-service attacks. However, it is effective against chosen-ciphertext attacks, since all the ensuing ciphertexts will not be decrypted, and therefore a new session with new keys has to be re-negotiated. This makes such attacks more detectable and less likely to succeed. Third, we do not include the padding method of SCP03 (recommended in ISO/IEC 10116:2006 [26]), since Paterson et al. prove that padding has no negative impact on security when it is used in encryption schemes following the EtM construction (like SCP03) [37]. Fourth, the MAC construction is quite peculiar: only half of the MAC (i.e. 8 bytes) is included with the ciphertext, and the remainder is reconstructed during MAC verification. The other half is somehow used as a 'state' between the sender and the receiver. To the best of our knowledge, GlobalPlatform has never provided the rationale behind this unusual construction that complicates the analysis of SCP03. However, we can plausibly assume that this choice was made to reduce the communication overhead incurred by SCP03. Indeed, the transmission rate with the card is low and it greatly increases with respect to the number of the communicated packets (as a matter of fact, the packet length is limited to 255 bytes) [38]. Therefore, despite being so small in other contexts, the overhead of transferring some extra 8 bytes might not be negligible in the case of smart cards.

4.2   Security Models

At first glance, SCP03 seems to fall into the EtM paradigm. Naturally, this raises no question regarding its security, since its generic security is proved in [8]. Here, we prove that SCP03 offers more than the standard security notions.

The construction of SCP03 described in Sect. 4.1 brings out three points that should be underlined. First, both the encryption and decryption algorithms involve the use of two variables that maintain their values and get updated after each call. These two variables must be '*in-sync*' between the sender and the receiver, otherwise $\mathcal{D}_k(.)$ returns $\perp$. Second, the encryption of messages could be seen as a stateful nonce-based CBC encryption scheme. Third, the `chained` variable serves much the same purpose that a tweak does. Taking into consideration these three notes, we can turn the EtM construction of SCP03 into another composite. We start by introducing the two underlying blocks that will compose our new equivalent construction of SCP03.

ANALYZING SCP03 VIA A NEW CONSTRUCTION.

Definition 6 *(Stateful Nonce-based Symmetric Scheme (Sf-n$\mathcal{SE}$)).* Let $n\mathcal{SE} = (n\mathcal{K}, n\mathcal{E}, n\mathcal{D})$ be a nonce-based encryption scheme. Let `counter` be a static variable initialized by 0 and which maintains its value between calls. For a message M, we define the associated stateful scheme Sf-n$\mathcal{SE} = (n\mathcal{K}\text{-Sf}, n\mathcal{E}\text{-Sf}, n\mathcal{D}\text{-Sf})$ as follows: $n\mathcal{E}_k\text{-Sf}(M) = n\mathcal{E}_k(\texttt{counter++}, M)$ and $n\mathcal{D}_k\text{-Sf}(C) = n\mathcal{D}_k(\texttt{counter++}, C)$.

Definition 7 *(Tweak Chaining MAC ($\mathcal{TC}\text{-}\widetilde{\mathcal{MA}}$)).* Let $\widetilde{F}_k : \texttt{TWEAK} \times \texttt{MSG} \longrightarrow \texttt{TWEAK}$ be a tweakable MAC function for all key $\mathsf{K} \in \texttt{Key}$. Then, we define the associated chaining scheme $\mathcal{TC}\text{-}\widetilde{\mathcal{MA}} = (\widetilde{\mathcal{K}}, \widetilde{\mathcal{T}}, \widetilde{\mathcal{V}})$:

Tagging $\widetilde{\mathcal{T}}_k(M)$

1: $\tau_1 \| \tau_2 \longleftarrow \widetilde{F}_k(\texttt{chained}, M)$
2: $\texttt{chained} \longleftarrow \tau_1 \| \tau_2$
3: **return** τ_1

Verification $\widetilde{\mathcal{V}}_k(M, \tau)$

1: $\tau_1 \| \tau_2 \longleftarrow \widetilde{F}_k(\texttt{chained}, M)$
2: $b \longleftarrow [\tau_1 = \tau]$
3: $\texttt{chained} \longleftarrow \tau_1 \| \tau_2$
4: **return** b

Construction 2 *(Stateful Nonce-based Encrypt-then-Tweak (Sf-nEtTw)).* Let Sf-n$\mathcal{SE} = (n\mathcal{K}\text{-Sf}, n\mathcal{E}\text{-Sf}, n\mathcal{D}\text{-Sf})$ be a stateful nonce-based symmetric scheme. Let $(\mathsf{Enc}, \mathsf{Dec})$ be a prefix-free encoding scheme. Let $\mathcal{TC}\text{-}\widetilde{\mathcal{MA}} = (\widetilde{\mathcal{K}}, \widetilde{\mathcal{T}}, \widetilde{\mathcal{V}})$ be a tweak chaining MAC. Given a message M, we define the composite stateful nonce-based Encrypt-then-Tweak scheme $\mathbf{Sf\text{-}nEtTw} = (\widetilde{\mathcal{K}}\text{-Sf}, \widetilde{\mathcal{E}}\text{-Sf}, \widetilde{\mathcal{D}}\text{-Sf})$:

Encryption $\widetilde{\mathcal{E}}_k\text{-Sf}(M)$

1: $C \longleftarrow n\mathcal{E}_{k1}\text{-Sf}(M)$
2: $C' \longleftarrow \mathsf{Enc}(C)$
3: $\tau \longleftarrow \widetilde{\mathcal{T}}_{k2}(C')$
4: **return** $C' \| \tau$

Decryption $\widetilde{\mathcal{D}}_k\text{-Sf}(C)$

1: Parse C as $C' \| \tau$
2: $C'' \longleftarrow \mathsf{Dec}(C')$ or **return** $\perp$
3: **if** $\widetilde{\mathcal{V}}_{k2}(C', \tau) \neq 1$ **then**
4:     **return** $\perp$ and halt
5: **end if**
6: **return** $n\mathcal{D}_{k1}\text{-Sf}(C'')$

Now, let's see if the Construction 1 actually implies the definition of Construction 2. We start by examining whether the SCP03 operation $\mathcal{T}_k(\texttt{chained} \| C)$ is indeed a secure tweakable MAC function. We notice that the MAC computation in SCP03 is based on CMAC as specified in [16]. As mentioned by the author, CMAC is equivalent to OMAC that is defined in [28]. We rely on the result of [10] in which authors prove that $\mathsf{OMAC}(T \| M)$ is an $\widetilde{\mathsf{IND}}$-CPA tweakable extension of OMAC. Hence, $\mathcal{T}_k(\texttt{chained} \| C) = \widetilde{F}_k(\texttt{chained}, C)$, where $\widetilde{F}_k$ is a tweakable function. Then, we investigate the security of the SCP03 encryption scheme that could be seen as a stateful variant of CBC1 recommended by the NIST in [15] and broken in [39]. CBC1 is a nonce-based scheme that encrypts the nonce to use it as IV. Unlike the insecure CBC1, the stateful CBC1 is IND-CPA secure. The intuition behind this is that attacks against CBC1 generally involve a craftily chosen nonce, and therefore they are not applicable against the stateful CBC1 where nonces are taken as a counter. A full proof is given in Theorem 17 in [4].

SECURITY NOTIONS. A new concrete security treatment is required in order to capture the power of Sf-nEtTw. Here, we outline the security concepts that we will use to study SCP03 and that are formalized by Bellare et al. in [6,9].

Definition 8 *(Indistinguishability Under Stateful CCA (IND-SFCCA))*. Conventionally, we consider an experiment in which the adversary **A** has access to a *left-or-right* encryption oracle $\mathcal{E}_k(\mathcal{LR}(.,.,b))$ and a decryption oracle $\mathcal{D}_k(.)$. $\mathcal{D}_k$ returns the result of the decryption when **A** makes an *out-of-sync* query. A query is out-of-sync if it satisfies one of these conditions: (1) there are more queries to the decryption oracle than to the encryption one; (2) the ciphertext inside the decryption query is different from the last one computed by $\mathcal{E}_k(\mathcal{LR}(.,.,b))$. As long as **A** does not make out-of-sync queries, $\mathcal{D}_k$ updates its internal state, but returns nothing.

Definition 9 *(Integrity of Stateful Ciphertext (INT-SFCTXT))*. Here, we consider an experiment in which the adversary **A** has access to an encryption oracle $\mathcal{E}_k(.)$ as well as a decryption oracle $\mathcal{D}_k(.)$. The scheme is INT-SFCTXT secure if for all polynomial-time adversaries, it is hard to find an out-of-sync C, such that $\mathcal{D}_k(C) \neq \perp$ and C was not produced by $\mathcal{E}_k$. Similarly to IND-SFCCA, $\mathcal{D}_k$ updates its internal state and returns nothing if no out-of-sync query is sent.

Definition 10 *(Algorithm-Substitution Attacks (ASA))*. Motivated by the potential threat of subverting implementations of cryptographic algorithms, Bellare et al. in [9] have recently defined ASA security by identifying two adversarial goals – *conducting surveillance* and *avoid detection*. In the ASA experiment, given user's key K and a subversion key $\widetilde{K}$, the adversary $\mathcal{B}$ (also called big brother) wants to subvert the encryption algorithm $\mathcal{E}_k$ by another one $\widetilde{\mathcal{E}}_{\widetilde{k}}$. $\mathcal{B}$ requires that the subversion be both successful and undetectable. Here, we focus solely on the surveillance goal (SURV). SURV means that from observing ciphertexts, $\mathcal{B}$ can compromise confidentiality. Stated formally, SURV is defined as a classical distinguishing experiment when given oracle access to one of these two algorithms (i.e. $\mathcal{E}_k$ and $\widetilde{\mathcal{E}}_{\widetilde{k}}$). Indeed, $\mathcal{B}$, who has access to K but not to $\widetilde{K}$, is required to distinguish $\mathcal{E}_k$ from $\widetilde{\mathcal{E}}_{\widetilde{k}}$. We say that an encryption scheme is ASA secure if no adversary $\mathcal{B}$ can succeed the SURV distinguishing game.

Definition 11 *(Unique Ciphertexts (UQ-CTXT))*. Following their work to defeat ASA, Bellare et al. define the notion of 'Unique Ciphertexts' as follows. Let $\mathcal{SE} = (\mathcal{K}, \mathcal{E}, \mathcal{D})$ be a symmetric encryption scheme. Given a secret key K, a message M, and a state τ, let $\mathcal{C}_{\mathcal{SE}}(K, M, \tau)$ be the set of all ciphertexts such that $\mathcal{D}_k^\tau(C)$ (also denoted $\mathcal{D}_k(C_\tau)$) returns M. We say that $\mathcal{SE}$ has unique ciphertexts (i.e. UQ-CTXT secure) if the set $\mathcal{C}_{\mathcal{SE}}(K, M, \tau)$ has size at most one for all K, M, τ. Stated differently, for any given key, message and state, there exists at most one ciphertext that decrypts to the message in question.

Result 4.1 [*Unique Ciphertexts* $\implies$ *ASA Resilience* [9]]. In other words, let $\mathcal{SE} = (\mathcal{K}, \mathcal{E}, \mathcal{D})$ be a unique ciphertext symmetric encryption scheme, and let $\mathcal{B}$ be a SURV adversary. Then, $\mathcal{B}$ cannot succeed the SURV experiment; which means that $\mathcal{SE}$ is resilient to ASA.

5 SCP03 Security Results

We now state our security results regarding SCP03. We provably show that SCP03 protects the integrity and the confidentiality of messages against chosen-plaintext and chosen-ciphertext attacks. In addition, it resists replay, out-of-delivery and algorithm-substitution attacks (ASAs). Indeed, authors of [6,9] prove that cryptographic schemes satisfying IND-SFCCA, INT-SFCTXT and Unique Ciphertexts meet all the security notions mentioned above.

5.1 Sf-nEtTw Security Analysis

In order to prove that SCP03 is IND-SFCCA and INT-SFCTXT secure, we start by analyzing the composite encryption scheme Sf-nEtTw. The following proposition concerns the security properties of $\mathcal{TC}\text{-}\widetilde{\mathcal{MA}}$.

Proposition 1 *(Upper Bound of* $\mathbf{Adv}_{\mathcal{TC}\text{-}\widetilde{\mathcal{MA}}}^{suf\text{-}cma}(A)$*).* Let $\widetilde{F}_k : \{0,1\}^n \times \mathsf{MSG} \longrightarrow \{0,1\}^n$ be a tweakable function and let $\mathcal{TC}\text{-}\widetilde{\mathcal{MA}}$ be its associated chaining scheme. Let $\mathbf{A}$ be an SUF-CMA adversary against $\mathcal{TC}\text{-}\widetilde{\mathcal{MA}}$ who queries q messages. Then, we can construct a distinguisher $\mathbf{D}$ against $\widetilde{F}$ such that

$$\mathbf{Adv}_{\mathcal{TC}\text{-}\widetilde{\mathcal{MA}}}^{suf\text{-}cma}(A) \leq \mathbf{Adv}_{\widetilde{F}}^{\widetilde{ind}\text{-}cpa}(D) + \frac{q^2}{2^n} + \frac{1}{2^{n/2}} + \Pr[\mathsf{Col_q}]$$

Proof. The proof is given in Appendix A.

We now show how schemes following the construction of Sf-nEtTw protect their stateful integrity of ciphertext (i.e. INT-SFCTXT).

Theorem 1. *(Upper Bound of* $\mathbf{Adv}_{\text{Sf-nEtTw}}^{int\text{-}sfctxt}(A)$*).* Let Sf-nEtTw be a scheme of stateful nonce-based encryption Sf-n$\mathcal{SE}$ = $(\mathcal{K}\text{-Sf}, n\mathcal{E}\text{-Sf}, n\mathcal{D}\text{-Sf})$ associated to a tweak chaining MAC $\mathcal{TC}\text{-}\widetilde{\mathcal{MA}} = (\widetilde{\mathcal{K}}, \widetilde{\mathcal{T}}, \widetilde{\mathcal{V}})$ and a prefix-free encoding scheme (Enc, Dec) as described in Construction 2. Let $\widetilde{F}_k : \{0,1\}^n \times \mathsf{MSG} \longrightarrow \{0,1\}^n$ be the tweakable MAC function related to $\mathcal{TC}\text{-}\widetilde{\mathcal{MA}}$. Consider any INT-SFCTXT adversary $\mathbf{A}$ against Sf-nEtTw who asks to encrypt q messages, we can construct an SUF-CMA adversary $\mathbf{B}$ against $\mathcal{TC}\text{-}\widetilde{\mathcal{MA}}$ such that:

$$\mathbf{Adv}_{\text{Sf-nEtTw}}^{int\text{-}sfctxt}(A) \leq \mathbf{Adv}_{\mathcal{TC}\text{-}\widetilde{\mathcal{MA}}}^{suf\text{-}cma}(B) + \Pr[q\text{-Col}]$$

where, given a message M and a list S containing q outputs of $\widetilde{F}_k$, $\Pr[q\text{-Col}]$ is the probability that $\widetilde{F}_k(M) \in \mathsf{S}$.

Proof. The proof is given in Appendix B.

5.2 SCP03 Security Analysis

Now, we give our concrete security results for the particular case of SCP03. This requires to compute the different collision probabilities when $\widetilde{\mathsf{OMAC}}_k(T, M) = \mathsf{OMAC}_k(T \| M)$ is used as the tweakable function $\widetilde{F}_k(.,.)$ for all tweak T and message M. Two results about OMAC collisions are stated in Appendix C.1.

SCP03 Is both INT-SFCTXT and IND-SFCCA. We show here that SCP03 protects its stateful confidentiality and integrity against powerful adversaries who can perform chosen-ciphertext attacks (CCA).

Theorem 2 *(SCP03 is INT-SFCTXT Secure).* Let E_k be a block cipher of size n and let $OMAC[E_k](.)$ be its associated OMAC scheme. Let $\widetilde{OMAC}_k(.,.)$ be a tweakable function defined as $\widetilde{OMAC}_k(T, M) = OMAC[E_k](T \,\|\, M)$ for all tweak T and message M. Given a prefix-free encoding scheme (Enc, Dec), a stateful nonce-based encryption $Sf\text{-}n\mathcal{SE} = (\mathcal{K}\text{-}Sf, n\mathcal{E}\text{-}Sf, n\mathcal{D}\text{-}Sf)$ and a tweak chaining MAC $\mathcal{TC}\text{-}\widetilde{\mathcal{MA}} = (\widetilde{\mathcal{K}}, \widetilde{\mathcal{T}}, \widetilde{\mathcal{V}})$ whose tweakable MAC function is $\widetilde{OMAC}_k$, we define SCP03 to be the composite scheme formed by following the Construction 2. Consider any INT-SFCTXT adversary **A** attacking SCP03 and asking to encrypt q messages, we can construct a distinguisher **D** against $\widetilde{OMAC}$ and a negligible function negl such that:

$$\mathbf{Adv}^{int\text{-}sfctxt}_{scp03}(A) \le \mathbf{Adv}^{\widetilde{ind\text{-}cpa}}_{\widetilde{OMAC}}(D) + \mathsf{negl}$$

Proof. Since SCP03 is a composite scheme formed by following the Sf-nEtTw construction, it satisfies the relations given in Sect. 5.1. By using Proposition 1 and Theorem 1, we can obtain that

$$\mathbf{Adv}^{int\text{-}sfctxt}_{scp03}(A) \le \mathbf{Adv}^{\widetilde{ind\text{-}cpa}}_{\widetilde{OMAC}}(D) + \frac{q^2}{2^n} + \frac{1}{2^{n/2}} + \Pr[\mathsf{Col}_q] + \Pr[\mathsf{q\text{-}Col}]$$

where $\Pr[\mathsf{Col}_q]$ is the collision probability of the tweakable function $\widetilde{OMAC}_k$ after q messages and $\Pr[\mathsf{q\text{-}Col}]$, given a message M and a list S containing q outputs of $\widetilde{OMAC}_k$, is the probability that $\widetilde{OMAC}_k(M) \in \mathsf{S}$.

Now, we use the following lemma to conclude our proof.

Lemma 5.1. Given $n \in \mathbb{N}$, there is a negligible function negl such that:

$$\frac{q^2}{2^n} + \frac{1}{2^{n/2}} + \Pr[\mathsf{Col}_q] + \Pr[\mathsf{q\text{-}Col}] \le \mathsf{negl}$$

where $\Pr[\mathsf{Col}_q]$ and $\Pr[\mathsf{q\text{-}Col}]$ are as defined above.

Proof. The proof is given in Appendix C.2.

Theorem 3 *(SCP03 is IND-SFCCA Secure).* Let E_k be a block cipher of size n and let $OMAC[E_k](.)$ be its associated OMAC scheme. Let $\widetilde{OMAC}_k(.,.)$ be a tweakable function defined as $\widetilde{OMAC}_k(T, M) = OMAC[E_k](T \,\|\, M)$ for all tweak T and message M. Given a prefix-free encoding scheme (Enc, Dec), a stateful nonce-based encryption $Sf\text{-}n\mathcal{SE} = (\mathcal{K}\text{-}Sf, n\mathcal{E}\text{-}Sf, n\mathcal{D}\text{-}Sf)$ and a tweak chaining MAC $\mathcal{TC}\text{-}\widetilde{\mathcal{MA}} = (\widetilde{\mathcal{K}}, \widetilde{\mathcal{T}}, \widetilde{\mathcal{V}})$ whose tweakable MAC function is $\widetilde{OMAC}_k$, we define SCP03 to be the composite scheme formed by following the Construction 2. Consider any IND-SFCCA adversary **A** against SCP03, we can construct an IND-CPA adversary **B** against Sf-$n\mathcal{SE}$ and an INT-SFCTXT adversary **F** against $\mathcal{TC}\text{-}\widetilde{\mathcal{MA}}$ such that:

$$\mathbf{Adv}^{ind\text{-}sfcca}_{\text{scp03}}(A) \leq \mathbf{Adv}^{ind\text{-}cpa}_{\text{Sf-}n\mathcal{SE}}(B) + \mathbf{Adv}^{int\text{-}sfctxt}_{\mathcal{TC}\text{-}\widetilde{\mathcal{MA}}}(F)$$

Proof. This theorem follows directly from the implication proved by Bellare et al. [6]: IND-CPA $\wedge$ INT-SFCTXT $\implies$ IND-SFCCA. This means that if an encryption scheme is both IND-CPA and INT-SFCTXT secure, then it is also IND-SFCCA secure. Regarding the INT-SFCTXT security of SCP03, we have just proved it in Theorem 2. Now, let us consider the IND-CPA security property of SCP03. Notice that SCP03 is a variant of Encrypt-then-MAC. Therefore, it inherits the IND-CPA property of its encryption scheme [8]. Stated otherwise, if the underlying encryption scheme Sf-$n\mathcal{SE}$ is IND-CPA secure, then SCP03 is also IND-CPA secure, which concludes our proof.

SCP03 is ASA Resilient. Finally, we prove that SCP03 defends against ASA, hence also against mass surveillance.

Theorem 4 *(SCP03 has Unique Ciphertexts).* Let $\widetilde{\text{OMAC}}_k$ be a tweakable function as defined previously. Given a stateful nonce-based encryption Sf-$n\mathcal{SE} = (\mathcal{K}\text{-Sf}, n\mathcal{E}\text{-Sf}, n\mathcal{D}\text{-Sf})$ and a tweak chaining MAC $\mathcal{TC}\text{-}\widetilde{\mathcal{MA}} = (\widetilde{\mathcal{K}}, \widetilde{\mathcal{T}}, \widetilde{\mathcal{V}})$ whose tweakable MAC function is $\widetilde{\text{OMAC}}_k$, we define SCP03 to be the scheme formed by following the Construction 2. Then, SCP03 is UQ-CTXT secure.

Proof. Let C_i denote the ciphertext produced by encrypting the message M on the state i. Considering the SCP03 design (see Construction 2), we have

$$C_i = \sigma_i \,\|\, \tau_i = n\mathcal{E}_{\text{k1}}\text{-Sf}(M) \,\|\, \widetilde{\mathcal{T}}_{\text{k2}}(\sigma_i)$$

where K1 and K2 are two independent keys. Now, we study the probability of finding a triplet $(\mathsf{K} = \mathsf{K1}\|\mathsf{K2}, M, i)$ so that $|\mathcal{C}_{\text{scp03}}(\mathsf{K}, M, i)| > 1$. By definition, this is equal to the probability of finding a ciphertext C_i' such that: (1) $C_i' \neq C_i$ and (2) $\mathcal{D}_{\mathsf{k}}\text{-SCP03}(C_i') = M'$, where $M' = M$. We distinguish two cases.

Case 1 $(\sigma_i' \neq \sigma_i)$. Here, we prove that this case and the event of finding C' are contradictory, thereby proving that $\Pr[\text{case 1}] = 0$. Indeed, recall that $n\mathcal{SE} = (\mathcal{K}, n\mathcal{E}, n\mathcal{D})$ encrypts messages using a deterministic algorithm. Therefore, as a matter of fact, for a fixed nonce N, $n\mathcal{E}_{\text{k1}}(N, M_1) \neq n\mathcal{E}_{\text{k1}}(N, M_2)$ implies that $M_1 \neq M_2$. Also, we notice that the definition of the set $\mathcal{C}_{\text{scp03}}$ involves that the associated encryption scheme Sf-$n\mathcal{SE} = (n\mathcal{K}\text{-Sf}, n\mathcal{E}\text{-Sf}, n\mathcal{D}\text{-Sf})$ has called $n\mathcal{SE}$ algorithms with the same nonce for each state i. Then, the event $\sigma_i' \neq \sigma_i$ entails $\sigma_i' = n\mathcal{E}_{\text{k1}}\text{-Sf}(M') \neq n\mathcal{E}_{\text{k1}}\text{-Sf}(M) = \sigma_i$, which implies $M' \neq M$. This concludes our proof, since the definition of $\mathcal{C}_{\text{scp03}}$ includes that $M' = M$.

Case 2 $(\sigma_i' = \sigma_i)$. Since $C_i' \neq C_i$, this case implies that $\tau_i' \neq \tau_i$. Following the same argument of case 1, we prove that this case and the event of finding C' are contradictory, thereby proving that $\Pr[\text{case 2}] = 0$. Indeed, recall that the tweakable MAC function $\widetilde{\mathrm{OMAC}}_{k2}$ generates its tag using a deterministic algorithm. Therefore, as a matter of fact, for a fixed tweak T, $\widetilde{\mathrm{OMAC}}_{k2}(T, \sigma_1) \neq \widetilde{\mathrm{OMAC}}_{k2}(T, \sigma_2)$ implies that $\sigma_1 \neq \sigma_2$. Similarly, the definition of $\mathcal{C}_{\mathrm{scp03}}$ involves that the associated chaining MAC scheme $\mathcal{TC}\text{-}\mathcal{MA} = (\widetilde{\mathcal{K}}, \widetilde{\mathcal{T}}, \widetilde{\mathcal{V}})$ has called $\widetilde{\mathrm{OMAC}}_{k2}$ with same tweak for each state i. Then, the event $\tau_i' \neq \tau_i$ entails $\tau_i' = \widetilde{\mathcal{T}}_{k2}(\sigma_i') \neq \widetilde{\mathcal{T}}_{k2}(\sigma_i) = \tau_i$, which implies $\sigma_i' \neq \sigma_i$. This concludes our proof, since the definition of case 2 includes that $\sigma_i' = \sigma_i$.

6   Discussion

An important aspect of any cryptanalysis is what it implies in practice. Our study reveals interesting facts about the family of SCP. In particular, two protocols are concerned: SCP02 and SCP03. Here, we discuss our findings.

While discussing our results, we are aware that provable security is not a silver bullet for security, as authors of [13] notice that several cryptographic schemes have been proved secure and then broken some years later. We argue that this fact does not nullify the interest of such a powerful security tool. Indeed, despite being imperfect, provable security has greatly helped ruling out a large class of attacks in security protocols. In addition, although its findings should not be taken as absolute, they constitute a general direction that aims at designing better cryptographic schemes.

THE VULNERABLE, YET POPULAR, SCP02. In Sect. 3, we see that, unlike extensive evaluation, provable security for certified products provides a strong guarantee of security without promoting complexity. Indeed, we demonstrated a theoretical attack against the protocol SCP02. In addition, we showed how some technical details about SCP02 make the attacker likely to succeed in the context of smart cards. Surprisingly, the presented attack arises from a fundamental design flaw in SCP02, which is the use of CBC mode with no IV.

It is not clear that why the SCP02 designers made such a choice. However, we might suspect that the reasons behind this are twofold. First, when the first variant of SCP02 was published in 2000, cryptographic results about using CBC mode with stateful nonce-based IVs were not well-established yet. Second, designers chose not to use random IVs in order to reduce the overhead of SCP02. Indeed, a random IV must be appended to the sent ciphertext, thereby increasing the communication overhead with the smart card. In addition, the implementations of CBC mode in smart cards have been optimized to pre-generate some objects during the initialization of the cipher object. The problem is that choosing the IV is uniquely done together with the choice of the encryption key during the initialization phase. Therefore, constantly modifying the IV implies constant initialization of the cipher object that can no longer performs its optimization in advance. Thus, we argue that the real challenge of SCP02 was to achieve good performance in a limited environment, like a smart card, and still ensuring security. In the complex GP card specifications, the tiny detail of 'just keep using the same IV' might have passed unnoticed, especially that to the best of our knowledge, no formal analysis of SCP02 has been performed before.

Furthermore, identifying such a well-known vulnerability tells us something: smart cards industry has difficulty in catching up with the advances on cryptography. Finalized in 2003, SCP02 keeps existing, while other protocols have continuously been updated. Ironically, the stringent requirements of smart cards about security are both its strongest and weakest point: they do not make this technology only secure and trustworthy, but also so slow to improve. We illustrate by three examples. First, EMV [17], which is the actual standard of payment, still mandates the use of Triple DES with two independent keys instead of using AES (see Sect. 5.7 in the EMV Card Personalization Specification [18]). Second, numerous card manufacturers continue relying on SCP02, although SCP03 was published in 2009. For instance, NXP instructs the support of SCP02 and makes it optional for SCP03 for all its JCOP products that are certified EAL5+ [35]. Third, the SCP family (i.e. SCP02 and SCP03) still requires encrypting data using the CBC mode. As a matter of fact, Mitchell in [34] (and more recently Rogaway in [40]) promotes abandoning CBC for future designs.

THE POWERFUL SCP03. Introduced as an amendment in 2009, we have analyzed SCP03 in Sects. 4 and 5 and have found that it provably satisfies strong security notions. Of a particular interest, we proved that SCP03 resists against the algorithm substitution attacks (ASAs) that could lead to secret mass surveillance [9]. This result is significant, as it increases the trust in the closed industry of smart cards. The advantages offered by SCP03 are clear: it is provably secure and it is being gradually implemented by card manufacturers. It is true that the added security comes with additional cost: maintaining a 2-byte counter (i.e. state) per session as well as one more block cipher invocation per message (recall that the counter is encrypted in order to be used as an IV). However, modern smart cards include a dedicated cryptographic co-processor, hence the incurred overhead is very small.

Standards are particularly susceptible to significant modification. Therefore, we feel that the recently created GP 'Crypto Sub-Task Force' [24] may have a hard time justifying to wholly reconsider the design of the SCP family. Therefore, we advocate the deprecation of SCP02 as soon as possible and the switch over to SCP03 that should be included in the main specification instead of being an amendment. Our goal is to provide enough information to the GP community so that the Crypto Sub-Task Force can take an informed decision when deciding how to fix the current problems with SCP02. At this point, a quote from [6] seems appropriate: *"in the modern era of strong cryptography, it would seem counterintuitive to voluntarily use a protocol with low security when it is possible to fix the security (...) at low cost"*.

A   Proof of Proposition 1

We start by providing three definitions that we will use throughout our proof.

MAC Function. Here, we just recall how a MAC scheme is related to its MAC function. Let $\mathcal{MA}[F] = (\mathcal{K}, \mathcal{T}, \mathcal{V})$ be a MAC scheme based on the MAC function F. F takes as input a key K and a message M to output a tag τ. The tagging algorithm $\mathcal{T}_k$ and the verification algorithm $\mathcal{V}_k$ are defined as follows:

Tagging $\mathcal{T}_k(M)$

1: $\tau \longleftarrow F_k(M)$
2: **return** τ

Verification $\mathcal{V}_k(M, \tau)$

1: **if** $F_k(M) = \tau$ **then**
2:     **return** 1
3: **else**
4:     **return** 0
5: **end if**

Truncated MAC. Let $T : \{0,1\}^n \longrightarrow \{0,1\}^{n_T}$ be a transformation function. Let $\mathcal{MA}[F] = (\mathcal{K}, \mathcal{T}, \mathcal{V})$ be a MAC scheme based on the MAC function F. We define the transformed MAC scheme $To\mathcal{MA} = (\mathcal{K}, To\mathcal{T}, To\mathcal{V})$ that uses ToF as its MAC function, where o denotes the composition operator. A *truncated MAC* is a transformed MAC in which $T(.)$ is the $\mathtt{MSB}_l(.)$ function that takes a message as input and returns the l most significant (i.e. left-most) bits.

Tweak Chaining MAC2 (TC-$\widetilde{\mathcal{MA}}$2). Let $\widetilde{F}_k : \{0,1\}^n \times \mathtt{MSG} \longrightarrow \{0,1\}^n$ be a tweakable function and let $TC\text{-}\widetilde{\mathcal{MA}}$ be its associated chaining scheme. We define $TC\text{-}\widetilde{\mathcal{MA}}2$ as $TC\text{-}\widetilde{\mathcal{MA}}$ except that $TC\text{-}\widetilde{\mathcal{MA}}2$ operates on the entire tag returned by $\widetilde{F}(.,.)$ and not only on its half as in $TC\text{-}\widetilde{\mathcal{MA}}$. Stated differently, $TC\text{-}\widetilde{\mathcal{MA}}2$ is a MAC scheme in which the MAC function $F2$ is defined as follows:

MAC Function $F2_k(M)$

$\tau \longleftarrow \widetilde{F}_k(\mathtt{chained}, M)$
$\mathtt{chained} \longleftarrow \tau$
return τ

where $\mathtt{chained}$ is a static variable (i.e. maintains its value between calls) that was initialized with $\mathbf{0}^n$.

Having thus presented the above definitions, we are now on a position to make our proof. Let $\widetilde{F}_k : \{0,1\}^n \times \mathtt{MSG} \longrightarrow \{0,1\}^n$ be a tweakable function and let $TC\text{-}\widetilde{\mathcal{MA}}2[F2]$ be its associated tweak chaining MAC2 scheme. We notice that the $TC\text{-}\widetilde{\mathcal{MA}} = (\widetilde{\mathcal{K}}, \widetilde{\mathcal{T}}, \widetilde{\mathcal{V}})$ scheme presented in Definition 7 can be seen as the truncated MAC of $TC\text{-}\widetilde{\mathcal{MA}}2[F2]$, where $T(.) = \mathtt{MSB}_{n/2}(.)$. Thus, we denote the MAC function of $TC\text{-}\widetilde{\mathcal{MA}}$ as $ToF2$.

Consider any polynomial-time SUF-CMA adversary **A** against $TC\text{-}\widetilde{\mathcal{MA}}$. Recall that **A** can make two types of queries: tagging queries and verification queries. We suppose that **A** makes q tagging queries. We associate two adversaries to **A**: an sPRF adversary **B** against the MAC function $F2$ (or equivalently against $TC\text{-}\widetilde{\mathcal{MA}}2[F2]$), and an $\overline{\mathtt{IND}}$-CPA distinguisher **D** against the tweakable function $\widetilde{F}_k$. Now, we state the following lemmas in which we define how the adversaries **A**, **B** and **D** interact between each other and from which the Proposition 1 follows directly.

Lemma A.1. $\mathbf{Adv}_{TC\text{-}\widetilde{\mathcal{MA}}}^{suf\text{-}cma}(A) = \mathbf{Adv}_{F2}^{sprf}(B) + 1/2^{n/2}$

Lemma A.2. $\mathbf{Adv}_{F2}^{sprf}(B) \leq \mathbf{Adv}_{\widetilde{F}}^{\widetilde{ind}\text{-}cpa}(D) + \Pr[\mathsf{Col}] + \Pr[\mathsf{Col_q}]$

Lemma A.3. $\Pr[\mathsf{Col}] \leq q^2/2^n$

Proof of Lemma A.1: Recall that **B** has access to the oracle $\mathcal{O}$ and her goal is to distinguish whether $\mathcal{O}$ is the MAC function $F2$ or the stateful random oracle $\mathcal{R_S}$. Recall also that the MAC function of $TC\text{-}\widetilde{\mathcal{MA}}$ is $ToF2$. The algorithm **B** is described below:

Algorithm. $\mathbf{B}^{\mathcal{O}}$

1: **repeat**
2:     **if A** queries (M) **then**
3:         $\tau \longleftarrow To\mathcal{O}(M)$
4:             **output** τ to **A**
5:     **end if**
6:     **if A** queries (M, τ) **then**
7:         $b \longleftarrow [\tau = To\mathcal{O}(M)]$
8:             **output** b to **A**
9:     **end if**
10: **until A** ends
11: **if A** forges **then**
12:     **return** 1
13: **else**
14:     **return** 0
15: **end if**

We can see that **B** perfectly simulates the answers to **A**. In addition, **B** returns 1 (i.e. guesses that the oracle $\mathcal{O}$ is the MAC function $F2$) when **A** succeeds in forging a tag. Therefore, the following relation holds:

$$\Pr[\mathbf{A}^{To\mathcal{O}} \text{ forges}] = \Pr[\mathbf{B}^{\mathcal{O}} \Rightarrow 1] \tag{1}$$

where we use the equivalent notation in which we note that the adversary **A** has access to the MAC function as oracle instead of the tagging/verification oracles.

By definition of strong unforgeability of the MAC scheme $TC\text{-}\widetilde{\mathcal{MA}}$ (see Definition 2), the advantage of **A** is defined by the probability of her success when she has access to the oracle $ToF2$. Therefore, we have:

$$\mathbf{Adv}_{TC\text{-}\widetilde{\mathcal{MA}}}^{suf\text{-}cma}(\mathbf{A}) = \Pr[\mathbf{A}^{T \circ F2} \text{ forges}]$$

$$= \Pr[\mathbf{A}^{T \circ F2} \text{ forges}] + \left(\Pr[\mathbf{A}^{T \circ \mathcal{R}_S} \text{ forges}] - \Pr[\mathbf{A}^{T \circ \mathcal{R}_S} \text{ forges}]\right)$$

$$= \left(\Pr[\mathbf{A}^{T \circ F2} \text{ forges}] - \Pr[\mathbf{A}^{T \circ \mathcal{R}_S} \text{ forges}]\right) + \Pr[\mathbf{A}^{T \circ \mathcal{R}_S} \text{ forges}]$$

$$= \left(\Pr[\mathbf{B}^{F2} \Rightarrow 1] - \Pr[\mathbf{B}^{\mathcal{R}_S} \Rightarrow 1]\right) + \Pr[\mathbf{A}^{T \circ \mathcal{R}_S} \text{ forges}] \text{ (from 1)}$$

$$= \mathbf{Adv}_{F2}^{sprf}(B) + \Pr[\mathbf{A}^{T \circ \mathcal{R}_S} \text{ forges}]$$

Now, we examine $\Pr[\mathbf{A}^{T \circ \mathcal{R}_S} \text{ forges}]$, which is equal to the probability that $\mathbf{A}$ forges against a MAC scheme that has $T \circ \mathcal{R}_S$ as its MAC function. Recall that $\mathcal{R}_S$ is a random oracle. Let us suppose that (M, τ) is the forging query that $\mathbf{A}$ uses to break the scheme. Therefore, the following relations holds: $\tau = T(\mathcal{R}_S(M))$. Thus, we conclude our proof by showing that we have:

$$\Pr[\mathbf{A}^{T \circ \mathcal{R}_S} \text{ forges}] = \Pr[x \xleftarrow{R} \{0,1\}^n,\ T(x) = \tau]$$

$$= \frac{1}{2^{n/2}} \qquad \left(\text{since } T(.) = \mathrm{MSB}_{n/2}(.)\right)$$

Proof of Lemma A.2: Here, we consider any sPRF adversary $\mathbf{B}$ against $F2$ and we associate it to a particular IND-CPA distinguisher $\mathbf{D}$ against the tweakable function $\widetilde{F}_k : \{0,1\}^n \times \mathrm{MSG} \longrightarrow \{0,1\}^n$. Recall that $\mathbf{D}$ has access to the oracle $\mathcal{O}(.,.)$ and her goal is to distinguish whether $\mathcal{O}$ is $\widetilde{F}_k(.,.)$ or $\widetilde{\mathcal{R}}(.,.)$, where $\widetilde{\mathcal{R}}(.,.)$ is a function that, on input (T, M), returns n-bit random strings. Recall also that $\mathbf{D}$ is a tweak-respecting adversary (i.e. does not repeat tweak). We define the algorithm of $\mathbf{D}$ as follows:

Algorithm. $\mathbf{D}^{\mathcal{O}}$

1: $t \longleftarrow \mathbf{0}^n$
2: $\mathsf{S} \longleftarrow \{t\}$
3: **repeat**
4:     **if B queries** (M) **then**
5:         $t \longleftarrow \mathcal{O}(t, M)$
6:         $\mathsf{S} \longleftarrow \mathsf{S} \cup \{t\}$
7:         **output** t **to B**
8:         **if** S contains duplicate values **then**
9:             **return** 1
10:         **end if**
11:     **end if**
12: **until B outputs** b'
13: **return** b'

---

where S is a multiset in which values can repeat. We argue that when S does not contain the same value twice, $\mathbf{D}$ is perfectly simulating $\mathbf{B}$'s execution environment. This is true because $\widetilde{F}(.,.)$ is no distinguishable from the random oracle $\widetilde{\mathcal{R}}(.,.)$ only against tweak-respecting adversaries. We illustrate the importance of such a condition by an example. In our example, we take $\widetilde{\mathrm{OMAC}}(T, M)$ $(= \mathrm{OMAC}(T\|M))$ as the tweakable function $\widetilde{F}(.,.)$. Now, we show that $\mathbf{B}$ can easily see under the simulation environment that she is not interacting with a random oracle. $\mathbf{B}$ knows that the initial tweak (i.e. state) is $\mathbf{0}^n$ and queries $M_1 = \mathbf{0}^n$ to receive τ_1 from her oracle. Then, let T be a tweak that repeats twice. For the first occurrence of T, $\mathbf{B}$ queries $M_2 = \mathbf{0}^n$ to receive τ_2 and for its second occurrence she queries $M_2 = \mathbf{0}^n\| \tau_2 \|\mathbf{0}^n$ to receive τ_3. It is easy to see that $\tau_1 = \tau_3$ when $\mathcal{O} = \widetilde{F}_k(.,.)$ $(\neq\widetilde{\mathcal{R}}(.,.))$. Indeed, we have

$$\tau_1 = E_k\left(E_k(\mathbf{0^n})\right)$$
$$\tau_2 = E_k\left(E_k(T)\right)$$
$$\tau_3 = E_k\left(E_k\left(\cancel{E_k(E_k(T))} \oplus \cancel{\tau_2}\right) \oplus \mathbf{0^n}\right)$$

Thus, from $\mathbf{D}$'s algorithm, we can see that

$$\Pr[\mathbf{D}^{\widetilde{F}} \Rightarrow 1] = \Pr[\mathbf{B}^{F2} \Rightarrow 1] + \Pr[\mathsf{S}|\widetilde{F}]$$
$$\Pr[\mathbf{D}^{\widetilde{\mathcal{R}}} \Rightarrow 1] = \Pr[\mathbf{B}^{\mathcal{R}_S} \Rightarrow 1] + \Pr[\mathsf{S}|\widetilde{\mathcal{R}}]$$

where $\Pr[\mathsf{S}]$ is the probability that the multiset S contains duplicate values.

By using the two above relations, we get

$$\mathbf{Adv}_{F2}^{sprf}(B) = \mathbf{Adv}_{\widetilde{F}}^{\widetilde{ind}\text{-}cpa}(D) + \overbrace{\Pr[\mathsf{S}|\widetilde{\mathcal{R}}]}^{\Pr[\mathsf{Col}]} - \overbrace{\Pr[\mathsf{S}|\widetilde{F}]}^{\Pr[\mathsf{Col_q}]}$$
$$\leq \mathbf{Adv}_{\widetilde{F}}^{\widetilde{ind}\text{-}cpa}(D) + \Pr[\mathsf{Col}] + \Pr[\mathsf{Col_q}]$$

where $\Pr[\mathsf{Col_q}]$ is the collision probability of the tweakable function $\widetilde{F}$ after q messages. Thus, our proof ends.

Proof of Lemma A.3: Informally speaking, the lemma means that the set $\{x : x_0 = \mathbf{0}^n, \; x_i = \mathcal{R}(x_0, .)\}$ has asymptotically negligible probability to include duplicate values. Recall that q is the number of $\mathbf{B}$'s queries. We start our proof by making induction on q. For all $q \geq 1$, we prove that

$$\Pr[\mathsf{Col}] = \frac{q(q+1)}{2^{n+1}} \tag{2}$$

Then, we conclude our proof by noticing that $q(q+1)/2^{n+1} \leq q^2/2^n$.

Base case. When $q = 1$, the right side of (2) is $1/2^n$. Now, let's look at the left side. After only one call, there are two elements in S: $\{\mathbf{0}^n, y\}$, where $y \xleftarrow{R} \mathcal{R}(\mathbf{0}^n, .)$. Thus, $\Pr[\mathsf{Col}] = \Pr[x \xleftarrow{R} \{0,1\}^n, x = \mathbf{0}^n]$, which is equal to $1/2^n$.

Induction step. Suppose that the Eq. 2 is true for $q = m - 1$. Here, x_i denotes the ith element of the multiset S. After $q = m$ calls, we have

$$\Pr[\mathsf{Col}] = \overbrace{\Pr[\mathsf{Col} \text{ after } m - 1 \text{ calls}]}^{\text{induction hypothesis}} + \Pr[x_m \in S]$$

$$= \frac{m(m - 1)}{2^{n+1}} + \frac{m}{2^n}$$

$$= \frac{m(m + 1)}{2^{n+1}}$$

Hence, the Eq. 2 holds for $q = m$, and the induction step is complete.

B   Proof of Theorem 1

Recall that **A** can make two types of queries: encryption queries and decryption queries. We denote **A**'s i-th encryption query as M_i and the returned ciphertext as $C_i = \sigma_i \| \tau_i$. We denote **A**'s i-th decryption query as $C'_i = \sigma'_i \| \tau'_i$ and the returned message as m_i. We associate to **A** an SUF-CMA forger **F** against $\widetilde{TC\text{-}MA}$. This association is similar to the one given in the Case 1 of Theorem 4: **F** generates a key $\mathsf{K1} \in \mathsf{Key}$ that she uses for the encryption/decryption algorithms of Sf-n$\mathcal{SE}$. We recall that the forger **F** has access to two oracles: a tagging oracle $\widetilde{T}_{\mathsf{k2}}$ and a verification oracle $\widetilde{V}_{\mathsf{k2}}$, where the key $\mathsf{K2}$ is independent from $\mathsf{K1}$. Below, we describe our trivial association.

1. When **A** makes an encryption query M, **F** outputs $\sigma \longleftarrow \mathsf{Enc}\,(n\mathcal{E}_{\mathsf{k1}}\text{-Sf}(M))$. Then, she queries σ to her tagging oracle $\widetilde{T}_{\mathsf{k2}}$ and receives τ in response. Finally, she outputs $C = \sigma \| \tau$ to **A**.
2. When **A** makes a decryption query $C = \sigma \| \tau$, the forger **F** queries τ to her verification oracle $\widetilde{V}_{\mathsf{k2}}$ and receives a binary value b. If b is false, then **F** halts after outputting $\perp$. Otherwise, **F** computes $n\mathcal{D}_{\mathsf{k1}}\text{-Sf}\,(\mathsf{Dec}(\sigma))$ and outputs the result to **A**.
3. When **A** wins in her INT-SFCTXT experiment, namely providing a new valid out-of-sync decryption query $C = \sigma \| \tau$, then **F** stops and attempts to evaluate the pair (σ, τ) in order to see whether she succeeds in her forgery. The different cases are presented below in the proof of Lemma B.1.

Now, suppose **A** has made q encryption queries and d decryption ones. Let j be the index of **A**'s first out-of-sync decryption query. We only consider the first out-of-sync query because if it fails, the decryption algorithm will return $\perp$ and halt for all ensuing queries (see our discussion about the approach of halting state in Sect. 4.1). We define two events in case the **A**'s j-th decryption query succeeds: (1) Col: $\exists i \leq q$ such that $\tau'_j = \tau_i$ and $i \neq j$; (2) Bad: $q \geq j$, $\tau'_j = \tau_j$ and $m_j = M_j$. We state the following lemmas from which Theorem 1 follows directly (using Proposition 1).

Lemma B.1. $\mathbf{Adv}_{\text{Sf-nEtTw}}^{\text{int-sfctxt}}(A) \leq \mathbf{Adv}_{TC\text{-}\widetilde{MA}}^{\text{suf-cma}}(F) + \Pr[\mathsf{q\text{-}Col}] + \Pr[\mathsf{Bad}]$

Lemma B.2. $\Pr[\mathsf{Bad}] = 0$

Proof of Lemma B.1: As said previously, $\mathbf{A}$ made q encryption queries before her first out-of-sync query ($\mathcal{Q}$) which is the j-th decryption query ($C'_j = \sigma'_j \,\|\, \tau'_j$). We define the following events.

E : $\mathcal{Q}$ correctly verifies

E_1 : E occurs and $\tau'_j \notin \{\tau_1, ..., \tau_q\}$

E_2 : E occurs and $\tau'_j \in \{\tau_1, ..., \tau_q\}$

$E_{2,1}$: E_2 occurs and either $q < j$ or $\tau'_j \neq \tau_j$

$E_{2,2}$: E_2 occurs and $q \geq j$ and $\tau'_j = \tau_j$

$E_{2,2,1}$: $E_{2,2}$ occurs and $m_j = M_j$

$E_{2,2,2}$: $E_{2,2}$ occurs and $m_j \neq M_j$

If $\mathcal{Q}$ fails, then $\mathbf{A}$ cannot win any more, since the decryption algorithm will return $\perp$ for any subsequent query. Therefore, $\mathbf{Adv}^{int\text{-}sfctxt}_{\text{Sf-nEtTw}}(A) = \Pr[E]$. Considering the different events, we have $\Pr[E] = \Pr[E_1 \vee E_{2,2,2}] + \Pr[E_{2,1}] + \Pr[E_{2,2,1}]$.

Now, we study the probabilities of these events. We can see that $E_{2,1}$ corresponds to the event Col, since it implies that τ'_j has already been produced before and that was not during the j-th encryption query (this includes the fact that $\mathbf{A}$ might not have made j encryption queries yet). Concerning $E_{2,2,1}$, it is easy to see that it satisfies the definition of the Bad event. Consequently, we have

$$\mathbf{Adv}^{int\text{-}sfctxt}_{\text{Sf-nEtTw}}(A) = \Pr[E_1 \vee E_{2,2,2}] + \Pr[\mathsf{Col}] + \Pr[\mathsf{Bad}]$$

We conclude the proof by examining $\Pr[E_1 \vee E_{2,2,2}]$ and $\Pr[\mathsf{Col}]$.

$\mathbf{Pr[E_1 \vee E_{2,2,2}]}$. We notice that when the event $E_1 \vee E_{2,2,2}$ occurs, (i.e. the j-th decryption oracle $C'_j = \sigma'_j \,\|\, \tau'_j$ does not return $\perp$), then the forger $\mathbf{F}$ succeeds in finding an SUF-CMA forgery against $\mathcal{TC}\text{-}\widetilde{\mathcal{MA}}$, since the two events ensure that the pair (m_j, τ'_j) was never produced before by the oracle $\widetilde{\mathcal{T}}_{\mathsf{k2}}$.

Indeed, the event E_1 implies that τ'_j has never been queried to $\widetilde{\mathcal{T}}_{\mathsf{k2}}$, while the event $E_{2,2,2}$ implies that the tag τ'_j has never been obtained from querying the oracle $\widetilde{\mathcal{T}}_{\mathsf{k2}}$ with σ'_j as input. This is because for any state i, the following implication is asymptotically true (i.e. $n\mathcal{E}_{\mathsf{k}}\text{-Sf}(.)$ is injective):

$$M_i \neq M'_i \implies n\mathcal{E}_{\mathsf{k1}}\text{-Sf}(M_i) \neq n\mathcal{E}_{\mathsf{k1}}\text{-Sf}(M'_i)$$

Therefore, $\tau'_j \,(= \tau_j)$ was computed for $\sigma_j = n\mathcal{E}_{\mathsf{k1}}\text{-Sf}(M_j)$ which is different from σ'_j (i.e. $\sigma_j \neq \sigma'_j$), since $\sigma'_j = n\mathcal{E}_{\mathsf{k1}}\text{-Sf}(m_j)$ and $M_j \neq m_j$.

Thus, we have

$$\Pr[E_1 \vee E_{2,2,2}] = \Pr[\mathbf{F}\,forges] = \mathbf{Adv}^{suf\text{-}cma}_{\mathcal{TC}\text{-}\widetilde{\mathcal{MA}}}(F)$$

$\mathbf{Pr[Col]}$. As previously pointed out, $\Pr[\mathsf{Col}] = \Pr[\exists i \neq j \text{ such that } \tau'_j = \tau_i]$. This means that for two different states the following equality holds:

$$\widetilde{\mathcal{T}}_{\mathsf{k2}}(\mathsf{Enc}(n\mathcal{E}_{\mathsf{k1}}\text{-Sf}(m_j))) = \widetilde{\mathcal{T}}_{\mathsf{k2}}(\mathsf{Enc}(n\mathcal{E}_{\mathsf{k1}}\text{-Sf}(M_i)))$$

The above relation supposes that the adversary should find a collision against $\mathcal{TC}\text{-}\widetilde{\mathcal{MA}}$ after q invocations to the $\widetilde{\mathcal{T}}_{k2}(.)$ oracle, which corresponds to find a state $i(\neq j)$ such that the related MAC tag is equal to the one computed for the state j. By looking at the construction of $\mathcal{TC}\text{-}\widetilde{\mathcal{MA}}$ in Definition 7, we find that $\Pr[\mathsf{Col}]$ is equivalent to the probability of encountering a collision against the underlying tweakable function $\widetilde{F}_{k2}(.,.)$. Stated differently, we have

$$\Pr[\mathsf{Col}] = \Pr[\mathsf{q\text{-}Col}]$$

where, we recall that, given a message M and a list S containing q outputs of $\widetilde{F}_{k2}$, $\Pr[\mathsf{q\text{-}Col}]$ is the probability that $\widetilde{F}_{k2}(M) \in \mathsf{S}$.

Proof of Lemma B.2: The event $E_{2,2,1}$ includes all the following events: (1) $q \geq j$; (2) the decryption query $C'_j = \sigma'_j || \tau'_j$ is out-of-sync, hence $C_j \neq C'_j$; (3) $\sigma'_j \neq \sigma_j$, since $\tau'_j = \tau_j$; and (4) $m_j = M_j$. We notice that the events 3 and 4 are contradictory, and therefore $\Pr[\mathsf{Bad}] = 0$. Indeed, recall that $n\mathcal{SE} = (\mathcal{K}, n\mathcal{E}, n\mathcal{D})$ encrypts messages using a deterministic algorithm. Therefore, for a fixed nonce N, $n\mathcal{E}_{k1}(N, M_1) \neq n\mathcal{E}_{k1}(N, M_2)$ implies that $M_1 \neq M_2$. Also, we notice that the encryption and the decryption states were in-sync prior to the j-th decryption query. This means that the associated $\mathsf{Sf}\text{-}n\mathcal{SE} = (\mathcal{K}\text{-}\mathsf{Sf}, n\mathcal{E}\text{-}\mathsf{Sf}, n\mathcal{D}\text{-}\mathsf{Sf})$ has called $n\mathcal{SE}$ algorithms with the same nonce for each state. Thus, the event 3 entails $\sigma'_j = n\mathcal{E}_{k1}\text{-}\mathsf{Sf}(m_j) \neq n\mathcal{E}_{k1}\text{-}\mathsf{Sf}(M_j) = \sigma_j$, which implies $m_j \neq M_j$. This concludes our proof, since the event 4 is $m_j = M_j$.

C   Collision Probabilities

C.1   OMAC Collision Probabilities

Here, we state two Results proved in [28] about collisions in OMAC.

Result C.1 [$\Pr[\mathsf{Col}]_2$]. Let E_k be a block cipher of size l and let $\mathsf{OMAC}[E_k]$ be its associated OMAC scheme. For the sake of simplicity, we only consider messages M whose length is a multiple of l (i.e. $|M|/l$ is an integer). Given a message M, we denote by μ the number of its blocks, namely $\mu = |M|/l$. Consider two messages M and M', then the following relation characterizes the probability of the OMAC collision:

$$\Pr[\mathsf{Col}_2] = \Pr[\mathsf{Col}(M, M')] \leq \frac{(\mu + \mu')^2}{2^l}$$

Result C.2 [$\Pr[\mathsf{Col}]_q$]. Let E_k be a block cipher of size l and let $\mathsf{OMAC}[E_k]$ be its associated OMAC scheme. For the sake of simplicity, we only consider messages M whose length is a multiple of l (i.e. $|M|/l$ is an integer). Given a message M, we denote by μ the number of its blocks, namely $\mu = |M|/l$. Given a list $\mathcal{Q}$ of q messages, the following relation characterizes the probability of the OMAC collision on $\mathcal{Q}$:

$$\Pr[\mathsf{Col}_q] = \Pr[\mathsf{Col}(\mathcal{Q})] \leq \frac{\left(\sum_{i=1}^{q} \mu_i\right)^2}{2^l}$$

C.2   Proof of Lemma 5.1

We need to compute both $\Pr[\mathsf{Col_q}]$ and $\Pr[\mathsf{q\text{-}Col}]$. The case of $\Pr[\mathsf{Col_q}]$ is easy and it can be immediately obtained from Result C.2. Concerning the case $\Pr[\mathsf{q\text{-}Col}]$, it can be calculated from Result C.1. Indeed, given a message M and a list S, $\Pr[\mathsf{Col_q}]$ can be expressed as the sum of the collision probabilities $\Pr[\mathsf{Col}_2^i]$ between M and a message M_i for all $M_i \in S$. Here, $M_{\max}$ denotes any message of maximum length and $\mu_{\max}$ denotes its number of blocks. Therefore, we have

$$\Pr[\mathsf{q\text{-}Col}] \leq \sum_{i=1}^{q} \Pr[\mathsf{Col}(m_{\max}, m_i)] \leq \sum_{i=1}^{q} \frac{(\mu_{\max} + \mu_i)^2}{2^n}$$

From all the relations above, we have

$$\epsilon = \frac{q^2}{2^n} + \frac{1}{2^{n/2}} + \Pr[\mathsf{Col_q}] + \Pr[\mathsf{q\text{-}Col}]$$

$$\leq \frac{1}{2^{n/2}} + \frac{q^2}{2^n} + \frac{\left(\sum_{i=1}^{q} \mu_i\right)^2}{2^n} + \frac{\sum_{i=1}^{q}(\mu_{\max} + \mu_i)^2}{2^n}$$

$$\leq \frac{1}{2^{n/2}} + \frac{q^2}{2^n} + \frac{\left(\sum_{i=1}^{q} \mu_i\right)^2}{2^n} + \frac{3q\mu_{\max}^2 + \sum_{i=1}^{q} \mu_i^2}{2^n}$$

$$\leq \frac{1}{2^{n/2}} + \frac{q\left(q + (2\mu_{\max})^2\right) + \left(\sum_{i=1}^{q} \mu_i\right)^2 + \sum_{i=1}^{q} \mu_i^2}{2^n}$$

which is asymptotically negligible.

References

1. Aumüller, C., Bier, P., Fischer, W., Hofreiter, P., Seifert, J.-P.: Fault attacks on RSA with CRT: concrete results and practical countermeasures. In: Kaliski, B.S., Koç, K., Paar, C. (eds.) CHES 2002. LNCS, vol. 2523, pp. 260–275. Springer, Heidelberg (2003). doi:10.1007/3-540-36400-5_20
2. Bard, G.V.: A challenging but feasible blockwise-adaptive chosen-plaintext attack on SSL. In: Proceedings of the International Conference on Security and Cryptography. SECRYPT 2006, pp. 7–10. INSTICC Press (2006)
3. Béguelin, S.Z.: Formalisation and verification of the GlobalPlatform card specification using the B method. In: Barthe, G., Grégoire, B., Huisman, M., Lanet, J.-L. (eds.) CASSIS 2005. LNCS, vol. 3956, pp. 155–173. Springer, Heidelberg (2006). doi:10.1007/11741060_9
4. Bellare, M., Desai, A., Jokipii, E., Rogaway, P.: A concrete security treatment of symmetric encryption. In: Proceedings of the 38th Annual Symposium on Foundations of Computer Science. FOCS 1997, pp. 394–403. IEEE (1997)
5. Bellare, M., Kilian, J., Rogaway, P.: The security of the cipher block chaining message authentication code. J. Comput. Syst. Sci. 61(3), 362–399 (2000)
6. Bellare, M., Kohno, T., Namprempre, C.: Authenticated encryption in SSH: provably fixing the SSH binary packet protocol. In: Proceedings of the 9th ACM Conference on Computer and Communications Security. CCS 2002, pp. 1–11. ACM (2002)

7. Bellare, M., Namprempre, C.: Authenticated encryption: relations among notions and analysis of the generic composition paradigm. In: Okamoto, T. (ed.) ASIACRYPT 2000. LNCS, vol. 1976, pp. 531–545. Springer, Heidelberg (2000). doi:10.1007/3-540-44448-3_41

8. Bellare, M., Namprempre, C.: Authenticated encryption: relations among notions and analysis of the generic composition paradigm. J. Cryptol. **21**(4), 469–491 (2008)

9. Bellare, M., Paterson, K.G., Rogaway, P.: Security of symmetric encryption against mass surveillance. In: Garay, J.A., Gennaro, R. (eds.) CRYPTO 2014. LNCS, vol. 8616, pp. 1–19. Springer, Heidelberg (2014). doi:10.1007/978-3-662-44371-2_1

10. Bellare, M., Rogaway, P., Wagner, D.: The EAX mode of operation. In: Roy, B., Meier, W. (eds.) FSE 2004. LNCS, vol. 3017, pp. 389–407. Springer, Heidelberg (2004). doi:10.1007/978-3-540-25937-4_25

11. Chen, Z.: Java Card Technology for Smart Cards: Architecture and Programmer's Guide. Addison-Wesley Longman Publishing Co. Inc., Boston (2000)

12. Dai, W.: An attack against SSH2 protocol, email to the SECSH Working Group. ftp://ftp.ietf.org/ietf-mail-archive/secsh/2002-02.mail

13. Degabriele, J.P., Paterson, K., Watson, G.: Provable security in the real world. IEEE Secur. Priv. **9**(3), 33–41 (2011)

14. Duong, T., Rizzo, J.: Here come the XOR Ninjas (2011). Unpublished

15. Dworkin, M.: Recommendation for block cipher modes of operation: methods and techniques. National Institute of Standards and Technology (NIST), NIST Special Publication 800–38A., December 2001

16. Dworkin, M.: Recommendation for block cipher modes of operation: the CMAC mode for authentication. National Institute of Standards and Technology (NIST), NIST Special Publication 800–38B, November 2001

17. EMVCo: EMVCo Specification. https://www.emvco.com/specifications.aspx

18. EMVCo: EMV card personalization specification - version 1.1. https://www.emvco.com/specifications.aspx?id=20

19. Feix, B., Thiebeauld, H.: Defeating ISO9797-1 MAC Algo 3 by combining side-channel and brute force techniques. Cryptology ePrint Archive, Report 2014/702 (2014)

20. Fouque, P.-A., Joux, A., Martinet, G., Valette, F.: Authenticated on-line encryption. In: Matsui, M., Zuccherato, R.J. (eds.) SAC 2003. LNCS, vol. 3006, pp. 145–159. Springer, Heidelberg (2004). doi:10.1007/978-3-540-24654-1_11

21. GlobalPlatform: The standard for managing applications on secure chip technology. https://www.globalplatform.org

22. GlobalPlatform: Secure channel protocol '3' - card specification v2.2 - amendment d v1.1.1. http://www.globalplatform.org/specificationscard.asp

23. GlobalPlatform: GlobalPlatform card specification v2.3. http://www.globalplatform.org/specificationscard.asp

24. GlobalPlatform: About GlobalPlatform - security task force activities and achievements - 2016 activities and priorities (2016). https://www.globalplatform.org/aboutustaskforcesSecurity.asp

25. Hemme, L.: A differential fault attack against early rounds of (triple-)DES. In: Joye, M., Quisquater, J.-J. (eds.) CHES 2004. LNCS, vol. 3156, pp. 254–267. Springer, Heidelberg (2004). doi:10.1007/978-3-540-28632-5_19

26. ISO/IEC JTC 1/SC 27: Information technology - security techniques - modes of operation for an n-bit block cipher. Technical report, International Organization for Standardization, February 2006

27. ISO/IEC JTC 1/SC 6: Information technology - ASN.1 encoding rules: specification of Basic Encoding Rules (BER), Canonical Encoding Rules (CER) and Distinguished Encoding Rules (DER). Technical report, International Organization for Standardization, December 2002

28. Iwata, T., Kurosawa, K.: OMAC: one-key CBC MAC. In: Johansson, T. (ed.) FSE 2003. LNCS, vol. 2887, pp. 129–153. Springer, Heidelberg (2003). doi:10.1007/978-3-540-39887-5_11

29. Joux, A., Martinet, G., Valette, F.: Blockwise-adaptive attackers revisiting the (in)security of some provably secure encryption modes: CBC, GEM, IACBC. In: Yung, M. (ed.) CRYPTO 2002. LNCS, vol. 2442, pp. 17–30. Springer, Heidelberg (2002). doi:10.1007/3-540-45708-9_2

30. Katz, J., Lindell, Y.: Introduction to Modern Cryptography, 2nd edn. Chapman & Hall Book, Boca Raton (2015)

31. Katz, J., Yung, M.: Unforgeable encryption and chosen ciphertext secure modes of operation. In: Goos, G., Hartmanis, J., Leeuwen, J., Schneier, B. (eds.) FSE 2000. LNCS, vol. 1978, pp. 284–299. Springer, Heidelberg (2001). doi:10.1007/3-540-44706-7_20

32. Liskov, M., Rivest, R.L., Wagner, D.: Tweakable block ciphers. In: Yung, M. (ed.) CRYPTO 2002. LNCS, vol. 2442, pp. 31–46. Springer, Heidelberg (2002). doi:10.1007/3-540-45708-9_3

33. Markantonakis, C.: The case for a secure multi-application smart card operating system. In: Okamoto, E., Davida, G., Mambo, M. (eds.) ISW 1997. LNCS, vol. 1396, pp. 188–197. Springer, Heidelberg (1998). doi:10.1007/BFb0030420

34. Mitchell, C.J.: Error Oracle attacks on CBC Mode: is there a future for CBC mode encryption? In: Zhou, J., Lopez, J., Deng, R.H., Bao, F. (eds.) ISC 2005. LNCS, vol. 3650, pp. 244–258. Springer, Heidelberg (2005). doi:10.1007/11556992_18

35. NXP Semiconductors Germany Gmbh: Nxp j3e081_m64, j3e081_m66, j2e081_m64, j3e041_m66, j3e016_m66, j3e016_m64, j3e041_m64 secure smart card controller. Common Criteria for Information Technology Security Evaluation, certification Report: NSCIB-CC-13-37761-CR2, August 2014

36. Oracle: Java card protection profile - closed configuration. Common Criteria for Information Technology Security Evaluation, certification Report: ANSSI-CC-PP-2010/07, December 2012

37. Paterson, K.G., Watson, G.J.: Authenticated-encryption with padding: a formal security treatment. In: Naccache, D. (ed.) Cryptography and Security: From Theory to Applications. LNCS, vol. 6805, pp. 83–107. Springer, Heidelberg (2012). doi:10.1007/978-3-642-28368-0_9

38. Rankl, W., Effing, W.: Smart Card Handbook, 4th edn. Wiley, Chichester (2010)

39. Rogaway, P.: Nonce-based symmetric encryption. In: Roy, B., Meier, W. (eds.) FSE 2004. LNCS, vol. 3017, pp. 348–358. Springer, Heidelberg (2004). doi:10.1007/978-3-540-25937-4_22

40. Rogaway, P.: Evaluation of some blockcipher modes of operation. Technical report, Cryptography Research and Evaluation Committees (CRYPTREC) for the Government of Japan (2011)

NFC Payment Spy: A Privacy Attack on Contactless Payments

Maryam Mehrnezhad$^{(\boxtimes)}$, Mohammed Aamir Ali, Feng Hao,
and Aad van Moorsel

School of Computing Science, Newcastle University, Newcastle upon Tyne, UK
{m.mehrnezhad,m.a.ali2,feng.hao}@newcastle.ac.uk,
aad.vanmoorsel@ncl.ac.uk

Abstract. In a contactless transaction, when more than one card is presented to the payment terminal's field, the terminal does not know which card to choose to proceed with the transaction. This situation is called *card collision*. EMV (which is the primary standard for smart card payments) specifies that the reader should not proceed when it detects a card collision and that instead it should notify the payer. In comparison, the ISO/IEC 14443 standard specifies that the reader should choose one card based on comparing the UIDs of the cards detected in the field. However, our observations show that the implementation of contactless readers in practice does not follow EMV's card collision algorithm, nor does it match the card collision procedure specified in ISO.

Due to this inconsistency between the implementation and the standards, we show an attack that may compromise the user's privacy by collecting the user's payment details. We design and implement a malicious app simulating an NFC card which the user needs to install on her phone. When she aims to pay contactlessly while placing her card close to her phone, this app engages with the terminal before the card does. The experiments show that even when the terminal detects a card collision (the app essentially acts like a card), it proceeds with the EMV protocol. We show the app can retrieve from the terminal the transaction data, which include information about the payment such as the amount and date. The experimental results show that our app can effectively spy on contactless payment transactions, winning the race condition caused by card collisions around 66 % when testing with different cards. By suggesting these attacks we raise awareness of privacy and security issues in the specifications, standardisation and implementations of contactless cards and readers.

Keywords: NFC payment · NFC phone · Contactless payment · Privacy attack · EMV · Card collision

1 Introduction

Near Field Communication (NFC) payment is already very popular. The statistics show that as of February 2016, £1,318.3 m was spent in the UK in the month

© Springer International Publishing AG 2016
L. Chen et al. (Eds.): SSR 2016, LNCS 10074, pp. 92–111, 2016.
DOI: 10.1007/978-3-319-49100-4_4

using a contactless card. This is an increase of 19.1 % on the previous month and an increase of 306.8 % over the year[1]. Apart from contactless cards, other types of technologies for contactless payment are suggested to the users. Examples include mobiles, tablets, watches, bPay bands, and bPay Stickers (bpay.co.uk). In fact, there are more than 350 different types of NFC-enabled devices on the market now[2].

NFC technology is based on Radio Frequency Identification (RFID) technology. Security and privacy issues of RFID communication, and in particular NFC, have been studied intensively in the literature. Contactless cards are always on and a malicious reader in the proximity of such a device is able to trigger a response from the card, without the user's awareness. A number of security and privacy violations have been reported in the literature exploiting such unauthorised readings [17]. More security attacks include different types of relay attacks such as Man-in-The-Middle and Mafia attacks [18, 21, 30, 35].

On the other hand, there are many works showing how malicious apps compromise user's security/privacy by listening to different mobile sensor data via a background process. Examples include accelerometer and gyroscope [13, 15, 22–24, 28, 36], camera and microphone [31], light [32], and Geolocation [14]. Most of these attacks work by accessing sensor data through a background process activated by a mobile app, which requires installation and user permission. Users normally install many different apps without even reviewing the app permissions. Thus, even if there is a permission request from the users, they normally ignore it [14]. This behaviour leaves the doors open for the attackers to obtain access to sensors. In this paper, we also rely on such a behaviour; we develop an app using the phone's NFC functionality which the user needs to install.

Contributions. In this paper, for the first time, we show that the NFC functionality on the victim's mobile phone can be used to compromise her contactless payment activities. This happens due to a particular situation in contactless payment which is called *card collision* or *card clash*. Card collision is the situation when more than a contactless card (or NFC-enabled device) is available in the reader's field at the same time. Card collision has been explained and addressed by EMV [10] and ISO 14443 [4][3], as the two main contactless payment references for developers to implement the contactless systems. We study these standards and propose attacks based on our findings. In particular, the contributions are:

- We explain the race condition caused by card collision and study the approaches suggested by EMV and ISO on this. We perform experiments to discover the behaviour of contactless terminals when a card collision occurs. The results show that the implementation on contactless terminals match neither EMV nor ISO.

---

[1] theukcardsassociation.org.uk/contactless_contactless_statistics/.

[2] nfcworld.com/nfc-phones-list/.

[3] For the rest of this paper, unless noted otherwise, by ISO standard we mean ISO/IEC 14443, and by EMV standard, we mean EMV Contactless Specifications.

Fig. 1. Different card holder cases: flip wallet, back cover/stand, Opanable back cover, sticker cover, transparent cover.

- We show that due to this inconsistency, it is possible to track the user's contactless payment activities, for instance through a malicious app. The malicious app would have a chance to intercept payment messages and data if the phone is closely located to the contactless payment card (Fig. 1). We propose an attack vector following EMV contactless specifications by requesting the Processing Options Data Object List (PDOL) from the terminal when the malicious app wins the race and connects with the terminal first.
- We develop an Android app and perform experiments to support our claim. The results show that our attack can effectively break users' privacy and discover the pattern of their contactless payment activities.

This research highlights vulnerabilities in the standards and implementations of contactless cards and readers when a collision occurs in a contactless transaction.

2 Card Collision

In this section, first we present a real-world example of card collision which is called *Card Clash* by Transport for London (TfL) [34]. Next, we explain the approaches suggested by EMV and ISO to handle card collision.

2.1 Oystercard and Bank Card Clash

Card clash is a well-known phenomenon for a metro traveller. For example in the London metro, a traveller can either use an Oystercard or a contactless bank card[4] to pay for her journey. While swiping a wallet containing Oystercard and bank cards, the reader gets confused and does not know which card to take payment from. This causes discomfort for the users as follows [33,34]:

- The commuter might inadvertently pay for her travel with a card she did not intend to use.
- The reader might refuse to work under this situation and the gate won't open.

---

[4] In the rest of this paper unless noted otherwise, by bank card we mean contactless payment card.

- The passenger could be charged two maximum fares for the same journey. This happens when the reader charges one card when she touches in and another card when she touches out.
- Even if the reader selects the contactless bank card over Oystercards for both start and end of journey, the passenger might end up being charged two times since she has already paid for a weekly travelcard on the Oystercard.

The only way to find out if any card clash happened is to sign into the user online accounts and check records of payment. If the user has been charged a maximum fare on two separate cards for the same journey, she can apply for a refund provided by TfL [34]. In fact, when TfL introduced card payments as an additional payment method to paper tickets and Oystercards in September of 2014, a huge number of double payments occurred in just a few weeks. Many of those were automatically refunded within 3–5 working days. TfL has automatically handed back about £300,000 to about 50,000 customers, with refunds averaging £5.93. Although the Card Clash issue was publicised very well, surprisingly, TFL estimates that around 1,500 instances of it are occurring every day [25]. Accordingly, different solutions have been suggested to passengers to avoid card clash [16, 20, 25, 33] which include:

- To choose the card that you want to pay with and take it out from the wallet.
- To register the Oystercard online, so that you can regularly check the online account for auditing.
- To check your bank statements regularly to find out if you have been charged on the wrong card.
- In the case of a double payment, to claim the refund by applying to the TfL website.
- To use protective cases for your contactless cards that you do not aim to pay with. Actually, Metro Bank gives free card protectors out to all of its customers.
- To switch to contactless payments. TfL has fixed the problem of weekly travelcards by applying them automatically both on Oystercards and contactless bank cards. Hence, the cost would not differ that much if a passenger switches to a contactless bank card. There are reports which show that it is even cheaper if costumers move to contactless bank cards [29].
- To use a Barclaycard contactless bPay wristband (bpay.co.uk) and pay with a wave of your hand. Any UK Visa or MasterCard debit or credit card can be linked to the bPay wristband.

Among the above solutions, those which suggest to replace the Oystercard by contactless cards or bands seem more user friendly. However, not all passengers are happy with paying for a bPay and wearing it all the time. On the other hand, people normally carry multiple bank cards. Hence even in the absence of the Oystercard, other contactless cards are still subject to card clash. Therefore, we believe that a fundamental approach is needed to overcome this real-world problem.

2.2 EMV Contactless Specifications

EMV is the primary protocol standard for smart card payments. The EMV standards are managed by EMVCo (emvco.com), a consortium of multinational companies such as Visa, MasterCard, and American Express. EMV has specifically defined specifications for contactless payment in books A, B, C and D [6–10]. ISO/IEC 14443 on the other hand, is an international standard that defines proximity cards used for identification, and the transmission protocols used for communication between the card and host. Generally, there are two ISO/IEC 14443 communication signal interfaces: Type A and Type B. They use different Radio Frequency Field (RF) modulation methods for the Proximity Coupling Device (PCD, Reader) to Proximity Integrated Circuit Card (PICC, Card) and the PICC to PCD communication. In this paper, the focus is Type A, which is the mainstream technology [26]. Android supports it, and all of our tested bank cards are Type A.

EMV Contactless Book D [10] defines *Collision* as follows: "Transmission by two or more PICCs in the same PCD energizing field and during the same time period, such that the PCD [reader] is unable to distinguish from which PICC [card] the data originated". Based on this definition, in different parts of EMV documents, the aim is to describe how EMV anti-collision mechanism handles the situation when there is more than a card in the field. Here we generally review the whole process for a contactless transaction from the reader's point of view.

According to EMV contactless Book D [10], the terminal is constantly running a main loop as illustrated in Fig. 2. In the polling phase, the reader ensures that there only exists one type of technology (Type A or B) in the field by using Wake UP command e.g., WUPA for type A. Then it checks if there is only one card from the same technology in the field. If so, it activates the card. Remember that contactless bank cards are passive, and the reader creates an energising RF (the operating field) that enables the card to power up. Next, the terminal application performs the transaction.

On the other hand, if there exists more than a card in the field, a collision is detected. Accordingly, the terminal will not initiate a transaction in this situation. The collision detection procedure is applicable either on different technologies (Type A, B, and others), or on multiple cards from the same technology. If more than one technology is in the field, the reader must report a collision, reset the operating field, and return to the polling phase. For Type A collision detection, the terminal performs a specific procedure as follows (illustrated in Fig. 5; see Appendix B). Type A cards respond to Wake UP command synchronously using Manchester coding. This allows the terminal to detect the collision in the bit level. After the terminal waits for an interval t_p, it sends WUPA command. In all parts of this algorithm, if the terminal detects a transmission error in response to the WUPA and Anti-Collision (AC) commands, it reports a collision, resets, and returns to the polling procedure. Otherwise, the reader sends an AC command which is used to obtain the complete UID of a Type A card, and to detect whether more than one Type A card is in the field. Depending on the UID

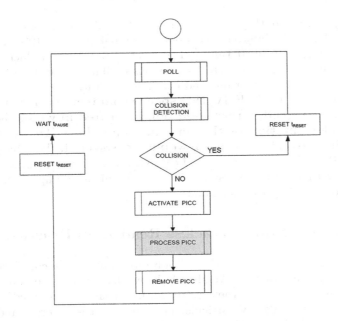

Fig. 2. Terminal Main Loop, taken from EMV contactless Book D.

size of the card, the response to the AC is different. In summary, regardless of the card collision procedure, according to EMV, **once a collision is detected, the terminal should not proceed any more; instead it should reset the field and go back to the polling procedure**.

2.3 ISO/IEC 14443

Payment cards (contact and contactless) are based on ISO/IEC 7816 [12] and ISO/IEC 14443 [2–5]. Mobile NFC payment technologies, such as Android Host-based Card Emulation (HCE) [1], are also based on ISO/IEC 14443, which is an international standard in four parts, defining the technology-specific requirements for proximity cards [2–5]. The third part of this standard [4], namely, Part 3: Initialization and anticollision, presents the same definition for collision as EMV. However, handling collision is different as we explain (presented in Fig. 6, see Appendix B).

In this standard, anticollisions are detected based on conflict in the bits of the UIDs (started from uid0 as the most significant byte). The least significant bit (LSB) of each byte is transmitted first. As an example, consider two cards as follows. Card 1: UID size = 4 bytes (single), value of uid0 = '10', and Card 2: UID size = 7 bytes (double). After both cards respond to the reader's command, the terminal performs the first cascade level for the anticollision loop. As response the first card sends back the four UID bytes (uid0 uid1 uid2 uid3) plus some extra data. However since the second card's UID is double, it sends back the cascade tag (CT) and the first three bytes ('88' uid0 uid1 uid2), plus some extra data. Hence the bits received in the terminal side are: (00001000)b and (00010001)b, respectively. If the implementation pads (1)b (which is what a typical implementation does [4]) to the previous similar bits, the terminal chooses the second card over the first one and continues with it.

As it can be seen unlike EMV, **ISO specifies no termination in the case of a collision. Instead, a race condition is created in which depending on the implementation of the terminal, and the UIDs of the cards available in the field one card would be selected.** This inconsistency between EMV and ISO perhaps would cause confusion when it comes to practical implementations of these systems. We believe this is an important issue and should be addressed by the community.

3   Experiments on Contacless Readers in Practice

In this section, we examine the anticollision procedure on the contactless terminals implemented in practice. We already know that in the case of a card clash in the London metro system, the card reader may either not proceed or pick one card over others without any particular pattern [34]. It is also reported that the cards that are picked up at the start and the end of a journey may be different (in this case the passenger can apply for a refund). This explanation by TfL suggests that the implementation in practice is not consistent with either EMV or ISO. To investigate this issue further, we performed an experiment to observe how payment terminals handled card collision in practice.

Before running the experiment, we tested the NFC chipsets on the cards and the phones that we used in our experiments by writing a reader app using the getId() function[5]. Our Nexus 5 mobiles returned random 4-byte UIDs which always start with '08'. The first byte represents the brand of the technology [27]. All our tested bank cards including TSB visa debit, Barclays visa debit, and barclaycard visa have fixed 4-byte UIDs, as presented in Table 1.

Table 1. Cards' information, LSB: Least Significant Bit

Card	Technology	UID size	UID0 Hex	UID0 Binary (LSB)	ISO winner
TSB visa debit- Card 1	A	4	0 × 35	(10101100)b	✓
TSB visa debit- Card 2	A	4	0 × 65	(10100110)b	✗
Barclays visa debit- Card 1	A	4	0 × E7	(11100111)b	✓
Barclays visa debit- Card 2	A	4	0 × 87	(11100001)b	✗
barclaycard Platinum visa- Card 1	A	4	0 × 67	(11100110)b	✗
barclaycard Platinum visa- Card 2	A	4	0 × DF	(11111011)b	✓
Nexus 5	A	4	x08	(00010000)b	✗

---

[5] developer.android.com/reference/android/nfc/Tag.html#getId

In this experiment, we examined three pairs of contactless cards as presented in Table 1. Each pair has been requested and issued from the same banks and roughly at the same time. (The two TSB visa debit, and the two Barclays visa debit, were requested at the exact same time, and the two barclaycard Platinum visa, were requested and received within a month. The TSB card 1 had been in use more than card 2, and the barclaycard card 2 had been in use much more than card 1.) We presented each pair to different contactless terminals several times in order to put them in race conditions. We made sure that both cards were

Table 2. The results of putting card pairs in the race condition. MS stands for Metro Station. In the case of No operation, the cards were presented 3 times to the POS for the same transaction. msg1: "Only present one card", msg2: "Card read failed".

No.	POS	Issuing bank	Facing card to reader	Result	Note
1	MS 1, POS 1	TSB	Card 1	No operation	
2	MS 1, POS 1	TSB	Card 2	No operation	
3	MS 2, POS 1	TSB	Card 1	No operation	
4	MS 2, POS 1	TSB	Card 2	No operation	
5	MS 1, POS 2	TSB	Card 1	No operation	
6	MS 1, POS 2	TSB	Card 2	Card 1 won	msg1
7	MS 1, POS 2	TSB	Card 1	Card 2 won on 2nd try	msg1
8	MS 2, POS 2	TSB	Card 2	Card 1 won	
9	MS 2, POS 2	TSB	Card 1	No operation	
10	MS 2, POS 2	TSB	Card 1	No operation	
11	MS 1, POS 2	Barclays	Card 2	Card 1 won	
12	MS 1, POS 2	Barclays	Card 1	Card 2 won	
13	MS 1, POS 2	Barclays	Card 2	Card 1 won	msg1
14	MS 1, POS 2	Barclays	Card 1	Card 2 won	
15	MS 2, POS 1	Barclays	Card 2	Card 1 won	
16	MS 2, POS 1	Barclays	Card 1	Card 2 won	msg1
17	MS 2, POS 1	Barclays	Card 2	Card 1 won	msg1
18	MS 1, POS 3	barclaycard	Card 2	Card 1 won	
19	MS 1, POS 3	barclaycard	Card 1	Card 1 won	
20	MS 1, POS 3	barclaycard	Card 2	Card 1 won	
21	MS 1, POS 3	barclaycard	Card 1	Card 1 won	
22	MS 2, POS 2	barclaycard	Card 2	Card 1 won	
23	MS 2, POS 2	barclaycard	Card 1	Card 1 won	
24	MS 1, POS 1	barclaycard	Card 2	Card 1 won on 2nd try	msg2
25	MS 1, POS 1	barclaycard	Card 1	Card 1 won	
26	MS 2, POS 3	barclaycard	Card 2	Card 1 won	
27	MS 2, POS 3	barclaycard	Card 1	Card 1 won	

attached to each other from the same side -contactless chipsets on each other. More specifically, when tapping the cards together to the reader, we put one of the cards on top of the other one for half of the experiments, and exchanged them for the rest of the tests.

The results are presented in Table 2. As it can be seen, these results do not match the anticollision algorithms suggested by either EMV or ISO. Generally, we can not find any specific pattern in the behaviour of these terminals when facing more than a card. Interestingly, in a few cases, the terminal shows this message: "only present one card", yet it proceeds with the payment. Based on this observation, in the next sections, we demonstrate an attack which can compromise user's privacy.

4   Attack Design

In this section, first we present the context of the attack. Then, we explain the feasibility of our attack by designing it based on the existing contactless payment specifications.

4.1   Threat Model and Attack Scenario

The context of this attack is when a user aims to pay for something by her contactless card where her card and phone are close to each other and both are presented to the reader's field. If the phone manages to hijack a few initial NFC signals that the card is meant to receive from the terminal, the attack is successful. In this situation, the phone is able to learn a lot about this contactless payment by requesting PDOL data (details in Sect. 4.2). The data can then be sent to a remote server controlled by the attacker. However, the malicious app would not continue further communication with the reader at some point (since it does not simulate the entire payment) and the user would realise that the payment is not being processed. In order to not disappoint the user on her second effort to pay, the NFC service on the mobile should be turned off for a few minutes once it hears from the reader. In this way, the user is able to complete the payment on the second try.

There are different ways in which the user might keep her card very close to her phone. For example, different models of card holder mobile cases are available in the market now. These cases are capable of containing a few cards as shown in Fig. 1. These types of wallets are already very popular with users since they offer an easy way to travel light and keep wallet essentials close to hand. When it comes to contactless payment, these accessories are even more popular since the users do not even need to take the card out of the case. Users can slide their contactless card that is kept inside the mobile case and easily tap it against the reader for daily purchases. After the increase of the cap limit from £20 to £30 in 2015, more retailer shops started to accept contactless payments for small item purchases[6].

---

[6] theukcardsassociation.org.uk/Contactless_(our_views)/index.asp.

Third parties are very interested in this sort of information, e.g., for advertising purposes. The collected information could be used in several ways. Third parties normally stimulate the users to purchase items by providing them customized ads based on this information. In addition, they can perform data mining programs to extract the patterns of people's shopping behaviours. An advanced attack might even pretend to be the user's bank by presenting this shopping information to her and tricking her to reveal her credentials via social engineering techniques. This attack in this paper can be even more impactful if the malicious app turns into the reader mode and extracts the card's information as suggested by Emms et al. [17]. Once the information is extracted, the app goes to the card mode for the rest of the attack. In this way, the attacker can easily pretend to be the user's bank by having her card information and her shopping records. We believe that these sorts of information are private to the users and should not be collected and shared without their permission.

4.2   Designing the Attack Based on NFC Payment Protocols

In this section, we cover a few key points in relation to contactless payment protocols in which we are going to refer in our implementation. EMV Contactless Book B [7] covers the Entry Point Specification. This specification defines the reader requirements necessary to enable the discovery and selection of a contactless application, and activation of the appropriate kernel for processing the transaction. Different kernels are used for different Application Definition File (ADF) names. (e.g., for a MasterCard ADF name, Kernel 2 will be used, and for a Visa ADF name, Kernel 3 will be used.) Based on the chosen Kernel, different procedures will run to complete a payment. However, the entry point protocols are the same for all card schemes.

Entry Point is designed around the use of a Proximity Payment System Environment (PPSE) as the selection mechanism. For multi-brand acceptance, this allows a reader to quickly obtain all the available brands and applications with a single command and to make an immediate choice based on priority and kernel availability. The Entry Point command and response Application Protocol Data Units (APDUs) are presented in Fig. 3. The File Control Information (FCI) as the response to the PPSE command from the card side includes the Directory Definition File (DDF) covering a product supported by the card, the Kernel Identifier of the kernel required for the specific application underpinning the product (conditional), and the priority of the Combination (conditional). The product is indicated by its ADF name in the card. Hence, it is the card which decides what kernel to choose and talk to. Entry Point finds Combinations by matching pairs of data elements (ADF Name) and Kernel Identifier in the card with pairs of data elements in the reader (AID and Kernel ID). Once all supported Combinations have been found and the highest priority Combination has been identified, Entry Point selects the associated card application by sending a SELECT (AID) command with the ADF Name of the selected Combination. Depending on the selected AID and the kernel in the selected Combinations, a specific kernel is called to take care of the rest of the payment.

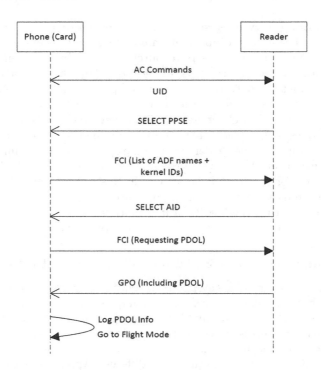

Fig. 3. The sequence diagram of the communication between our app and the reader.

As a part of the response to SELECT AID command, the card requests Processing Options Data Object List (PDOL). Generally, a Get Processing Option (GPO) command is returned in response to this FCI command (SELECT AID) which includes the Terminal Transaction Qualifiers (TTQ), Unpredictable Number, Amount, Authorised, Transaction Currency Code, and other tags [11].

As shown Fig. 3 and we explain in the next section, our attack app is going to take the proper action in response to each command from the terminal in order to retrieve as much information as possible about each transaction.

5   Implementation

In this section we present the technical implementation of our attack.

5.1   Android HCE

Android supports emulating cards that are based on the NFC-Forum ISO-DEP specification (based on ISO/IEC 14443-1 to 4) and processes Application Protocol Data Units (APDUs) as defined in the ISO/IEC 7816-4 specification. In compliance with ISO/IEC 7816-4, each HCE application has an Application ID (AID). This ID enables the reader app to select the correct service.

In our implementation, we declared an AID group including an AID filter of a Visa card (0xA0000000031010) in an XML resource to be pointed by a `SERVICE_META_DATA` tag in the manifest declaration. On the other hand, Android does not interpret the PPSE selection command and, consequently, it does not generate or send a list of available payment applications. Hence we have to handle the PPSE command in the app. Typically, an HCE payment application based on EMV standards would register for both: the payment application AID and the PPSE ADF name. Note that from a protocol perspective there is no difference between an ADF name and an AID, so we can register for it in our service XML file with an AID filter for the ADF name ("2PAY.SYS.DDF01") in its ASCII hexadecimal representation of 0x325041592E5359532E4444463031. In the same file, we set the `android:requireDeviceUnlock` attribute to `false` in order to avoid the user being asked for unlocking her device.

The `HostApduService` class is extended for implementing an HCE service with two abstract methods: `processCommandApdu` and `onDeactivated`. The former is called whenever the card receives an APDU from an NFC reader and enables half-duplex communication with the reader. The latter is called when either the NFC link is broken or the reader wishes to talk to another service. According to EMV, the first two APDUs (SELECT PPSE and SELECT AID) are for service selection. That is where we request PDOL, as shown in Fig. 3. After a successful service selection, the card and reader can exchange any type of data. When the app receives the first GPO command including the requested data, it logs the data in a file, and the attack terminates. Accordingly, our app turns the NFC off by going to the flight mode to allow the user to complete the purchase on the second try.

5.2 Android Flight Mode

Android does not offer any API for turning the NFC controller on/off programmatically. Therefore, developers usually set the NFC settings in a way that prompts the user to turn it on/off manually. In our attack, once our app hears from the terminal, it needs to turn off the NFC, so that the user can successfully pay on her second try. One possible way to control the NFC adapter is to change the phone's airplane mode setting. However, only those apps with the superuser permissions can change the Airplane mode setting which requires `WRITE_SETTINGS` and `WRITE_SECURE_SETTINGS` to be declared in the manifest file. Starting from Android 4.2, turning on/off airplane mode is not supported by android APIs any more. Hence, this part of our attack only works on a rooted device.

On the other hand, this attack needs to keep the phone's screen on since, at the moment, NFC does not work when the phone is off [1]. An advanced attack would turn the screen on only when the user wants to pay by using accelerometer and gyroscope sensor measurements in order to recognise such a gesture. Li et al. in [19] show that it is effectively possible to use the tap gesture to unlock the phone for NFC applications based on accelerometer data. By augmenting such a gesture recognition feature to our code, we will have a complete application that is able to compromise users privacy in contactless payments.

6   Experiments and Results

We performed an experiment by installing the app on Android phones (Nexus 5). We attached the card to the back of the phone in two different positions, as shown in Fig. 4. The position that the card was attached to the phone was important in our experiments since it effected the results, as we explain later. In all experiments, the back of the phone was faced to the terminal (hence, the card was in a closer distance to the terminal than the phone).

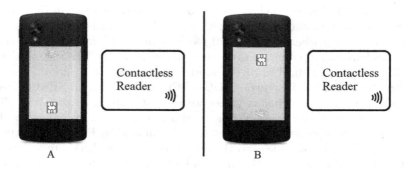

Fig. 4. Contactless card attached to the phone in two different positions for the experiments; A (left): the NFC chipset was down, B (right): the NFC chipset was up.

6.1   Expected Results

According to the EMV specifications, regardless of the UID of the card and the phone, the terminal should not proceed in the case of a card collision. ISO standards, however, suggest to opt one of the UIDs (typically with higher values) in the race condition. The first UID byte (UID0) of mobile phones that we tested is always '08' (LSB: 00010000), and it is a single UID. As presented in Table 1, all of our cards should always win over the phone if it is a typical ISO implementation. In the following experiments, we show that the expected behaviour does not happen in practice, and the phone wins with a high probability.

6.2   Experiment A: Card and Phone Collision

In this experiment, we tested a few different contactless cards by presenting each card with the phone to a few terminals (contactless metro ticket machines). We tested multiple cards including two TSB visa debit, and two Barclays visa debit on different machines. During this experiment, we asked a few users to pay for metro tickets with different contactless cards that we provided to them.

These cards were attached to mobile phones (Nexus 5). These participants were informed of the purpose of the experiment, but were not asked to follow any particular procedure. We asked them to naturally pay contactlessly. We observed the behaviour of the terminals as summarized in Table 4 (see Appendix A).

The results show that when the card is attached to the phone in position A (the card's NFC chipset is down), the phone can hear the reader's signal first with a very high probability. On the other hand, when the card's NFC chipset is positioned to the top of the phone (position B), the chance of the card winning is slightly more than the phone. Nevertheless, an average user might put the card in any of these two positions close to the phone. Based on our experiment, generally our app is able to recognise about 66 % of the user's contactless payment activities. Over time, this success rate would allow the attacker to accumulate information about the user's contactless payment patterns.

Our observations show that contactless terminals present different messages on the display based on the situation. When select to pay, it displays: "Insert, swipe or tap for GBP 0.80" as the first message. If it can not choose either the card or the phone it displays: "Card read failed", and it goes back to the first message. The fail message happened when our users tapped the card and the phone very quickly, hence none of them were presented to the field for a sufficient time. Similar to our experiments in Sect. 3, the terminal may show another message: "Only present one card", but it still proceeds with the transaction.

Table 3. Exchanged APDUs of experiment B

Sender	APDU	Command
Terminal	00A404000E325041592E5359532E444446303100	SELECT PPSE
Phone	6F3C840E325041592E5359532E4444463031A52A BF0C2761254F07A0000000031010870101501042 4152434C41594341524442056495341BF6304DF20 01809000	FCI
Reader	00A4040007A000000003101000	SELECT AID
Phone	6F4B8407A0000000031010A5405010424152434C 41594341524420564953418701019F38189F6604 9F02069F03069F1A0295055F2A029A039C019F37 045F2D02656EBF0C089F5A0531082608269000	FCI including PDOL request
Terminal	80A800002383213000000000000000000080000000 000000082600000000000082616052300161267 3900	GPO including PDOL data

6.3 Experiment B: PDOL Data

In order to show the impact of the attack more visibly, we performed another experiment. While purchasing a ticket, we presented our final app to a payment terminal in a metro station. Our app logged the PDOL data of the transaction and then went to the Airplane mode. We built our card app in a way that it responded to the two SELECT commands – PPSE and AID – before asking for PDOL data (see Fig. 3).

The exchanged command and response APDUs are shown in Table 3. As it can be seen, when the card sends the second FCI, by sending PDOL tag ('9F38'), it requests different sort of information about the transaction such as the amount (tag='9F02', Amount, Authorised (Numeric)) and transaction date (tag='9A'). Accordingly, the terminal responds with the first GPO command including the requested items for PDOL ('83') i.e. amount ('000000000080' = 0.80 pence) and date ('160523' = 2016 May 23) [11].

As it can be seen, the attacker can easily build such a table for all transactions and discover the user's payment patterns.

7 Conclusion

In this paper, we discussed a real world problem concerning the card collision when making contactless payments. We studied the EMV and ISO standards on card collision, and by performing experiments we discovered that the implementation in practice matches neither of them. Based on this inconsistency, we described and implemented an attack on the privacy of contactless payments. In this attack, we simulated a card within an app and tracked the user's contactless payment transactions by requesting PDOL data from the terminal. When the phone and the card are both presented to a contactless terminal, our app could successfully win the race condition over the card in the majority of test cases.

Our findings suggest vulnerabilities in the current infrastructure which needs to be addressed. More specifically, the results of our experiments show that when tapping the terminal with more than a card, in most cases (Tables 2 and 4), the terminal does not even identify the card collision. Nevertheless, even if the terminal identifies the presence of more than a card in the field (by showing a message), it still proceeds with the transactions. The selection of the card appears random. A countermeasure to this identified privacy attack is updating the implementation of the payment terminals according to EMV's card collision algorithm: i.e., the process should not proceed when more that one card is detected in the field. Updating some parts of EMV's protocol and protecting the PDOL data would also mitigate the introduced attack. Finally, the EMV and ISO standards would need to be updated to have a consistent algorithm to handle card collision.

Acknowledgement. We would like to thank Dr. Michael Ward from EMV and Digital Devices for his valuable help towards our better understanding of EMV contactless specifications. We would like to thank Dr. Martin Emms and Mr. Ehsan Toreini from Newcastle University for their help on performing the experiments of this work. We also thank all the anonymous reviewers of this paper. All experiments gained approval through Newcastle University's research ethics processes. Feng Hao was supported by ERC Starting Grant No 306994, Aad van Moorsel was supported by EPSRC grant K006568.

A   Experiment Results

In this section, we provide the detailed results of our Card and Phone Collision experiment. These results are presented in Table 4.

B   EMV and ISO Flowcharts

The collision detection procedure of EMV specification and Anticollision loop flowchart of ISO are presented in Figs. 5 and 6, respectively.

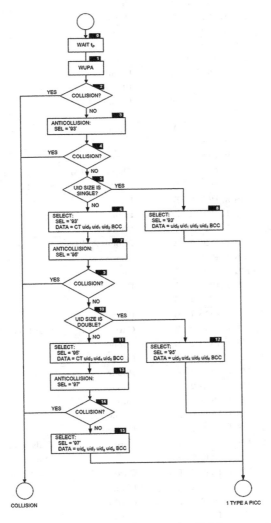

Fig. 5. Type A collision detection, taken from EMV contactless Book D.

Table 4. Results of experiment A

No.	Card	Terminal	Position	Winner	Msg
1	TSB 1	MS 1, POS 2	A	Phone	
2	TSB 1	MS 2, POS 2	A	Phone	
3	TSB 1	MS 2, POS 2	A	Card	
4	TSB 1	MS 2, POS 2	A	Phone	
5	TSB 1	MS 1, POS 1	B	Card	
6	TSB 1	MS 1, POS 1	B	Card	
7	TSB 1	MS 1, POS 1	B	Phone	
8	TSB 1	MS 1, POS 1	B	Phone	
9	TSB 1	MS 2, POS 2	B	Card	
10	TSB 1	MS 2, POS 2	B	Card	
11	TSB 2	MS 1, POS 2	A	Phone	
12	TSB 2	MS 1, POS 2	A	Phone	
13	TSB 2	MS 1, POS 2	A	Phone	
14	TSB 2	MS 1, POS 2	A	Phone	
15	TSB 2	MS 1, POS 2	A	Phone	
16	TSB 2	MS 3, POS 1	A	Phone	
17	TSB 2	MS 3, POS 2	B	Card	
18	TSB 2	MS 3, POS 2	B	Phone	
19	TSB 2	MS 3, POS 2	B	Phone, 2nd try	"Card read failed"
20	TSB 2	MS 3, POS 2	B	Card, 2nd try	"Card read failed"
21	TSB 2	MS 3, POS 2	B	Phone	
22	Barclays 1	MS 1, POS 1	A	Phone	
23	Barclays 1	MS 1, POS 1	A	Phone	
24	Barclays 1	MS 1, POS 1	A	Phone, 2nd try	"Card read failed"
25	Barclays 1	MS 1, POS 1	A	Phone	
26	Barclays 1	MS 1, POS 1	A	Phone	
27	Barclays 1	MS 1, POS 1	A	Phone	
28	Barclays 1	MS 1, POS 1	B	Card	
29	Barclays 1	MS 1, POS 1	B	Phone	
30	Barclays 1	MS 1, POS 2	B	Card, 2nd try	"Card read failed"
31	Barclays 1	MS 1, POS 2	B	Phone	
32	Barclays 1	MS 1, POS 2	B	Card	
33	Barclays 1	MS 1, POS 2	B	Phone	
34	Barclays 2	MS 1, POS 2	A	Phone	
35	Barclays 2	MS 1, POS 2	A	Phone	
36	Barclays 2	MS 1, POS 2	A	Phone	
37	Barclays 2	MS 1, POS 2	A	Phone	
38	Barclays 2	MS 1, POS 2	A	Card	"Only present one card"
39	Barclays 2	MS 1, POS 2	B	Card	"Only present one card"
40	Barclays 2	MS 1, POS 2	B	Card, 2nd try	"Card read failed"
41	Barclays 2	MS 1, POS 2	B	Phone	
42	Barclays 2	MS 1, POS 1	B	Card	
43	Barclays 2	MS 1, POS 1	B	Card	
44	Barclays 2	MS 1, POS 1	B	Phone, 2nd try	"Card read failed"

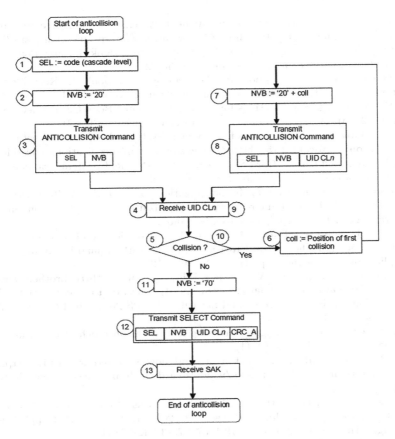

Fig. 6. Anticollision loop, flowchart for PCD, taken from ISO/IEC 14443-3.

References

1. Host-based card emulation. http://developer.android.com/guide/topics/connectivity/nfc/hce.html.
2. International Organization for Standardization, BS ISO, IEC 14443–1: 2008+A1: 2012 Identification cards. Contactless integrated circuit cards. Proximity cards. Physical characteristics (2012). http://www.bsol.bsigroup.com
3. International Organization for Standardization, BS ISO, IEC 14443–2: 2010+A2: 2012 Identification cards. Contactless integrated circuit cards. Proximity cards. Radio frequency power and signal interface (2012). http://www.bsol.bsigroup.com
4. International Organization for Standardization, BS ISO, IEC 14443–3: 2011+A6: 2014 Identification cards. Contactless integrated circuit cards. Proximity cards. Initialization and anticollision (2014). http://www.bsol.bsigroup.com
5. International Organization for Standardization, BS ISO, IEC 14443–4: 2008+A4: 2014 Identification cards. Contactless integrated circuit cards. Proximity cards. Transmission protocol (2014). http://www.bsol.bsigroup.com

6. EMV Contactless Specifications for Payment Systems, Book A: Architecture and General Requirements (2015). http://www.emvco.com/specifications.aspx?id=21

7. EMV Contactless Specifications for Payment Systems, Book B: Entry Point (2015). http://www.emvco.com/specifications.aspx?id=21

8. EMV Contactless Specifications for Payment Systems, Book C2: Kernel 2 Specification (2015). http://www.emvco.com/specifications.aspx?id=21

9. EMV Contactless Specifications for Payment Systems, Book C3: Kernel 3 Specification (2015). http://www.emvco.com/specifications.aspx?id=21

10. EMV Contactless Specifications for Payment Systems, Book D: Contactless Communication Protocol (2015). http://www.emvco.com/specifications.aspx?id=21

11. EMV Integrated Circuit Card Specifications for Payment Systems, Book 3 (2011). http://www.emvco.com/specifications.aspx?id=223

12. International Organization for Standardization, BS ISO, IEC 7816-4: 2013, Identification cards. Integrated circuit cards. Organization, security and commands for interchange (2013). http://www.bsol.bsigroup.com

13. Aviv, A.J., Sapp, B., Blaze, M., Smith, J.M.: Practicality of accelerometer side channels on smartphones. In: Proceedings of the 28th Annual Computer Security Applications Conference, pp. 41–50. ACM (2012)

14. Balebako, R., Jung, J., Lu, W., Cranor, L.F., Nguyen, C.: "little brothers watching you": Raising awareness of data leaks on smartphones. In: Proceedings of the Ninth Symposium on Usable Privacy and Security, SOUPS 2013, pp. 12:1–12:11. ACM, New York (2013)

15. Cai, L., Chen, H.: Touchlogger: inferring keystrokes on touch screen from smartphone motion. In: HotSec (2011)

16. Curphey, M.: Card clash, what is it, and how to avoid ir (2014). http://uk.creditcards.com/credit-card-news/what-is-card-clash-and-how-to-avoid-it-1372.php

17. Emms, M., Arief, B., Little, N., Moorsel, A.: Risks of offline verify PIN on contactless cards. In: Sadeghi, A.-R. (ed.) FC 2013. LNCS, vol. 7859, pp. 313–321. Springer, Heidelberg (2013). doi:10.1007/978-3-642-39884-1_26

18. Halevi, T., Ma, D., Saxena, N., Xiang, T.: Secure proximity detection for NFC devices based on ambient sensor data. In: Foresti, S., Yung, M., Martinelli, F. (eds.) ESORICS 2012. LNCS, vol. 7459, pp. 379–396. Springer, Heidelberg (2012). doi:10.1007/978-3-642-33167-1_22

19. Li, H., Ma, D., Saxena, N., Shrestha, B., Zhu, Y.: Tap-wave-rub: lightweight malware prevention for smartphones using intuitive human gestures. In: Proceedings of the Sixth ACM Conference on Security and Privacy in Wireless and Mobile Networks, WiSec 2013, pp. 25–30. ACM, New York (2013)

20. Marshall, G.: Travel using contactless cards: an update from tfl (2014). http://londonist.com/2014/07/travel-using-contactless-cards-an-update-from-tfl

21. Mehrnezhad, M., Hao, F., Shahandashti, S.F.: Tap-tap and pay (TTP): preventing the mafia attack in NFC payment. In: Chen, L., Matsuo, S. (eds.) SSR 2015. LNCS, vol. 9497, pp. 21–39. Springer, Heidelberg (2015). doi:10.1007/978-3-319-27152-1_2

22. Mehrnezhad, M., Toreini, E., Shahandashti, S.F., Hao, F.: Touchsignatures: identification of user touch actions based on mobile sensors via javascript. In: Proceedings of the 10th ACM Symposium on Information, Computer and Communications Security, ASIA CCS 2015, pp. 673–673. ACM, New York (2015)

23. Mehrnezhad, M., Toreini, E., Shahandashti, S.F., Hao, F.: Touchsignatures: identification of user touch actions and pins based on mobile sensor data via javascript. J. Inf. Secur. Appl. **26**, 23–38 (2016)

24. Miluzzo, E., Varshavsky, A., Balakrishnan, S., Choudhury, R.R.: Tapprints: your finger taps have fingerprints. In: Proceedings of the 10th International Conference on Mobile Systems, Applications, and Services, pp. 323–336. ACM (2012)

25. Morley, K.: Contactless cards: how to avoid paying twice (2014). http://www.tele graph.co.uk/finance/personalfinance/money-saving-tips/11215583/Contactless-cards-how-to-avoid-paying-twice.html

26. ISO 14443, ISO 18092, Type-A, Type-B, Type-F, Felica, Calypso NFCIP, NFC-HELP! (2009). http://www.nfc.cc/2009/01/03/iso-14443-iso-18092-type-a-type-b-type-f-felica-calypso-nfcip-nfc-help/

27. AN10927, MIFARE and handling of UIDs. By NXP, Company Public (2013)

28. Owusu, E., Han, J., Das, S., Perrig, A., Zhang, J.: Accessory: password inference using accelerometers on smartphones. In: Proceedings of the Twelfth Workshop on Mobile Computing Systems & Applications, p. 9. ACM (2012)

29. Saul, H.: Oyster card users pay up to £91 more each week than peopleusing new contactless payment (2014). http://www.independent.co.uk/news/uk/home-news/oyster-card-users-pay-up-to-91-more-each-week-than-people-using-new-contactless-payment-9843642.htmll

30. Shrestha, B., Saxena, N., Truong, H.T.T., Asokan, N.: Drone to the rescue: relay-resilient authentication using ambient multi-sensing. In: Christin, N., Safavi-Naini, R. (eds.) FC 2014. LNCS, vol. 8437, pp. 349–364. Springer, Heidelberg (2014). doi:10.1007/978-3-662-45472-5_23

31. Simon, L., Anderson, R.: Pin skimmer: inferring pins through the camera and microphone. In: Proceedings of the Third ACM Workshop on Security and Privacy in Smartphones and Mobile Devices, SPSM 2013, pp. 67–78. ACM, New York (2013)

32. Spreitzer, R.: Pin skimming: exploiting the ambient-light sensor in mobile devices. In: Proceedings of the 4th ACM Workshop on Security and Privacy in Smartphones and Mobile Devices, SPSM 2014, pp. 51–62. ACM, New York (2014)

33. Why contactless cards can leave you with a losing deal (2014). http://www.theguardian.com/money/2013/may/25/contactless-cards

34. Watch out for card clash. https://tfl.gov.uk/fares-and-payments/contactless/card-clash

35. Vila, J., Rodríguez, R.J.: Practical experiences on NFC relay attacks with android. In: Mangard, S., Schaumont, P. (eds.) RFIDSec 2015. LNCS, vol. 9440, pp. 87–103. Springer, Heidelberg (2015). doi:10.1007/978-3-319-24837-0_6

36. Xu, Z., Bai, K., Zhu, S.: Taplogger: inferring user inputs on smartphone touch-screens using on-board motion sensors. In: Proceedings of the Fifth ACM Conference on Security and Privacy in Wireless and Mobile Networks, pp. 113–124. ACM (2012)

Security Analysis of the W3C Web Cryptography API

Kelsey Cairns[1], Harry Halpin[2(✉)], and Graham Steel[3]

[1] Washington State University, PO Box 442, Seattle, WA 98194, USA
kelsey.cairns@email.wsu.edu
[2] INRIA, 2 Simone Iff, 75012 Paris, France
harry.halpin@inria.fr
[3] Cryptosense, 19 Boulevard Poissonnire, 75022 Paris, France
graham@cryptosense.com

Abstract. Due to the success of formal modeling of protocols such as TLS, there is a revival of interest in applying formal modeling to standardized APIs. We argue that formal modeling should happen as the standard is being developed (not afterwards) as it can detect complex or even simple attacks that the standardization group may not otherwise detect. As a case example of this, we discuss in detail the W3C Web Cryptography API. We demonstrate how a formal analysis of the API using the modeling language AVISPA with a SAT solver demonstrates that while the API has no errors in basic API operations and maintains its security properties for the most part, there are nonetheless attacks on secret key material due to how key wrapping and usages are implemented. Furthermore, there were a number of basic problems in terms of algorithm selection and a weakness that led to a padding attack. The results of this study led to the removal of algorithms before its completed standardization and the removal of the padding attack via normalization of error codes, although the key wrapping attack is still open. We expect this sort of formal methodology to be applied to new standardization efforts at the W3C such as the W3C Web Authentication API.

1 Introduction

The World Wide Web Consortium (W3C) has commenced work on the Web Cryptography API [3], which defines cryptographic primitives to be deployed across browsers and native Javascript environments. This process has begun in the W3C Web Cryptography Working Group, driven by all major browsers and also open to the wider community.[1] Started in 2012, the W3C Web Cryptography Working Group is finalizing the standard for completion by the end of 2015, with the design being led by Ryan Sleevi of Google with Mark Watson of Netflix as co-editor. The API is already implemented across Chrome 37 and above (including Android), Mozilla version 36 and above, Opera 27 and above, Safari 8 and above,

---

[1] http://www.w3.org/2012/webcrypto/.

© Springer International Publishing AG 2016
L. Chen et al. (Eds.): SSR 2016, LNCS 10074, pp. 112–140, 2016.
DOI: 10.1007/978-3-319-49100-4_5

and Internet Explorer 11 and Microsoft Edge. Thus, the W3C Web Cryptography API is the primary Web-facing cryptography API for the foreseeable future.

Like any API, the Web Cryptography API (informally called the "WebCrypto API") needs an impartial and thorough analysis to determine its security properties. Cryptographic APIs, and even cryptographic libraries such as OpenSSL, that have not received such an analysis until after widespread deployment have resulted in dangerous security incidents in validating TLS certificates [20]. Given that the W3C's mission including security reviews, the W3C explicitly worked with the larger community discover possible security vulnerabilities and formally prove the guarantees that the Web Cryptography API could provide. Due to an unfortunate tendency of Web developers to bring incorrect expectations (brought from other environments) to Javascript and to (incorrectly) believe that the Web Cryptography API 'magically' makes the Javascript browser environment a suitable platform for secure Web applications, it is important to be able to state precisely the security properties of the Web Cryptography API and what attacks are inherent in the API design as well as its operation in the Javascript browser environment. In the future, these kinds of attacks need to be mitigated so that the use of the Web Cryptography API matches intuitive developer expectations around the use of security APIs.

Section 2 explains in detail the role of formal modeling. Section 3 overviews existing background on Javascript cryptography, followed by relevant literature describing the formal analysis of APIs and Web applications. In Sect. 4, we describe the formal modeling of the Web Cryptography API using the AVISPA language, and describe the experiments we used to verify various security properties in a number of scenarios, including a successful attack on key-wrapping that can be generalized to attacks on key exchange. The behavior of key wrapping and key usages in the API would seem to violate the expectations of most developers who want to use the API. In Sect. 5 we discuss algorithm selection in the WebCrypto API, pointing out well-known errors in their algorithm selection and error codes, and these problems were accepted and our proposed fixes became part of the current WebCrypto API. In Sect. 6 we summarize what properties future standards need to improve the security properties of the Web Cryptography API in particular and the future application of formal API modeling to new standardized APIs and protocols at the W3C.

2   The Role of Formal Modeling in Standardization

In the process of standardization, there is a desire to offer as much functionality to developers as possible, while simultaneously preventing them from making mistakes. In terms of cryptographic APIs like the WebCrypto API, this can lead to handing the application developers a "kitchen sink" of cryptographic primitives, which inadvertently may give a developer "enough rope to hang themselves." Unlike protocols, APIs typically do not have precisely stated threat models and security properties. This is a mistake, as security flaws at the API level are automatically inherited by application that deploy the API and the primitives provided by the API.

Although there is a reasonable argument to give developers only "high level" APIs that may include suitable defaults, these APIs by nature must build on "low level" APIs that provide access to a large range of cryptographic primitives even if the "low level" API is not accessible or hidden from the developer. In the Web Cryptography API, it was chosen to release the "low level" WebCrypto API and not explicitly work on a "high level" cryptographic API or provide defaults. While it seems that users will generally use the highest-level of abstraction available to them, the Working Group has decided that given that the field of cryptography is in flux around issues such as elliptic curves and attacks on RSA, it would be unwise to provide any defaults that may become outdated in the standard. Instead, a 'high-level' API with appropriate defaults can be created that would build from the primitives in the Web Cryptography API.

The process of standardization in the field of security needs to incorporate formal methodology in order to state the security properties and discover attacks *before* a standard is released. As security standardization is difficult due to the complexity of maintaining security properties throughout the lifetime of a standardization process, there is a clear use-case for formal modeling.

The general insight behind formal modeling is that the traditional method of discovering new attacks on security APIs (and security protocols in general), by being based on human insight, may miss important attacks. While a single human may be able to discover by sheer insight an important attack, the state-space of possible combinations of items such as keys, messages, cryptographic primitives, and various desired properties may simply be difficult to discern without the assistance of automated or semi-automated tools. Similar to the automated discovery of proofs, the ideal automatic security checker would essentially be a "machine attacker" that would try out an large number of attacks using all possible combinations of cryptographic primitives and their parameters over messages in all possible states. The general technique is the reduction of maintaining security properties to a boolean satisfiability problem (SAT), where a model-checker is used to see if the security properties hold via automatically checking the property exhaustively (rather than theorem-proving) [18]. Although the problem is well-known to be undecidable, efficient SAT solvers exist for large classes of problem. Once a problem is detected via formal modeling, it may be fixed in the standard before deployment. If the standard has already been implemented, the flaw is usually then tested against real-world implementations, hopefully to be fixed once the flaw is shown to be valid.

This approach of formal modeling has shown itself to be successful against many already deployed protocols, in particular against TLS 1.2 [10]. Sometimes attacks on standards incorporate errors in the choice of cryptographic primitives, which are usually widespread in standardization as the time it takes to update. While usually the choice of a vulnerable cryptographic primitives is easily discovered, attacks on the protocol itself can be discovered years after the release of the protocol [9] due to fundamental problems in the protocol such as the lack of a well-defined state machine.

One area where formal modeling is just beginning to be applied to in standardization is in security API design. A *security API* consists of a set of functions that are offered to some other program that uphold some security properties, regardless of the program making the function calls and what functions are called [13]. For example, one would hope that an API like PKCS#11 that provides access to key material in hardware tokens would prevent any private key material from being tampered with, regardless of the application [17]. These kinds of security properties are particularly critical in many applications, and classically security APIs have been studied in the realm of hardware security modules [13].

Early work did not use generalizable formal techniques, but customized each technique for the API at hand [13]. Only more recently has fully automated analysis in terms of model-checking and theorem-proving been deployed, usually based on the Dolev-Yao (DY) abstract model where cryptographic primitives are given as functions on bitstrings in an abstract algebra [19]. This methodology has shown to be successful by its ability to compromise from non-standardized solutions such as an authentication server and steal private keys from the Yubikey USB hardware token [27]. Formal modeling has then be used to successfully reveal a number of API-based attacks on standards, including the commercially available tamper-resistant hardware security tokens PKCS#11 [17]. Currently, a large number of security APIs are under process of standardization at the IETF and W3C. Although formal modeling is not part of the current required security review of protocols in the IETF and the optional security review of protocols in the W3C, we believe it should be encouraged in the future as a mandatory part of the security review before and after implementation.

3   Background

In Sect. 3.1 we give relevant background on Javascript Web Cryptography. Section 3.2 reviews the existing academic literature on formal modeling that serves as the basis of our work on the Web Cryptography API, as well as mentioning previous usages of formal modeling for security properties on the Web. Section 3.3 summarizes the W3C Web Cryptography API (abbreviated as the "Web Cryptography API").

3.1   Javascript Cryptography

As an increasing number of applications transition to the Web, the need of ordinary users to have more secure Web applications has increased and Web developers are attempting to match those expectations. Although there was initial hostility to the idea of cryptography in Javascript as exemplified by "Javascript Cryptography Considered Harmful,"[2] there has nonetheless been widespread interest in creating secure Web applications [21]. Yet without the

---

[2] http://matasano.com/articles/javascript-cryptography/.

proper cryptographic primitives working cross-browser, Javascript cryptography would indeed be dangerous. For example, the initial version of the 'Crypto.cat' encrypted chat application initially not only recreated their own cryptographic routines in Javascript but also deployed these Javascript libraries insecurely.[3] In a remarkable turn-around, Crypto.cat has since become the first formally verified Javascript-based cryptographic application. Although a number of well-designed Javascript cryptographic libraries exist such as the Stanford Javascript Crypto Library [38], there are certain properties even the most well-designed Javascript cryptography library presents, such as the problem of accessing the library itself securely. Although well-designed libraries can prevent this, common libraries *OpenPGP.js*[4] are vulnerable to side-channel attacks and critically use built-in weak number generation given by default by *Math.random*.[5] Furthermore, even well-designed libraries that feature native Javascript password-based key derivation using algorithms such as PBKDF2 are still simply too slow for widespread high security deployment (i.e. if a sufficient number of iterations are used). After a public workshop in 2012,[6] the W3C decided to create a cross-browser Web Cryptography API that would offer a number of standardized, constant-time primitives to be accessed by Web developers. This API does not address larger concerns with the Web Security Model, such as cross-origin code injection (as currently addressed by the Web Application Security Group[7]) and completely trusted servers (i.e. Javascript as remote code execution), as well as problems inherent in Javascript itself such as prototype inheritance and the lack of availability of efficient big integer operations.

3.2   Formal Modeling Literature Review

There is still no single dominant formal modeling language for modeling security. Alloy [22], a language based on the Z specification language that uses SAT solving, has been popular and used against APIs such as the Trusted Platform Module 1.2 API [40]. It has recently been used for discovering security vulnerabilities in Web applications, although it was not used to investigate the properties of the Web Cryptography API [30]. Alloy is a well-developed framework that allows infinite models. Scyther can work with an unbounded number of sessions but does not allow the modeling of control flows [16]. ProVerif is a cryptographic protocol verifier that works as a sequence of Horn clause and allows unbounded verification on smaller protocols [11]. Tamarin also provides unbounded session support with the required mutable global state [36].

AVISPA provides automatic validation and verification of security protocols based on the DY formalism given by re-writing rules, where the knowledge of

---

[3] https://crypto.cat/.

[4] http://openpgpjs.org/.

[5] See the results of the 2014 penetration testing report by Cure53.de available here: https://cure53.de/pentest-report_openpgpjs.pdf.

[6] The workshop was called 'Identity in the Browser,' archived at http://www.w3.org/2011/identity-ws/.

[7] https://www.w3.org/2011/webappsec/.

the attacker can also be modeled using standard re-write rules rather than an entirely different set of rules based on, for example, belief logic. AVISPA supports multiple model-checkers over bounded sessions, and features both high and low-level formats for specifying protocols. Although unbounded sessions are of interest for some scenarios, given that in our scenarios the Web application operates over bounded sessions given the ephemeral nature of Javascript sessions (with the exception of 'cookies'). We chose AVISPA for our analysis since it takes into account mutable global state shared between sessions, i.e. in particular keys in a key store that have attributes that change over time and that affect the execution semantics of protocols for operations such as signing and encryption in an API.

Earlier work in formal analysis of the Web did conceptual work such as dividing the attacker spaces of web attackers, who attack Javascript run-time environments in the browser via cross-site scripting (XSS) attacks, from network attackers who would attack the underlying TCP/IP connections between sites and attack the certificate authority infrastructure [2]. More recent work has used Proverif to model the properties of so-called "safe" cloud storage providers via the Web [4], verifying subsets of Javascript [39], and interactive proofs of security properties of Web applications [30]. However, none of these previous works were aimed at the Web Cryptography API. This paper presents the first security analysis and formal modeling of the Web Cryptography API.

3.3   W3C Web Cryptography API

The Web Cryptography API is a low-level API that exposes cryptographic functionality via a number of components specified as a WebIDL. A WebIDL is a way of specifying Javascript functions, although it may also in principle be bound to programming languages outside Javascript.[8] The main features of the Web Cryptography API are as follows, with much more detail given in the specification itself [3]:

1. *RandomSource*: Pseudorandom number generation.
2. *CryptoKey*: JSON object for key material.
3. *CryptoOperation*: Functions such as encryption and wrapping, along with error codes.

RandomSource. The *RandomSource* interface represents an interface to a cryptographically strong pseudo-random number generator (PRNG). Implementations should generate cryptographically random values using well-established cryptographic pseudo-random number generators seeded with high-quality entropy. Currently it provides no lower-bound on the information theoretic entropy present in cryptographically random values, but implementations should make a best effort to provide as much entropy as practicable and may provide platform or application specific entropy-related error messages.

---

[8] http://www.w3.org/TR/WebIDL/.

CryptoKey. The *CryptoKey* object represents an opaque reference to keying material that is managed by the user agent. There are three types of keys: secret keys (for symmetric encryption), public keys, and private keys (for asymmetric encryption). Most importantly, the API does not expose key material itself, but instead only pass handlers to the key material itself in Javascript and so access to secret key material is forbidden. The only exception is when a key is explicitly given a boolean *extractable* set to true and then exported (even then, it would have the same-origin and structured clone properties). Keys that are not marked explicitly as private, secret, or as non-extractable (i.e. *extractable* set to false) will be accessible to the server with same-origin policy if key export is done. A simplified (types not being given for all values) Javascript WebIDL interface for CryptoKeys is given in Fig. 1.

```
KeyType { public, private, secret };

KeyUsage { encrypt, decrypt, sign, verify,
           deriveKey, deriveBits, wrapKey, unwrapKey };

CryptoKey { KeyType type;  boolean extractable;
            object algorithm; object usages; };
```

Fig. 1. CryptoKey WebIDL

In the Web Cryptography API, we use the *structured clone* algorithm to store keys.[9] This algorithm is an abstraction on top of existing Web storage mechanisms such as *IndexedDB*[10] that has the same lifetime guarantees as the rest of Web storage. This would allow a user to clear their key material at the same time they 'wipe' cookies from their browser storage. So keys are restricted to the same origin policy in storage and are essentially ephemeral as they can be removed when session state is cleared.

CryptoOperation. The *CryptoOperation* is the heart of every cryptographic primitive. Given a algorithm and a set of parameters (usually including a handler to a key), the *CryptoOperation* will attempt to commit some operation. Every *CryptoOperation* can be thought of as a named finite state machine with an internal state, an associated algorithm, an internal count of available bytes, and a list of pending data. Every member of the list of pending data represents data that should undergo the associated cryptographic transformation if the operation as a whole is successful. The order of items when added to the list is preserved in processing, so that the first data that is added being the data processed. If the cryptographic operation fails (such as when the key type is wrong or when the algorithm is not supported), the *CryptoOperation* then terminates and

---

[9] See https://developer.mozilla.org/en-US/docs/DOM.
[10] See http://www.w3.org/TR/IndexedDB/.

```
encrypt(algorithm, key, data);
decrypt(algorithm, key, data);
sign(algorithm, key, data);
verify(algorithm, key, signature, data);
digest(algorithm, data);
generateKey(algorithm, extractable, keyUsages );
deriveKey(algorithm, baseKey, derivedKeyType,
          extractable, keyUsages );
deriveBits(algorithm, baseKey, length);
importKey(format, keyData, algorithm,
          extractable, keyUsages );
exportKey(format, key);
wrapKey(format, key,wrappingKey, wrapAlgorithm);
unwrapKey(format, wrappedKey, unwrappingKey,
          unwrapAlgorithm,  unwrappedKeyAlgorithm,
          extractable, keyUsages);
```

Fig. 2. CryptoOperation WebIDL

Table 1. CryptoOperations per Algorithm

Algorithm	encrypt	decrypt	sign	verify	digest	generateKey	deriveKey	deriveBits	importKey	exportKey	wrapKey	unwrapKey
RSAES-PKCS1-v1_5	•	•				•			•	•	•	•
ECDSA			•	•		•			•	•		
RSASSA-PKCS-v1_5			•	•		•			•	•		
RSA-PSS			•	•		•			•	•		
RSA-OAEP	•	•				•			•	•	•	•
ECDSA			•	•		•			•	•		
ECDH						•	•	•	•	•		
AES-CTR	•	•				•			•	•	•	•
AES-CBC	•	•				•			•	•	•	•
AES-CMAC			•	•		•			•	•		
AES-GCM	•	•				•			•	•	•	•
AES-CFB	•	•				•			•	•	•	•
AES-KW						•			•	•		•
HMAC			•	•		•			•	•		
DH						•	•	•	•	•		
SHA-1					•							
SHA-256					•							
SHA-384					•							
SHA-512					•							
CONCAT							•	•	•			
HKDF-CTR							•	•	•			
PBKDF2						•	•	•	•			

produces an error code. A simplified (no types) Javascript WebIDL interface for CryptoOperations is given in Fig. 2. Each algorithm then gives support for a number of operations as given in Table 1.

Examples may clarify the usage of the API. An example generate a signing key pair and sign some data is given in Fig. 3. More examples, including symmetric key encryption, are given in the specification [3].

Supported Algorithms. Each algorithm type is given by the CryptoOperation and the key generation. Keys generated with particular algorithms thus can have

```
var algorithmKeyGen = {
  name: "RSA-PSS",
  modulusLength: 2048,
  publicExponent: new Uint8Array([0x01, 0x00, 0x01]),
};

var algorithmSign = {
  name: "RSA-PSS",
  saltLength: 32,
  hash: {
    name: "SHA-256"
  }
};

window.crypto.subtle.generateKey(algorithmKeyGen, false, ["sign","verify"]).then(
  function(key) {
    var dataPart1 = convertPlainTextToArrayBufferView("hello,");
    var dataPart2 = convertPlainTextToArrayBufferView(" world!");
    return window.crypto.subtle.sign(algorithmSign, key.privateKey)
      .process(dataPart1)
      .process(dataPart2)
      .finish();
  },
  console.error.bind(console, "Unable to generate a key")
).then(
  console.log.bind(console, "The signature is: "),
  console.error.bind(console, "Unable to sign")
);
```

Fig. 3. Public Key signature example

their usages restricted to only those CryptoOperations permitted by the algorithm. We expect the Web Cryptography Working Group to be maintained over the long-term by the W3C, any requests for new algorithms can be sent to the Working Group for consideration and discussion with implementers. As the API is meant to be extensible in order to keep up with future developments within cryptography and to provide flexibility, there are no strictly required algorithms. However, in order to promote interoperability for developers, there are a number of algorithms that the API supports by default: RSA-PSS, RSA-OAEP, ECDSA, AES-CTR, AES-CMAC, AES-CFB, AES-KW, AES-CBC, HMAC, PKCS-v3 Diffie-Hellman (DH), the SHA family, CONCAT, HKDF-CTR, and PBKDF2. RSAES-PKCS1-v1_5 was supported but removed due to attacks described in this paper, see Sect. 5. These will be tested in the test-suite of the Web Cryptography API so developers will be able to easily ascertain with certainty if they can use these operations across browsers.

4   Formal Analysis

4.1   Threat Model

The threat model needs to be realistic in terms of actual attacks on the Web, and not too powerful. If we assume the origin is completely untrusted or compromised by an attacker, then the attacker can easily steal the application's secrets directly before they are encrypted. Thus, we assume the origin is trusted when the WebCrypto API is initialized and secrets are successfully encrypted and stored on the client.

Our threat model is then a temporary compromise of the Javascript environment being used by the server or client after secrets have been encrypted by WebCrypto and stored on the client. This accurately models most cross-site scripting (XSS) attacks on the Web, including DOM-based attacks on the client and temporary compromises of Javascript delivered by the server.

The security property that we want to maintain is that access to the raw key material that is private, secret, or explicitly typed as non-extractable should not be accessible to Javascript. These keys should only be accessible to a server with same-origin policy if key export is explicitly done to extractable key material.

The goal of the attacker is to retrieve previously encrypted secrets. This threat model's assumptions are built into our formalization, as seen from the rule definitions in Fig. 4. The inputs and outputs to each rule are either known by the attacker or stored on the client device.

4.2   Model

The models we used were constructed using the AVISPA toolset,[11] which was built to enable easy translation from protocol to model. The AVISPA toolset forms a hierarchical set of languages which take in a high-level protocol description and translate it through a series of steps to a low level description that functions as input to a model checking engine. Since AVISPA's high level language is tailored towards protocols and not API's, we designed our models in AVISPA's intermediate format (IF). AVISPA's IF format describes protocols modeled as an infinite state machine whose semantics is given via set re-writing.[12] Protocols are described unambiguously by sets of typed predicates which define states and rules which define state transitions. For example a predicate might take the following form:

$$keystore(K) : key \rightarrow fact$$

Which represents a $fact$-type predicate relating to a variable K of type key. States are defined by a list of applicable predicates. Transition rules take the form of having a list of predicates on the left hand side which must be true for the transition to occur. The right hand side lists predicates which are true

---

[11] http://www.avispa-project.org/.
[12] The formal semantics of AVISPA's higher-level HLPSL that subsumes IF are out of scope but are given here: http://www.avispa-project.org/delivs/2.1/d2-1.pdf.

$generateKey(key\ K, type\ T)$: $\rightarrow keystore(K,T) \wedge usages(K,T) \wedge extractable(K,T)$
$importKey(key\ K, type\ T)$: $iknows(K)$ $\rightarrow keystore(K,T) \wedge usages(K,T) \wedge extract(K,T)$
$extractkey(key\ K, type\ T)$: $keystore(K,T) \wedge extract(K,T)$ $\rightarrow iknows(K,T)$
$encrypt(key\ K, type\ T, message\ M)$: $keystore(K,T) \wedge encryptUsage(K) \wedge pub(T)$ $\rightarrow iknows(crypt(K,M))$
$sencrypt(key\ K, type\ T, message\ M)$: $keystore(K,T) \wedge encryptUsage(K) \wedge sym(T)$ $\rightarrow iknows(scrypt(K,M))$
$decrypt(key\ K, type\ T, message\ M)$: $keystore(K,T) \wedge decryptUsage(K) \wedge iknows(crypt(K,M)) \wedge priv(T)$ $\rightarrow iknows(M)$
$sdecrypt(key\ K, type\ T, message\ M)$: $keystore(K,T) \wedge decryptUsage(K) \wedge iknows(scrypt(K,M)) \wedge sym(T)$ $\rightarrow iknows(M)$
$sign(key\ K, type\ T, message\ M)$: $keystore(K,T) \wedge signUsage(K) \wedge priv(T)$ $\rightarrow iknows(crypt(K,M))$
$verify(key\ K, type\ T, message\ M)$: $keystore(K,T) \wedge verifyUsage(K) \wedge iknows(crypt(K,M)) \wedge pub(T)$ $\rightarrow iknows(M)$
$wrap(key\ K, type\ T, key\ WK)$: $keystore(K,T) \wedge wrapUsage(K) \wedge pub(T) \wedge keystore(WK) \wedge extract(WK)$ $\rightarrow iknows(crypt(K,WK))$
$swrap(key\ K, type\ T, key\ WK)$: $keystore(K,T) \wedge wrapUsage(K) \wedge sym(T) \wedge keystore(WK) \wedge extract(WK)$ $\rightarrow iknows(scrypt(K,WK))$
$unwrap(key\ K, type\ T, key\ WK, type\ WT)$: $keystore(K,T) \wedge unwrapUsage(K) \wedge iknows(crypt(K,WK)) \wedge priv(T)$ $\rightarrow keystore(WK,WT) \wedge extract(WK) \wedge usages(WK)$
$sunwrap(key\ K, type\ T, key\ WK, type\ WT)$: $keystore(K,T) \wedge unwrapUsage(K) \wedge iknows(scrypt(K,WK)) \wedge sym(T)$ $\rightarrow keystore(WK,WT) \wedge extract(WK) \wedge usages(WK)$

Fig. 4. Model for each API call. Note that all usages are allowed for created and imported keys, simplifying the model and giving the advantage to the attacker.

following the transition. The following shows an example rule which models encryption:[13]

$do\_encrypt(M, K) :=$
$\quad private\_data(M) \wedge keystore(K)$
$\quad \Rightarrow private\_data(scrypt(K, M))$

Initial states are described by declaring initial terms and predicates on them. Lowercase letters are used to represent instantiated terms. Uppercase letters denote free terms that may be bound to instance of the same type.

$k, K : key$
$m, M : message$

Initial predicates use instantiated terms:

$private\_data(m)$
$keystore(k)$

This example would initialize a state machine with the predicates $keystore(k)$ and $private\_data(m)$. The $do\_encrypt$ rule is applicable when $M = m$ and $K = k$.

AVISPA assumes an attacker following the standard DY model (where the attacker is called the "intruder") and is represented functionally by an $iknows$ predicate which dictates information known to the attacker. Further, the attacker has basic cryptographic capabilities. For example, the following rules would be applicable to the attacker independently of the modeled protocol:

$i\_encrypt(M, K) :=$
$\quad iknows(M) \wedge iknows(K)$
$\quad \Rightarrow iknows(scrypt(K, M))$
$i\_decrypt(M, K) :=$
$\quad iknows(scrypt(K, M)) \wedge iknows(K)$
$\quad \Rightarrow iknows(M)$

Consistent with the DY model, information communicated over the channel between actors is predicated with $iknows$. Thus, inputs to rules may be attacker created values and outputs are assumed to be learned to the by the attacker. This paradigm allows us to model compromised Javascript, where inputs may come from any source and outputs may be sent anywhere. The only state accessible to the API is the keys stored on the host, which we modeled with a $keystore$ predicate. The attacker in this model uses keys stored on the host. Our API rules use $iknows$ or $keystore$ to predicate inputs:

$api\_encrypt(M, K) :=$
$\quad iknows(M) \wedge keystore(K)$
$\quad \Rightarrow iknows(scrypt(K, M))$

The attacker goal states specify the conditions of a successful attack. For example, an attacker goal when testing confidentiality would be defined as a state in

---

[13] Throughout this paper we omit many AVISPA-specific constructs in order to focus on the underlying model. This includes statements that are necessary for modeling protocols but not APIs, but will nonetheless cause errors if omitted. The complete rules are available here: http://www.w3.org/2012/webcrypto/webcrypto_if_files.tgz.

which both the *iknows* predicate applies to a variable already declared secret by the *secret* predicate, for example:

Goal: $secrecy(M) := iknows(M) \wedge secret(M)$

4.3 API Model

To test properties of the API, we built a general API model which we then varied slightly to perform different tests. Creation of the general model includes custom predicates, transition rules representing API calls, and handling of key objects. The API call transition rules are built from both AVISPA's default predicates (*crypt, scrypt, iknows*, etc.) and custom predicates. The modeling for each rule is described in Fig. 4.

In addition to AVISPA's default predicates, several custom predicates were necessary to handle the modeling of key objects. The actual CryptoKey objects associates raw key data and the following set of attributes:

Type   Public, private or secret (symmetric)

Extractable A boolean specifying whether the key material may be exported to Javascript

Algorithm   The algorithm used to create the key

Usages   attributes which specify the key's allowed operations

Our modeled CryptoKey objects only represent the parts of the actual CryptoKey object. For efficiency reasons, our model expresses keys as *(type, value)* pairs. A key's attributes (*extractable, usages*) are represented by inclusion of that key in a set representing the particular attribute. For example, all keys with the *encrypt* usages are contained in a set named *Javascript_encrypt*. We ignore the algorithm attribute in our model.

Each entity is associated with a store of keys known to that entity. Each WebCrypto operation requires that the keys it will use be present in its associated entity's key store. Some operations (*generate, import, unwrap*) will add a key to the key store.

WebCrypto calls were translated directly into transition rules for our model. The predicates used are a combination of AVISPA defined (*crypt, scrypt, iknows*, etc.) and some that were specifically defined for this model. The predicates we defined are:

$$keystore(K, T):\text{ key is stored in local storage}$$
$$extract(K):\quad\quad \text{in extractable set}$$
$$usages(K):\quad\quad \text{all usages apply to key}$$
$$xUsage(K):\quad\quad \text{usage } x \text{ applies to key}$$
$$sym(T):\quad\quad\quad \text{key type is symmetric}$$
$$pub(T):\quad\quad\quad \text{key type is public}$$
$$priv(T):\quad\quad\quad \text{key type is private}$$

Modeling Specific Scenarios. Each individual scenario was created by customizing the models initial state and attack goal. After this step is done, the discovery of attacks is then fully automated by AVISPA. Some scenarios also included additional transition rules which allow more control over the behavior of the model. The additional rules serve as "unit operations" for each scenario. These operations model the equivalent of a sequence of individual API operations. Building unit operations for each test had two advantages. First, it optimizes the number of steps needed by the model checker in order to find attack sequences that include this sequence of steps. Second, constraints can be added to the model which require any found attack sequences to contain these operations. This allows modeling a scenario with the requirement that either the server or client fulfilled their role properly. A large number of scenarios were formalized, building up from simple to more complex in terms of properties by the use of these unit operations.

As an example, we look at the model used to check confidentiality of wrapped key exchange messages sent from client to server. This model is initialized with three key objects. The intent is to model two keys that belong to the client: one (*swkey*) for wrapping and the other (*skey*) to be exchanged securely. The third (*ikey*) key is known to the attacker and can be used in whatever way aids the attacker:

Instance Variables : $skey, swkey, ikey : key$
$$st, iwt, it : type$$

Initial State : $sym(st) \wedge secret(skey) \wedge secret(swkey)$
$$\wedge\ keystore(skey, st) \wedge keystore(swkey, swt)$$
$$\wedge\ keystore(ikey) \wedge usages(ikey)$$
$$\wedge\ iknows(ikey) \wedge extract(skey)$$
$$\wedge\ wrapUsage(swkey) \wedge unwrapUsage(skey)$$

The predicates in the initial state describe the properties of the keys using the predicates as described earlier. The goal state for this case was described by:

Goal : $secrecy(K) : secret(K) \wedge iknows(K)$

This goal specifies that for some variable key K, K has been defined to be both secret and known by the attacker. This goal was trivially achieved because $extract(skey)$ lets a secret key be marked as extractable which allows the attacker to export $skey$ and learn its value.

To force the model to find attack sequences that show how export attacks can effect operations such as key exchange with the key being explicitly extractable (as would be the case with secret key material by default), we modified our model slightly. First, we remove $extract(skey)$ from the initial state. Next we added a $c\_send()$ unit operation which wraps and sends a key without requiring either keys to be extractable:

$c\_send(key\ K, type\ T, key\ WK, type\ WT)$:
$$keystore(K, T) \wedge wrapUsage(K) \wedge keystore(WK, WT)$$
$$\Rightarrow iknows(\{WK\}_K) \wedge has\_sent(K) \wedge has\_sent(WK)$$

The *has_sent* fact is used to force this rule to be used. This is accomplished by modifying the goal state to be require that *has_sent(K)* be true, which can only happen after the *c_send* rule is used:

Goal: $secrecy(K) : secret(K) \wedge iknows(K) \wedge has\_sent(K)$

The attack found by the model checker for this set of modification is discussed in Sect. 4.4.

4.4   Tests and Results

We tested security properties by systematically modeling different use cases and assessing the resulting attacks. The attacks we found existed due to potentially unintuitive traits of the API, which would have negative security implications if misunderstood by a large audience. The interesting attacks fell into two types:

- **Export Attack:** Exporting extractable key data and changing usages.
- **API Attacks:** Using client API calls to recover clear text of encrypted communication via an attack on key wrapping.

To summarize, our analysis found that keys managed by the API, if wrapped and then unwrapped, then lose their usage properties. In particular this can be used to subvert operations such as key exchange and so reveal private key material.

Export Attack. While unextractable keys are appear safe, our attack shows there are no safeguards in place to preserve the usage attributes on extractable keys. Furthermore, any wrapped key can be unwrapped and then given arbitrary usage attributes. Thus, there is no guarantee that a key transmitted by wrapping will be used with the intended usages.

The test that revealed this property was modeled with a client initialized with two symmetric keys. One was an unextractable key with the wrap and unwrap usage enabled. The other key was extractable but had no usages enabled. The initial state and goal state are given below, where *skey* is the secret key and *ikey* is the key being under possession of the attacker (note that i is used as the "attacker" is called "the intruder" in AVISPA):

Instance Variables: $key, ikey : key$
$$st : type$$

Initial State: $sym(skey) \wedge sym(ikey)$
$$\wedge\ keystore(skey, st) \wedge keystore(ikey, st)$$
$$\wedge\ extract(skey) \wedge usages(ikey)$$

Goal: $addUsage() : encryptUsage(skey)$

Not only the *encrypt* usage, but all usages could be added simply by wrapping and unwrapping the extractable key: $wrap(skey, ikey), unwrap(skey, ikey)$. This simple single-host attack extends to wrapped keys transmitted between multiple hosts, and demonstrates the lack of control over usages: Once a key has been wrapped, the original usages with which it was created are lost, and new usages, as well as the choice to designate a key extractable, can be added during the unwrap operation.

Key Exchange API Attacks. The test case in Sect. 4.4 revealed the lack of key attribute preservation, and an attacker can be successful in deploying this strategy to reveal secret key material in key exchange and message passing protocols that use the WebCrypto API. A set of experiments, also done with the AVISPA model, involved keys sent between a client and server using various combinations of authentication and key wrapping.

Enumerating these cases also gives us insight into the security of general message exchanges based on WebCrypto: As key wrapping is a composition of export and encrypt, if an attack existed on a wrapped key, then the same attack would apply to an encrypted message. The combinations of encryption and authentication our model discovered compromises in are:

Symmetric encryption – The sender wraps the key using a symmetric key shared with the receiver who unwraps the key
Asymmetric encryption – The sender wraps the key using public key for the receiver who unwraps with the corresponding private key
Symmetric encryption with asymmetric signing – The symmetric encryption case augmented by signing with the sender's private key
Asymmetric encryption with asymmetric signing – The asymmetric encryption case augmented by signing with the sender's private key

Each test was initialized with enough keys to allow the client and server's task to be modeled as well as the attacker. We modeled multiple versions of each scenario: one matching the current API specification and a second restricted version designed to show changes that could reduce attacks. The attacks are described in a number of tables. Operations in the attack sequences are prepended with an identifier specifying the entity that performed the operation: **ijs-** malicious Javascript controlled by the attacker, **i-** the attacker, **c-** the client Javascript running honestly, and **s-** the honest server.

Table 2 shows attacks found by testing confidentiality of keys sent from client to server. A successful attack involves the attacker learning a key that was also defined as secret. In the cases using symmetric encryption, the basic model used a symmetric wrapping key that had both wrap and unwrap usages enabled. These cases allowed API attacks where the secret key was unwrapped and given export privileges and then extracted. The restricted cases were modeled by removing the unwrap usage from the client's wrapping key, which removed this attack as well as the export attack on the key. The asymmetric case did allow export attacks but not API attacks.

Table 2. Client → Server confidentiality attacks

Scenario	Export	API
Symmetric Encryption		
Single key for wrap and unwrap	Yes	*c-send, ijs-unwrap, ijs-extractKey*
Different key for each direction	Yes	*None*
Asymmetric Encryption		
No Restrictions	Yes	*None*
No key extraction	None	*None*
Symmetric Encryption with Asymmetric Authentication		
No Restrictions	Yes	*c-send, i-verify, ijs-unwrap, ijs-extractKey*
Client wrapping key cannot unwrap	None	*None*
Asymmetric Encryption with Asymmetric Authentication		
No Restrictions	Yes	*None*
No key extraction	None	*None*

Table 3. Server → Client confidentiality attacks

Scenario	API
Symmetric Encryption	
No Restrictions	*s-send, ijs-unwrap, ijs-extractKey*
Different keys for wrap and unwrap	*s-send, s-unwrap, s-extractKey*
Asymmetric Encryption	
No Restrictions	*s-send, ijs-unwrap, ijs-extractKey*
Different keys for wrap and unwrap	*s-send, s-unwrap, s-extractKey*
Symmetric Encryption with Asymmetric Authentication	
No Restrictions	*s-send, i-verify, ijs-unwrap, ijs-extractKey*
Asymmetric Encryption with Asymmetric Authentication	
No Restrictions	*s-send, i-verify, ijs-unwrap, ijs-extractKey*

Table 3 covers confidentiality attacks but this time for keys sent from server to client. In these scenarios all base cases were susceptible to an API attack which caused the key received from the server to be imported as extractable and then immediately exported. No modifications were found which prevented this attack.

Table 4 shows integrity attacks on the same set of scenarios as Table 2. The successful attack was modeled as a key, originally known only to the attacker, being stored in the server's key store. For most cases, both symmetric and asymmetric, API attacks allowed an attacker to send a key to the server by importing that key into the client and using API calls to wrap and possibly sign the key. The only modification we found preventing this attack was to disallow use of one of the keys, but this may not be practical in real world use cases.

Table 4. Client → Server integrity attacks

Scenario	API
Symmetric Encryption	
Single key for wrap and unwrap	*ijs-importKey, ijs-wrap, s-receive*
Different key for each direction	*ijs-importKey, ijs-wrap, s-receive*
Asymmetric Encryption	
No Restrictions	*ijs-encrypt, s-receive*
Signing key removed before malicious code runs	*None*
Symmetric Encryption with Asymmetric Authentication	
No Restrictions	*ijs-importKey, ijs-wrap, ijs-sign, s-receive*
Client wrapping key cannot unwrap	*None*
Asymmetric Encryption with Asymmetric Authentication	
No Restrictions	*ijs-importKey, ijs-wrap, ijs-sign, s-receive*
Signing key removed before malicious code runs	*None*

Table 5. Server → Client integrity attacks.

Scenario	API
Symmetric Encryption	
Same key for wrap and unwrap	*ijs-importKey, ijs-wrap, c-receive*
Different keys for wrap and unwrap	*None*
Asymmetric Encryption	
No Restrictions	*i-wrap, c-receive*
Symmetric Encryption with Asymmetric Authentication	
No Restrictions	*None*
Asymmetric Encryption with Asymmetric Authentication	
No Restrictions	*None*

The integrity attacks shown in Table 5 on keys sent from server to client yield fewer API attacks. API attacks exist for the cases where the attacker has access to the wrapping key. This is the symmetric case where the client's key has wrap and unwrap usages as well as the asymmetric case where the encryption key is public by default. With authentication required, no API attacks were found.

These results lead to a few general observations. Export attacks are often available because keys that can be wrapped are also then extractable; any key that can be exported from the client can be retrieved in the clear by an attacker even though the wrapping is intended to keep the key secret. The found API attacks have a common element of using a key stored on the client to perform cryptographic operations. Some of these attacks are caused by the fact that the *extractable* attribute and *usages* array are not preserved for wrapped keys, and unwrapped keys can be given any new combination of attributes, including *extractable*. Other attacks could be mitigated by limiting the usability of stored keys. For example in the symmetric encryption case, if one key is used for both directions, the attacker can use the client's keys to both encrypt and decrypt the communication. However, using distinct keys for each direction of communication and reinforcing this behavior with *usages* attributes prevents this type of attack assuming the usages are not changed. Thus, the successful API attacks could be prevented if usages were bound to key material in general and not allowed to be altered while the key is being stored. Lastly, authenticating via asymmetric keys where extractability of key material is not allowed prevents the attacks on confidentiality and integrity of keys from the server to the client.

5   Algorithm-Level Analysis

In our formal analysis, we treated algorithms as "black boxes" in the analysis of cryptographic primitives. This is because some of the attacks on security APIs are beyond the scope of the DY model employed by AVISPA. For example, formal models do not in general deal with attacks like *oracle attacks* that observe the error messages that are returned by the API. Furthermore, some algorithms have well-known weaknesses.

In this review, we limit ourselves to peer-reviewed results on the algorithms which have been included in the first Candidate Recommendation version of the WebCrypto API, although the precise algorithms are still in flux due to interoperability testing. Table 6 summarizes the results. Although none of these results or attacks are new in terms of cryptanalysis, the fact that they were present in the WebCrypto API should be explicitly noted. After this analysis, RSAES-PKCS1-v1_5 was removed from the specification and the problems with padding error return codes were corrected.

There is at least one annual publication, the ENISA "Algorithms, Key Size and Parameters Report," whose aim is to track ongoing developments, which discusses a much larger set of algorithms in much greater depth. Our results are in general the same except for algorithms ENISA does not cover like PBKDF2 and AES-KW [37].[14] We note that HKDF has security proofs [26] but needs more study. Security models for password-based key derivation functions are still in a state of flux [42]. PBKDF2 has known weaknesses [43], and many implementations do not use enough iterations.

In detail, the main problematic algorithm originally included in WebCrypto was *RSAES-PKCS1-v1_5*, which has been known to be vulnerable to a chosen ciphertext attack (CCA) since 1998 [12]. The attack has recently been improved to require a median of less than 15 000 chosen ciphertexts on the standard oracle [5]. Instances of the attack in widely-deployed real-world systems continue to be found [23]. Finally, note also that as of version 1.3, RSAES-PKCS1-v1_5 will be dropped from the TLS standard.[15] In terms of alternatives, there are no publicly known attacks on RSASSA-PKCS1-v1_5 but no security proofs and

---

[14] Note as of September 2016, the 2014 report is currently under revision.

[15] http://www.ietf.org/mail-archive/web/tls/current/msg12362.html.

Table 6. Algorithm summary

Algorithm/Mode	Ok legacy	Ok future	Note
RSAES-PKCS1-v1_5	×	×	
RSA-OAEP	✓	✓	
RSASSA-PKCS1-v1_5	✓	×	No security proof
RSA-PSS	✓	✓	
ECDSA	✓	×	Weak provable security results
ECDH	✓	✓	
AES-CBC	✓	✓	NB not CCA secure
AES-CFB	✓	✓	NB not CCA secure
AES-CTR	✓	✓	NB not CCA secure
AES-GCM	✓	✓	
AES-CMAC	✓	✓	
AES-KW	✓	×	No public security proof
HMAC	✓	✓	
DH	✓	✓	
SHA-1	×	×	See text
SHA-256	✓	✓	
SHA-384	✓	✓	
SHA-512	✓	✓	
CONCAT	✓	✓	
HKDF-CTR	✓	✓	
PBKDF2	✓	×	Known weaknesses (see text)

no advantages compared to other RSA-based schemes, while RSA-PSS has a security proof due to Bellare and Rogaway [8] in the random oracle model.

There are also some inevitable issues with elliptic curve cryptography, which is in an ongoing state of flux in both WebCrypto and wider internet standards. In particular, ECDSA has some provable security results but only in weak models [42]. There is debate on elliptic curves.[16] ECDH has provable security results [14], but like other plain DH modes it offers no authenticity, so this must be handled separately. A proposal exists to include Curve25519 [32] after the browsers are finished implementing the CFRG recommendations. In general, we recommend using only named curves with wide public review.

In terms of AES, there are well-known issues with *AES-CBC* mode that are not currently believed to pose a practical threat [25], and it is not CCA secure. Both *AES-CBC* and *AES-CFB* are secure against chosen plaintext attacks (CPA-secure) if the IV is random, but not if the IV is a nonce [35]. In particular *AES-CFB* does not tolerate a padding oracle [41] - indeed, in practice,

---

[16] http://safecurves.cr.yp.to/.

padding oracle attacks are common [29, 31, 33]. The padding mode [24] is exactly that which gives rise to most of these attacks. *AES-KW* has received various criticisms, for example being inconsistent in its notions of security (requiring IND-CCA from a deterministic mode), but though it has no public security proof, it has no known attacks either [34]. *AES-CTR* is probably the best mode of the traditional AES modes, although the mode is easy to mis-use and thus in general *AES-GCM* should be preferred (ideally with an explicit safeguard to prevent re-usage of the IV). Since WebCrypto does not contain guidance on composing AES modes with a MAC and does not prevent the re-usage of an IV, care needs to be taken by developers.

Due to the inclusion of AES-CBC and the consideration of RSAES-PKCS1-v1.5, padding attacks against these protocols would be a threat to both encrypted

Table 7. Explanation of padding attacks

	Attacking Encrypted Text	Attacking Wrapped Keys
PKCS1-v1.5	**Potential Attack** – PKCS1-v1.5 padding is susceptible to known oracle attacks when an attacker can discern that decryption failed due to incorrect padding. The API specifies that failure to decrypt should result in a `OperationError`. Causes of this failure are incorrect padding (either incorrect leading bytes or not enough padding) and a cipher text that is out of range of the RSA modulus. (The latter can be prevented in the attack.) These are the only possible causes of the `OperationError` from PKCS1-v1.5 decryption, leading to the possibility that a decryption oracle is exposed to the attacker	**Potential Attack** – Similarly to the attack against encryption, the error given when unwrapping an incorrectly padded key is an `OperationError`. However, the error that results from a correctly padded but incorrectly formatted key (which would be used in the attack) is a `DataError`. If the difference in errors in not concealed from attackers, an attack would be able to recover wrapped keys
AES-CBC	**Potential Attack** – AES-CBC is known to be susceptible to padding oracle attacks when an attacker can discern that a particular cipher text cannot be decrypted due to a padding error. The API specifies that this error is a `DataError`. The only other source of this error during the *decrypt* operation is an incorrect initialization vector length, which the attacker could check given access to the IV	**No Obvious Attack** – A successful attack requires the ability to differentiate between keys that cannot be unwrapped due to 1) incorrect padding and 2) incorrect key length or structure that cannot be parsed. In both cases, the error specified by the API is the same and no other test is apparent to distinguish between the two

messages and wrapped keys in WebCrypto. Table 7 explains how these vulnerabilities manifest themselves in the Webcrypto API. After these attacks were discussed with the W3C Web Cryptography Working Group due to the analysis presented in this paper, *RSAES-PKCS1-v1_5* had its support removed from the W3C Web Cryptography specification. Also, errors that could lead to attacks on AES-CBC wrapped keys, such as *DataError*, were removed from the spec where necessary and replaced with *OperationError* that could not distinguish between a key and padding operation. This should be considered a good example of a standards-based Working Group working well with knowledge from the cryptographic community.

5.1 AES-CBC Wrapped Keys

It is worth noting that despite the API's resistance to padding attacks against AES-CBC wrapped keys, this vulnerability could easily emerge through implementation errors or misuse of the API. To guard against implementation errors, we recommend the following checks:

- All errors caused by improper padding or incorrect key length/formatting are indistinguishable. (Padding errors will be returned from a different subroutine than the other errors and be discovered first, so any information about the *source* of the error is potentially a distinguishing factor.)
- Lengths of unwrapped keys are verified to match one of the predefined key lengths.
- All bytes of padding are checked for conformance.

Of these three recommendations, the first was accepted in to the specification. Additionally, the specific key lengths reduce the search space of a brute force attack against 192 and 256 bit keys. Unwrapping a 256 bit key as if it was 192 bits requires guessing only the 64 bits that need to be (wrongly) interpreted as padding for unwrapping to be successful. Thus the problem is reduced to finding a 192 bit key. These, in turn, require guessing another 64 bits in order to be unwrapped as if they were 128 bit keys. From there, the problem is equivalent finding a 128 bit key. Thus, brute forcing 192 and 256 bit keys takes at most $2^{128} + 2^{64}$ and $2^{128} + 2^{65}$ guesses respectively, which is less than the traditional brute force attack. Lastly, it should be mentioned that if the attacker is given an oracle that uses the *decrypt* operation instead of the *unwrap* operation with the same key used for wrapping, a standard padding attack may be able to recover wrapped keys.

5.2 High-Level API Recommendations

Although the API does not provide "safe" defaults, the IRTF CFRG (CryptoForum Research Group) created a document to track known security flaws, attacks, and the status of formal security proofs for each algorithm in the API.[17] From

---

[17] https://www.w3.org/2012/webcrypto/draft-irtf-cfrg-webcrypto-algorithms-01.
html.

our analysis, it is quite clear what the recommend modes should be in general for a developer-friendly "high-level" API that also automatically took care of IV vector initialization and other parameters. For RSA-based algorithms, *RSA-PSS* should be used for signing and verification while *RSA-OAEP* should be used for encryption and decryption. It is likely that Curve 25519 support should be added. Standardised by NIST, *AES-GCM* is gaining traction in standards such as IPsec, MACSec, P1619.1, and TLS [35]. Regarding *DH*, more protocols are now favoring *ECDH* as attacks against "weak" standard Diffie-Hellman groups are not as powerful against elliptic curves due to a loss of a clear precomputation-based advantage [1]. HMAC has well-studied security proofs, even if the underlying hash function is not (weak) collision resistant [7]. In terms of hashing functions, of course *SHA-2* is to be preferred due to the amount of increased feasibility of practical methods of obtaining collisions for SHA-1.[18] As regard key size, in-line with NIST and ENISA [37], larger key sizes should be preferred such as RSA keys of at least 2048 bits and 256 bits for symmetric keys and elliptic curve cryptography.

6   Conclusions

6.1   Fixing the Web Cryptography API

In summary, the Web Cryptography API had three attacks, of which only one still stands. The attack that is still present is that the usages of keys are not preserved upon export that can be exploited in numerous ways to reveal not only wrapped secret key material sent from between the client and server but also disrupt authenticated key exchange. A number of simple mitigations would prevent this attack. The most general solution would be to prevent usages from being changed, but this binds key usages to a key throughout its lifespan. A more limited mitigation that would address only the unique case of wrapping would be to have key wrapping require that the properties of a wrapped and then unwrapped key be preserved, and not require the export of the wrapped key before wrapping. Wrapping could be done outside the general Javascript environment and only the wrapped key material exposed. One way to implement this option would be to inherit the property of being unextractable from the wrapping key to the wrapped key by default. Another more restrictive option would be to prevent wrapping and unwrapping. Earlier errors involving padding attacks being made possible due to error types were corrected, and the $RSAES-PKCS1-v1\_5$ algorithm was correctly removed from the specification due to the analysis presented in this paper. However, the API does not suffer from the fatal errors in its key management that can be detected via formal modeling, such as PKCS#11 [17] or the Yubikey [27].

In detail, the handling of key attributes in the API does not create a clear intuition about their actual effect as the *usages* may not always be supported, and so will confuse developers about key management across the boundary

---

[18] https://sites.google.com/site/itstheshappening/.

between client and server. For any key transported between either client and server or server and client, the *usages* array may be changed arbitrarily. In other words, the originating host has no control over the usages a key has once imported onto another host. Another limitation is that keys are either extractable or not, and must be extractable in order to be wrapped. As demonstrated, extractable keys are easily attacked and can be retrieved (including maliciously) from a client with a single API call. Although seemingly harmless insofar as we would assume a correctly designed Web application would only allow keys to be extractable on purpose, this produces counter-intuitive results when mixed with wrapping, as restricting keys to be wrapped to be extractable forces the aforementioned vulnerabilities. This wrapping attack was verified in all conformant Web Crypto implementations, including Chrome, Edge, and Fire-Fox. Furthermore, it prevents WebCrypto for being used for use-cases such as those proposed by Netflix to ensure secure delivery of key material to clients. This attack also prevents users from sharing long-term private keys that are unknown to the server between sessions by virtue of wrapping and sending to the server and then downloading the wrapped keys into private local storage when a successful authentication is completed. This is a widely requested feature for those wanting some ability to authenticate without the server being able to easily impersonate a user by having access to all the user's secrets.

The lack of a long-term key storage model combined with a lack of persistent key usages may be detrimental to the usage of Web Cryptography. Without guidance, developers may make poor choices that do not meet expectations when storing key material, as the lifetime of these keys is tied to the execution environment. While this provides many positive security and privacy benefits, to retain a key for use in later sessions developers will need to make use of a persistent key storage service on the server using the previously described problematic key exporting and wrapping routines. As it would be expected then that key wrapping in order to send keys from the client to the server (and back again upon revisiting the page) will be used to preserve long-term keys, the key wrapping attacks mentioned earlier are particularly dangerous. One suggestion is that future versions of the specification should likely tie private keys and wrapping operations with special processing outside of the normal Javascript environment, or even more ambitiously try to use a trusted environment to secure keys and cryptographic operations. This may require some kind of tie between hardware tokens for keys and their operations. Recently, the W3C has been exploring adding hardware token access to the Web Cryptography API in their "Web Cryptography v.Next" workshop, and so the next version of the API may support both secure multi-session key storage and cryptographic operations on those keys via some form of a trusted execution environment[19] as well as access via

---

[19] Such as ARM TrustZone.

next-generation authentication APIs such as FIDO[20] to origin-bound platform-held keys via call-response requests that do not reveal the secret key material.[21]

Standards to assure the end user of the integrity of Javascript code would prevent many of these attacks. Only recently has the W3C begun to develop standards to secure Javascript code, and these tend to be quite simple such as the Sub-resource Integrity W3C standard that allows the hash of Javascript to be checked before running [15] or Content Security Policy [6] that restricts the domain of Javascript being run. In detail, Sub-resource Integrity requires Javascript linked or imported as a script to match a particular hash before execution and so could prevent some of these cross-scripting attacks or where a third-party library has been exploited in order to gain access to the origin. There does not yet exist for Javascript a way to securely install code, such as has been done via signed code in Linux-based operating systems, much less the more comprehensive necessary precautions taken into account by The Update Framework.[22] While signed Javascript may seem difficult, many other systems such as native applications have moved to such a model and so it should not be surprising if the Web itself may need to adopt signed code. In fact, the hashes of popular Javascript code could even be imagined to be stored in a Merkle-tree based append-only log such as those being designed in Certificate Transparency [28]. Also, there does not exist a standard way to defend the entry in cleartext of data in locally-running Javascript from the server.

These kinds of attacks could also be countered by creating higher-level libraries that make it easier to use the Web Cryptography API and avoid having developers make decisions of key usages and key exporting. This design could be validated if there was a large-scale study of the usage of the Web Cryptography API amongst web developers attempting to solve common tasks with the API, with an eye towards common errors and mistakes with defaults and for attacks such as those detailed in this paper.

6.2   Next Steps for Standards Research

More formal research is needed on the larger framework of the Web Cryptography API and the Web security model, with a focus on the possible interactions between Web Cryptography and other APIs that are part of HTML5. Ideally, the entire Web Security Model needs to be formalized and modeled, and it only makes sense formalizing the security analysis of the Web Cryptography as part of this larger analysis as most applications will use multiple APIs with possibly contradictory security policies. It would make sense to engage in a thorough study to be able to determine important security properties such as safe key storage in both the specification and implementations thereof when the WebCrypto

---

[20] http://www.fidoalliance.org.

[21] For details of the W3C Web Cryptography v.Next workshop that dealt with hardware tokens, FIDO, and trusted execution environments, see http://www.w3.org/2012/webcrypto/webcrypto-next-workshop/.

[22] http://theupdateframework.com/.

API is used in combination with other APIs that allow low-level access to a browser's localstorage.

The process of formal modeling would be helpful if integrated into the standardization process to understand the security properties of APIs and their complex interactions with other APIs. One approach would be to include it at the early stages of the design of the standard. If it were, it could both correct early flaws, but would require considerable investment in updating the model. Another option would be do the formal model as part of the security review, although such a security review is currently optional at the W3C. Another option would be to include the formal modeling as part of the test-suite necessary to reach standardiation, where the test-suite must demonstrate security properties. One possible incentive structure is that just as currently W3C specifications require conformance testing via a test-suite to be done manually, the automatic generation of a test-suite using formal methods would both save the developers time and lead to a more thorough test-suite. The formally-generated test-suite could then be tested against real-world implementations in order to prove interoperability and conformance. The use of formal methods for testing is currently under development for the new Web Authentication API (formerly the "FIDO 2.0" API) that attempts to supplement passwords with one-factor cryptographic authentication.[23] In general, we hope that formal analysis of Web APIs will lead to a more secure Web that is better understood and easier to use for developers.

References

1. Adrian, D., Bhargavan, K., Durumeric, Z., Gaudry, P., Green, M., Halderman, J.A., Heninger, N., Springall, D., Thomé, E., Valenta, L., et al.: Imperfect forward secrecy: how Diffie-Hellman fails in practice. In: Proceedings of the 22nd ACM SIGSAC Conference on Computer and Communications Security, pp. 5–17. ACM (2015)
2. Akhawe, D., Barth, A., Lam, P.E., Mitchell, J., Song, D.: Towards a formal foundation of web security. In: Proceedings of the 2010 23rd IEEE Computer Security Foundations Symposium, CSF 2010, pp. 290–304. IEEE Computer Society, Washington, DC, USA (2010)
3. Sleevi, R., Watson, M.: Web Cryptography API. Candidate recommendation, IETF (2014). http://www.w3.org/TR/WebCryptoAPI/
4. Bansal, C., Bhargavan, K., Delignat-Lavaud, A., Maffeis, S.: Keys to the cloud: formal analysis and concrete attacks on encrypted web storage. In: Basin, D., Mitchell, J.C. (eds.) POST 2013. LNCS, vol. 7796, pp. 126–146. Springer, Heidelberg (2013). doi:10.1007/978-3-642-36830-1_7
5. Bardou, R., Focardi, R., Kawamoto, Y., Simionato, L., Steel, G., Tsay, J.-K.: Efficient padding oracle attacks on cryptographic hardware. In: Safavi-Naini, R., Canetti, R. (eds.) CRYPTO 2012. LNCS, vol. 7417, pp. 608–625. Springer, Heidelberg (2012). doi:10.1007/978-3-642-32009-5_36
6. Barth, A., Veditz, D., West, M.: Content Security Policy level 1.1. Working draft, W3C (2012). http://www.w3.org/TR/2014/WD-CSpp.11-20140211/

---

[23] https://www.w3.org/TR/webauthn.

7. Bellare, M.: New proofs for NMAC and HMAC: security without collision-resistance. In: Dwork, C. (ed.) CRYPTO 2006. LNCS, vol. 4117, pp. 602–619. Springer, Heidelberg (2006). doi:10.1007/11818175_36

8. Bellare, M., Rogaway, P.: The exact security of digital signatures-how to sign with RSA and Rabin. In: Maurer, U. (ed.) EUROCRYPT 1996. LNCS, vol. 1070, pp. 399–416. Springer, Heidelberg (1996). doi:10.1007/3-540-68339-9_34

9. Beurdouche, B., Bhargavan, K., Delignat-Lavaud, A., Fournet, C., Kohlweiss, M., Pironti, A., Strub, P.-Y., Zinzindohoue, J.K.: A messy state of the union: taming the composite state machines of TLS. In: 2015 IEEE Symposium on Security and Privacy (SP), pp. 535–552. IEEE (2015)

10. Bhargavan, K., Lavaud, A.D., Fournet, C., Pironti, A., Strub, P.-Y.: Triple handshakes and cookie cutters: breaking and fixing authentication over TLS. In: 2014 IEEE Symposium on Security and Privacy (SP), pp. 98–113. IEEE (2014)

11. Blanchet, B.: An efficient cryptographic protocol verifier based on prolog rules. In: Proceedings of the 14th IEEE Workshop on Computer Security Foundations, CSFW 2001, pp. 82–96. IEEE Computer Society, Washington, DC, USA (2001)

12. Bleichenbacher, D.: Chosen ciphertext attacks against protocols based on the RSA encryption standard PKCS #1. In: Krawczyk, H. (ed.) CRYPTO 1998. LNCS, vol. 1462, pp. 1–12. Springer, Heidelberg (1998). doi:10.1007/BFb0055716

13. Bond, M., Anderson, R.: API-level attacks on embedded systems. Computer 34(10), 67–75 (2001)

14. Boneh, D., Shparlinski, I.E.: On the unpredictability of bits of the elliptic curve Diffie-Hellman scheme. In: Kilian, J. (ed.) CRYPTO 2001. LNCS, vol. 2139, pp. 201–212. Springer, Heidelberg (2001). doi:10.1007/3-540-44647-8_12

15. Braun, F., Akhawe, D., Weinberger, J., West, M.: Subresource Integrity. Working draft, W3C (2014). http://www.w3.org/TR/SRI/

16. Cremers, C.J.F.: The Scyther tool: verification, falsification, and analysis of security protocols. In: Gupta, A., Malik, S. (eds.) CAV 2008. LNCS, vol. 5123, pp. 414–418. Springer, Heidelberg (2008). doi:10.1007/978-3-540-70545-1_38

17. Delaune, S., Kremer, S., Steel, G.: Formal security analysis of PKCS#11 and proprietary extensions. J. Comput. Secur. 18(6), 1211–1245 (2010)

18. Dennis, G., Chang, F.S.-H., Jackson, D.: Modular verification of code with SAT. In: Proceedings of the ACM/SIGSOFT International Symposium on Software Testing and Analysis, ISSTA 2006, 17–20 July 2006, Portland, Maine, USA, pp. 109–120 (2006)

19. Dolev, D., Yao, A.: On the security of public key protocols. IEEE Trans. Inf. Theory 29(2), 198–208 (1983)

20. Georgiev, M., Iyengar, S., Jana, S., Anubhai, R., Boneh, D., Shmatikov, V.: The most dangerous code in the world: validating SSL certificates in non-browser software. In: Proceedings of the 2012 ACM Conference on Computer and Communications Security, CCS 2012, pp. 38–49. ACM, New York (2012)

21. Halpin, H.: The W3C web cryptography API: motivation and overview. In: Proceedings of the Companion Publication of the 23rd International Conference on World Wide Web Companion, WWW Companion 2014, pp. 959–964, Republic and Canton of Geneva, Switzerland. International World Wide Web Conferences Steering Committee (2014)

22. Jackson, D.: Alloy: a lightweight object modelling notation. ACM Trans. Softw. Eng. Methodol. 11(2), 256–290 (2002)

23. Jager, T., Schinzel, S., Somorovsky, J.: Bleichenbacher's attack strikes again: breaking PKCS#1 v1.5 in XML encryption. In: Foresti, S., Yung, M., Martinelli, F. (eds.) ESORICS 2012. LNCS, vol. 7459, pp. 752–769. Springer, Heidelberg (2012). doi:10.1007/978-3-642-33167-1_43

24. Kaliski, B.: PKCS #7: Cryptographic Message Syntax. RSA Security Inc., v1.5. https://www.ietf.org/rfc/rfc2315.txt

25. Kaminsky, A., Kurdziel, M., Radziszowski, S.: An overview of cryptanalysis research for the advanced encryption standard. In: 2010 Military Communications Conference - MILCOM 2010 (2010)

26. Krawczyk, H.: Cryptographic extraction and key derivation: the HKDF scheme. In: Rabin, T. (ed.) CRYPTO 2010. LNCS, vol. 6223, pp. 631–648. Springer, Heidelberg (2010). doi:10.1007/978-3-642-14623-7_34

27. Künnemann, R., Steel, G.: YubiSecure? Formal security analysis results for the Yubikey and YubiHSM. In: Jøsang, A., Samarati, P., Petrocchi, M. (eds.) STM 2012. LNCS, vol. 7783, pp. 257–272. Springer, Heidelberg (2013). doi:10.1007/978-3-642-38004-4_17

28. Laurie, B., Langley, A., Kasper, E.: RFC 6962 Certificate Transparency. Experimental, IETF (2013). https://tools.ietf.org/html/rfc6962

29. Mitchell, C.J.: Error Oracle attacks on CBC mode: is there a future for CBC mode encryption? In: Zhou, J., Lopez, J., Deng, R.H., Bao, F. (eds.) ISC 2005. LNCS, vol. 3650, pp. 244–258. Springer, Heidelberg (2005). doi:10.1007/11556992_18

30. Near, J.P., Jackson, D.: Derailer: interactive security analysis for web applications. In: Proceedings of the 29th IEEE/ACM International Conference on Automated Software Engineering (ASE), pp. 587–598. IEEE/ACM (2014)

31. Paterson, K.G., Yau, A.: Padding Oracle attacks on the ISO CBC mode encryption standard. In: Okamoto, T. (ed.) CT-RSA 2004. LNCS, vol. 2964, pp. 305–323. Springer, Heidelberg (2004). doi:10.1007/978-3-540-24660-2_24

32. Perrin, T.: Web Cryptography API. Editor's draft, W3C (2014). http://github.com/trevp/curve25519_webcrypto

33. Rizzo, J.: Duong., T.: Practical padding Oracle attacks. In: Proceedings of the 4th USENIX Conference on Offensive Technologies, WOOT 2010, pp. 1–8. USENIX Association, Berkeley, CA, USA (2010)

34. Rogaway, P., Shrimpton, T.: A provable-security treatment of the key-wrap problem. In: Vaudenay, S. (ed.) EUROCRYPT 2006. LNCS, vol. 4004, pp. 373–390. Springer, Heidelberg (2006). doi:10.1007/11761679_23

35. Rogaway, P.: Evaluation of some blockcipher modes of operation. Technical report, University of California, Davis, Evaluation carried out for the Cryptography Research and Evaluation Committees (CRYPTREC) for the Government of Japan, February 2011

36. Schmidt, B., Sasse, R., Cremers, C., Basin, D.: Automated verification of group key agreement protocols. In: 2014 IEEE Symposium on Security and Privacy (SP), pp. 179–194. IEEE (2014)

37. Smart, N.P., Rijmen, V., Warinschi, B., Watson, G., Patterson, K., Stam, M.: Algorithms, key sizes and parameters report: 2014 recommendations. Technical report, November 2014. ENISA Report. Version 1.0

38. Stark, E., Hamburg, M., Boneh, D.: Symmetric cryptography in Javascript. In: Proceedings of the 2009 Annual Computer Security Applications Conference, ACSAC 2009, pp. 373–381. IEEE Computer Society, Washington, DC, USA (2009)

39. Taly, A., Erlingsson, Ú., Mitchell, J.C., Miller, M.S., Nagra, J.: Automated analysis of security-critical Javascript APIs. In: Proceedings of the 2011 IEEE Symposium on Security and Privacy, SP 2011, pp. 363–378. IEEE Computer Society, Washington, DC, USA (2011)
40. Torlak, E., Taghdiri, M., Dennis, G., Near, J.P.: Applications and extensions of alloy: past, present and future. Math. Struct. Comput. Sci. **23**(4), 915–933 (2013)
41. Vaudenay, S.: Security flaws induced by CBC padding — applications to SSL, IPSEC, WTLS. In: Knudsen, L.R. (ed.) EUROCRYPT 2002. LNCS, vol. 2332, pp. 534–545. Springer, Heidelberg (2002). doi:10.1007/3-540-46035-7_35
42. Wen, C.C., Dawson, E., González Nieto, J.M., Simpson, L.: A framework for security analysis of key derivation functions. In: Ryan, M.D., Smyth, B., Wang, G. (eds.) ISPEC 2012. LNCS, vol. 7232, pp. 199–216. Springer, Heidelberg (2012). doi:10.1007/978-3-642-29101-2_14
43. Yao, F.F., Yin, Y.L.: Design and analysis of password-based key derivation functions. In: Menezes, A. (ed.) CT-RSA 2005. LNCS, vol. 3376, pp. 245–261. Springer, Heidelberg (2005). doi:10.1007/978-3-540-30574-3_17

Algorithm Agility – Discussion on TPM 2.0 ECC Functionalities

Liqun Chen[1,2] and Rainer Urian[3(✉)]

[1] Hewlett Packard Laboratories, Palo Alto, USA
liqun.chen@hpe.com
[2] University of Surrey, Guildford, UK
liqun.chen@surrey.ac.uk
[3] Infineon Technologies AG, Neubiberg, Germany
rainer.urian@infineon.com

Abstract. The TPM 2.0 specification has been designed to support a number of Elliptic Curve Cryptographic (ECC) primitives, such as key exchange, digital signatures and Direct Anonymous Attestation (DAA). In order to meet the requirement that different TPM users may favor different cryptographic algorithms, each primitive can be implemented from multiple algorithms. This feature is called *Algorithm Agility*. For the purpose of performance efficiency, multiple algorithms share a small set of TPM commands. In this paper, we review all the TPM 2.0 ECC functionalities, and discuss on whether the existing TPM commands can be used to implement new cryptographic algorithms which have not yet been addressed in the specification. We demonstrate that four asymmetric encryption schemes specified in ISO/IEC 18033-2 can be implemented using a TPM 2.0 chip, and we also show on some ECDSA variants that the coverage of algorithm agility from TPM 2.0 is limited. Security analysis of algorithm agility is a challenge, which is not responded in this paper. However, we believe that this paper will help future researchers analyze TPM 2.0 in more comprehensive methods than it has been done so far.

Keywords: Algorithm Agility · Elliptic Curve Cryptography · Trusted Platform Module

1 Introduction

Trusted Platform Module (TPM) is an international standard for a tamper-resistant crypto processor. TPM's technical specification is developed by a computer industry standard body called Trusted Computing Group (TCG). The first broadly used TPM specification is TPM version 1.2 [29], which was released in 2003. International Organization for Standardization (ISO) and International Electrotechnical Commission (IEC) standardized this specification as ISO/IEC 11889 in 2009 [1].

The TPM 1.2 specification only supported a small number of cryptographic algorithms: RSA encryption and digital signatures, SHA-1 hash function, HMAC

© Springer International Publishing AG 2016
L. Chen et al. (Eds.): SSR 2016, LNCS 10074, pp. 141–159, 2016.
DOI: 10.1007/978-3-319-49100-4_6

message authentication code and Direct Anonymous Attestation (DAA) based on the RSA problem. This fixed algorithm coverage was not satisfactory to worldwide TPM users. Besides an obvious reason that SHA-1 is no longer suitable for digital signatures based on the attack in [31], people from different countries and regions may favor different cryptographic algorithms, especially elliptic curve cryptography. This required the TCG to revise the TPM specification.

As a reaction, the TCG now continuously revises the TPM specification, and the biggest step was to move from TPM 1.2 to TPM 2.0. The latest TPM 2.0 release is Trusted Platform Module Library Specification Revision 01.16 released in October 2014 [30]. ISO/IEC standardized this specification as ISO/IEC 11889 in December 2015 [2] and meanwhile the previous 2009 edition [1] was withdrawn.

Among many important modifications from TPM 1.2, the most attractive change from the authors of this paper's view point is that the TPM 2.0 supports **Algorithm Agility**, which means that each cryptographic primitive can be used by multiple cryptographic algorithms. This is managed by using the TCG Algorithm Registry [28].

Although algorithm agility is a well received property, the performance efficiency is still one of the most important requirements in the development of the TPM 2.0 family. In order to achieve a balance between algorithm agility and high performance, the TPM 2.0 specification allows a set of TPM commands to be shared by multiple algorithms.

The new cryptographic functionalities from TPM 1.2 include a number of Elliptic Curve Cryptographic (ECC) primitives, such as Elliptic Curve (EC) based digital signatures, key exchange and DAA. This paper is focused on discussing the algorithm agility for TPM 2.0 ECC functionalities. We aim to make the following contributions:

1. Find whether the existing TPM 2.0 commands can be used to implement new cryptographic algorithms which have not yet addressed in the current specification [2,30]. We demonstrate that four asymmetric encryption schemes specified in ISO/IEC 18033-2 [4] can be implemented using a TPM 2.0 chip. We also show that the coverage of algorithm agility from TPM 2.0 is limited.
2. Show some obstacles one faces when implementing an algorithm in such way that it will be usable from many different standards.
3. Provide a concise description of the ECC functionalities in TPM 2.0, which is easier to follow by cryptographic researchers than the specification [2,30].

In the literature, there are many papers aimed to analyze security features of a TPM. They all focus on individual cryptographic algorithms or functions; for example, analyzing privacy-CA solution [15,19] and DAA [10,13,33]. To the best of our knowledge, a comprehensive security analysis of multiple TPM functionalities, such as algorithm agility, does not exist. This is a big challenge. We notice that one reason why this has not happened yet is because the TPM specification is not reader friendly for cryptographic researchers, with the evidence that the specification [2,30] is over 1500 pages long. Although this paper does not aim to provide a complete response to this challenge, we believe that the content of this paper will help the future cryptographic researcher analyst TPM 2.0 in more comprehensive methods than it has been done so far.

The remaining part of this paper is arranged as follows. In the next section, we will review the existing TPM 2.0 ECC functionalities, which include a short overview of the TPM's key handling method and commands, and the TPM ECC related commands. In Sect. 3 we list the EC-based cryptographic algorithms and protocols which were already addressed in the TPM 2.0 specification. In Sect. 4, we will discuss a number of asymmetric encryption algorithms, which can be implemented by using the existing TPM 2.0 ECC functionalities, although they have not been mentioned in the specification yet. In this section we also show the limitation of TPM algorithm agility by variants of ECDSA signature algorithms. In Sect. 5, taking an example of the EC-based Schnorr digital signature scheme, we will further discuss on some issues in compatibility. Section 6 will share our considerations about TPM performance. We will conclude the paper in Sect. 7 with an open question on how to define and prove security notions for the TPM 2.0 algorithm agility property.

2   Overview of the TPM 2.0 ECC Functionalities

In this section we give an overview of the Elliptic Curve Cryptographic (ECC) functionalities which are specified in the TPM 2.0 specification [2,30]. Because the TCG TPM 2.0 specification [30] is still under development, the information used in this section is based on a version of the TPM library published by ISO/IEC in 2015 [2]. We introduce a set of major TPM 2.0 commands that are used to implemented the TPM 2.0 ECC functions. After that we list all the EC-based cryptographic algorithms that are mentioned in the specification.

2.1   Introduction to TPM Keys

To describe ECC keys in the TPM 2.0 environment, we use the notation shown in Table 1.

TPM Key Structures. In the TPM 2.0 environment, TPM keys are arranged with key hierarchies. For the reason of limiting TPM resources, keys are normally stored outside. Each key except a root key is associated with a parent key, parentK, and the top parent key is a root key.

Let an ECC key be denoted by tk with a private potion tsk and a public potion tpk. Some system parameters about an ECC key, known by a TPM, include coefficients of the curve, a field modulus of the curve, an order of group elements on the curve and a generator of the group. For simplicity, we use tpk to cover all of these parameters. Each key tk is associated a key name denoted by tk.name, key blob denoted by tk.blob and key handle denoted by tk.handle, which have the following meanings.

Table 1. Notation used in this paper

Notation	Descriptions
tk	ECC key created by TPM
tpk/tsk	public/private portion of tk
parentK	a key used to introduce another key
k.name	name of key k used for identifying the key externally
k.blob	key blob of key k wrapped by its parentK
k.handle	handle of key k used for identifying the key internally by a TPM
KDF (s)	key derivation function using s as seed
MAC $_k(m)$	message authentication code of m computed using key k
$(m)_k$	encryption of m under symmetric key k
$x \| y$	concatenation of x and y
$\mathbb{G}_p$	an elliptic curve group of prime order p
G	a generator of $\mathbb{G}_p$

- *Key name:* tk.name is a message digest of tpk and the key's attributes. It is usually used for verifying the integrity of the key.
- *Key blob:* Each TPM key stored outside of the TPM is in a format of a key blob; tk.blob includes the following information: tsk encrypted under its parentK, tpk, and an integrity tag. The tag allows the TPM to verify integrity and authenticity of the key and is achieved by using a message authentication code (MAC). Both the encryption key SK and MAC key MK are derived from parentK by using a key derivation function (KDF). The following is a brief description of tk.blob:

$$(\text{SK}, \text{MK}) := \text{KDF}(\text{parentK}),$$
$$\text{tk.blob} := (\text{tsk})_{\text{SK}} \| \text{tpk} \| \text{MAC}_{\text{MK}}((\text{tsk})_{\text{SK}} \| \text{tpk.name}).$$

- *Key handle:* If tk is associated with multiple commands, the connection between these commands is presented as tk.handle that uniquely identifies the key. tk.handle is assigned by the TPM when tk is loaded into the TPM. Such a key handle is a 4 byte (word) value. The first byte designates the handle type and the remaining three bytes are uniquely referring the key. After the loading command, when tk is subsequently used in another command (or multiple commands), the handle is taken as input for each command. If more than one key are involved in a command, all handles of these keys are taken as input for the command.

The usage of each ECC key are classified by three key base attributes as *restricted, sign* and *decrypt*. Table 2 shows valid combinations.

The *sign* attribute is used to allow the key to perform signing operations, e.g. this key can be used for the TPM2_Sign() command.

Table 2. Key base attributes

Sign	Decrypt	Restricted	Description
0	0	0	no key, user defined data blob
0	0	1	not allowed
0	1	0	a decryption key but may not be a parentK
0	1	1	may be a parentK
1	0	0	a key for signing external date
1	0	1	a key for signing TPM generated data only
1	1	0	a general-purpose key
1	1	1	not supported

The *decrypt* attribute is used to allow the key to perform decryption operations, e.g. this key can be used for the TPM2_ECDH_ZGen() command.

The *restricted* attribute needs a bit more explanation. Let's first explain *restricted sign* keys. The TPM can be used to sign externally given messages or to sign internally generated data. For instance, the TPM2_Quote() command signs the values of some platform configuration registers and the TPM2_Certify() command signs a TPM generated key. A verifier must be assured that the signatures actually have been performed by those commands on internal TPM data. To do this, the TPM puts a special tag word called TPM_GENERATED_VALUE in the message header of the signature. This tag proves to the verifier that the signature belongs to TPM created data. If the signing key has the *restricted* attribute, the TPM will only sign an externally given message by TPM2_Sign(), if the message does not start with the TPM_GENERATED_VALUE tag. This protects that the TPM2_Sign() command cannot be misused to fake a platform attestation.

The *restricted decryption* attribute is mainly used for the parent key to protect a key blob. Here it must be targeted that only the TPM can decrypt the key blob. The *restricted* attribute protects this key from being used for general purpose decryption commands (e.g. TPM2_ECDH_ZGen()). If the key would not be *restricted* an attacker could simply use the TPM2_ECDH_ZGen() command to decrypt the key blob.

In addition to the base attributes there are other key attributes. We will not go into detail here but only mention the most important ones.

– userWithAuth and adminWithPolicy: they control authorization of the key.
– fixedTPM and fixedParent: they control if the key can be duplicated under another parent key of the same TPM or another one.

2.2 TPM 2.0 Key Handling Commands

All TPM functions are served by using a set of TPM commands. Most of the TPM commands have multiple options, regarding to different types of keys and applications. For simplicity, we only explain these options which are related to the implementation of the TPM ECC functions that will be discussed in the later part of the paper. For the same reason, we may also omit some input and output information if they are not relevant to our purposes.

Generate a Key: TPM2_Create(). An ECC key tk can be generated by using this command. The command takes a handle of a parent key (say parentK) that has already been loaded into the TPM and public parameters about the curve, algorithm identifier and so on as input, creates a fresh ECC key pair tk = (tpk, tsk), and outputs a wrapped key blob, tk.blob as described before.

In the context of the ECC functions, to respond to this command, the TPM performs the following steps:

1. TPM picks a random $x \leftarrow \mathbb{Z}_p$ and computes $Y = [x]G$, where the values p and G are a part of the public parameters dependent on the ECC algorithms that will be discussed in the next subsection.
2. TPM sets tpk := Y, tsk := x, and tk := (tpk, tsk).
3. TPM wraps tk with the parent key and outputs a key blob tk.blob.

A variation of this command is TPM2_CreatePrimary(), in which the private key tsk is derived from a primary seed of the TPM using a key derivation function (KDF). A primary seed is a secret key stored inside of the TPM. As a result, the key tk is a root key of the key hierarchy. The same primary seed can be used to create multiple root keys. In order to make each created key unique, some index value(s) shall be used. Primary keys will be used internally as root keys which protect a key hierarchy of ordinary keys. They will normally not be used for cryptographic services and we therefore ignore them in the remaining of this paper.

Load a Key into TPM: TPM2_Load(). When tk is created in TPM2_Create(), it is not stored inside of the TPM. In order to use tk, the key has to be loaded into the TPM using the command TPM2_Load(). This command takes as input a parent key handle and a key blob tk.blob. The TPM verifies integrity of the key by checking the validation of the blob under the parent key, optionally also verifies the user authorization and the attributes consistence. If all the verification succeeds, the TPM outputs a handle tk.handle and the name tk.name for the key. After TPM2_Load() has been called, tk is now stored inside the TPM and can be used for future operations.

Load an External Key to TPM: TPM2_LoadExternal(). An external key that is not part of a TPM key hierarchy can also be loaded into the TPM. This will normally be a public key only. For example, if a signature verification is the purpose, then the public verification key will be loaded into the TPM with this command.

2.3   TPM 2.0 ECC Commands

Commit an Ephemeral Secret for Signing: TPM2_Commit(). Several EC-based signature schemes are implemented using two phases: committing and signing. The committing process is achieved using the command TPM2_Commit(). It takes as input a key handle of a signing key tk, a point P_1 in $\mathbb{G}_p$, a string $\hat{s}$, and an integer $\hat{y}$, where $\hat{s}$ and $\hat{y}$ are used to construct another point P_2 in $\mathbb{G}_p$, see below for details. The TPM outputs three points R_1, R_2, K_2, and a counter ctr to the host, where ctr is used for identifying the random value r created by this command. To respond this command the TPM performs the following steps:

1. TPM computes $\hat{x} := H(\hat{s})$ where H is a collision-resistant hash function, and sets $P_2 := (\hat{x}, \hat{y})$.
2. TPM verifies P_1 and P_2 are elements in $\mathbb{G}_p$.
3. TPM chooses a random integer $r \leftarrow \mathbb{Z}_p$.
4. TPM computes $R_1 := [r]P_1$, $R_2 := [r]P_2$, and $K_2 := [\mathtt{tsk}]P_2$.
5. TPM outputs R_1, R_2, K_2 and ctr while keeping r internally.

Note that some input to this command can be empty. If $\hat{s}$ and $\hat{y}$ are empty, then R_2 and K_2 are not computed. If all the three elements P_1, $\hat{s}$ and $\hat{y}$ are empty, then $R_1 = [r]G$, where G is a long-term base in the curve parameters and was used in creating tk.

Sign: TPM2_Sign(). This command can be used as a one-phase signing operation or the second phase of the two-phase signing protocols. It takes as input a handle of the signing key tk, a message digest c_h, and optionally a counter value ctr, and outputs a signature σ on the message. The counter value ctr is only needed when the sign command is called after executing a commit command TPM2_Commit(). Standard digital signature algorithms can be used, such as RSA, ECDSA, or ECSchnorr signatures. If a conventional signature scheme is used, then there is no need to call the commit command. In the context of a two-phase signing protocol, the TPM responds to this command by performing the following steps:

1. TPM retrieves r from the commit command based on the ctr value.
2. TPM computes $s := r + c \cdot \mathtt{tsk} \bmod p$ and deletes r.
3. TPM outputs s.

Note: Recently Xi et al. [33] and Camenisch et al. [13] reported an issue in the security proof of [16], that requires to a modification of the scheme in [2] by adding the nonce n_t. Note also that the nonce n_t is in another version of EC-DAA schemes specified in ISO/IEC 20008-2 [6], so this issue does not require such a modification to ISO/IEC 20008-2. This modification has of course implications also to other protocols which rely on the ECDAA functionality. Here is the modified sign algorithms.

1. TPM created a nonce $n_t \to \mathbb{Z}_p$.
2. TPM computes $c := H(c_h, n_t)$.
3. TPM retrieves r from the commit command based on the ctr value.
4. TPM computes $s := r + c \cdot \mathtt{tsk} \bmod p$ and deletes r.
5. TPM outputs $\sigma = (n_t, s)$.

The TPM 2.0 specification also contains commands which perform a signature over TPM internally stored date. For instance, TPM2_Quote() is used to sign platform configuration registers and TPM2_Certify() will sign another TPM stored key. We will not go into detail of those commands.

Compute an Ephemeral Key: TPM2_ECDH_KeyGen(). This command takes as input the public portion of a loaded key including an EC point P in the curve, chooses an element d uniformly at random from the space of the ECC private key, computes $Q := [d]P$ and outputs P and Q. The TPM does not record or output the value d. Since the operation can be performed by software, no authorization is required to use the loaded key and the key may be either *sign* or *encrypt*.

Compute a Static DH Key: TPM2_ECDH_ZGen(). This command takes as input a loaded key with the private portion d along with the corresponding public parameters, and an elliptic curve point P. The TPM first verifies whether P matches with the public parameters. If the verification passes, the TPM computes $Z := [d]P$ and outputs Z. Since this operation uses the private portion of an ECC key, authorization of the key is required. The attributes of the key is the *restricted* attribute CLEAR and the *decrypt* attribute SET.

Commit an Ephemeral Secret for Key Exchange: TPM2_EC_Ephemeral(). This command takes as input the public parameters for an ECC key with the elliptic curve point G, generates an ephemeral private portion of an ECC key r by using a counter technique as used in TPM2_Commit(), and computes a public key $P := [r]G$. The value of P is returned to the caller along with the counter value associated with r.

Compute a DH Key: TPM2_ZGen_2Phase(). This command takes as input a scheme selector and the counter value returned by TPM2_EC_Ephemeral() along with the corresponding public parameters, recreates r and regenerates the associated public key. After that the TPM will "retire" the r value so that it will not be used again. This command can be used to achieve multiple key exchange protocols, which may have different operations. The scheme selector is used to tell the TPM which key exchange protocols should be implemented.

The TPM 2.0 specification also contains the TPM2_ActivateCredential() command which uses an ECC decryption algorithm internally. This command cannot be used for decryption of general purpose data. Therefore, we will not go into the detail of this commands.

3   Known ECC Use Cases for the TPM 2.0

The TPM 2.0 specification [2] supports three ECC primitives: conventional digital signatures, anonymous digital signatures that is called direct anonymous attestation, and Diffie-Hellman (DH) key exchange.

3.1   Conventional Digital Signatures

The following three conventional digital signature algorithms are mentioned in the TPM 2.0 specification [2].

1. ECDSA. The specification does not explain any details about this algorithm, but simply referring it to ISO/IEC 14888-3 [3]. This algorithm is originally described in NIST Fips 186-3 [23]. It is also defined in numerous other specifications, e.g. BSI TR-03111 [12].
2. ECSchnorr. The specification specifies an implementation of the EC Schnorr signature scheme, which is assigned as the **TPM_ALG_ECSCHNORR** scheme. The scheme includes the EC Schnorr signing operation and signature verification operation. The reference for the EC Schnorr signature scheme given in the TPM 2.0 specification is ISO/IEC 14888-3 [3].
3. SM2. The specification specifies the SM2 digital signature scheme, which is the Chinese EC-based signature scheme, originally published as the Chinese National Standard [27]. This digital signature scheme has recently been adopted by ISO/IEC and the process of adding it into an amendment of ISO/IEC 14888-3 [3] is in progress.

3.2   Direct Anonymous Attestation (DAA)

One of the main purposes of a TPM chip is to attest the state of the platform configuration to some verifier. This is basically been done by signing the values of platform configuration registers inside the TPM. It is an important privacy requirement that two attestations shall not be linkable. In the pre-DAA epoch, this has been accomplished by using a privacy certification authority (privacy CA). This basically worked in the following way. For each attestation, the TPM contacts the privacy CA and requests a new key, the "Attestation Identity Key" (AIK) together with a corresponding X.509 certificate. This enables privacy, because the verifier always sees a different public key. If the verifier gets two attestations, then he cannot tell if they came from two different TPMs or form the same one. In this case, the attestations are *unlinkable* from the verifier.

The downside of this approach is that the privacy CA is involved in every attestation. Furthermore this CA can link two signatures from the same TPM and can find which TPM was the signer. Therefore TGC were looking for a solution which didn't need the privacy CA: In the TCG history, DAA was the only cryptographic primitive that was designed to meet the TCG special privacy requirement. DAA is an anonymous digital signature. A DAA protocol accomplishes unlinkability by randomizing the signatures and associated certificates.

The first RSA DAA scheme was introduced by Brickell, Camenisch and Chen [10] for the TPM 1.2 specification [29]. The TPM 2.0 specification has been designed to support a new family of Elliptic Curve (EC) based DAA protocols. The TPM 2.0 specification [2] supports two different DAA protocols which are based on pairings over elliptic curves. The first [17] is based on Camenisch-Lysyanskana (CL) credentials [14] and the second one [11] is based on sDH credentials [9]. The paper from Chen and Li [16] shows how both DAA protocols can be used with a TPM 2.0 chip.

3.3 DAA with Attributes (DAA-A)

Chen and Urian [18] have recently preposed an extension of DAA by adding multiple attributes. This protocol is related to the U-Prove protocol but has a significant advantage over it: In contrast to the U-prove protocol, DAA-A is *multi-show unlinkable*. The DAA-A protocol comes in two variants, which correspond to the respective ECDAA protocols:

- the CL DAA-A protocol which corresponds to the CL ECDAA protocol.
- the sDH DAA-A protocol which corresponds to the sDH ECDAA (aka Epid) protocol.

In a nutshell, the DAA-A protocol works as follows: Each attribute value will be encoded as an exponent for an ECC key which is normally stored on the host but can also be for better security stored on the TPM. The DAA-A Issuer defines the list of attributes which shall be used in a DAA-A credential. According to the minimum disclosure principle, the TPM/host shall only reveal a minimum set of attributes to the Verifier. The TPM/host decide on each individual attestation what attributes they will reveal to the Verifier and what attributes they will hide form him. The revealed attributes will be sent by the TPM/host to the Verifier as part of the DAA-A Sign protocol. The correctness of the hidden attributes will be proved to the Verifier by a zero-knowledge proof.

Attributes can be stored on the host or on the TPM. TPM hosted attributes are stored as conventional signature keys. The DAA-A scheme uses the TPM2_Sign() and TPM2_Commit() commands, specified in ISO/IEC 11889 [2], as sub-protocols to aid in the generation of the DAA-A signature (see [18] for details).

Due to the proposed change of the TPM2_Sign() command for ECDAA (see Sect. 2.3), the integration of DAA-A with this command must also be changed. We leave how to handle this new adaption as an open problem, and from our point of view this problem is not trivial.

3.4 U-Prove

The U-Prove protocol [25] from Microsoft is an attribute based protocol with user controlled selective disclosure. The paper of Chen and Li [16] shows how U-Prove can be integrated with a TPM 2.0 chip. But the U-Prove protocol has the severe drawback that it is not multi-show unlinkable. The reason for this is that the authentication token of the U-Prove protocol is signed by a Schnorr-like signature and the signature value can be used as a correlation handle. To be unlinkable, a U-Prove token may only be used once.

3.5 Key Exchange

The following Diffie-Hellman (DH) based key exchange schemes in the EC setting are mentioned in the TPM 2.0 specification [2]. Interestingly this technique is called "secret sharing" in the TPM 2.0 specification. Secret sharing has been broadly used as a different cryptographic protocol, in which multiple entities each holds a share of a common secret and a number of these entities can work together and retrieve such a secret. In order to avoid any confusion, we name this technique "key exchange" throughout the paper.

1. One-Pass DH. The specification specifies the one-pass DH key exchange scheme and refers it to NIST SP800-56A [26].
2. Two-Pass DH. The specification specifies the two-pass DH key exchange scheme, which is also from NIST SP800-56A [26].
3. ECMQV. The specification specifies the two-pass DH key exchange scheme, which is known as EC-based MQV [26].
4. SM2 key exchange. The specification specifies the two-pass DH key exchange scheme from the SM2 family, the Chinese National Standard on ECC [27].

4 New ECC Use Cases for TPM 2.0

In this section we will discuss how cryptographic protocols can be used with a TPM 2.0, although they have not been mentioned in the specification yet. First we will show that a TPM can nicely be integrated in asymmetric encryption schemes. Then we will show the limitation of TPM integration by discussing some variants of signature algorithms.

4.1 Asymmetric Encryption

Based on the TPM 2.0 specification [2,30], ECC is not used directly for encryption. It is well-known that in ECC, a key exchange functionality is used to establish a symmetric key from an ECC key, and then a symmetric algorithm is used for data encryption, which is known as the hybrid encryption, i.e., Key Encapsulation Mechanism and Data Encapsulation mechanism (KEM-DEM). The TPM 2.0 specification does not specify any KEM-DEM scheme. In this section, we demonstrate how to use TPM 2.0 to implement the ElGamal based KEM schemes in the ECC setting from ISO/IEC 18033-2 [4]. For the performance consideration (as a TPM chip is not efficient for data encryption/decryption compared with software), a DEM scheme would likely be implemented by software, and therefore we do not discuss it in this paper.

Generally speaking, a KEM consists of three algorithms:

- A key generation algorithm KEM.KeyGen() that takes as input the public system parameters par and outputs a public-key/private-key pair (pk, sk).
- An encryption algorithm KEM.Encrypt() that takes as input (pk, par) and outputs a secret-key/ciphertext pair (K, C).
- A decryption algorithm KEM.Decrypt() that takes as input (sk, C, par) and outputs K.

The public system parameters par depend on the particular scheme, and in the ECC setting they should include an elliptic curve defined over a given finite field, a subgroup of the elliptic curve group with a prime order q and a generator G, a hash function HASH() and a key derivation function KDF(). For simplicity, we omit other items in par.

ISO/IEC 18033-2 [4] specifies three ElGamal-based KEM schemes in the ECC setting. Respectively, they are ECIES (Elliptic Curve Integrated Encryption Scheme) based on the work of Abdalla, Bellare, and Rogaway [7,8], PSEC (Provably Secure Elliptic Curve encryption) based on the work of Fujisaki and Okamoto [22] and ACE (Advanced Cryptographic Engine) based on the work of Cramer and Shoup [20,21]. Recently a new submission of the ElGamal-based KEM scheme in the ECC setting [24] has been adopted by ISO/IEC and an amendment of ISO/IEC 18033-2 specifying this new scheme is in progress. This scheme is called FACE (Fast ACE).

Table 3 shows the algorithms in these four KEMs. Note that we have changed the notation used in ISO/IEC 18033-2 for the purpose of this paper, because we want to demonstrate that the same set of TPM functions can be used for all the three KEMs.

By using a TPM 2.0 chip to operate a KEM, we mean that the TPM generates a public-key/private-key pair, stores the key pair in the TPM protected environment and uses the private-key to decrypt a secret key, which is used for the DEM operation in a later stage. For the best use of the TPM, we only make use of the TPM for the operations involving the private-key and leaves other operations, such as the KEM.Encrypt() algorithm, the KDF() function and the HASH() function, to the software. With this consideration, these three KEM schemes can be implemented by using the same TPM ECC functionalities.

Now, let us see how to implement the KEM.KeyGen() and KEM.Decrypt() algorithms in ECIES and PSEC using a number of TPM 2.0 commands, which were introduced in Sect. 2.2. We assume that a caller enabling to run these software operations mentioned before has authorization to use the TPM commands as follows.

1. In the KEM.KeyGen() algorithm, The caller first chooses an existing TPM key as a parent key parentK. If the key is stored outside of the TPM, the caller uses the TPM2_Load() command to load the key and receives a key handle parentK.handle from the TPM. In order to generate the public-key/private-key pair $\mathtt{tk} = (pk, sk)$, where $sk = x$ and $pk = Y = [x]G$, the caller calls

Table 3. Four KEMs in ISO/IEC 18033-2 [4] and ISO/IEC 18033-2/AMD1 [5]

	KEM.KeyGen(par)	KEM.Encrypt(pk, par)	KEM.Decrypt(sk, C, par)
ECIES [7,8]	$x \in [1, q)$	$r \in [1, q)$	$C_0 = C$
	$Y = [x]G$	$C_0 = [r]G,\ C = C_0$	$D = [x]C_0$
	$sk \leftarrow x$	$D = [r]Y$	$K = \text{KDF}(C_0\|D)$
	$pk \leftarrow Y$	$K = \text{KDF}(C_0\|D)$	Return K
	Return (pk, sk)	Return (K, C)	
PSEC [22]	$x \in [0, q)$	$seed \in \{0,1\}^{seedLen}$	Parse $C = C_0\|F$
	$Y = [x]G$	$t = u\|K = \text{KDF}(0\|seed)$	$D = [x]C_0$
	$sk \leftarrow x$	$r = u \mod q$	$E = \text{KDF}(1\|C_0\|D)$
	$pk \leftarrow Y$	$C_0 = [r]G,\ D = [r]Y$	$seed = F \oplus E$
	Return (pk, sk)	$E = \text{KDF}(1\|C_0\|D)$	$t = \text{KDF}(0\|seed) = u\|K$
		$C = C_0\|(seed \oplus E)$	$r = u \mod q$
		Return (K, C)	Return K, if $C_0 = [r]P$
			Otherwise, return Fail
ACE [20,21]	$x_1, x_2, x_3, x_4 \in [0, q)$	$r \in [0, q)$	Parse $C = C_0\|D_1\|E$
	$Y_1 = [x_1]G$	$C_0 = [r]G$	$\alpha = \text{HASH}(C_0\|D_1)$
	$Y_2 = [x_2]G$	$D_1 = [r]Y_1,\ D_4 = [r]Y_4$	$t = x_2 + x_3 \cdot \alpha \mod q$
	$Y_3 = [x_3]G$	$\alpha = \text{HASH}(C_0\|D_1)$	If $D_1 \neq [x_1]C_0 \vee E \neq [t]C_0$
	$Y_4 = [x_4]G$	$r' = \alpha \cdot r \mod q$	return Fail
	$sk \leftarrow (x_1, x_2, x_3, x_4)$	$E = [r]Y_2 + [r']Y_3$	Otherwise calculate
	$pk \leftarrow (Y_1, Y_2, Y_3, Y_4)$	$C = C_0\|D_1\|E$	$D_4 = [x_4]C_0$
	Return (pk, sk)	$K = \text{KDF}(C_0\|D_4)$	$K = \text{KDF}(C_0\|D_4)$
		Return (K, C)	Return K
FACE [24]	$a_1, a_2 \in [0, q)$	$r \in [0, q)$	Parse $C = U_1\|U_2\|T$
	$G_1 = [a_1]G$	$U_1 = [r]G_1$	$\alpha = \text{HASH}(U_1\|U_2)$
	$G_2 = [a_2]G$	$U_2 = [r]G_2$	$t_1 = x_1 + y_1 \cdot \alpha \mod q$
	$x_1, x_2, y_1, y_2 \in [0, q)$	$\alpha = \text{HASH}(U_1\|U_2)$	$t_2 = x_2 + y_2 \cdot \alpha \mod q$
	$C = [x_1]G_1 + [x_2]G_2$	$r' = \alpha \cdot r \mod q$	$V = t_1 U_1 + t_2 U_2$
	$D = [y_1]G_1 + [y_2]G_2$	$V = [r]C + [r']D$	$K\|T' = \text{KDF}(V)$
	$sk \leftarrow (x_1, x_2, y_1, y_2)$	$K\|T = \text{KDF}(V)$	Return K, if $T = T'$
	$pk \leftarrow (G_1, G_2, C, D)$	$C = U_1\|U_2\|T$	Otherwise, return Fail
	Return (pk, sk)	Return (K, C)	

TPM2_Create(), that takes as input the public system parameters par along with parentK.handle, generates the key pair tk and a key blob tk.blob, and outputs the blob. Recall that tk.blob includes sk encrypted under parentK, pk and a tag to check integrity.

2. In the KEM.Decrypt() algorithm, the caller first loads the key pair tk into the TPM using TPM2_Load() that will return a tk.handle. The caller then calls TPM2_ECDH_ZGen() with the input tk.handle and the value $C_0 = [r]P$. The TPM will computes and outputs $D = [x]C_0$. The caller can take care of the remaining operations using software to obtain the secret key K, and in

PSEC the K value can be obtained if the necessary check $C_0 = [r]P$ passes; otherwise the caller will get a Fail message.

In the ACE KEM, the key pair $tk = (pk, sk)$ consists of four private-key values $sk = (x_1, x_2, x_3, x_4)$ and four corresponding public-key values $pk = (Y_1, Y_2, Y_3, Y_4)$. The caller can treat them as four independent key pairs $tk_1 = (Y_1, x_1)$, $tk_2 = (Y_2, x_2)$, $tk_3 = (Y_3, x_3)$ and $tk_4 = (Y_4, x_4)$. In the KEM.KeyGen() algorithm, the caller runs the operation in the first bullet four times each obtaining one key pair tk_i for $i = [1, 4]$. In the KEM.Decrypt() algorithm, again the caller calls the same TPM commands in the second bullet four times, each with C_0 as input but loading a different key pair tk_i to obtain (D_1, D_2, D_3, D_4). Obviously the caller can verify the value E since $E = D_2 + [\alpha]D_3$ and $\alpha = \mathsf{Hash}(C_0 || D_1)$. By following the remaining part of the decryption algorithm, the caller can verify the ciphertext C and retrieve the secret key K if the verification succeeds or obtain a Fail message if the verification fails.

The FACE scheme first might need some explanation regarding the value T. The KDF function for this scheme does not only generate the bits for a key K, but instead generates some additional bits for the so called *Tag* value T. The size of the Tag value are defined in the system parameters.

The FACE KEM algorithm has four public keys and four private keys. But the private and public keys are not directly related. In the KEM.KeyGen() algorithm, one has to calculate two public points G_1 and G_2 without corresponding private keys. To use a TPM here, one can use two invocations of the TPM2_ECDH_KeyGen() TPM command to generate them as ephemeral points. Then four private keys x_1, x_2, y_1, y_2 must be generated and two further public keys: $C = [x_1]G_1 + [x_2]G_2$ and $D = [y_1]G_1 + [y_2]G_2$. The TPM calculates the intermediate points $X_1 = [x_1]G_1$, $X_2 = [x_2]G_2$, $Y_1 = [y_1]G_1$, $Y_2 = [x_2]G_2$ with four TPM2_ECDH_ZGen() command calls. The host then finalises the calculation by adding the points to get $C = X_1 + X_2$ and $D = Y_1 + Y_2$. In the KEM.Decrypt() algorithm, the receiver has to calculate $t_1 = x_1 + \alpha y_1$ and $t_2 = x_2 + \alpha y_2$ and then $V = [t_1]U_1 + [t_2]U_2$. In order to use the TPM, one must a bit rearrange the equations. The TPM calculates the intermediate points $X_1 = [x_1]U_1$, $X_2 = [x_2]U_2$, $Y_1 = [y_1]U_1$, $Y_2 = [y_2]U_2$ with four TPM2_ECDH_ZGen() command calls. The host then finalises the calculation by computing the point $V = X_1 + X_2 + [\alpha](Y_1 + Y_2)$.

4.2   Limitations of Algorithmic Agility

The ECDSA algorithm implemented in the TPM is described in NIST Fips 186-3 [23]. It is also defined in numerous other specifications, e.g. ISO/IEC 14888-3 [3] and BSI TR-03111 [12]. Despite this standard ECDSA scheme, [3] also describes three further national schemes:

- EC-GDSA (Elliptic Curve German Digital Signature Algorithm)
- EC-KCDSA (Elliptic Curve Korean Certificate-based Digital Signature Algorithm)
- EC-RDSA (Elliptic Curve Russian Digital Signature Algorithm)

It would be nice if the current TPM 2.0 specification could also be integrated in those schemes. But this seems to be impossible. Generally speaking, in order to integrate a TPM for implementing an algorithm, one has to split the algorithm into two parts in such a way that the TPM can calculate one part, and the host can calculate the remaining part. It is thereby crucial that the host only performs the operation that needs the public keys only. Every operation involving the private key must be done by the TPM. Such a splitting can be done easily if the underling primitive is as simple as an ECDH point multiplication. This was the case in the KEM schemes above. But the ECDSA-type of signature schemes require to make more complicated operations on the private key. For instance, there is no obvious way to calculate $[x^{-1}]G$ by using the existing TPM commands in which the public key is formed as $Y = [x]G$.

Now, instead of implementing each algorithm separately on a TPM, a suggestion for a future TPM related research could be to split the different signature algorithms in simple "atomic" pieces, where the private key parts can be easily implemented on a TPM.

5   Compatibility Issue in Algorithm Agility

Algorithm compatibility is crucial for algorithm agility. However it is a common practice in cryptographic standardization to ignore this. That means, different standards for the same cryptographic protocol often use different and incompatible implementation choices. This will not be an issue if the TPM has been considered at the time when the cryptographic protocol is designed. But it will be a problem if the TPM shall be used to enhance the security for an already existing cryptographic system.

The TCG noticed this especially for the elliptic curve based Schnorr signature scheme. Therefore, they decided to revise the current Schnorr implementation in the TPM 2.0 specification in order to optimize interoperability. By the date of writing this paper, the final version of this revision has not been done. The following discussion shows the problems one faces by trying to reach a maximum amount of interoperability.

The public system parameters *par* for the EC-based digital signature scheme also depend on the particular scheme, and they should include an elliptic curve defined over a given finite field, a subgroup of the elliptic curve group with a prime order q and a generator G, and a hash function HASH(). We use x to denote the private key and Y for the public key. For simplicity, again we omit other items in *par*.

The Schnorr signature algorithm basically consists of the following steps:

1. Choose a random value r and calculate the point $R = [r]G$.
2. Calculate the signature value c by hashing the x-coordinate R_x of the point R and a given message M, c = HASH(M, R_x). See the discussion below for the different choices how this hashing can be done on the bit level.
3. Calculate the signature value s. Here we have the two choices to calculate either (a) $s = r + c \cdot x \mod q$ or (b) $s = r - c \cdot x \mod q$.
4. Return the signature (c, s).

The Schnorr signature verification algorithm to the signature (c, s) for the message M consists of the following steps:

1. Calculate the point R'. Here we must use the correct version corresponding to the sign variant, i.e. either (a) $R' = [s]G - [c]Y$ or (b) $R' = [s]G + [c]Y$.
2. Calculate the signature value c' by hashing the x-coordinate R'_x of the point R' and message M as $c' = \text{HASH}(M, R'_x)$.
3. Return Accept, if $c = c'$ or Reject, otherwise.

Note that the different calculation variants for the signature value s can easily be transformed into each other by inverting the s value, i.e. if (c, s) is a signature for variant (a), then $(c, -s)$ will be a signature for variant (b) (and vice-versa).

Let us now discuss the different hash calculation variants. The first decision to make is the bit encoding of the value R_x. Since R_x is an element of the finite field with q elements, it can be encoded as a byte string of length $\lceil \log_{256}(q) \rceil$. Let this be the default encoding. This encoding can contain leading zero bytes. As an alternative encoding one can strip down those leading zeroes from the default encoding. Let the $\text{TRZ}(x)$ denote the function which truncates the leading zeroes from the default encoded byte string x. The next choice we must make is in which order the message M and the value R_x will enter the HASH function, i.e. either as $h = \text{HASH}(M \| R_x)$ or as $h = \text{HASH}(R_x \| M)$. The next choice regards the truncation of the value h. This is necessary only if the bit size λ of the hash result is bigger than the bit size l of the binary encoding of the number q, i.e. $l = \lceil \log_2 q \rceil$. Here one has the choices to either leave the value as it is or truncate the $\lambda - l$ least significant bits of h. Let us denote this truncation of a bit string x as $\text{TRH}(x)$. As a last choice, we can now set $c = h$ or reduce h first to $h' = h \bmod q$ and set $c = h'$.

For comparison, in Table 4, we list the three existing implementations of the EC Schnorr signature scheme in ISO/IEC 14888-3 [3], ISO/IEC 11889 [2] and BSI TR-03111 [12] respectively, and a new implementation proposed by the TCG recently [32].

6   Performance Considerations

TPM chips are optimized to provide a high level of hardware security. This means they have to be resistant against sophisticated physical attacks, like fault injection or side channel leakage. Security certifications according to Common Criteria or FIPS give evidence for this security level. TPM chips are also required to be cost optimized devices. This implies that they will be somewhat restricted regarding processor speed and memory resources. However the performance of TPM chips is continuously increasing due to higher clock frequencies, sophisticated cryptographic co-processors and firmware optimizations.

As a TPM chip is normally invoked by the software stack of an multitasking operating system, the performance also depends on that software part. It is therefore difficult to provide meaningful performance measurements for TPM chips.

Table 4. Different EC Schnorr implementation variants

	$\text{Sign}(par, x, M)$	$\text{Verify}(par, Y, s, c, M)$
ISO/IEC 14888-3 [3]	$r \in [1, q),\ R = [r]G$	$R' = [s]G - [c]Y$
	$c = \text{HASH}(R_x \| M)$	$c' = \text{HASH}(R'_x \| M)$
	$s = r + c \cdot x \mod q$	Accept, iff $c = c'$
BSI TR-03111 [12]	$r \in [1, q),\ R = [r]G$	$R' = [s]G + [c]Y$
	$c = \text{TRH}(\text{HASH}(M \| R_x))$	$c' = \text{TRH}(\text{HASH}(M \| R'_x))$
	$s = r - c \cdot sk \mod q$	Accept, iff $c = c'$
ISO/IEC 11889 [2]	$r \in [1, q),\ R = [r]G$	$R' = [s]G - [c]Y$
	$c = \text{HASH}(M \| (\text{TRZ}(R_x$ $\mod q)) \mod q$	$c' = \text{HASH}(M \| (\text{TRZ}(R'_x$ $\mod q)) \mod q$
	$s = r + c \cdot x \mod q$	Accept, iff $c = c'$
New TCG proposal [32]	$r \in [1, q),\ R = [r]G$	$R' = [s]G - [c]Yk$
	$c = \text{TRH}(\text{HASH}(R_x \| M))$	$c' = \text{TRH}(\text{HASH}(R'_x \| M))$
	$s = r + c \cdot x \mod q$	Accept, iff $c = c'$

The bottom line is that a host CPU is faster but provides no hardware security while the TPM chip is slower but provides a far high level of hardware security. Due to this performance/security asymmetry, it is very important to cleverly split the algorithm between the host CPU and the TPM chip. The TPM should only perform the operations involving the private key.

7   Conclusion with an Open Question

In this paper, we have shown that a TPM 2.0 chip is a reasonably powerful cryptographic engine, which can potentially achieve more than what have be specified in its published specification [2]. This benefits from the property of algorithm agility. However, the algorithm agility has made the environment much more complex than these algorithms individually implemented and analyzed in their original security proof. Therefore, it is a real challenge to make a sound security analysis for the entire TPM/host system. This paper has not done anything in this topic. We finish this paper with an open question: How to define the security notion of algorithm agility? On the other words, whether it is possible and then how to build a security model for TPM 2.0 ECC functionalities and to prove it?

References

1. ISO/IEC 11889:2009 (all parts) Information technology - Trusted platform module
2. ISO/IEC 11889:2015 (all parts) Information technology - Trusted platform module library
3. ISO/ IEC 14888–3:2016 Information technology - Security techniques - Digital signatures with appendix - Part 3: Discrete logarithm based mechanisms

4. ISO/IEC 18033–2:2006 Information technology - Security techniques - Encryption algorithms - Part 2: Asymmetric ciphers
5. ISO/IEC 18033–2, amd1 Encryption algorithms - Part 2: Asymmetric ciphers - Amendment 1
6. ISO/IEC 20008–2:2013 Information technology - Security techniques - Anonymous digital signatures - Part 2: Mechanisms using a group public key
7. Abdalla, M., Bellare, M., Rogaway, P.: DHAES: an encryption scheme based on the Diffie-Hellman problem. Cryptology ePrint Archive, Report 1999/007 (1999). http://eprint.iacr.org
8. Abdalla, M., Bellare, M., Rogaway, P.: The oracle Diffie-Hellman assumptions and an analysis of DHIES. In: Naccache, D. (ed.) CT-RSA 2001. LNCS, vol. 2020, pp. 143–158. Springer, Heidelberg (2001). doi:10.1007/3-540-45353-9_12
9. Boneh, D., Boyen, X.: Short signatures without random oracles. In: Cachin, C., Camenisch, J.L. (eds.) EUROCRYPT 2004. LNCS, vol. 3027, pp. 56–73. Springer, Heidelberg (2004). doi:10.1007/978-3-540-24676-3_4
10. Brickell, E., Camenisch, J., Chen, L.: Direct anonymous attestation. In: Proceedings of the 11th ACM Conference on Computer and Communications Security, pp. 132–145. ACM Press (2004)
11. Brickell, E., Li, J.: A pairing-based DAA scheme further reducing TPM resources. In: Acquisti, A., Smith, S.W., Sadeghi, A.-R. (eds.) Trust 2010. LNCS, vol. 6101, pp. 181–195. Springer, Heidelberg (2010). doi:10.1007/978-3-642-13869-0_12
12. BSI: Technical Guideline TR-03111, Elliptic Curve Cryptography, v2.0. BSI (2012). https://www.bsi.bund.de/SharedDocs/Downloads/EN/BSI/Publications/TechGuidelines/TR03111/BSI-TR-03111_pdf.html
13. Camenisch, J., Drijvers, M., Lehmann, A.: Universally composable direct anonymous attestation. In: Cheng, C.-M., Chung, K.-M., Persiano, G., Yang, B.-Y. (eds.) PKC 2016. LNCS, vol. 9615, pp. 234–264. Springer, Heidelberg (2016). doi:10.1007/978-3-662-49387-8_10
14. Camenisch, J., Lysyanskaya, A.: Signature schemes and anonymous credentials from bilinear maps. In: Franklin, M. (ed.) CRYPTO 2004. LNCS, vol. 3152, pp. 56–72. Springer, Heidelberg (2004). doi:10.1007/978-3-540-28628-8_4
15. Chen, L., Lee, M.-F., Warinschi, B.: Security of the enhanced TCG privacy-CA solution. In: Bruni, R., Sassone, V. (eds.) TGC 2011. LNCS, vol. 7173, pp. 121–141. Springer, Heidelberg (2012). doi:10.1007/978-3-642-30065-3_8
16. Chen, L., Li, J.: Flexible and scalable digital signatures in TPM 2.0. In: Proceedings of the 2013 ACM Conference on Computer and Communications Security, pp. 37–48. ACM Press (2013)
17. Chen, L., Page, D., Smart, N.P.: On the design and implementation of an efficient DAA scheme. In: Gollmann, D., Lanet, J.-L., Iguchi-Cartigny, J. (eds.) CARDIS 2010. LNCS, vol. 6035, pp. 223–237. Springer, Heidelberg (2010). doi:10.1007/978-3-642-12510-2_16
18. Chen, L., Urian, R.: DAA-A: direct anonymous attestation with attributes. In: Conti, M., Schunter, M., Askoxylakis, I. (eds.) Trust 2015. LNCS, vol. 9229, pp. 228–245. Springer, Heidelberg (2015). doi:10.1007/978-3-319-22846-4_14
19. Chen, L., Warinschi, B.: Security of the TCG privacy-CA solution. In: Proceedings of the 6th IEEE/IFIP International Symposium on Trusted Computing and Communications (TrustCom 2010), pp. 609–616. IEEE Press (2010)
20. Cramer, R., Shoup, V.: Design, analysis of practical public-key encryption schemes secure against adaptive chosen ciphertext attack. Cryptology ePrint Archive, Report 2001/108 (2001). http://eprint.iacr.org

21. Cramer, R., Shoup, V.: A practical public key cryptosystem provably secure against adaptive chosen ciphertext attack. In: Krawczyk, H. (ed.) CRYPTO 1998. LNCS, vol. 1462, pp. 13–25. Springer, Heidelberg (1998). doi:10.1007/BFb0055717

22. Fujisaki, E., Okamoto, T.: Secure integration of asymmetric and symmetric encryption schemes. In: Wiener, M. (ed.) CRYPTO 1999. LNCS, vol. 1666, pp. 537–554. Springer, Heidelberg (1999). doi:10.1007/3-540-48405-1_34

23. Gallagher, P.: Deputy Director Foreword, Cita Furlani Director: Fips pub 186–3 federal information processing standards publication digital signature standard (dss) (2009)

24. Kurosawa, K., Trieu Phong, L.: Kurosawa-Desmedt key encapsulation mechanism, revisited. In: Pointcheval, D., Vergnaud, D. (eds.) AFRICACRYPT 2014. LNCS, vol. 8469, pp. 51–68. Springer, Heidelberg (2014). doi:10.1007/978-3-319-06734-6_4

25. Microsoft U-Prove Community Technology: U-Prove cryptographic specification version 1.1 (2013). http://www.microsoft.com/u-prove

26. National Institute of Standards and Technology: Recommendation for pair-wise key estabishment schemes using discrete logarithm cryptography. Special Publication 800-56A, March 2007

27. Chinese National Standards: Public key cryptographic algorithm SM2 based on elliptic curves - Part 2: digital signature algorithm

28. TCG: TCG algorithm registry. Committee Draft, 7 January 2016

29. Trusted Computing Group: TCG TPM specification 1.2 (2003). www.trustedcomputinggroup.org

30. Trusted Computing Group: TCG TPM library 2.0 (2014). http://www.trustedcomputinggroup.org/tpm-library-specification/

31. Wang, X., Yin, Y.L., Yu, H.: Finding collisions in the full SHA-1. In: Shoup, V. (ed.) CRYPTO 2005. LNCS, vol. 3621, pp. 17–36. Springer, Heidelberg (2005). doi:10.1007/11535218_2

32. Wooten, D.: Final schnorr algorithm (2016). (email to TCG TPMWG)

33. Xi, L., Yang, K., Zhang, Z., Feng, D.: DAA-related APIs in TPM 2.0 revisited. In: Holz, T., Ioannidis, S. (eds.) Trust 2014. LNCS, vol. 8564, pp. 1–18. Springer, Heidelberg (2014). doi:10.1007/978-3-319-08593-7_1

Reactive and Proactive Standardisation of TLS

Kenneth G. Paterson and Thyla van der Merwe(⊠)

Information Security Group, Royal Holloway, University of London, Egham, UK
kenny.paterson@rhul.ac.uk, thyla.vandermerwe.2012@live.rhul.ac.uk

Abstract. In the development of TLS 1.3, the IETF TLS Working Group has adopted an "analysis-prior-to-deployment" design philosophy. This is in sharp contrast to all previous versions of the protocol. We present an account of the TLS standardisation narrative, examining the differences between the reactive standardisation process for TLS 1.2 and below, and the more proactive standardisation process for TLS 1.3. We explore the possible factors that have contributed to the shift in the TLS WG's design mindset, considering the protocol analysis tools available, the levels of academic involvement and the incentives governing relevant stakeholders at the time of standardisation. In an attempt to place TLS within the broader realm of standardisation, we perform a comparative analysis of standardisation models and discuss the standardisation of TLS within this context.

Keywords: Security · Standardisation · TLS

1 Introduction

The Transport Layer Security (TLS) protocol is used by millions, if not billions, of users on a daily basis and is the *de facto* standard when it comes to securing communications on the World Wide Web. The protocol was initially developed by Netscape Communications under the name Secure Sockets Layer (SSL) and then officially came under the auspices of the Internet Engineering Task Force (IETF) in the mid 1990s, eventually leading to the release of TLS 1.0 [32] in 1999. Subsequent versions were released in 2006 (TLS 1.1, [33]) and 2008 (TLS 1.2, [34]). Since then, TLS has received increasing amounts of attention from the security research community. Dozens of research papers on TLS have been published, containing both positive and negative results for the protocol. What began as a trickle of papers has, in the last five years, become a flood. Arguably, the major triggers for this skyrocketing in interest from the research community were the TLS Renegotiation flaw of Ray and Rex in 2009 and the BEAST and CRIME attacks in 2011 and 2012.

The many weaknesses identified in TLS 1.2 and below, as well as increasing pressure to improve the protocol's efficiency (by reducing its latency in establishing an initial secure connection) prompted the IETF to start drafting the next version of the protocol, TLS 1.3, in the Spring of 2014. Unlike the development process employed for earlier versions, the TLS WG has adopted an "analysis-prior-to-deployment" design philosophy, making a concerted effort to engage the

© Springer International Publishing AG 2016
L. Chen et al. (Eds.): SSR 2016, LNCS 10074, pp. 160–186, 2016.
DOI: 10.1007/978-3-319-49100-4_7

research community in an attempt to catch and remedy weaknesses before the protocol is finalised.

Given the critical nature of TLS, the recent shift in the IETF's design methodology for TLS 1.3, and TLS 1.3 now reaching the beginning of the end of the standardisation process, we think it pertinent that the TLS standardisation story be told. Prior to the standardisation of TLS 1.3, the TLS WG conformed to a reactive standardisation process: attacks would be announced and the WG would respond to these attacks by either updating the next version of the protocol or by releasing patches for the TLS standard. A number of factors contributed to the adoption of such a standardisation process. As we argue in the sequel, protocol analysis tools were not mature enough at the time of the design, the research community's involvement in the standardisation process was minimal, and until the first wave of attacks in 2009–2012, attacks on TLS were not considered to be of enough practical import to warrant making changes with urgency. In contrast, the on-going TLS 1.3 standardisation process has been highly proactive. The availability of more mature analysis tools, the threat of practical attacks, the presence of an engaged research community, and a far more open dialogue with that community have, we contend, enabled this shift in the TLS standardisation process.

This newer process has arguably been successful; several research works have helped build confidence in the protocol's design [12,35,36,42,57,64], and others have caught flaws in a timely fashion [18,31]. The design itself has also been significantly influenced by the research community [61], and the amount of communication between those who implement TLS and those who analyse TLS has probably never been greater.

Despite this relative success, we deem it important to reflect on whether or not the TLS 1.3 process could have been improved, and indeed to what extent it fits into the broader realm of standardisation. To this end, we briefly consider standardisation models as employed by differing standardisation bodies and examine their differences, advantages and disadvantages through the lens of TLS. Specifically, we focus on the IETF, the International Organization for standardisation (ISO) and the US government's National Institute for Standards and Technology (NIST). We conduct the thought experiment of identifying which model best suits a protocol such as TLS.

1.1 Contributions

In this paper we detail the TLS standardisation process, commenting on the recent shift in the design methodology employed by the IETF. We examine the era of post-deployment analysis, in which the IETF reacted to protocol vulnerabilities, as well as the era of pre-deployment analysis, in which the IETF is actively trying to preempt protocol weaknesses. Our contributions may be described as follows:

Pre- Versus Post-deployment Analysis. We present an account of the TLS standardisation process, examining factors which may have contributed to the different standardisation cycles employed for TLS 1.2 and below and TLS 1.3, respectively. We comment on the tools available for analysis, levels of academic involvement, as well as the incentives driving the agents involved in the standardisation process.

Further Improvements. We comment on how the TLS 1.3 standardisation process could have been improved and present an alternative standardisation cycle for security protocols.

Comparative Analysis. We perform a comparative analysis of standardisation models and discuss the merits and faults of these models by examining their suitability for the standardisation of critical protocols such as TLS.

1.2 Related Work

In work on standardisation transparency, Griffin [49] presents the Kaleidoscope Conference case study which details actions by the International Telecommunication Union (ITU) to host an academic conference aimed at encouraging openness in standards development, as well as cultivating academia as an important external source of new ideas and technologies. We cover the concept of conferences and workshops as a means of enhancing academic involvement but also show that in the case of TLS 1.3, academia serves as an internal source of ideas in the standardisation process.

Gutmann *et al.* discuss the importance of setting requirements for security protocols in [50], another topic which we touch upon. But they appear to do so in the post-analysis setting, as they discuss formal techniques for updating requirements in response to flaws found in already published standards.

We are unaware of any work covering the complete TLS standardisation process.

1.3 Paper Organisation

In Sect. 2 we briefly present background on TLS and the IETF. In Sect. 3 we discuss the standardisation process for TLS 1.2 and below. We cover the process that has been followed for TLS 1.3 in Sect. 4. In Sect. 5 we consider the standardisation of protocols beyond the realm of the IETF and we conclude in Sect. 6.

2   Background

2.1   TLS

We provide a high-level overview of the TLS protocol, describing only what is relevant to the standardisation discussions to follow. We direct the reader to [34,78] for further details.

TLS is a network protocol designed to provide security services for protocols running at the application layer. The primary goal of TLS is to facilitate the establishment of a secure channel between two communicating entities, namely the client and the server. The TLS protocol is made up of a number sub-protocols, the two most important being the Handshake Protocol and the Record Protocol. The Handshake Protocol negotiates all cryptographically relevant parameters (including what TLS version, what authentication and key exchange method, and what subsequent symmetric key algorithms will be used). It authenticates one (or both) of the communicating entities, and establishes the keys for the symmetric algorithms that will be used in the Record Protocol to protect application data. For instance, if a client and a server agree on the TLS_RSA_WITH_AES_128_CBC_SHA256 cipher suite during a TLS 1.2 handshake, then the server will provide an RSA certificate to be used for key exchange and entity authentication purposes. In this example, the Record Protocol will then make use of AES in CBC mode for the encryption of application data, and SHA-256 will be used in the HMAC algorithm to provide message authentication.

TLS 1.2 and Below. The message flows for an initial TLS 1.2 handshake are depicted in Fig. 1. Messages marked with an asterisk are optional or situation-dependent and braces of the type "[...]" indicate encryption with the application traffic keys. The client and the server exchange ClientHello and ServerHello messages in order to agree on a cipher suite and to exchange nonce values. The communicating entities also exchange cryptographic parameters (ServerKeyExchange, ClientKeyExchange) that allow for the derivation of the pre-master secret. Certificates and the corresponding verification information (Certificate, CertificateVerify) are sent for the purposes of entity authentication. A master secret is derived from the nonce values and the pre-master secret, and in turn used in the derivation of the application traffic keys to be employed by the Record Protocol. The Finished message comprises a MAC over the entire handshake, ensuring that the client and the server share an identical view of the handshake and that an active attacker has not altered any of the handshake messages.

The Handshake Protocol runs over the Record Protocol, initially with null encryption and MAC algorithms. The ChangeCipherSpec messages signal the intent to start using newly negotiated cryptographic algorithms and keys; they are not considered part of the handshake but instead are the messages of a peer protocol, the ChangeCipherSpec protocol. Because the Finished messages come after the ChangeCipherSpec messages, they are protected using the application data traffic keys derived in the handshake. These messages, then, are the first to be protected as part of the Record Protocol. They are followed by application data messages, now protected by the Record Protocol.

The cryptographic parameters established in the initial handshake constitute a TLS *session*. A session can be updated via a renegotiation handshake. This is a full handshake that runs under the protection of an already established TLS session. This mechanism allows cryptographic parameters to be changed (for

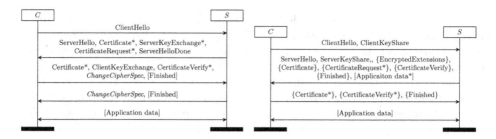

Fig. 1. TLS 1.2 handshake   **Fig. 2.** TLS 1.3 (EC)DHE handshake

example, upgraded), or client authentication to be demanded by a server. In order to avoid the expensive public key operations in repeated handshakes, TLS also offers a lightweight resumption handshake in which a new **master secret** is derived from the old **pre-master secret** and new nonces, thus forcing fresh application data keys. Each such resumption handshake leads to a new TLS *connection* within the existing session; many connections can exist in parallel for each session.

The Record Protocol, as already indicated, provides a secure channel for transmission of Application Data (as well as Handshake Protocol and Alert messages). In TLS 1.0 and 1.1, it uses a "MAC-then-Encode-then-Encrypt" (MEE) construction, with the MAC algorithm being HMAC instantiated with a range of hash functions and the encryption algorithm being instantiated with CBC-mode of a block cipher or the RC4 stream cipher. Sequence numbers are included in the cryptographic processing, creating a stateful secure channel in which replays, deletions and re-orderings of TLS records can be detected. TLS 1.2 added supported for Authenticated Encryption with Associated Data (AEAD) schemes, with AES-GCM being an increasingly popular option.

TLS 1.3. We provide a brief description of TLS 1.3 as defined in the current draft 15 of the standard [78], deferring discussion of the design rationale to Sect. 4. The design process for TLS 1.3 is on-going and several more drafts can be expected before it is complete. However, at the time of writing, the major components of the protocol appear to be fairly stable.

The message flows for an initial TLS 1.3 ephemeral Diffie-Hellman handshake are depicted in Fig. 2. Messages marked with an asterisk are optional or situation-dependent. Braces of the type "{...}" indicate protection under the handshake traffic key and braces of the type "[...]" indicate protection under the application traffic key. The client and the server exchange **ClientHello** and **ServerHello** messages in order to agree a cipher suite and to exchange nonce values. The entities also exchange freshly generated Diffie-Hellman (DH) key shares along with the associated set of groups (**ClientKeyShare**, **ServerKeyShare**).

The server's first message flight will also contain extensions not used for key establishment (**EncryptedExtensions**) as well as optional early application data. Certificates and the corresponding verification information (`Certificate`, `CertificateVerify`) are exchanged for the purposes of entity authentication; the client will provide this information if requested to do so by the server (`CertificateRequest`). The `Finished` messages comprise MACs over the entire handshake transcripts using a handshake traffic key derived from the DH key shares. These messages provide integrity of the handshake as well as key confirmation. As depicted in Fig. 2, the `Finished` messages are encrypted with handshake traffic keys, and no longer with application traffic keys as was the case in TLS 1.2 and below. The first records to be protected by the Record Layer are application data messages. TLS 1.3 only allows the use of AEAD schemes for the protection of this data.

Entities may also choose to use a pre-shared key (PSK) (`PreSharedKey`), or may make use of a PSK/DH combination for key exchange. In TLS 1.3, session resumption makes use of PSKs; the same is true for transmission of early client data, with the PSK used in both cases being established in an earlier handshake. This so-called *zero round-trip time (0-RTT)* capability allows the client to transmit data as part of its first flight of messages. Details pertaining to these handshake modes can be found in [78]. The renegotiation handshake as described in the TLS 1.2 RFC is no longer available in TLS 1.3.

2.2   The IETF

The IETF is a self-organized group of software developers, implementers, vendors and researchers focused on creating and maintaining engineering standards for the Internet. The IETF's mission is, simply, "to make the Internet work better" [2]. Participation by individuals is entirely voluntary and there is no formal membership or associated membership fees. The standardisation work done by the IETF is organised into areas, each of which contains several Working Groups (WGs). These areas cover all protocol layers, starting from IP [75] at the internet layer up to general application layer protocols such as HTTP [15], making the IETF the de facto technical forum for all matters concerning Internet protocol standards. The TLS WG falls into the Security Area of the IETF.

The IETF's standards are published free of charge as *Request for Comment* documents (RFCs). These are compiled using inputs from the WG mailing lists and the face-to-face discussions held at IETF meetings throughout the year. The TLS WG mailing list is remarkably active and serves as an important platform for discussion regarding the TLS RFCs. Once published, RFCs may be augmented via the use of *extensions*. These are RFCs intended to provide increased functionality and/or, in the case of TLS, security enhancements.

The IETF follows an open model of standards development. There are no barriers to entry with regards to membership and contributions, and there is a many-to-one development philosophy: all contributions are pooled in the production of one standard, with a consensus-based process being used to decide between competing options. Analysis of TLS results from a mixture of internal and external sources; WG members may provide analyses at formal IETF meetings or on the mailing list, and research originating outside of the WG may also be consulted. In reality, and in particular for TLS 1.3, the official IETF processes have been supplemented by a shadow process involving input from a small and time-varying group of cryptographic protocol design experts. This input has been fed in to the draft editor via e-mail and in informal meetings at various conferences and workshops. Since the IETF charges no fee for its standards there are no financial barriers to adoption.

3   Post-deployment Analysis

The standardisation process for TLS 1.2 and below can arguably be described as reactive. Following the announcement of attacks against the protocol, the TLS WG has responded by either making the necessary changes to the next version of the standard or by releasing interim recommendations or extensions. This conforms to what we will term the *design-release-break-patch* cycle of standards development. In what follows, we outline this development process as it pertains to TLS, highlighting attacks against the protocol and the IETF's responses to these attacks. We focus on attacks against the protocol rather than attacks on specific implementations (though the importance of these, for example Heartbleed and various certificate processing vulnerabilities, should not be underestimated).

We note that each TLS version builds on the previous version, incorporating changes where necessary. All TLS versions are currently in use, with clients and servers often supporting more than one version. At the time of writing, almost 98 % of sites probed in the SSL Pulse survey[1] support TLS 1.0, with support of TLS 1.1 and TLS 1.2 both being in the region of 80 %.

3.1   Design, Release, Break, Patch

The TLS standard officially sprang to life with a decision by the IETF to standardize a version of the Secure Sockets Layer (SSL) protocol[2] in 1996. The growing need to support e-commerce and hence the growing deployment of the SSL protocol prompted the IETF to this course of action. At this stage, two versions of SSL existed in the public domain, namely SSLv2 and SSLv3 [43]. SSLv2 had a number of weaknesses, in particular offering no defence against downgrade attacks. It was finally deprecated by the IETF in [84], published in 2011.

In 1998, Bleichenbacher published an attack on RSA when encryption used the PKCS #1 encoding scheme [26], affecting SSLv3. The attack targets the RSA-encrypted pre-master secret sent from client to server (see Sect. 2.1) by using the distinctive server-generated PKCS #1-padding error message as an oracle. Successive, adaptive calls to this oracle allow an attacker to narrow in on the value of the pre-master secret, and once this is obtained, the attacker is able to derive the symmetric keys used in the connection. The TLS 1.0 standard [32] briefly addresses this attack in a two-paragraph note that describes the

---

[1] https://www.trustworthyinternet.org/ssl-pulse/.
[2] Designed by Netscape Communications in the 1990s.

following countermeasure: a server that receives an incorrectly formatted RSA block should use a pre-generated, random 48-byte value as the pre-master secret instead, thereby eliminating the oracle. The Bleichenbacher attack has been re-enabled (in various forms) in several works [52,55,69], the most recent case being DROWN [13], a cross-protocol attack targeting all versions of TLS running on servers that also support SSLv2. Surprisingly, a large number of servers still support this legacy version of the protocol.[3]

Following the release of TLS 1.0 [32], the first significant attack against TLS seems to be Vaudenay's padding oracle attack [28,86]. This attack exploits the specific CBC-mode padding format used by TLS in its MEE construction in the Record Protocol. The TLS WG initially responded to the attack by adding an attack-specific countermeasure to the attack in the TLS 1.1 specification [33]. This was intended to equalise the running time of the reverse of the MEE process-ing – decryption, decoding, MAC verification (DDM). This knowingly left a small timing channel, but it was not believed to be exploitable. A decade later, in 2013, AlFardan and Paterson [8], in their Lucky 13 attack, showed that in fact it was exploitable in a sophisticated timing attack. Notably, the definitive patch against this attack required roughly 500 lines of new code in the OpenSSL implemen-tation, illustrating the difficulty of making the DDM operations constant time. Moreover, several follow-up papers [7,10,11] have shown that variants of the attack are still mountable in certain circumstances or for certain implemen-tations. The 2014 POODLE attack [71] on SSLv3 showed that SSLv3 was also vulnerable to a related but arguably more serious padding oracle attack, in which timing information was replaced with much more easy to measure error informa-tion. Because of weaknesses in the RC4 algorithm (that we discuss below), the only other encryption option in SSLv3, and because POODLE was essentially unpatchable, this attack left no other reasonable encryption options for SSLv3.

Following the release of TLS 1.2 [34] in 2008, we see more of a "patch" process being adopted by the TLS WG. During this time, we saw an explosion of attacks against TLS. We discuss some of these next.

In 2009 Ray and Rex more or less simultaneously discovered the TLS Rene-gotiation attack[4]. By exploiting the lack of a cryptographic binding between an attacker's initial handshake and a subsequent renegotiation handshake between an honest client and an honest server, the attacker is able to convince the server to interpret traffic – both the attacker-injected traffic and the honest client's traffic – as coming from the honest client. The WG's response to this attack was the announcement of a mandatory TLS extension [79] applicable to all versions of TLS. The extension proposed including the respective **Finished** messages in the client and server renegotiation **Hello** messages, thus creating a bind-ing between the two handshakes. Unfortunately, the Triple Handshake attack of Bhargavan et al. [20] resurrected the Renegotiation attack by cleverly exploiting

---

[3] At the time of writing, 7 % of the roughly 150 k servers surveyed by SSL pulse still do.

[4] See   http://www.educatedguesswork.org/2009/11/understanding_the_tls_renegoti. html for a description of the attack.

the interaction of various TLS resumption and renegotiation handshakes. The attack completely breaks client authentication.

In 2011 Duong and Rizzo announced the BEAST[5] attack [38]. The attack affects TLS 1.0 and makes use of the chained-IV vulnerability observed by Moeller [70] and Bard [14], though it has its roots in an observation of Rogaway [80] from as early as 1995. BEAST exploits the fact that in TLS 1.0, the final ciphertext block of a CBC-encrypted record becomes the IV for the next record to be encrypted. This enables an attacker with a chosen plaintext capability to recover low entropy plaintexts. The main significance of the BEAST attack is the clever use of malicious JavaScript running in a victim's browser to realise the low entropy, chosen plaintext requirement and thereby mount an HTTP session cookie recovery attack against TLS. However, it should be noted that the attack required a zero-day vulnerability in the browser in order to obtain the required fine control over chosen plaintexts. The malicious JavaScript techniques were leveraged a year later by the same authors in the CRIME[6] attack (see [82] for a useful description of the attack). Unlike BEAST, however, CRIME exploits the compression side-channel inherent to all versions of TLS, a vulnerability noted in theoretical form by Kelsey in 2002 [54]. Interestingly, whilst the BEAST and CRIME attacks can be seen as having triggered the flood of research that followed, neither came from the academic research community, but instead from the "hacker" community (which partly explains the lack of formal research papers describing the attacks). Both attacks required a strong understanding not only of the cryptographic aspects of the protocol, but also of how the protocol is deployed in the web context.

The widespread response to CRIME was to disable TLS's compression feature. However, this does not completely solve the problem of compression-based attacks because compression can also take place at the application layer and introduce similar side-channels (see the BREACH and TIME attacks). A common response to BEAST was to switch to using RC4 as the encryption method in the Record Protocol, since a stream cipher would not be susceptible to the CBC vulnerabilities. Unfortunately, the RC4 keystream has long been known to be biased [66], and in 2013, AlFardan et al. [9] exploited newly discovered and known keystream biases to obtain cookie recovery attacks when RC4 was used as the method of protection in TLS. Garman et al. [45] enhanced the statistical techniques of Al Fardan et al. and developed password recovery attacks that were of greater practical significance than those presented in [9]. The weaknesses in RC4 were further exploited by Vanhoef and Piessens [85] and Bricout et al. [27]. The IETF deprecated RC4 in March 2015 in [74]. Its usage has dropped rapidly as a consequence of the high profile nature of the attacks, the deprecation, and the decision by major vendors to disable RC4 in their browsers.[7]

---

[5] Browser Exploit Against SSL/TLS.

[6] Compression-Ratio Info-leak Made Easy.

[7] See, for example, http://www.infoworld.com/article/2979527/security/google-moz illa-microsoft-browsers-dump-rc4-encryption.html.

Other notable attacks to follow the BEAST, CRIME and RC4 attacks include the FREAK [17] and Logjam [6] attacks of 2015, and the SLOTH attack [24] of 2016. Both FREAK and Logjam exploit the enduring widespread support for weak export-grade cryptographic primitives. Whereas the FREAK attack affects certain TLS implementations, the Logjam vulnerability, in contrast, is the result of a protocol flaw and targets Diffie-Hellman key exchange in TLS. The attack requires a server to support export-grade cryptography, and for the client to be willing to use low security Diffie-Hellman groups. An active attacker can convince the server to provide an export-grade 512-bit group to a client that has requested a non-export DHE cipher suite, and the client will in turn accept this weak group as being valid for the DHE handshake. Clever use of a pre-computation phase for state-of-the-art discrete logarithm algorithms in [6] allowed for the quick computation of individual connections' secrets. An early intimation of these types of cross-cipher-suite attack can be found in the work of Wagner and Schneier [87] as early as 1996. The warning from this paper seems to have been either forgotten or ignored in subsequent developments of TLS. Moreover, from version 1.1 onwards, export-grade cipher suites were not supported by the TLS standards. However, as already noted, almost all servers do support TLS 1.0 and so become vulnerable to this class of attack.

The change in TLS 1.2 from supporting the MD5/SHA-1 hash function combination to supporting single hash functions for digital signatures meant that stronger hash functions such as SHA-256 could be supported but alas, so could weaker hash functions, such as MD5. Wang and Yu [88] described collision attacks against MD5 in 2005; the SLOTH attack [24] exploits this weakness to break client authentication in TLS 1.2 when MD5-based signatures are employed. The attacks presented are near-practical and falsify the belief of some practitioners that only second-preimage resistance is required of the hash functions used for TLS signatures.

We have described, at a high-level, a number of the most prominent attacks on TLS and the TLS WG's responses to these attacks. We now turn to examining whether or not these attacks were adequately addressed, and indeed, to what extent they could have been addressed by the standardisation process.

3.2   Effective Fixing, Implementation Constraints and Time Lags

The TLS 1.2 specification provides the following cautionary note with regards to the Bleichenbacher attack:

```
"a TLS server MUST NOT generate an alert if processing an
RSA-encrypted premaster secret message fails, or the version
number is not as expected. Instead, it MUST continue the handshake
with a randomly generated premaster secret. It may be useful
to log the real cause of failure for troubleshooting purposes;
however, care must be taken to avoid leaking the information to an
attacker (through, e.g., timing, log files, or other channels.)"
```

Upon first glance, the countermeasure appears adequate. However, as pointed out by Jager *et al.* [52], the discovery of new side-channels and the development of more sophisticated analysis techniques allow for the implementation of Bleichenbacher-style attacks even though the vulnerability was thought to be successfully patched. The attacks by Meyer *et al.* [69] on implementations of TLS serve as an example of this. One course open to the TLS WG was to remove the use of the PKCS#1 v1.5 encoding scheme in favour of the PKCS#1 v2.1 encoding scheme (implementing OAEP padding). This would have been more secure against the Bleichenbacher attack and all envisionable variants. However, as is explained in the TLS 1.1 and TLS 1.2 RFCs, in order to maintain compatibility with earlier TLS versions, this replacement was not made. We presume that the desire to maintain backwards compatibility and confidence in the *ad hoc* countermeasure trumped the evidently better security available from the use of PKCS#1 v2.1.

A very similar situation pertains to padding oracle attacks and Lucky 13: an implementation patch was put in place in TLS 1.1 and 1.2, but shown to be inadequate by the Lucky 13 attack [8]. With hindsight, it would have been less effort overall, and less damaging to the reputation of the protocol, to reform the MEE construction used in TLS at an earlier stage, replacing it with a modern design fully supported by theoretical analysis (notwithstanding the positive results of [58], whose limitations were pointed out in [73]). A repeated pattern in the development of TLS 1.2 and below is that the TLS community (a larger group of individuals and organisations than the TLS WG) seem to need to see concrete working attacks before addressing a potential vulnerability or adopting an intrinsically more secure solution, rather than applying a patch to each specific vulnerability.

In the case of attacks that exploit the existence of primitives or mechanisms that have long been known to exhibit weaknesses, the simple (but naive) solution is to simply consider removing a primitive or mechanism as soon as it is shown to be weak. However, this might not be straightforward given implementation and interoperability constraints. In the case of FREAK and Logjam, the standardisation process cannot be faulted: the weak export cipher suites were removed from TLS 1.1 and TLS 1.2 and these attacks exist as a result of poor implementation choices by practitioners. Similar remarks apply to the IV-chaining vulnerability, which while already known in 1995, was introduced to TLS 1.0 in 1999, but then removed in TLS 1.1 in 2006. Unfortunately, deployed versions of TLS did not move so quickly, with widespread support for TLS 1.0 in servers even today. On the other hand, all modern browsers will now prefer TLS 1.2 and AEAD cipher suites in an initial handshake attempt, thanks to the long line of attacks on TLS's CBC-mode and RC4 options. In the case of SLOTH, however, the issue might not be as clear-cut. MD5-based signature schemes should not have been re-introduced in the TLS 1.2 RFC. And RC4 has a very long track-record of weaknesses stretching back more than 15 years, meaning that its phasing out from TLS could arguably have been initiated much sooner than it was, instead of waiting for the attacks to become so powerful. In many cases, particularly where hardware support for AES is available, AES-GCM could have served as a better choice for encryption.

With the many research papers professing the security of the TLS Handshake Protocol, the existence of attacks exploiting the interaction of various TLS handshakes may have come as a surprise to the TLS community. However, even here, there were early signs that things were amiss with the 1996 cross-cipher-suite attack of Wagner and Schneier [87]. Perhaps the lack of a practical attack in that paper and in later papers such as [68] led to a more relaxed attitude being adopted by the TLS WG here. The subtle interactions of different TLS handshakes was never fully considered in any analysis of TLS prior to the Triple Handshake attack of 2014. It is therefore not surprising that attacks of this form would have slipped through the standardisation process. Yet it should be remembered that the Triple Handshake attack is a resurrection of the Renegotiation attack from 2009. This is indicative of insufficiently broad or powerful analysis having been available to the TLS WG in the period intervening between the two attacks.

We argue that, in general and in view of the extreme importance of TLS, a much more conservative approach to dealing with attacks on TLS is warranted. We do, however, appreciate that bringing about meaningful change is challenging given the large scale and wide diversity of TLS deployment, the historical reticence of the major implementations to code newer versions of the protocol (especially TLS 1.2), and the slowness with which users (particularly on the server side) have tended to update their TLS versions.

3.3   Impact and Incentives

In the design-release-break-patch standardisation cycle, maximal reward for researchers has come in the form of producing and promoting high impact attacks against TLS, and engagement of the research community was largely encouraged in a retroactive fashion. The obvious problem with this incentive model is that it leaves users of published standards vulnerable to attack and imposes a potential patch action on the TLS WG. In the next section we consider whether or not a shift in the standardisation cycle leaves the opportunity for researchers to have impact (of a different kind) whilst positively benefiting the standardisation process.

4   Pre-deployment Analysis

In contrast to the development of TLS 1.2 and below, the standardisation process for TLS 1.3 has been proactive in nature. It has followed what we describe as the *design-break-fix-release* cycle for standards development. Working more closely with the research community, the TLS WG has released multiple protocol drafts and welcomed analyses of the protocol before its final release. As the next section will show, this design philosophy has simultaneously led to the discovery of weaknesses and provided confidence in the WG's design decisions. We explore the factors that have enabled this newer process by considering the improvements in the protocol analysis tools available, as well as the shift in design attitudes and incentives. This approach, however, has not been without its complications. In what follows we also address the challenges inherent to such an approach and comment on ways in which the process, a far as TLS is concerned, could have been improved.

4.1   Design, Break, Fix, Release

The two broad design goals for TLS 1.3 are (i) to improve efficiency of the Handshake Protocol and (ii) to address the weaknesses identified in TLS 1.2 and below.[8] The initial challenge for the TLS WG was to go about achieving these goals without having to invent an entirely new protocol: in addition to requiring new code libraries, a new protocol might introduce new weaknesses. The development of Google's QUIC Crypto by Langley and Chang [63] in 2013, offering a zero round-trip time (0-RTT) capability for the QUIC protocol [81], put pressure on the TLS WG to consider ways of reducing handshake latency in TLS 1.3. And, after the flurry of attacks in the preceding years, the protocol was due an overhaul to remove weak or broken features.

In comparison to TLS 1.2 and below, the first few drafts of TLS 1.3 (beginning with draft 00 in April 2014) incorporated changes that aim to fortify the protocol against known attacks, such as the removal of support for compression, as well as the removal of static RSA and Diffie-Hellman key exchange mechanisms, leaving ephemeral Diffie-Hellman as the only method of key exchange. Handshake latency was also reduced by the introduction of a one round-trip time (1-RTT) TLS handshake (previously an initial handshake required two round trips before a client and a server could start exchanging application data).

Two important changes that were introduced in the drafts up to and including `draft-05` are the concept of a *session hash* and the removal of the renegotiation handshake. At the time of release of `draft-04`, the session hash constituted a hash value of all messages in a handshake starting with the `ClientHello`, up to and including the `ClientKeyExchange`. The session hash is then included in the key derivation process to prevent an active attacker from synchronizing the **master secret** across two different sessions, a trick employed in the Triple Handshake attack [21]. The removal of renegotiation prevents renegotiation-based attacks, the Triple Handshake attack again serving as an example of this class of attack.

In terms of analysis of TLS 1.3, Dowling *et al.* [35] and Kohlweiss *et al.* [57] published works on `draft-05`, the latter set of authors using a constructive-cryptography approach to provide security guarantees for the protocol. Their work highlights that the design choice in TLS 1.3 to separate out the Handshake and Record protocols helps with their analysis, and indeed with provable security

---

[8] See the TLS WG charter at https://datatracker.ietf.org/wg/tls/charter/ for further details.

approaches in general. (Recall that in TLS 1.2 and below, the application traffic keys derived in the Handshake Protocol were used to encrypt the Finished messages of the Handshake Protocol itself. This interaction adds significant complexity to analyses of TLS 1.2 and below, in particular because it violates the standard indistinguishability security goal for a key exchange protocol.)

Dowling *et al.* [35] used the multi-stage key exchange model of Fischlin and Günther [41] to show that the keys output by the Handshake Protocol could be securely used in the Record Protocol. Their work provided several comments on the design of TLS 1.3, thereby explicitly providing useful feedback to the TLS WG.

In draft-07 we see the most radical shift away from TLS 1.2, with the cryptographic core of the TLS handshake becoming strongly influenced by the OPTLS protocol of Krawczyk and Wee [62], with many OPTLS elements being incorporated into the draft. OPTLS has been expressly designed to be simple and modular, offering a 1-RTT, forward secure TLS handshake that employs ephemeral Diffie-Hellman key exchange. OPTLS also offers 0-RTT support as well as a pre-shared key (PSK) mode, capturing the use case in which a client and a server enter into the protocol having previously shared a key. This particular mode is of relevance from draft-07 onwards as the TLS 1.2-style resumption mechanism is replaced with a mechanism that makes use of PSKs. This draft included a 0-RTT handshake and key derivation schedule that is similar to that of OPTLS, employing the HKDF primitive designed by Krawczyk [59]. The OPTLS designers provided a detailed analysis of their protocol in [62], again providing the TLS WG with confidence in its design choices.

However, it should be noted that significant changes were made in adapting OPTLS to meet the needs of TLS. For example, OPTLS originally assumed that servers' long term keys would be Diffie-Hellman values, in turn supported by certificates. However, such certificates are not widely used in practice today, potentially hindering deployment of TLS 1.3. Thus, in the "translation" of OPTLS into TLS 1.3, a two-level process was assumed, with the server using a traditional signing key to authenticate its long-term Diffie-Hellman value. But this created yet another real-world security issue: if an attacker can gain access to a server's signing capability just once, then he would be able to forge a credential enabling him to impersonate a server on a long-term basis. Thus it was decided to change the signature scope to also include client-supplied, session-specific information, limiting the value of any temporary access to the signing capability. This reduces the efficiency of the protocol, since now a fresh signature must be produced by the server in each handshake.

Notable changes in draft-08 and draft-09 of the protocol include the removal of support for MD5-based signatures as well as the deprecation of SHA-1-based signatures, partly in response to the SLOTH vulnerability [24] and as result of pressure from practitioners and researchers to remove these weak primitives, as evidenced on the TLS mailing list [46, 47].

Cremers *et al.* [31] performed an automated analysis of TLS 1.3 using the Tamarin prover [83]. Their model covers draft-10 and their analysis showed that this draft meets the goals of authenticated key exchange. They showed this in a symbolic model in which secrecy properties are more coarse-grained than would be the case in a computational model, but where the interaction of the different handshake components is easier to analyze. Cremers *et al.* anticipated the inclusion of the delayed client authentication mechanism in the TLS 1.3 series of drafts. This feature enables a server to request authentication at any point after the handshake has completed, reminiscent of the functionality provided by the renegotiation handshake in TLS 1.2 and below. They discovered a potential interaction attack which would break client authentication. The attack highlighted the strict necessity of expanding the session hash scope to include `Finished` messages. This prevents the attacker from replaying a client signature across sessions by binding the signature to the session for which it is intended. Their attack was communicated to the TLS WG, and `draft-11`, which officially incorporated the delayed client authentication mechanism, included the necessary fix as part of the design. In concurrent work, Li *et al.* [64] analysed the interaction of the various TLS 1.3 handshake modes in the computational setting using their "multi-level&stage" security model. They found `draft-10` to be secure in this model. The delayed authentication threat was not identified in this work presumably because this mechanism was not officially part of `draft-10`.

In February of 2016, just prior to the release of `draft-12`, the Internet Society hosted a "TLS Ready or Not?" (TRON) workshop. The workshop showcased analyses of TLS 1.3, both published and under development, bringing together members of the TLS Working Group, researchers and industry professionals with the aim of testing the readiness of TLS 1.3 in its then current form. Besides the aforementioned work by Kohlwiess *et al.*, Krawczyk and Wee, and Cremers *et al.*, there were several other presentations highlighting progress in the protocol's development, as well as the challenges still facing the TLS WG. Dowling *et al.* updated their previous analysis to cover `draft-10` [36], showing the full (EC)DHE handshake to be secure in the multi-stage key exchange setting. Bhargavan *et al.* introduced ProScript [18], a JavaScript variant of their verified TLS implementation, miTLS [3,22]. Interestingly, ProScript also allows for the extraction of a symbolic model for use within the ProVerif protocol analysis tool [4,25]. This work highlighted the potential dangers of incorporating certificate-based authentication into PSK handshakes, a potential protocol extension being considered by the TLS WG. Work on the secure of implementation of TLS 1.3 by Berdouche *et al.* [16] considered how to maintain compatibility with current TLS versions whilst protecting against downgrade attacks, and highlighted simplifications to the protocol which could be beneficial from an implementation point of of view.

Importantly, the TRON workshop led to discussions between the WG and the research community regarding potential simplifications and enhancements to the protocol. Some of these discussions are still ongoing and have informed subsequent drafts of the protocol. The workshop also fostered an in-depth discussion regarding the security requirements for TLS 1.3. This has led to a call for contributions from researchers and practitioners alike [5]. It may seem surprising that security requirements analysis was taking place at such a late stage in the process. We comment on this further below.

At around the same time as the TRON workshop, an analysis by the Cryptographic protocol Evaluation towards Long-Lived Outstanding Security (CELLOS) Consortium, using the ProVerif tool, was announced on the TLS WG mailing list [12,67]. This work showed the initial (EC)DHE handshake of draft-11 to be secure in the symbolic setting.

Further publications of relevance to TLS 1.3 include the work on downgrade resilience by Bhargavan *et al.* [19] and the work on key confirmation by Fischlin *et al.* [42]. The first provides suggestions on how to strengthen downgrade security in TLS 1.3 and the second provides assurances regarding the key confirmation mechanisms used.

A smaller *ad hoc* meeting informally called "TRON2" took place in May 2016. At this meeting, the latest changes to the protocol were discussed, further formal analysis was presented, and TLS 1.3 implementations were compared.[9]

4.2   Available Tools

Since the release of TLS 1.2 in 2008, cryptographic protocol analysis tools have developed and matured to the extent that they can now effectively serve a proactive standardisation process, thereby contributing to, and perhaps even enabling, a more collaborative design effort for TLS 1.3. Significant advances have been made across all fronts, from lower-level primitives such as key derivation and authenticated encryption, to higher level primitives such as authenticated key exchange and cryptographic modelling of secure channels.

An early analysis of the TLS protocol itself can be found in the work of Gajek *et al.* [44] in 2008. However, their analysis only covers unauthenticated key exchange. Many refinements and advances in the area of provable security for TLS have since been made. A major on-going challenge has been to provide accurate modelling of the protocol and to capture the complexity of its many interacting components and modes. In 2010, Morrissey *et al.* [72] also analysed the TLS Handshake Protocol. However, their work only considered a truncated version of the protocol (with no encryption of Finished messages), assumed that a CCA-secure encryption scheme was used for key transport (which is unrealistic given that TLS implementations employ PKCS#1 v1.5-based RSA encryption), and relied on the random oracle model. In 2012, Jager *et al.* [51] introduced the Authenticated and Confidential Channel Establishment (ACCE) security model in an attempt to handle the unfortunate mixing of key usage in the Handshake and Record protocols; they used the ACCE model to analyse certain Diffie-Hellman-based key exchanges in TLS. Their work built in part on a 2011 work of Paterson *et al.* [73], who introduced the notion of length-hiding Authenticated Encryption, which models desired security goals of the TLS Record Protocol. Further important works include those by Krawczyk *et al.* [60] and Kohlar *et al.* [56]. The former work analysed multiple, different TLS

---

[9] See https://www.mitls.org/tron2/ for details.

key exchange methods using a single, uniform set of proof techniques in the ACCE setting, while the latter extended the work of Jager *et al.* to show that the RSA and DH handshakes can be proven secure in the mutual authentication setting. Li *et al.* [65] performed a similar task for pre-shared key cipher suites. Giesen *et al.* [48] explicitly consider multiple Handshake protocol runs and their interactions in their formal treatment of the security of TLS renegotiation, while Dowling and Stebila [37] examined cipher suite and version negotiation in TLS. All of these works offer techniques that could be harnessed, and potentially extended, in the analysis of TLS 1.3, prior to its final release. Moreover, they represent a growth in interest in the TLS protocol from the research community, a necessary precursor to their greater involved in the TLS 1.3 design process.

A major step forward in the domain of program verification for TLS came with the first release of the miTLS reference implementation in 2013 [3,22]. The miTLS implementation integrates software security and computational cryptographic security approaches so as to obtain security proofs for running code. This approach aims to eliminate the reliance on the simplifying assumptions employed by the more traditional provable security techniques – those tend to analyse abstract and somewhat high-level models of TLS and tend to ignore many implementation details in order to obtain tractable models (in the form of pseudo-code) suitable for the production of hand-generated proofs; moreover, they tend to focus on "fragments" of the TLS protocol suite rather than the entire system. Using this approach, Bhargavan *et al.* provided an epoch-based security analysis of the TLS 1.2 handshake as implemented in miTLS [23]. The miTLS implementation provides a reference for the secure implementation of TLS 1.2 and below, and interoperates with all major web browsers and servers. Not only has the miTLS project lead to the discovery of vulnerabilities such as the Triple Handshake attack and FREAK, but it has also left the TLS community with tools such as FlexTLS [1] which allows for the rapid prototyping and testing of TLS implementations. These tools are now being harnessed to assess TLS 1.3.

The rise of automated protocol analysis tools such as ProVerif [4] and the Tamarin Prover [83] can also be counted as a boon for the TLS WG. The more recent Tamarin tool, for instance, offers exceptional support for DH-based protocols and allows for the instantiation of an unbounded number of protocol participants and sessions, making it a good choice for the modelling and consequent symbolic analysis of TLS 1.3. Once established, this type of model can also be easily adapted in response to protocol changes, making this tool invaluable in an ongoing development process.

The advances in the areas of provable security, program verification and formal methods have contributed to a development environment in which a design-break-fix-release standardization cycle can thrive. Previously, the absence of these techniques, or the limited experience in applying them to real protocols like TLS, would have limited the amount of pre-release analysis that could have been performed, making a design-release-break-patch standardisation cycle understandable, natural even, for TLS 1.2 and below.

4.3   Involvement, Impact and Incentives

In the development of TLS 1.3, the WG has taken many positive steps in aiming to protect the protocol against the various classes of attacks mentioned in Sect. 3. Removal of support for weak hash functions, renegotiation, and non-AEAD encryption modes, as well as the introduction of the session hash mechanism serve as illustrative examples. The WG has also made design choices that have eased the analysis of the protocol, such as making a clean separation of the Handshake and Record Protocols, for instance. This is undoubtedly a positive step by the WG to respond to the research community's needs, marking a shift in the WG's design mindset. The TRON workshop also displays a desire by the WG to involve the research community in the design of TLS 1.3, and to incorporate its contributions. The research community, on the other hand, has gained a much greater awareness of the complexities of the TLS protocol and its many use cases, and has tried to adapt its analyses accordingly. In view of the rising interest in and focus on TLS in the research community over a period of years, and the attendant refinement of its analysis tools, this community has been in a much better position to contribute to the TLS 1.3 design process than it was for former editions of the protocol.

The ability to adapt the protocol in response to potential attacks, such as those identified by Cremers et al. [31] and Bhargavan et al. [18], makes for a stronger protocol and has allowed the WG to implement changes pre-emptively, hopefully reducing the need to create patches post-release. In comparison to the previous process described in Sect. 3, the design-break-fix-release standardisation cycle appears to leave the incentives for researchers unchanged, with a number of top-tier papers being produced prior to the protocol's finalisation. However, it's notable that these papers provide positive security results about TLS 1.3 rather than new attacks. We consider this to be as a result of the research community's stronger appreciation of the importance of TLS and its greater awareness of the value in contributing to its standardisation than in former development cycles.

4.4   Areas for Improvement

Although a positive step with regards to collaboration between researchers faced with analyzing TLS and the engineers faced with implementing TLS, the analysis-prior-to-deployment design strategy is not without its difficulties. Greater numbers of contributions, be they from researchers and/or implementers, have led to conflicting design opinions, potentially creating a greater administrative overhead for the TLS WG. The increase in uncoordinated contributions has also meant that the TLS 1.3 draft specification has become a rapidly moving target. This has increased the amount of analysis work required and has rendered some analyses 'outdated' within the space of few months, potentially frustrating those engaged in analysis of the protocol. The varied contributions have also created tension between the researchers looking at TLS 1.3, with those focused on implementation concerns suggesting improvements to the potential detriment of those concerned with the provable security aspects of the protocol. This has been an on-going issue in the area of key derivation and key separation, for example. The time scales for analysis could also potentially be more favourable: not only do rapid changes require quick analysis, but with the WG/IETF wanting official publication of TLS 1.3 within a few months of publishing the final (or a near-final) draft, this does not leave much time for detailed analysis of the final version of TLS 1.3. This is unfortunate for a protocol of such critical importance.

It is also the case that, due to the inevitable gaps in understanding between the scientific community and the more engineering-focussed participants in the TLS WG, there is the potential for miscommunication (in both directions). While we are not aware of specific instances where miscommunication or misunderstanding has seriously hampered the development of TLS 1.3, it is true that the formal security analyses presented to the WG by the research community do involve assumptions concerning attacker capabilities and the strength of the used cryptographic primitives. Sometimes these assumptions, while well understood in one community, may not be so obvious to another. One example of this would be the use of idealised cryptographic assumptions in some of the analyses based on formal methods; another (in the other direction) would be constraints on the TLS 1.3 handshake stemming from the use of Hardware Security Modules for storing server private keys.

A related area of potential improvement in the process is that of the identification of security and functionality requirements for TLS 1.3. We noted previously that only after the TRON workshop in February 2016 did it become apparent that a complete and explicit set of requirements was missing. This suggests that a different design process for TLS 1.3 could have been adopted: *requirements analysis, design, prove, release.* Instead, it appears that while some of the requirements were established early on, many others emerged only through discussion during the design phases. It is perhaps naive to hope that such a linear process would be possible for a protocol as complex as TLS, with its many use cases and with many stakeholders being involved in the development process. Certainly, multiple cycles of the "design" and "prove" steps might be needed. On the other hand, perhaps a TRON-like workshop could have been held at the commencement of the process, with the objective of flushing out the design requirements.

Finally, an issue throughout the process has been uncertainty over the degree of change permitted in TLS 1.3 relative to TLS 1.2. Initially, changes were to be incremental, potentially limiting the thinking of some participants to consider only less radical designs. Now, it is hard to argue that TLS 1.3 is anything other than a complete protocol redesign — a TLS 2.0 rather than a TLS 1.3, let us say. What novel ideas might have been brought forward had that been clear from the start?

5   Beyond TLS 1.3

Given its importance and pervasive nature, it is possible that the successful rolling out of the highly collaborative, fast-paced, proactive standardisation process may be unique to TLS. To what extent can the TLS case serve as a trendsetter, paving the way for the IETF, and indeed other standardisation bodies, to foster stronger ties with security researchers? Or is TLS an outlier in this regard? Involvement of researchers is by no means unheard of in the standardisation of security mechanisms and protocols but does the importance of TLS increase the willingness of the research community to get involved in the process?

We now examine how the newer, proactive standardisation process for TLS compares to the processes inherent to other standardisation models, such as those employed by ISO and NIST, and question to what extent these differing models would have been suitable for the standardisation of TLS. We also comment on the extent to which these models encourage active participation from the security community.

ISO. This standards body conforms to a closed model for standardisation. As with the IETF, standardisation work is organised into areas which are managed by technical committees. These committees are further broken down into subcommittees, with subcommittee 27 (SC27) being responsible for the creation and maintenance of standards concerning security techniques[10]. Within this subcommittee, WG2 is responsible for the standardisation of cryptographic mechanisms. The members of an ISO WG are not individuals but rather National Bodies (NBs) and standardisation decisions are made by the WG based on comments and contributions received from participating NBs. The formation and make-up of these NBs undoubtedly varies from nation to nation, but by and large, this type of model is characterised by barriers to entry as far as contributions are concerned as the process is far more "members only" in comparison to the open model employed by the IETF.

The development philosophy is arguably many-to-one as many members provide inputs to one standard but an ISO security standard will generally contain a number of mechanisms aimed at providing a security service, and will not be dedicated to one protocol, as is the case with the TLS RFCs. Inclusion of mechanisms in SC27 WG2 standards is usually subject to the mechanisms meeting certain maturity conditions – research from external sources is consulted and where required, NBs may perform additional analyses. This maturity requirement would potentially not suit a dynamically shifting protocol such as TLS 1.3, and the closed nature of the standardisation process potentially discourages high levels of external academic involvement. Also, ISO imposes a fee for its standards, creating a financial barrier to adoption, a less than ideal situation for a critical protocol such as TLS. The NB structure of ISO also brings into question the possible motives of state actors that may be involved in the standardisation process, a potential concern for a ubiquitous protocol such as TLS.

---

[10] Other ISO subcommittees also standardise security mechanisms, such as SC17 which focuses on cards and personal identification but we focus our discussion here on SC27.

NIST. We focus here on the competition model used by NIST. This model was employed successfully in the development of AES [40] and SHA-3 [39]. This model exhibits no barriers to entry as the competitions are public and the development philosophy is one-to-one, since only one proposed candidate is selected for standardisation and contributions from the respective competitors are not pooled in the creation of the final standard. A necessity of the competition model is that algorithm/protocol requirements are clearly established and communicated. The announcement of the SHA-3 competition in the Federal Register in 2007 [77], for instance, contained sections covering minimum criteria as well as evaluation criteria. Analysis of the SHA-3 candidates was performed by NIST and the larger cryptographic community, with many comments being communicated on the public hash forum set up for the competition. Many of the analyses culminated in top-tier publications (see [29] for a comprehensive list), thereby productively serving academic incentives as part of the standardisation process. NIST also held several SHA-3 conferences as a means of obtaining public feedback.

Some of the elements of the SHA-3 standardisation narrative overlap with the TLS 1.3 standardisation process discussed in Sect. 4. The analysis-prior-to-deployment development methodology, the use of public mailing lists and the hosting of public conferences/workshops are all aspects in which the TLS 1.3 process is similar. But the process differs in that the requirements for TLS 1.3 were not fully expressed before the design commenced. There is of course no *explicit* element of competition, differentiating the competition model from the open model. On the other hand, individual researchers and research teams do stand to gain greatly by having their ideas adopted in TLS 1.3, whether through personal kudos or recognition that is internal (promotion, company awards) or external (prizes, paper citations). Finally, the SHA-3 competition ran for several years (from 2007 to 2012), allowing more time for detailed analysis.

Like the open model, there is no cost associated with the final product and this model could most certainly work for TLS. However, it is doubtful whether such a model would allow for the rapid development of the protocol, as we have seen with TLS 1.3. The competition model has proven to be suitable for cryptographic primitives like block ciphers and hash functions. A complex protocol such as TLS might be too large in scope for any one research team to design in its entirety, perhaps making a collaborative standardisation model more appropriate.

6   Conclusion

We have presented an account of TLS standardisation, starting with the early versions of TLS, right up until TLS 1.3, which is, at the time of writing, nearing completion. We have described how the process for TLS 1.2 and below fits the design-release-break-patch cycle of standards development and how a shift in the process has resulted in the standardisation of TLS 1.3 conforming to the design-break-fix-release development cycle. We have commented on the factors that have influenced the shift in the TLS WG's design methodology, namely, the protocol analysis tools available, the levels of involvement from the research community, and the incentives driving the relevant stakeholders. This newer process exhibits benefits over the cycle employed previously as it allows for the preemptive detection and fixing of weaknesses, thus producing a potentially stronger protocol and reducing the need for patches post-release. We have gone on to suggest that the process for TLS 1.3 could have been enhanced even further by the WG considering a requirements analysis-design-prove-release cycle for development of the standard. We have also examined the standardisation of TLS in relation to a number of varying standardisation models. We find that the current, collaborative process under the open model of the IETF shows promise in producing a strong protocol but that the competition model as employed by NIST would also potentially have suited a protocol such as TLS.

We believe our work to be the first attempt at a TLS standardisation diegesis, and that a detailed classification of standardisation models, based on further case studies, would make for interesting future work.

Acknowledgements. Paterson was supported in part by a research programme funded by Huawei Technologies and delivered through the Institute for Cyber Security Innovation at Royal Holloway, University of London, and in part by EPSRC grant EP/M013472/1. Van der Merwe was supported by the EPSRC as part of the Centre for Doctoral Training in Cyber Security at Royal Holloway, University of London. We thank Eric Rescorla and the anonymous reviewers of SSR 2016 for their valuable feedback on the paper.

References

1. FlexTLS: A Tool for Testing TLS Implementations. https://mitls.org/pages/flextls
2. Getting Started in the IETF. https://www.ietf.org/newcomers.html. Accessed 06 Aug 2016
3. miTLS: A Verified Reference Implementation of TLS. https://mitls.org/
4. ProVerif: Cryptographic protocol verifier in the formal model. http://prosecco.gforge.inria.fr/personal/bblanche/proverif/
5. TLS 1.3 Security Properties. https://github.com/tls13properties/tls13-properties
6. Adrian, D., Bhargavan, K., Durumeric, Z., Gaudry, P., Green, M., Halderman, J.A., Heninger, N., Springall, D., Thomé, E., Valenta, L., VanderSloot, B., Wustrow, E., Béguelin, S.Z., Zimmermann, P.: Imperfect forward secrecy: how Diffie-Hellman fails in practice. In Ray et al. [76], pp. 5–17
7. Albrecht, M.R., Paterson, K.G.: Lucky Microseconds: A timing attack on amazon's $s2n$ implementation of TLS. In: Fischlin, M., Coron, J.-S. (eds.) EUROCRYPT 2016. LNCS, vol. 9665, pp. 622–643. Springer, Heidelberg (2016). doi:10.1007/978-3-662-49890-3_24
8. AlFardan, N., Paterson, K.G.: Lucky thirteen: breaking the TLS and DTLS record protocols. In: Sommer, R. (ed.) Proceedings of the 2013 IEEE Symposium on Security and Privacy (S&P 2013) (2013)
9. AlFardan, N.J., Bernstein, D.J., Paterson, K.G., Poettering, B., Schuldt, J.C.N.: On the security of RC4 in TLS. In: King, S.T. (ed.) Proceedings of the 22nd USENIX Security Symposium, Washington D.C., August 2013, pp. 305–320. USENIX (2013)

10. Almeida, J.B., Barbosa, M., Barthe, G., Dupressoir, F.: Verifiable side-channel security of cryptographic implementations: constant-time MEE-CBC. In: Peyrin, T. (ed.) FSE 2016. LNCS, vol. 9783, pp. 163–184. Springer, Heidelberg (2016). doi:10.1007/978-3-662-52993-5_9

11. Apecechea, G.I., Inci, M.S., Eisenbarth, T., Sunar, B.: Lucky 13 strikes back. In: Bao, F., Miller, S., Zhou, J., Ahn, G.-J. (eds.) Proceedings of the 10th ACM Symposium on Information, Computer and Communications Security, ASIA CCS 2015, Singapore, 14–17 April 2015, pp. 85–96. ACM (2015)

12. Arai, K.: Formal Verification of TLS 1.3 Full Handshake Protocol Using Proverif. Technical report, Cryptographic protocol Evaluation toward Long-Lived Outstanding Security Consortium (CELLOS), February 2016. https://www.cellos-consortium.org/studygroup/TLS1.3-fullhandshake-draft11.pv

13. Aviram, N., Schinzel, S., Somorovsky, J., Heninger, N., Dankel, M., Steube, J., Valenta, L., Adrian, D., Halderman, J.A., Dukhovni, V., Käsper, E., Cohney, S., Engels, S., Paar, C., Shavitt, Y.: DROWN: breaking TLS using SSLv2. In: Holz, T., Savage, S. (eds.) 25th USENIX Security Symposium, USENIX Security 16, Austin, 10–12 August 2016, pp. 689–706. USENIX Association (2016)

14. Bard, G.V.: A challenging but feasible blockwise-adaptive chosen-plaintext attack on SSL. In: Malek, M., Fernández-Medina, E., Hernando, J. (eds.) SECRYPT, pp. 99–109. INSTICC Press (2006)

15. Berners-Lee, T., Fielding, R., Frystyk, H.: The Hypertext Transfer Protocol HTTP/1.0. RFC 1945 (Informational), May 1996

16. Beurdouche, B., Bhargavan, K., Delignat-Lavaud, A., Fournet, C., Ishtiaq, S., Kohlweiss, M., Protzenko, J., Swamy, N., Zanella-Bguelin, S., Zinzindohou, J.K.: Towards a Provably Secure Implementation of TLS 1.3. Presented at TRON 1.0, San Diego, 21 February 2016

17. Beurdouche, B., Bhargavan, K., Delignat-Lavaud, A., Fournet, C., Kohlweiss, M., Pironti, A., Strub, P.-Y., Zinzindohoue, J.K.: A messy state of the union: taming the composite state machines of TLS. In: 2015 IEEE Symposium on Security and Privacy, SP 2015, San Jose, 17–21 May 2015, pp. 535–552. IEEE Computer Society (2015)

18. Bhargavan, K., Kobeissi, N., Blanchet, B.: ProScript T.L.S.: Building a TLS 1.3 Implementation with a Verifiable Protocol Model. Presented at TRON 1.0, San Diego, 21 February 2016

19. Bhargavan, K., Brzuska, C., Fournet, C., Green, M., Kohlweiss, M., Zanella-Bèguellin, S.: Downgrade resilience in key-exchange protocols. In: 2016 IEEE Symposium on Security and Privacy, SP 2016, San Jose, 23–25 May 2016

20. Bhargavan, K., Delignat-Lavaud, A., Fournet, C., Pironti, A., Strub, P.-Y.: Triple handshakes, cookie cutters: breaking and fixing authentication over TLS. In: 2014 IEEE Symposium on Security and Privacy, SP 2014, Berkeley, 18–21 May 2014, pp. 98–113. IEEE Computer Society (2014)

21. Bhargavan, K., Delignat-Lavaud, A., Fournet, C., Pironti, A., Strub, P.-Y., Handshakes, T., Cutters, C.: Breaking and fixing authentication over TLS. In: 2014 IEEE Symposium on Security and Privacy, SP 2014, Berkeley, 18–21 May 2014, pp. 98–113 (2014)

22. Bhargavan, K., Fournet, C., Kohlweiss, M., Pironti, A., Strub, P.-Y.: Implementing TLS with verified cryptographic security. In: 2013 IEEE Symposium on Security and Privacy, SP 2013, Berkeley, 19–22 May 2013, pp. 445–459. IEEE Computer Society (2013)

23. Bhargavan, K., Fournet, C., Kohlweiss, M., Pironti, A., Strub, P.-Y., Zanella-Béguelin, S.: Proving the TLS handshake secure (as it is). In: Garay, J.A., Gennaro, R. (eds.) CRYPTO 2014. LNCS, vol. 8617, pp. 235–255. Springer, Heidelberg (2014). doi:10.1007/978-3-662-44381-1_14

24. Bhargavan, K., Leurent, G.: Transcript collision attacks: breaking authentication in TLS, IKE, and SSH. In: 23rd Annual Network and Distributed System Security Symposium, NDSS 2016, San Diego, 21–24 February 2016

25. Blanchet, B.: An efficient cryptographic protocol verifier based on prolog rules. In: 14th IEEE Computer Security Foundations Workshop (CSFW-14 2001), 11–13 June 2001, Cape Breton, pp. 82–96 (2001)

26. Bleichenbacher, D.: Chosen ciphertext attacks against protocols based on the RSA encryption standard PKCS #1. In: Krawczyk, H. (ed.) CRYPTO 1998. LNCS, vol. 1462, pp. 1–12. Springer, Heidelberg (1998). doi:10.1007/BFb0055716

27. Bricout, R., Murphy, S., Paterson, K.G., Van der Merwe, T.: Analysing and exploiting the Mantin biases in RC4. IACR Cryptology ePrint Archive, 2016:63 (2016)

28. Canvel, B., Hiltgen, A., Vaudenay, S., Vuagnoux, M.: Password interception in a SSL/TLS channel. In: Boneh, D. (ed.) CRYPTO 2003. LNCS, vol. 2729, pp. 583–599. Springer, Heidelberg (2003). doi:10.1007/978-3-540-45146-4_34

29. Chauhan, S., Sobti, R., Geetha, G., Anand, S.: Cryptanalysis of SHA-3 candidates: a survey. Res. J. Inf. Technol. 5, 149–159 (2013)

30. Chen, L., Mitchell, C. (eds.): SSR 2014. Security and Cryptology. LNCS, vol. 8893. Springer (2014)

31. Cremers, C., Horvat, M., Scott, S., van der Merwe, T.: Automated analysis and verification of TLS 1.3: 0-RTT, resumption and delayed authentication. In: 2016 IEEE Symposium on Security and Privacy, SP 2016, San Jose, 23–25 May 2016

32. Dierks, T., Allen, C.: The TLS Protocol Version 1.0. RFC 2246, Internet Engineering Task Force, January 1999

33. Dierks, T., Allen, C.: The Transport Layer Security (TLS) Protocol Version 1.1. RFC 4346, Internet Engineering Task Force, April 2006

34. Dierks, T., Rescorla, E.: The Transport Layer Security (TLS) Protocol Version 1.2. RFC 5246, Internet Engineering Task Force, August 2008

35. Dowling, B., Fischlin, M., Günther, F., Stebila, D.: A cryptographic analysis of the TLS 1.3 handshake protocol candidates. In: Ray et al. [76], pp. 1197–1210

36. Dowling, B., Fischlin, M., Günther, F., Stebila, D.: A cryptographic analysis of the TLS 1.3 draft-10 full and pre-shared key handshake protocol. Cryptology ePrint Archive, Report 2016/081 (2016). http://eprint.iacr.org/

37. Dowling, B., Stebila, D.: Modelling ciphersuite and version negotiation in the TLS protocol. In: Foo, E., Stebila, D. (eds.) ACISP 2015. LNCS, vol. 9144, pp. 270–288. Springer, Heidelberg (2015). doi:10.1007/978-3-319-19962-7_16

38. Duong, T., Rizzo, J.: Here come the ⊕ Ninjas. Unpublished manuscript (2011)

39. Dworkin, M.J.: SHA-3 Standard: permutation-based hash and extendable-output functions. FIPS 202, August 2015

40. Dworkin, M.J., Barker, E.B., Nechvatal, J.R., Foti, J., Bassham, L.E., Roback, E., Dray, Jr., J.F.: Announcing the Advanced Encryption Standard (AES). FIPS PUB 197, November 2001

41. Fischlin, M., Günther, F.: Multi-stage key exchange and the case of Google's QUIC protocol. In: Proceedings of the 2014 ACM SIGSAC Conference on Computer and Communications Security, Scottsdale, pp. 1193–1204, 3–7 November 2014

42. Fischlin, M., Günther, F., Schmidt, B., Warinschi, B.: Key confirmation in key exchange: a formal treatment and implications for TLS 1.3. In: 2016 IEEE Symposium on Security and Privacy, SP 2016, San Jose, 23–25 May 2016

43. Freier, A., Karlton, P.: The Secure Sockets Layer (SSL) Protocol Version 3.0. RFC 6101 (Historic Document), August 2011
44. Gajek, S., Manulis, M., Pereira, O., Sadeghi, A.-R., Schwenk, J.: Universally composable security analysis of TLS. In: Baek, J., Bao, F., Chen, K., Lai, X. (eds.) ProvSec 2008. LNCS, vol. 5324, pp. 313–327. Springer, Heidelberg (2008). doi:10. 1007/978-3-540-88733-1_22
45. Garman, C., Paterson, K.G., Van der Merwe, T.: Attacks only get better: password recovery attacks against RC4 in TLS. In Jung and Holz [53], pp. 113–128
46. Garret, D.: Banning SHA-1 in TLS 1.3, a new attempt. TLS mailing list post, October 2015. http://www.ietf.org/mail-archive/web/tls/current/msg17956.html
47. Garret, D.: MD5 diediedie (was Re: Deprecating TLS 1.0, 1.1 and SHA1 signature algorithms). TLS mailing list post, January 2016. http://www.ietf.org/ mail-archive/web/tls/current/msg18977.html
48. Giesen, F., Kohlar, F., Stebila, D.: On the security of TLS renegotiation. In: Sadeghi, A.-R., Gligor, V.D., Yung, M. (eds.) 2013 ACM SIGSAC Conference on Computer and Communications Security, CCS 2013, Berlin, 4–8 November 2013, pp. 387–398. ACM (2013)
49. Griffin, P.H.: Standardization transparency - an out of body experience. In: Chen and Mitchell [30], pp. 57–68
50. Guttman, J.D., Liskov, M.D., Rowe, P.D.: Security goals and evolving standards. In: Chen and Mitchell [30], pp. 93–110
51. Jager, T., Kohlar, F., Schäge, S., Schwenk, J.: On the security of TLS-DHE in the standard model. In: Safavi-Naini, R., Canetti, R. (eds.) CRYPTO 2012. LNCS, vol. 7417, pp. 273–293. Springer, Heidelberg (2012). doi:10.1007/978-3-642-32009-5_17
52. Jager, T., Schwenk, J., Somorovsky, J.: On the security of TLS 1.3 and QUIC against weaknesses in PKCS#1 v1.5 encryption. In: Proceedings of the 22nd ACM SIGSAC Conference on Computer and Communications Security, Denver, 12–16 October 2015, pp. 1185–1196 (2015)
53. Jung, J., Holz, T., (eds.): 24th USENIX Security Symposium, USENIX Security 15, Washington, D.C., 12–14 August 2015. USENIX Association (2015)
54. Kelsey, J.: Compression and information leakage of plaintext. In: Daemen, J., Rijmen, V. (eds.) FSE 2002. LNCS, vol. 2365, pp. 263–276. Springer, Heidelberg (2002). doi:10.1007/3-540-45661-9_21
55. Klíma, V., Pokorný, O., Rosa, T.: Attacking RSA-based sessions in SSL/TLS. In: Walter, C.D., Koç, Ç.K., Paar, C. (eds.) CHES 2003. LNCS, vol. 2779, pp. 426–440. Springer, Heidelberg (2003). doi:10.1007/978-3-540-45238-6_33
56. Kohlar, F., Schäge, S., Schwenk, J.: On the security of TLS-DH and TLS-RSA in the standard model. IACR Cryptology ePrint Archive, 2013:367 (2013)
57. Kohlweiss, M., Maurer, U., Onete, C., Tackmann, B., Venturi, D.: (De-)constructing TLS. IACR Cryptology ePrint Archive, 2014:20 (2014)
58. Krawczyk, H.: The order of encryption and authentication for protecting communications (or: how secure is SSL?). In: Kilian, J. (ed.) CRYPTO 2001. LNCS, vol. 2139, pp. 310–331. Springer, Heidelberg (2001). doi:10.1007/3-540-44647-8_19
59. Krawczyk, H.: Cryptographic extraction and key derivation: the HKDF scheme. In: Rabin, T. (ed.) CRYPTO 2010. LNCS, vol. 6223, pp. 631–648. Springer, Heidelberg (2010). doi:10.1007/978-3-642-14623-7_34
60. Krawczyk, H., Paterson, K.G., Wee, H.: On the security of the TLS protocol: a systematic analysis. In: Canetti, R., Garay, J.A. (eds.) CRYPTO 2013. LNCS, vol. 8042, pp. 429–448. Springer, Heidelberg (2013). doi:10.1007/978-3-642-40041-4_24
61. Krawczyk, H., Wee, H.: The OPTLS protocol and TLS 1.3. IACR Cryptology ePrint Archive, 2015:978 (2015)

62. Krawczyk, H., Wee, H.: The OPTLS protocol and TLS 1.3. In: IEEE European Symposium on Security and Privacy, EuroS&P 2016, Saarbrücken, 21–24 March 2016, pp. 81–96. IEEE (2016)
63. Langley, A., Chang, W.: QUIC Crypto, June 2013. https://docs.google.com/document/d/1g5nIXAIkN_Y-7XJW5K45IblHd_L2f5LTaDUDwvZ5L6g/
64. Li, X., Xu, J., Zhang, Z., Feng, D., Hu, H.: Multiple handshakes security of TLS 1.3 candidates. In: 2016 IEEE Symposium on Security and Privacy, SP 2016, San Jose, 23–25 May 2016
65. Li, Y., Schäge, S., Yang, Z., Kohlar, F., Schwenk, J.: On the security of the pre-shared key ciphersuites of TLS. In: Krawczyk, H. (ed.) PKC 2014. LNCS, vol. 8383, pp. 669–684. Springer, Heidelberg (2014). doi:10.1007/978-3-642-54631-0_38
66. Mantin, I., Shamir, A.: A practical attack on broadcast RC4. In: Matsui, M. (ed.) FSE 2001. LNCS, vol. 2355, pp. 152–164. Springer, Heidelberg (2002). doi:10.1007/3-540-45473-X_13
67. Matsuo, S.: Formal verification of TLS 1.3 full handshake protocol using ProVerif (Draft-11). TLS mailing list post, February 2016. https://www.ietf.org/mail-archive/web/tls/current/msg19339.html
68. Mavrogiannopoulos, N., Vercauteren, F., Velichkov, V., Preneela, B.: A cross-protocol attack on the TLS protocol. In: Yu, T., Danezis, G., Gligor, V.D. (eds.) Proceedings of the 2012 ACM Conference on Computer and Communications Security (CCS 2012), Raleigh, pp. 62–72. ACM Press, October 2012
69. Meyer, C., Somorovsky, J., Weiss, E., Schwenk, J., Schinzel, S., Tews, E.: Revisiting, SSL/TLS implementations: new Bleichenbacher side channels and attacks. In: Fu, K., Jung, J., (eds.) Proceedings of the 23rd USENIX Security Symposium, San Diego, 20–22 August 2014, pp. 733–748. USENIX Association (2014)
70. Moeller, B.: Security of CBC ciphersuites in SSL/TLS: problems andcounter-measures. Unpublished manuscript, May 2004. http://www.openssl.org/~bodo/tls-cbc.txt
71. Möller, B., Duong, T., Kotowicz, K.: This POODLE bites: exploiting the SSL 3.0 fallback, September 2014
72. Morrissey, P., Smart, N.P., Warinschi, B.: The TLS handshake protocol: a modular analysis. J. Cryptol. **23**(2), 187–223 (2010)
73. Paterson, K.G., Ristenpart, T., Shrimpton, T.: Tag size *Does* matter: attacks and proofs for the TLS record protocol. In: Lee, D.H., Wang, X. (eds.) ASIACRYPT 2011. LNCS, vol. 7073, pp. 372–389. Springer, Heidelberg (2011). doi:10.1007/978-3-642-25385-0_20
74. Popov, A.: Prohibiting RC4 Cipher Suites. RFC 7465 (Proposed Standard), February 2015
75. Postel, J.: Internet Protocol. RFC 791, Internet Engineering Task Force, September 1981
76. Ray, I., Li, N., Kruegel, C., (eds.) Proceedings of the 22nd ACM SIGSAC Conference on Computer and Communications Security, Denver, 12–6 October 2015. ACM (2015)
77. Federal Register. Announcing Request for Candidate Algorithm Nominations for a New Cryptographic Hash Algorithm (SHA 3) Family. Federal Register, November 2007
78. Rescorla, E.: The Transport Layer Security (TLS) Protocol Version 1.3, Draft 15. Internet draft, Internet Engineering Task Force, August 2016
79. Rescorla, E., Ray, M., Dispensa, S., Oskov, N.: Transport Layer Security (TLS) Renegotiation Indication Extension. RFC 5746 (Proposed Standard), February 2010

80. Rogaway, P.: Problems with proposed IP cryptography. Unpublished manuscript (1995). http://www.cs.ucdavis.edu/~rogaway/papers/draft-rogaway-ipsec-comments-00.txt
81. Roskind, J.: QUIC: Quick UDP Internet Connections, April 2012. https://docs.google.com/document/d/1RNHkx_VvKWyWg6Lr8SZ-saqsQx7rFV-ev2jRFUoVD 34/edit?pref=2&pli=1
82. Sarkar, P.G., Fitzgerald, S.: Attacks on SSL - a comprehensive study of BEAST, CRIME, TIME, BREACH, Lucky 13 and RC4 biases, August 2013
83. Tamarin prover GitHub repository (develop branch) (2015). https://github.com/tamarin-prover/tamarin-prover
84. Turner, S., Polk, T.: Prohibiting Secure Sockets Layer (SSL) Version 2.0. RFC 6176 (Proposed Standard), March 2011
85. Vanhoef, M., Piessens, F.: All your biases belong to us: breaking RC4 in WPA-TKIP and TLS. In Jung and Holz [53], pp. 97–112
86. Vaudenay, S.: Security flaws induced by CBC padding — applications to SSL, IPSEC, WTLS. In: Knudsen, L.R. (ed.) EUROCRYPT 2002. LNCS, vol. 2332, pp. 534–545. Springer, Heidelberg (2002). doi:10.1007/3-540-46035-7_35
87. Wagner, D., Schneier, B.: Analysis of the SSL 3.0 protocol. In: USENIX Electronic Commerce (1996)
88. Wang, X., Yu, H.: How to break MD5 and other hash functions. In: Cramer, R. (ed.) EUROCRYPT 2005. LNCS, vol. 3494, pp. 19–35. Springer, Heidelberg (2005). doi:10.1007/11426639_2

Extending the UML Standards to Model Tree-Structured Data and Their Access Control Requirements

Alberto De la Rosa Algarín[1]([✉]) and Steven A. Demurjian[2]

[1] Loki Labs Inc, Baltimore, USA
alberto@lokilabs.io
[2] Department of Computer Science and Engineering,
University of Connecticut, Storrs, USA
steven.Demurjian@uconn.edu
http://www.lokilabs.io
http://www.cse.uconn.edu

Abstract. Secure data sharing between computational systems is a necessity to many workflows across domains such as healthcare informatics, law enforcement and national security. While there exist many approaches towards securing data for the purpose of dissemination, the vast majority follows the traditional thought of security engineering that occurs as the last step of the overall software engineering process. In this paper we extend the Unified Modeling Language (UML) standard to: (1) modeling tree-structured data and associated schemas and (2) information security via role-based, lattice-based, and discretionary access control; both push it towards the forefront of the software development life-cycle. Tree structured data and associated schemas are dominant in information modeling and exchange formats including: the eXtensible Markup Language (XML), JavaScript Object Notation (JSON), etc. New UML artifacts for tree-structured data and schemas would allow the modeling of generalized information solutions from which XML, JSON, RDF, etc., could be generated; this is akin to generating different object-oriented programming language code from UML class diagrams. This UML extension also allows security experts to model and define information security requirements at the schema level as well, before code is written. The end-result is the assurance of information security for the purpose of sharing across computational systems.

1 Introduction

Information modeling is focused on representing the information that is used and exchanged in large-scale applications and system-to-system operability with a common representation for scalable reuse. The implementation of information modeling has been predominately pursued using standards that utilize languages that facilitate structure, such as the eXtensible Markup Language (XML) [8], which models documents as schemas that dictate and enforce the required format for instances. Sample application areas and standards that use XML include: healthcare via the Health Level 7's Clinical Document Architecture (HL7 CDA) [12, 14]; cXML [20] for e-commerce

© Springer International Publishing AG 2016
L. Chen et al. (Eds.): SSR 2016, LNCS 10074, pp. 187–204, 2016.
DOI: 10.1007/978-3-319-49100-4_8

communication; finance via the Open Financial Exchange (OFX) [22], and other standards [23]. While XML has become the de-facto standard for information modeling implementation, other formats exist that share similar capabilities: the Resource Description Framework (RDF) [17], the Web Ontology Language (OWL) [19], and the JavaScript Object Notation (JSON) [9]. XML, RDF, OWL, and JSON can all model data utilizing a tree-structure of index and entity nodes that allows for information to be represented via schemas (that define structure), which can then be used as blueprints for the creation of new documents (instances) and their validation (enforcement), with some of them providing semantic modeling capabilities as well (RDF and OWL).

This paper proposes extensions to the Unified Modeling Language (UML) [2, 15] standard with new constructs that achieve a two-fold objective. The first objective supports the modeling of tree-structured data and schemas with new UML diagrams to allow generalized design from which target schemas/instances in XML, JSON, RDF, etc., can be generated. The second objective supports the definition of new UML diagrams from role-based access control (RBAC) [13], lattice-based access control (LBAC) [30], and discretionary access control (DAC) [31]) for tree-structure schemas and their instance. The end result is the ability to model tree-structured schemas at a generalized level including access thereby elevating the process of secure information design as a first-class citizen of the software engineering process. By tackling the problem from a perspective of tree-structured schemas, any document format that is represented by such a structure (e.g. XML, specialized JSON structures, RDF, OWL, etc.) can be modeled, secured and safely shared. This effectively allows us to provide separation of concerns with respect to information modeling and RBAC, LBAC, and DAC by defining the information model itself and security requirements in a software process phase.

The remainder of this paper is organized as follow: Sect. 2 provides background knowledge on UML utilized in the paper. Section 3 details the initial set of UML extensions for tree-structured data. Section 4 utilizes this initial set of extensions to UML and builds upon the need for RBAC, LBAC and DAC support by presenting diagram extensions that allow a security engineer to define access control requirements on tree-structured data. Section 5 presents the automated strategy utilized to generate enforcement policies via the proposed UML diagrams. Section 6 discusses related work. Section 7 concludes the paper.

2   Background

UML is a general-purpose modeling language for object-oriented systems [15, 32]. Currently managed by the Object Management Group (OMG), UML can be used throughout the software development cycle by combining data, business and object modeling. UML provides the benefit of reducing misinterpretation and promoting simple communication of domain requirements with its visual notation. However, while UML can be utilized to define security requirements, what is lacking in the UML standard is actual diagrams that are dedicated to, in our interest, access control models (RBAC, LBAC, and DAC) that allow the definition of security requirements using new security UML diagrams that seamlessly integrate with the UML model and unified

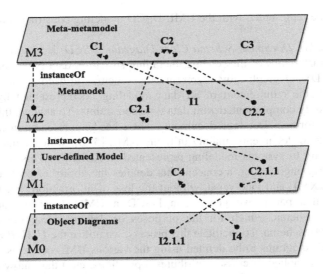

Fig. 1. UML's Meta-Object Facility layers.

design process. This is particularly true for domains such as healthcare where the information to be utilized is private and often governed by legal constructs that assure its proper use and dissemination [1, 3, 4].

UML can be extended via the use of the meta-model architecture developed by OMG. This meta-model architecture, called the Meta-Object Facility [27], consists of four layers. As shown in Fig. 1, the M3 layer consists of the meta-meta model. M2-models are built using the M3 language. In turn, M2-models describe the elements of the M1-layer, while the M1-models describe the elements of the M0-layer (the runtime instance of the modeled system). Due to the inclusion of UML into ISO as a standard [2] for software systems, several tools (and development environments) exist to aid in UML modeling, including: ArgoUML [28], StarUML [18], Eclipse [21], Visual Studio [29], NetBeans [7], and others. The UML meta-model will be utilized in this paper to support the definition of new UML diagrams that are capable of modeling tree-structured data and RBAC, LBAC, and DAC requirements for said data.

3   Extending UML with New Diagrams for Tree-Structured Schemas

This section supports the modeling of tree-structured data and schemas by extending UML with new UML to allow generalized design from which target schemas/instances in XML, JSON, RDF, etc., can be generated. The presentation is in two parts. First, section introduces the new UML Document Schema Class Diagram (DSCD), a UML extension that can handle any tree-structured schema to model the data and realize the instance. Second, the DSCD is demonstrated at an instance level utilizing the HL7 CDA schema, which are specializations of a tree-structure document whose structure can be represented with the UML DSCD modeling construct called the UML Profile.

The new *UML Document Schema Class Diagram (DSCD)* is an artifact that holds all of the characteristics of the schema, including structure, data type, and value constraints. The DSCD graphically represents the schemas utilized by an information system. Recall the requirement of all data modeling be represented by a tree-like structure, possibly complimented with data type constraints. To achieve this, we utilize a UML profile for tree-structured documents. There has been research in UML profiles for tree-structured documents, mainly utilizing XML [5, 6], which range from information modeling to systems modeling represented in XML [8]. This work also considers round-trip engineering, a concept that denotes the ability of producing a UML diagram from XML and vice-versa, without the loss of information. For the scope of the work in this paper, we generate a DSCD a UML diagram from a source tree-document schema, which for the purposes or demonstrating the concepts, is actually an XML schema. To facilitate this process, we utilize the *UML Profile* concept that allows new diagrams to be defined using the various UML concepts (stereotypes, tags, constraints applied to classes, attributes, operations, etc.) that allow a tree structured document to be transitioned into DSCD, and for the particular purposes of this section, to demonstrate the way that an XML schema (a tree structured format) can be transitioned to the new UML DSCD diagram; this is shown in Table 1.

While it is possible to utilize the UML profile to represent an entire schema as a UML package, we instead have chosen to represent each schema as a tree of stereotyped classes. This approach was chosen in order to capture the hierarchical structure of a schema as a series of related classes. Table 1 has three columns: the first column

Table 1. Specialized UML profile for tree-structured document to DSCD with XML cases.

Tree-Structured Document Component	XML Analog	DSCD Component
General Element	Element	UML Class
General Element Name	Element Name	UML Class Name
General Element Attribute	Generic Attribute	Stereotyped Attribute
Parent – child relationship of a schema (tree-subtree)	Tree - Subtree	UML Dependency Relationship
Complex Type of Elements and/or Attributes	XML xs:complexType	Stereotyped «complexType» UML Class
Sequential Element Order	XML xs:sequence	Stereotyped «sequence» UML Class
Aggregation of Attributes	XML xs:attributeGroup	Stereotyped «attributeGroup» UML Class
Grouping of Elements to form a complex type	XML xs:group	Stereotyped «group» UML Class
Acceptable Values for Elements	XML constraints via minOccurs, maxOccurs	Stereotyped «constraint» class member
Indirect Reference of Elements	XML ref	Stereotyped «ref» name class member
Parent – child relationship of non-named Elements	XML Element – non-named child element	UML Directed Association Relationship

represents the features of tree structured document, the second column defines the corresponding XML equivalents of these features, and the third column transitions the second column into the equivalent UML profile concept. In the first row of Table 1, a general element in the tree-structured document is equivalent to an XML element (xsd:element) and is realized as a UML class; the second row maps the element name to a UML class name. In the third row of Table 1, an element attribute in the tree-structured document is equivalent to a generic attribute in XML which can be mapped to a «stereotyped» attribute in UML. The fourth row corresponds to a patient – child relationship at the schema level to identify a tree and its subtrees, which in XML is observed as nested elements, and is represented as a UML dependency relationship in the DSCD. The fifth row of Table 1 describes complex elements (those that are built out of many sub-elements), which in XML are denoted as xsd:complexType and in the DSCD are denoted as a UML class with the «complexType» stereotype. The sixth row covers a similar case, considering sequences or lists of elements, which in XML are denoted as xsd:sequence and in the DSCD are denoted as a UML class with the «sequence» stereotype. Aggregation of attributes are handled with the seventh row of Table 1 and is represented as xsd:attributeGroup in XML and as a UML class with the «attributeGroup» stereotype in the DSCD. In the eighth row of Table 1, groups of elements in a tree-structured document are equivalent to an XML xsd:-group node and is represented as a UML class with the «group» stereotype in DSCD. The ninth row of Table 1 handles acceptable or allowable values for elements, which in XML are usually maxOccurs and minOccurs attributes to an XML element constraints, realized as a «constraint» stereotyped class member in DSCD. In the tenth row of Table 1, indirect references allow elements of a tree-structure document to be associated with one another, which in XML is a ref attribute on an element that are represented as a «ref» class member from UML profile in the DSCD. Lastly, in the eleventh row of Table 1, for tree-structured document, the parent-child relationship between non-named elements corresponds to non-named elements in XML (e.g., xsd:complexType, xsd:attributeGroup, etc.) and is represented with a UML directed association relationship between classes in the DSCD. Note that by using these mappings in Table 1 it is possible to develop an algorithm that operate over an XML schema to generate a DSCD equivalent in UML. Note also that there would need to be other versions of Table 1 for other data formats (e.g., JSON, RDF, etc.) where the second column of the table would be replaced with the relevant model constructs from the other formats.

As an example of utilizing the UML profile approach to convert a tree-structured data into a DSCD, lets utilize the MMUCC schema [16] that is utilized in the law enforcement domain. The conversion of the schema from Fig. 2 into a DSCD follows a mapping process guided by the profile of Table 1, resulting in a DSCD as shown in Fig. 3.

```
1.    <?xml version="1.0" encoding="utf-16"?>
2.    <xsd:schema
3.      xmlns:b=http://schemas.microsoft.com/BizTalk/2003
4.      xmlns=http://CDR.CollisionReport/V2/0
5.      elementFormDefault="qualified"
6.      targetNamespace=http://CDR.CollisionReport/V2/0
7.      xmlns:xsd="http://www.w3.org/2001/XMLSchema">
8.       <xsd:include
9.       schemaLocation=".\crashreportbase.xsd" />
10.       <xsd:annotation>
11.         <xsd:appinfo>
12.          <b:schemaInfo root_reference="CrashReport"
13.            xmlns:b="http://schemas.microsoft.com/BizTalk/2003" />
14.         </xsd:appinfo>
15.       </xsd:annotation>
16.       <xsd:element name="CrashReport">
17.       <xsd:complexType>
18.         <xsd:sequence>
19.           <xsd:element ref="CrashSummary" />
20.           <xsd:element minOccurs="1" maxOccurs="1" name="Vehicles">
21.           <xsd:complexType>
22.             <xsd:sequence>
23.              <xsd:element minOccurs="1" maxOccurs="unbounded"
24.                ref="CrashVehicle" />
25.             </xsd:sequence>
26.           </xsd:complexType>
27.           </xsd:element>
28.           <xsd:element minOccurs="0" maxOccurs="1" name="Persons">
29.           <xsd:complexType>
30.             <xsd:sequence>
31.                <xsd:element minOccurs="0" maxOccurs="unbounded"
32.                  ref="Person" />
33.             </xsd:sequence>
34.           </xsd:complexType>
35.           </xsd:element>
36.           <xsd:element minOccurs="0" maxOccurs="1" name="Charges">
37.           <xsd:complexType>
38.             <xsd:sequence>
39.                <xsd:element minOccurs="0" maxOccurs="unbounded"
40.                  ref="Charge" />
41.             </xsd:sequence>
42.           </xsd:complexType>
43.           </xsd:element>
44.           <xsd:element minOccurs="1" maxOccurs="1"
45.            ref="CrashDiagram" />
46.           <xsd:element minOccurs="0" maxOccurs="1" name="Images">
47.           <xsd:complexType>
48.             <xsd:sequence>
49.                <xsd:element minOccurs="0" maxOccurs="unbounded"
50.                  ref="CrashImage" />
51.             </xsd:sequence>
52.           </xsd:complexType>
53.           </xsd:element>
54.         </xsd:sequence>
55.       </xsd:complexType>
56.       </xsd:element>
57.    </xsd:schema>
```

Fig. 2. Segment of MMUCC from Alaska Collision Report 12-200 Schema.

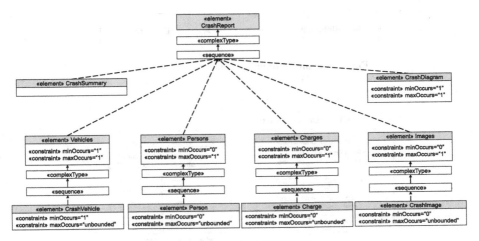

Fig. 3. A DSCD for the MMUCC Segment.

4 Extending UML Extensions to Model RBAC, LBAC, and DAC of Tree-Structured Schemas

This section presents a set of new UML diagrams from role-based access control (RBAC), lattice-based access control (LBAC), and discretionary access control (DAC) for tree-structure schemas and their instance. This is accomplished by detailing UML standard extension via a metamodel built on top of the foundation of the security model in Sect. 3. UML provides a large variety of diagrams for the visualization of different software requirements: class, component, deployment, activity, use-case, state-machine, communication, sequence, etc. [15] The work presented in this section leverages off of early work that has extended UML with new diagrams for RBAC, MAC, and DAC capabilities [24] from an object-oriented perspective. The extensions presented in this section are achieved via the UML Meta-Object Facility (MOF), which allows the extension of the modeling language with several degrees of formality, as reviewed in Sect. 2.

The tree-document schemas, as shown in the example DSCD in Fig. 3, can be constrained to identify those portions of the schema that require security control. To achieve this, we introduce the new UML *Secure Information Diagram*, which identifies those portions (elements and subtrees) of an application's schema (DSCD in Fig. 3) on which both RBAC permissions and LBAC classifications will be defined. For the SID, the M2 metamodel is shown in Fig. 4 where each class that is part of the SID is represented as meta-class (SecureInformation) associated with many possible instances of any given schema element as represented with the Element meta-class. Following the example of the MMUCC, the realization of the SID is shown in Fig. 5, a subset of the information from Fig. 3 that needs to be secure.

The next extension is the new Document Role-Slice Diagram (DRSD), with the purpose of supporting RBAC of operations that target schemas and their instances and to enable granular LBAC labeling of elements. The DRSD organizes the roles into a

Fig. 4. Secure Information Diagram M2 metamodel.

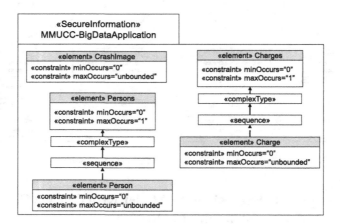

Fig. 5. SID with MMUCC elements.

hierarchy. The metamodel for the DRSD (as shown in Fig. 6) consists of the RoleSlice meta-class represents the role slices that will be defined with permissions against the SID (see Fig. 5 again) with respect to the schema(s) of the application to be secured. The Permission meta-class represents the permissions allowed over the instances validated against the secured schema (read, aggregate, insert, update, delete) that define what a role can and can't do for the elements in a schema. In order to create a relation between the RoleSlice meta-class (which contains all of the DRSD instances) and the Permission meta-class (which contains all of the schema targeting permissions), it is necessary to create a relation between the users and their roles. In Fig. 6, the UserRole meta-class is a parent-class of the RoleSlice meta-class and a sibling class of the Permission meta-class. The connections between the UserRole and Permission meta-classes are given by the permitted permission (PP) relation. The Element meta-class in turn represents all of the instances of elements (from the schema) that are targeted by the different permissions. This connection is tagged with the targeted

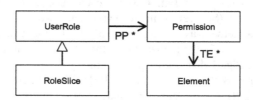

Fig. 6. Document Role Slice Diagram M2 metamodel.

element (TE) label in Fig. 6. Again, following the example of the MMUCC, the realization of the DRSD with sample roles against the SID of Fig. 5 is shown in Fig. 7.

Next, the new LBAC Secure Information Diagram (LSID) is shown in Fig. 8, a UML package with the stereotype «SecureInformation» that decorates the SID and contains all of the respective classes of elements from the schema to be secured per access modes (ams) and classifications (cls). The meta-model for the LSID consists of four meta-classes: User, AccessMode, Element, and SensitivityLevel. These meta-classes are interconnected to represent the relations between the user (User), its clearance level (Sensitivity), and access modes (read, aggregate, insert, update, delete; AccessMode) for each of the elements (xs:element, xs:complexTyp, etc.; Element) from the SID that need to be protected. To represent the relation between User and SensitivityLevel, an arrow with a UC (user clearance) tag is used. This relation indicates that the user could either have a clearance level or is without a clearance level, therefore the utilization of the 0..1 cardinality constraint. Element and Sensitivity are similarly related, represented with the arrow tagged EC (element classification). The relationship between Element and AccessMode is represented with the 1.. + cardinality constraint to cover the case of an element with different possible access modes. The result of the metamodel instantiation with the MMUCC example is shown in Fig. 9.

Next, at the metamodel layer (M2) of the MOF, the new User Diagram (UD) extension is presented in Fig. 10. The interplay of users, their roles and delegation permissions (for RBAC), their clearance levels (for LBAC), and their authorization permissions (DAC) require the proper definition of a user concept. The work in secure software engineering [26] proposed a UML extension for users via a User Diagram. In this paper, we build upon this first iteration of the User Diagram to extend to include both LBAC and RBAC user features directly to the metamodel. The metamodel of the UD is composed of six major meta-classes as given in Fig. 10: User, SensitivityLevel, UserRole, RoleSlice, SOD, and ME. The User meta-class represents all of the possible instances of users in a particular application. Both the User meta-class and the Role-Slice meta-class, is a subtype of the UserRole meta-class. The UR tag represents

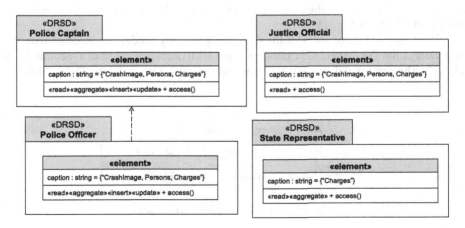

Fig. 7. DRSD Role hierarchy for MMUCC access in the law enforcement scenario.

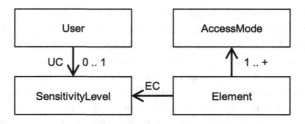

Fig. 8. LSID M2 metamodel.

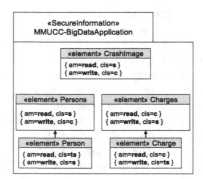

Fig. 9. LSID for MMUCC access.

user-role assignments (RBAC), the separation of duty (SOD) meta-class represents the separation of duty relations, and, the mutual exclusion (ME) meta-class represents the mutual exclusion relations between roles. The SensitivityLevel meta-class, which represents the sensitivity as related to LBAC is a clearance level for a user and is tied to the User meta-class. This distinction shows an important feature of the security framework presented in this dissertation, namely, that RBAC and LBAC capabilities are orthogonal. Following the examples of the roles in Fig. 7, we show an example UD for the MMUCC in Fig. 11.

The delegation component of the underlying security model is supported with the new Delegation Diagram (DD) extension to the UML standard given as a metamodel in Fig. 12. The metamodel consists of three meta-classes: OriginalUser, DelegableUser,

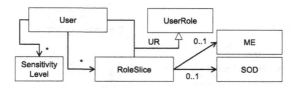

Fig. 10. User Diagram M2 metamodel.

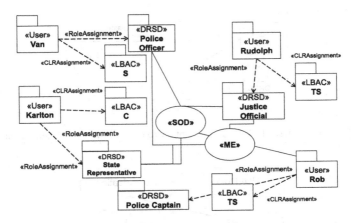

Fig. 11. User Diagram for the Law Enforcement Scenario.

and RoleSlice. The OriginalUser meta-class, along with the RoleSlice meta-class represents the original users of the application and their assigned roles. The DelegableUser, connected to the RoleSlice meta-class, represents the user/role pairs of authorized delegations. In turn, the Delegation tag in the connection between OringalUsers and DelegableUsers represents the ability to perform the delegation operation. Figure 13 shows a sample instantiation of the DD metamodel would look in the example of the MMUCC.

The final extension of the UML standard to support the security model consists of new the Authorization Diagram (AD) metamodel in Fig. 14 that consists of four meta-classes: UserRole, Authorization, Instance, and Schema. The UserRole meta-class represents the specific user/role pair in a similar fashion as the case of the UD in Fig. 6. The Authorization meta-class is connected to the Instance and Schema meta-classes to represent whether an authorization to an instance or schema exists and is represented with the 0.. + tag on the directional connection. This metamodel definition allows scenarios in which a user might not be authorized to any schema/instance, or any combination of the two (e.g. all schemas and all instances). Figure 15 shows an MMUCC related AD with the users and roles utilized from Figs. 11 and 7, respectively.

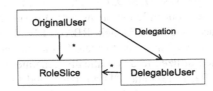

Fig. 12. Role Delegation Diagram M2 metamodel.

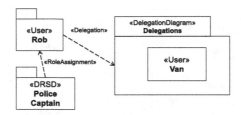

Fig. 13. DD for User Rob in police captain role in a law enforcement scenario.

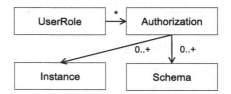

Fig. 14. Authorization Diagram M2 metamodel.

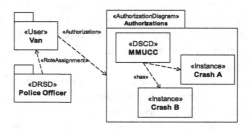

Fig. 15. AD for user van in the law enforcement scenario.

5   Generating Enforcement Policies from UML Extensions to XACML

In this section, we provide a high-level view of the security policy generation process that combines the access control concepts and capabilities of our security model with the new UML diagrams into an architecture. As shown in Fig. 16, the new UML extensions in the first column (DSCD, SID, DRSD, LBAC, UD, DD, and AD) are used in various combinations (see four different arrow types) in order to start a process that can map them through access control models RBAC, LBAC, DAC delegations, and authorizations (see column two) in order to identify the key policy components (see column three) that are then utilized to automatically generate a security policy (fourth column). First, DSCD, SID, DRSD and UD are combined to produce an RBAC ori-ented policy for each user/role combination; as a result, multiple security policies are generated on a user/role basis. Second, DSCD, SID, LSID, and UD are combined to produce an LBAC oriented policy for each user; again, specific security policies are generated for each user. Third, DRSD, UD, and DD are combined to produce a security policy that defines the delegable users and the role that can be delegated; again, this results in a separate policy each user/role combination. Finally, DSCD, DRSD, UD, and AD are combined to generate the policy that identifies the schemas and instances are authorized for a specific user. For each of these combinations, there is a transition to the policy components that form the basis of the generated policies. The last step in the process, illustrates the alternative policies that can be generated, including XACML (the focus of this dissertation), SQL DDL code for a relational database system, and aspect-oriented programing (AOP) for an object-oriented application [25].

The process of generating an XACML policy from the new UML standard extensions can be automated with an algorithm, as shown by Fig. 17. From a high-level perspective, the first step is to iterate over every user of the information system that requires security. Once a user is selected, the next step is to find that user's role and the respective DRSD that describes all of the permissions over every element. Then, by iterating over every permission in the relevant DRSD, the algorithm creates an XACML <Rule> object that would map the role to the <Subject>, the elements to the <Resources>, and the permissions (operations) to the <Actions> . Then, after that initial mapping is done, a check for LBAC features is done. If any LBAC features exist, such as simple-security, simple-integrity, etc., a <Condition> element is added to that rule. This process is repeated over every permission, resulting in one <Rule> with a <Condition> element if LBAC is needed for each permission in the DRSD. This iteration is repeated for every role the user might hold. After the mappings over RBAC and LBAC capabilities are complete, then delegations and authorizations are tackled. For each delegation and authorization, a <Rule> element is created that would map the schemas and instances to <Resources> inside the rule for authorization, or roles and delegable users to <Resources> and <DelegationTargets> respectively, for delegation. The end result of this high-level process is the creation of one XACML policy instance

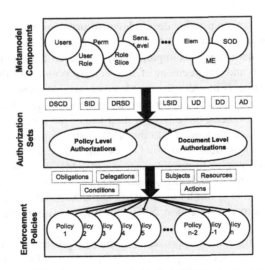

Fig. 16. Generating policies from UML diagrams.

```
1.   RBAC_LBAC_DAC_XACML_generation(DSCD, SID, DRSD, LSID, UD, DD, AD)
2.   {
3.     Generate_XACML_Description_Header()
4.     foreach(User as currentUser)
5.     {
6.       role_list = Find_Role(UD, DRSD);
7.       foreach(role_list as currentRole)
8.       {
9.         permission_list = Find_permissions(DRSD);
10.        foreach(permission_list as currentPermission)
11.        {
12.          XACML.createRule();
13.          XACML.mapSubject(UD,DRSD);
14.          XACML.mapResources(DSCD,SID,DRSD);
15.          XACML.mapActions(DRSD,SID);
16.          if(LBAC)
17.          {
18.            XACML.createCondition(UD,DSCD,SID,LSID);
19.          }
20.        }
21.      }
22.    }
23.    foreach(Delegation)
24.    {
25.      XACML.createRule();
26.      XACML.mapResources(DRSD,DD);
27.      XACML.mapTargets(UD,DRSD,DD);
28.    }
29.    foreach(Authorization)
30.    {
31.      XACML.createRule();
32.      XACML.mapSubject(UD,AD);
33.      XACML.mapResources(AD,DSCD);
34.    }
35.  }
```

Fig. 17. Pseudo-code for XACML policy instance generation algorithm.

per user, which could be readily deployed. Figure 18 shows the culmination of the MMUCC example with a sample policy created by this process.

6   Related Work

There have been attempts to provide design level security for tree-structured data in the past, though the majority of the efforts focus on securing document formats such as XML in real-life scenarios. For example, [10] presents an access control system that embeds the definition and enforcement of the security policies in the structure of the XML DTD and documents in order to provide customizable security. This is similar to our work in that security policies act in both a descriptive level of the XML instances and target the XML instances, but differs in their use of the outdated XML DTD's and their security policies are embedded into the XML instance for a high cost for security updates (recall Sect. 1). Another effort by [11] details a model that tries to combine the two discussed methodologies to provide security to XML datasets with three security attributes (access, condition and dirty) with changes updated in the both the XML schema its instances. This is similar to our work at the XACML policy level, but differs by our also taking into consideration XML document writing; their XPath's design only allows reads.

In terms of applying similar approaches to the one presented in this paper, but for functional aspects of a software system, work in [24] provides the most influential effort for the research presented in this paper by extending UML to represent RBAC

```
1.   <Policy PolicyId="ada-policy-law" RuleCombiningAlgId="deny-overrides">
2.   <Description>Law Enforcement Example Policy.</Description>
3.   <Target>
4.     <Subjects>
5.     <user><id>500</id><name>Rob</name></user>
6.     </Subjects>
7.     <Resources><AnyResource/></Resources>
8.     <Actions><AnyAction/></Actions>
9.   </Target>
10.  <Rule RuleId="simple-RBAC+LBAC-rule" Effect="Permit">
11.    <Target>
12.    <Subjects>
13.    <role><roleID>21</roleID><roleName>Polie Captain</roleName></role>
14.    </Subjects>
15.    <Resources><element>
16.    <elementID>el-26</elementID>
17.    <elementName>Crash Images</elementName>
18.    </element></Resources>
19.    <Actions><operation>
20.    <operationName>update</operationName>
21.    <opAccessMode>write</opAccessMode>
22.    </operation></Actions>
23.    </Target>
24.    <Condition>
25.    <Apply FunctionId="…:integer-greater-than-or-equal">
26.    <Apply FunctionId="…:integer-one-and-only">
27.    <AttributeValue DataType="…#integer">Top Secret</AttributeValue>
28.    </Apply>
29.    <AttributeValue DataType="…#integer">Secret</AttributeValue>
30.    </Apply>
31.    </Condition>
32.  </Rule>
33.  … // Remainder of permissions omitted due to space
34.  <Rule RuleId="simple-delegation-rule" Effect="Permit">
35.    <Target>
36.    <Subjects>
37.    <user><id>500</id><name>Rob</name></user>
38.    </Subjects>
39.    <Resources>
40.    <Roles><role>
41.    <roleID>21</roleID><roleName>Police Captain</roleName>
42.    </role></Roles>
43.    </Resources>
44.    <DelegationTargets>
45.    <user><id>23</id><name>Van</name></user>
46.    </DelegationTargets>
47.    </Target>
48.  </Rule>
49.  <Rule RuleId="simple-authorization-rule" Effect="Permit">
50.    <Target>
51.    <Subjects>
52.    <user><id>500</id><name>Rob</name></user>
53.    </Subjects>
54.    <Resources><Schemas><schema>
55.    <schemaID>50</schemaID>
56.    <schemaName>Schema 50</schemaName>
57.    </schema></Schemas>
58.    <Instances><instance>
59.    <instanceID>50,234</instaneID>
60.    <instanceName>Crash Report 234</instanceName>
61.    </instance></Instances></Resources>
62.    </Target>
63.  </Rule>
64.  </Policy>
```

Fig. 18. Resulting XACML policy for user rob and role PoliceCaptain.

and DAC via the introduction of the Role Slice Diagram, the User Diagram, the Delegation Diagram, and MAC extensions coupled with a Secure Subsystem Diagram. The work in [24] aims to provide security to the functional aspects of a software component, down to the granularity of methods in classes (in contrast, our work aims to provide the same level of security assurance to the information/data aspect of the software). To achieve this, the Secure Subsystem Diagram presented by [24] denotes the subset of an application's overall classes and methods that are restricted and require permissions to be in place for authorized users. The Role Slice Diagram, similar to the Document Role Slice in this paper, denotes RBAC policies from a role perspective. From an enforcement perspective, once defined, the diagrams are utilized to generate aspect-oriented enforcement code in AspectJ that is able to verify, at runtime, whether the active user has a role with permissions over the protected method and grants or denies access accordingly.

7 Conclusion

Information modeling is focused on representing, using, and exchanging data in large-scale applications or system-to-system operability. The work presented in this paper is a comprehensive approach that enables the modeling tree-structured schema in UML with the addition of the modeling of access control requirements (RBAC, LBAC, DAC) on said data for implementation solutions such as XML, JSON, and RDF. There were main contributions presented in the paper. The first contribution Sect. 3 supported the modeling of tree-structured data and schemas with the proposal of a new *UML Document Schema Class Diagram (DSCD)* in Sect. 3 that allowed generalized design from which target schemas/instances in XML, JSON, RDF, etc., can be generated. The second contribution in Sect. 4 proposed new UML diagrams for RBAC, LBAC, and DAC via the *Secure Information Diagram (SID)*, the *Document Role-Slice Diagram (DRSD)*, the *LBAC Secure Information Diagram (LSID)*, the *User Diagram (UD)*, the *Delegation Diagram (DD)*, and the *Authorization Diagram (AD)*. The combination of DSCD in Sect. 3 along with the security diagrams presented in Sect. 4 allowed the automatic generation of enforcement code via XACML as presented in Sect. 5. The end result is an underlying information security model that abstracts away from specific document formats and considers their most basic form as tree-structured containers while supporting access control capabilities as an integrated solution; and abstracting the comprehensive information security model with new UML diagrams that are capable of modeling tree-structured schemas and their associated RBAC, LBAC, and DAC.

References

1. HITECH act enforcement interim final rule (2014). http://www.hhs.gov/ocr/privacy/hipaa/administrative/enforcementrule/hitechenforcementifr.html
2. UML ISO standard. Object Management Group (2014). http://www.omg.org/spec/UML/
3. Annas, G.J.: HIPAA regulations—a new era of medical-record privacy? N. Engl. J. Med. **348**, 1486–1490 (2003)
4. Baumer, D., Earp, J.B., Payton, F.C.: Privacy of medical records: IT implications of HIPAA, pp. 137–152 (2006)

5. Bernauer, M., Kappel, G., Kramler, G.: Representing XML schema in UML–A comparison of approaches, pp. 767–769 (2004)
6. Bernauer, M., Kappel, G., Kramler, G.: Representing XML schema in UML-an UML profile for XML schema (2003)
7. Boudreau, T., Glick, J., Greene, S., Spurlin, V., Woehr, J.J.: NetBeans: The Definitive Guide. O'Reilly Media Inc., Sebastopol (2002)
8. Bray, T., Paoli, J., Sperberg-McQueen, C.M., Maler, E., Yergeau, F.: Extensible markup language (XML) (1998)
9. Crockford, D.: JSON: the fat-free alternative to XML (2006)
10. Damiani, E., Capitani, De, di Vimercati, S., Paraboschi, S., Samarati, P.: Design and implementation of an access control processor for XML documents. Comput. Netw. **33**, 59–75 (2000)
11. Damiani, E., Fansi, M., Gabillon, A., Marrara, S.: A general approach to securely querying XML. Comput. Stand. Interfaces **30**, 379–389 (2008)
12. Dolin, R.H., Alschuler, L., Boyer, S., Beebe, C., Behlen, F.M., Biron, P.V., Shvo, A.S.: HL7 clinical document architecture, release 2. J. Am. Med. Inform. Assoc. **13**, 30–39 (2006)
13. Ferraiolo, D.F., Sandhu, R., Gavrila, S., Kuhn, D.R., Chandramouli, R.: Proposed NIST standard for role-based access control. ACM Trans. Inform. Syst. Secur. **4**, 224–274 (2001)
14. Ferranti, J.M., Musser, R.C., Kawamoto, K., Hammond, W.: The clinical document architecture and the continuity of care record: A critical analysis. J. Am. Med. Inform. Assoc. **13**, 245–252 (2006)
15. Fowler, M.: UML distilled: a brief guide to the standard object modeling language. Addison-Wesley Professional, Boston (2004)
16. Guideline, M.: Model minimum uniform crash criteria. 811, 631 (2012)
17. Klyne, G., Carroll, J.J., McBride, B.: Resource description framework (RDF): Concepts and abstract syntax. 10 (2004)
18. Lee, M., Kim, H., Kim, J., Lee, J.: StarUML 5.0 developer guide' (2005)
19. McGuinness, D.L., Van Harmelen, F.: OWL web ontology language overview. 10, 10 (2004)
20. Merkow, M.: cXML: a new taxonomy for E-commerce (1999)
21. Moore, B., Dean, D., Gerber, A., Wagenknecht, G., Vanderheyden, P.: Eclipse development. 379 (2004)
22. OFX, Open Financial Exchange Specification
23. Ogle, J.H., Alluri, P., Sarasua, W.: MMUCC and MIRE: the role of segmentation in safety analysis (2011)
24. Pavlich-Mariscal, J., Michel, L., Demurjian, S.: Enhancing UML to model custom security aspects (2007)
25. Pavlich-Mariscal, Jaime A., Michel, Laurent, Demurjian, Steven A.: A formal enforcement framework for role-based access control using aspect-oriented programming. In: Briand, Lionel C., Williams, Clay (eds.) MoDELS 2005. LNCS, vol. 3713, pp. 537–552. Springer, Heidelberg (2005)
26. Pavlich-Mariscal, J.A., Demurjian, S.A., Michel, L.D.: A framework for security assurance of access control enforcement code. Comput. Secur. **29**, 770–784 (2010)
27. Poernomo, I.: The meta-object facility typed, pp. 1845–1849 (2006)
28. Ramirez, A., Vanpeperstraete, P., Rueckert, A., Odutola, K., Bennett, J., Tolke, L., van der Wulp, M.: ArgoUML user manual: a tutorial and reference description (2003)
29. Randolph, N., Gardner, D., Anderson, C., Minutillo, M.: Professional Visual Studio 2010. Wiley, Hoboken (2010)
30. Sandhu, R.S.: Lattice-based access control models. Computer **26**, 9–19 (1993)

31. Sandhu, R.S., Samarati, P.: Access control: principle and practice. IEEE Commun. Mag. **32**, 40–48 (1994)
32. Warmer, J.B., Kleppe, A.G.: The object constraint language: Precise modeling with uml (addison-wesley object technology series) (1998)

Attribute-Based Access Control Architectures with the eIDAS Protocols

Frank Morgner[1], Paul Bastian[1], and Marc Fischlin[2]([✉])

[1] Bundesdruckerei GmbH, Berlin, Germany
[2] Technische Universität Darmstadt, Darmstadt, Germany
marc.fischlin@cryptoplexity.de

Abstract. The extended access control protocol has been used for the German identity card since November 2010, primarily to establish a cryptographic key between a card and a service provider and to authenticate the partners. The protocol is also referenced by the International Civil Aviation Organization for machine readable travel documents (Document 9303) as an option, and it is a candidate for the future European eIDAS identity system. Here we show that the system can be used to build a secure access system which operates in various settings (e.g., integrated, distributed, or authentication-service based architectures), and where access can be granted based on card's attributes. In particular we prove the protocols to provide strong cryptographic guarantees, including privacy of the attributes against outsiders.

1 Introduction

The extended access control (EAC) protocol has originally been proposed by the German Federal Office for Information Security (BSI) for identity cards and machine readable travel documents [1]. Indeed, it is listed as an option in Document 9303 of the International Civil Aviation Organization for protecting machine readable travel documents [19]. In the latest version of the BSI document [2] it has also been proposed as a part of the candidate for the European electronic identities, authentication, and trust services (eIDAS) system. Technically, the protocol establishes a cryptographic key between an eID card, connected to a local reader, and a remote service provider, via the so-called terminal authentication (TA) step and the chip authentication (CA) step. The protocol also mutually authenticates the parties. See Fig. 1.

1.1 EAC for Attribute-Based Access Control

Here we discuss how the EAC protocol can be adapted for more general (physical) access system architectures. Furthermore, using the established cryptographic key in the EAC protocol one can use its channel protocol, called secure messaging, to have the card send further attributes on which the access decision can be based, too. The advantage is that only mild changes to the existing infrastructure of the German identity card and candidate eIDAS system are necessary.

© Springer International Publishing AG 2016
L. Chen et al. (Eds.): SSR 2016, LNCS 10074, pp. 205–226, 2016.
DOI: 10.1007/978-3-319-49100-4_9

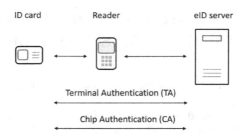

Fig. 1. Extended Access Control (EAC), consisting of the terminal authentication (TA) step and the chip authentication (CA) step.

Ample Architecture Scenarios. The first extension refers to broader architectures in which the verifying party can be distributed across various entities. The common settings, also displayed in Fig. 2, include:

- In the *integrated terminal architecture*, as in the border control scenario for travel documents, the reader implements the service provider functionality, and only forwards the attributes (sent over the secure messaging channel) for verification to the back-end management (via a secure connection like TLS). The reader then potentially grants access.
- In the *distributed terminal architecture*, as in the eID service scenario, the reader mainly connects the card to a controller which executes the EAC protocol with the card. The controller again calls the back-end management about the attributes.
- In the *eID-service architecture* an external service provider takes care of the cryptographic operations and forwards the attributes to the controller.
- In the *authentication-service architecture* the signature generation in the TA step of the EAC protocol is outsourced to a dedicated authentication server which holds the long-term signing key. The other steps are carried out again by the controller.

Restoring Sessions. Another extension concerns the possibility to authenticate faster through recognition. Here we can rely on the session contexts provided by the EAC protocol, version 2. Roughly, the EAC protocol offers the possibility to store the derived keys for secure messaging (and the send sequence counter) and to re-establish a connection with these keys. In EAC this allows to switch session contexts when changing communication partners.

By using the session context switching mechanism we can add a recognition step to our authentication procedure (for any setting). That is, the responding party checks if it has already successfully authenticated the card (and stored the session context under some identifier) and tries to re-establish the session with the card. If the card is responsive then both parties re-start the secure channel under the stored keys and the card transmits its attributes. By this the parties do not have to perform the more expensive public-key operations again.

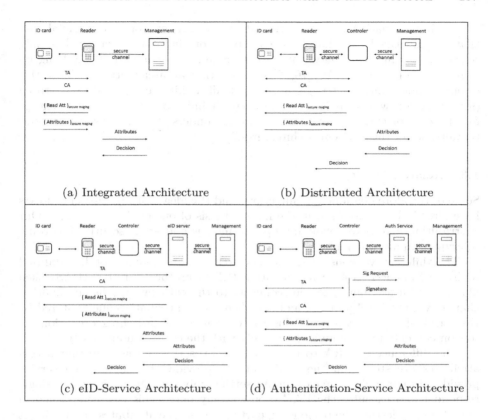

Fig. 2. Architectures for attribute-based access control.

1.2 Security of the Architectures

Our main result is to show that the proposed protocols provide strong security guarantees in a cryptographic sense. This boils down to two important security properties: *impersonation resistance*, preventing the adversary to trick the responding party into falsely accepting a card, and *attribute-privacy*, preventing the adversary from learning the attributes transmitted by genuine cards. The latter may be necessary in cases where the attributes carry confidential data, such as general access information or data facilitating the identification of the person using the card.

We envision very strong adversarial capabilities in attacks against either property, such that showing infeasiblity of attacks gives strong security guarantees. The adversary in our security model corresponds to similar attackers on key exchange protocols (such as in the Bellare-Rogaway model [8]), giving the adversary full control over the network, and allowing it to modify or inject messages in communications, and to corrupt parties.

For impersonation resistance the adversary wins except in the trivial case that the identified card has been corrupted, or that the adversary has only relayed communication between the reader and the genuine card. Relying on previous results about EAC [16, 22] we show that all architectures achieve this strong notion. Analogously, we argue that all architectures satisfy our strong privacy notion which postulates indistinguishability of used attributes, except for the case of corrupt cards or corrupt responders. We also discuss security peculiarities of the different architectures.

1.3   Related Work

Some of the aforementioned architectures and the idea of using session contexts have already been discussed in the master thesis of one of the authors [6]. Our contribution here is to define appropriate models and argue security according to cryptographic standards.

The different versions of the access architectures should not be confused with the Enhanced Role Authentication (ERA) protocol for the eIDAS token [2]. There, an attribute provider connects to the card by establishing another channel via the EAC protocol and can then access attribute requests stored by the terminal on the card. For this the card uses the switching operation for session contexts to communicate securely with the corresponding party.

The difference of ERA to our setting here is that we assume that access attributes are stored on the card and not provided by an external service provider. In particular, the card in our setting only communicates with a single responder and executes the EAC protocol only once. This is accomplished in our setting by letting the responding party read out the attributes and having it forward them to the management system. The protocol here also uses the session contexts to re-establish connections, instead of switching channels between the various communication partners. This also means that the session contexts are stored persistently here, whereas eIDAS tokens use them transiently only.

In a related proposal, Bundesdruckerei [5] introduces the possibility to secure transactions data, such as mobile phone numbers, on top of the EAC protocol and its existing eID architecture (requiring only minor modifications to the reader). The proposed transaction system has been analyzed cryptographically in [22]. This idea is orthogonal to our setting here where we discuss different access architectures including attributes. Yet, due to the resemblance with the EAC protocol we can partly use their results in order to show that the various access systems provide the common authentication guaranteed, even if the responding party cannot communicate with the management system for checking the attributes.

The EAC protocol (and its related protocols for the German identity card resp. the eIDAS tokens) has been analyzed in [9–12, 15–18, 21]. We merely rely on the EAC analysis in [16] and results related to secure composition of key exchange (like EAC) with secure channels (such as secure messaging).

2 The EAC Protocol and Adaptations

Since the access system strongly relies on the EAC protocol we first recall that protocol and then discuss the modifications.

2.1 The EAC Protocol

The Extended Access Control (EAC) protocol is a two-party key agreement protocol between a chip card and a terminal. It consists of a terminal authentication (TA) step and a chip authentication (CA) step. We omit explicit mentioning of the passive authentication step in between, in which the chip forwards passively authenticated data to the terminal, since the details of this step is irrelevant to our security concerns here.

At the outset both parties each hold a certified long-term key pair, on the card's side for generating a Diffie-Hellman key, and on the terminal's side for signing. Both parties also hold a card identifier id_C which in the execution of the German identity card equals the compressed version of the public-key of the preceding PACE protocol with which the card connects securely to the local reader (see Sect. 2.3). The PACE step is omitted in our setting. One may for now simply assume that id_C is empty.

In the TA step the terminal authenticates to the chip card. For this it chooses a session-specific ephemeral key pair (esk_T, epk_T), sends over its certificate for the long-term key pk_T (which is also included in its certificate $cert_T$) and a compressed version $\mathrm{Compr}(epk_T)$ of the ephemeral public key. The compression function can be for example the projection onto the x-coordinate of the elliptic curve point. The card returns a random nonce r_C which the terminal signs, together with $\mathrm{Compr}(epk_T)$ and id_C (if present). The terminal sends the signature to the card and the card accepts only if verification succeeds.

Upon successful completion of the TA phase, the card then executes the Chip Authentication (CA) step. For this the chip sends its certificate $cert_C$ and public key pk_C, and the terminal replies with its (uncompressed) ephemeral public key epk_T. The card checks that this value matches the previously sent compressed version. Both parties then compute the Diffie-Hellman key of pk_C and epk_T with the corresponding secret key they hold, and derive an encryption key K_{enc} and the MAC key K_{mac}. This step requires the card to pick another random nonce r'_C and include it in the key derivation process. The chip computes the MAC over epk_T and sends it together with the nonce r'_C to the terminal.

In the protocol description in Fig. 3 we also include the so-called session identifiers sid for compatibility with previous analyses [16,22]. These session identifiers can be roughly seen as unique session-specific labels. These cryptographic identifiers, determined by the protocol communication and used in the proof, should not be confused with the integer-valued session *context* identifiers used by the parties of the EAC protocol. Similarly, we include the partner identifiers pid which refer to the designated partner and are taken from the unique identifier in the certificate.

Chip :	Terminal :
key pair sk_C, pk_C	key pair sk_T, pk_T
certificate $cert_C$ for pk_C	certificate $cert_T$ for pk_T
card identifier id_C	card identifier id_C

Setup: domain parameters D_C, certification key pk_{CVCA}

Terminal Authentication (TA)

$$\longleftarrow \quad cert_T$$

check $cert_T$ with pk_{CVCA}
abort if $cert_T$ invalid
extract pk_T from $cert_T$ generate (esk_T, epk_T) for domain D_C

$$\longleftarrow \quad \mathrm{Compr}(epk_T)$$

pick $r_C \leftarrow \{0,1\}^n$

$$\xrightarrow{\quad r_C \quad}$$
$$\xleftarrow{\quad s_T \quad} \qquad s_T \leftarrow \mathsf{Sig}(sk_T, id_C||r_C||\mathrm{Compr}(epk_T))$$

abort if $\mathsf{SVf}(pk_T, s_T, id_C||r_C||\mathrm{Compr}(epk_T))$

$$sid = (\mathrm{Compr}(epk_T), r_C)$$

Chip Authentication (CA)

$$\xrightarrow{\quad pk_C, cert_C, D_C \quad} \qquad \text{check } pk_C, cert_C \text{ with } pk_{\mathrm{CVCA}}$$
$$\text{abort if invalid}$$

$$\xleftarrow{\quad epk_T \quad}$$

check pk_T against $\mathrm{Compr}(epk_T)$
abort if invalid
pick $r'_C \leftarrow \{0,1\}^n$
$K = \mathrm{DH}_{D_C}(sk_C, epk_T)$
$K_{\mathrm{enc}} = \mathsf{KDF}_{\mathsf{Enc}}(K, r'_C)$
$K_{\mathrm{mac}} = \mathsf{KDF}_{\mathsf{MAC}}(K, r'_C)$

$\tau = \mathsf{MAC}(K_{\mathrm{mac}}, epk_T)$ $\qquad \xrightarrow{\quad \tau, r'_C \quad}$

$\qquad\qquad K = \mathrm{DH}_{D_C}(pk_C, esk_T)$
$\qquad\qquad K_{\mathrm{enc}} = \mathsf{KDF}_{\mathsf{Enc}}(K, r'_C)$
$\qquad\qquad K_{\mathrm{mac}} = \mathsf{KDF}_{\mathsf{MAC}}(K, r'_C)$
$\qquad\qquad$ abort if $\mathsf{MVf}(K_{\mathrm{mac}}, \tau, epk_T) = 0$

$sid = (\mathrm{Compr}(epk_T), r_C)$	
$pid = \mathrm{id}$ in $cert_T$	$pid = \mathrm{id}$ in $cert_C$
accept	accept

Fig. 3. Terminal Authentication (TA) and Chip Authentication (CA). All number-theoretic operations are modulo q resp. over the elliptic curve.

2.2   Restoring Session Context

A session context in the domain of the German identity card consists mainly of some (session context) identifier, the cryptographic keys for secure messaging, the send sequence counter (and possibly additional entries like the auxiliary data which can be used in the EAC protocol) [2]. A new session context is usually stored after successful reception of the first secure messaging transmission. The card is usually restricted to store at most 127 session contexts (or even less). To restore a session the terminal is supposed to send the context identifier to the card, encapsulated into a corresponding protocol message.

When storing the sequence counter it must be ensured that this value does not interfere with the actual counter value used for secure messaging. The suggested method is to round the current value up to the next multiple of 16 and store this value. Only if the current value reaches this bound then one again needs to update the stored value to the next multiple of 16. For us here the details are irrelevant as long it is guaranteed that sequence counters are used only once in the context of a session.

We note that the card is supposed to immediately delete a session context if an erroneous secure messaging transmission arrives. Similarly, if a terminal tries to re-initialize a session context but receives an error (say, if some other terminal has overwritten the context under the identifier meanwhile) then the terminal should start from scratch running the EAC protocol.

2.3   Modifications

In this part we describe the modifications of the EAC protocol

Omitting the PACE step. First, we do not assume that the password-authenticated connection establishment (PACE) protocol between the card and the reader is executed before initializing the EAC protocol. The PACE protocol requires the card holder to type in the PIN at the reader and then establishes a secure channel between card and reader for the wireless data exchange.

As pointed out in [16] the EAC protocol itself already provides a secure key exchange protocol between card and terminal whose security does not rely on the strength of the PACE protocol. We therefore start with the assumption that card and reader have not executed the PACE protocol. This, however, also means that the card identifier value id_C has not been set yet, because it usually corresponds to data derived during the run of PACE. We simply assume that id_C is empty.

Adding Attributes. Besides completing the (modified) EAC protocol access permission may depend on the attributes a card can provide. We assume that the responder may request to see the attributes and then the card sends the stored data. Note that these steps are carried out over the secure-messaging channel. If the terminal requests to see the attributes then we set on the card's side, upon successful completion of this step, the cryptographic session identifier to be (sid, C) for the transmitted ciphertext C of the attributes.

We stress again that, if the management system is unreachable, the ordinary authentication process of the EAC protocol is still in effect such that reading the attributes after executing the EAC protocol may be optional. For restored sessions, however, reading out attributes over the secure channel is the only mechanism to ensure that the card actually holds the secret keys.

Persistent Session Contexts. Session contexts for the German identity card are supposed to be deleted when the card becomes unpowered or is being reset. In contrast we may assume that session contexts are stored over longer periods of time. One may even continuously use a stored context for "cascaded" executions.

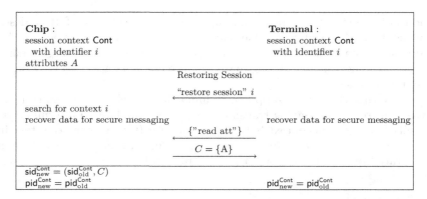

Fig. 4. Restoring sessions and reading out attributes in the case of the distributed architecture (with the controller acting as the terminal). Here, {. . . } denotes protocol messages sent via secure messaging. Note that the updated cryptographic session identifier is augmented by the ciphertexts of the attributes.

Furthermore, we do not make any restrictions on the number of stored contexts; the number may depend on the card's architecture.

In addition, we do not pose any stipulations on the choice of the identifiers of session contexts but advise some "collision-free" choice. For example, important responders may be assigned a fixed identifier whereas other terminals may select identifiers at random. Since the choice only affects efficiency but not security we do not discuss possible strategies here further.

We let the cryptographic session identifier sid monotonously grow with the number of restored contexts, because we append the card's latest authenticated ciphertext of the attributes, sent via secure messaging, to the current identifier value $\mathsf{sid}^{\mathsf{Cont}}_{\mathsf{old}}$ of the context upon acceptance. Partner identifiers and attributes remain unaltered. An execution example of a restored session of the distributed architecture is given in Fig. 4.

3   Access Systems and Their Security

Before discussing the security of our (modified) EAC protocol we first abstractly introduce access systems and their desired security features.

3.1   Access Systems

An access system $\mathcal{AS}$ consists of efficient algorithm $(\mathsf{KG}_C, \mathsf{KG}_R, \Pi_S, \Pi_R)$ for generating keys (and attributes) for the card, $(pk_C, sk_C, cert_C) \leftarrow \mathsf{KG}_C(1^n)$. We note that we will later add attributes to cards but in a session-specific way. More formally, we assume that the attributes A are provided "from the outside" and all attributes are stored externally in some list $\mathcal{ATT}$ and given to the managing party. Similarly, the system comprises a key generator for the responding party,

$(pk_R, sk_R, cert_R) \leftarrow \mathsf{KG}_R(1^n)$, and stateful algorithms Π_C, Π_R for the party's protocol messages. We sometimes omit mentioning certificates for the public keys explicitly, and that there must be a certification authority; all the details are relevant when taking an in-depth look at EAC, but we are mainly concerned with the fact that EAC provides a secure key exchange protocol.

We assume the usual completeness property, saying that for genuine keys, the card holding attribute $A \in \mathcal{ATT}$, and faithful execution of the algorithms Π_S, Π_R the responder eventually accepts the card. Here, to cover restored sessions we assume that the responder may accept multiple times within a session. Formally, this is captured by running Π_S and Π_R in modes init and restore, and we assume that at the end of the first execution of init on genuine data (involving $A \in \mathcal{ATT}$) the responder accepts, as well at the end of each execution in mode restore. Note that every time the session continues, triggered via a restore command, the party goes from an accepting state to an unaccepting one.

3.2   Security Model

In all versions of the access system we assume a powerful adversary controlling the network.

Attack Model. We assume that all parties, divided exclusively into cards from set $\mathcal{C}$ and responders from a set $\mathcal{R}$, receive their (certified) key pairs as initial input at the outset of the attack. Since we do not want to make any assumptions about the structure of card attributes we leave it up to the adversary to assign attributes to cards upon initialization of a new session.

The adversary has full control over the network and can, in particular, initiate new sessions of parties and decide when to deliver protocol messages (and potentially to modify such messages or even inject new ones). Formally, this is modeled by giving the adversary the following oracle access:

– INIT: The adversary can initiate a new card or responder session by calling INIT(id) for some identity id $\in \mathcal{C} \cup \mathcal{R}$. We assume that the identifier id uniquely determines a certificate and vice versa. In case of a card the adversary also has to provide some attribute A. The adversary may thus choose to hand out the same attribute to each card or change attributes depending on the concrete session. This attribute is immediately stored in a list $\mathcal{ATT}$. Upon such a call we spawn a new session of the party for attribute A and assign it a unique label ℓ for administrative purposes. The label ℓ is returned to the adversary and we write $\ell \leftarrow \text{INIT}(\text{id}, [A])$.
– SEND: The adversary can send any protocol message m to a session with label ℓ via the SEND(ℓ, m) command. If the session has not been initialized before, then the oracle immediately returns $\perp$. Else, it makes the corresponding party compute the next protocol message and this message is returned to the adversary (potentially also returning $\perp$ to express rejection).
  In particular, we assume that the adversary may make the party switch to modes, from init to restore or starting a new restore session, if receiving

Send(ℓ, restore). If the party has not finished successfully the previous mode yet, it may reject. In case the execution is successfully completed, the adversary is informed that the party has accepted.

- CORRUPT: The adversary can corrupt a party with identity id by using the Corrupt(id) command. It receives the party's long-term keys and internal state in return, and we put id in the (initially empty) set Corrupt of corrupt parties. From now on, we assume that the adversary does not send further commands to that session.

To facilitate the notation we use the following mappings. We write $\mathsf{ACC}(\ell)$ for the (current) acceptance status of the (responder) session (true or false), and $\mathsf{ID}(\ell)$ for the identity id of the session owner, and $\mathsf{PID}(\ell)$ for the intended partner pid, possibly pid $= \bot$ at this point. Similarly, $\mathsf{SID}(\ell)$ denotes the current value of the session identifier. We also denote by $\mathsf{ATT}(\ell)$ for a session the attribute A the card has been initialized with resp. the attribute the responder it has received (if at all).

Impersonation Resistance. Impersonation resistance of the access system now says that the adversary cannot make the responder accept, unless in the trivial case that a card with attribute A is accepted and the adversary has corrupted a card with these attributes (in which it could easily access the system by using that card), or if the adversary has merely relayed the communication between an honest card and the reader. This is formalized in Fig. 5.

While Fig. 5 describes the flow of the attack, the predicate ImpResPred in Fig. 6, which is evaluated at the end of the attack, determines when the adversary wins. There are two cases when we declare the adversary to win. The first case is when the adversary has managed to make an honest responder accept an honest card which has not participated in the execution (or with different attributes). This corresponds to the **foreach** loop in Line 3 in Fig. 6. The second case, covering replay resistance, is that partnered sessions are unique between cards and responders, or else the adversary wins, too. In particular, there

---

Experiment $\mathsf{ImpRes}_{\mathcal{A}}^{\mathcal{AS}}(n)$

1 : **foreach** $i \in \mathcal{C} \cup \mathcal{S}$ **do**
2 :   **if** $i \in \mathcal{C}$ **then** $(sk_i, pk_i, cert_i) \leftarrow \mathsf{KG}_{\mathcal{C}}(1^n)$ **fi**
3 :   **if** $i \in \mathcal{R}$ **then** $(sk_i, pk_i, cert_i) \leftarrow \mathsf{KG}_{\mathcal{R}}(1^n)$ **fi**
4 : **endforeach**
5 : $pks \leftarrow \{(pk_i, cert_i) \mid i \in \mathcal{C} \cup \mathcal{R}\}$
6 : $\mathcal{A}^{\mathrm{INIT}(\cdots),\mathrm{SEND}(\cdots),\mathrm{CORRUPT}(\cdot)}(1^n, pks)$
7 : $b \leftarrow \mathsf{ImpResPred}$ // evaluate predicate ImpResPred on execution state
8 : **return** $\bar{b}$

Fig. 5. Security of an access system.

Predicate ImpResPred on execution state

---

1 : $p \leftarrow \texttt{true}$

2 :   // accepting responder session must have honest partner with sid (or corrupt partner)

3 :   **foreach** $\ell \in \{\ell \mid \mathsf{ID}(\ell) \in \mathcal{R} \setminus \mathsf{Corrupt} \wedge \mathsf{ACC}(\ell) = \texttt{true}\}$ **do**

4 : $p \leftarrow p \wedge [\mathsf{PID}(\ell) \in \mathcal{C} \cap \mathsf{Corrupt}$

5 : $\vee \, \exists \ell' \neq \ell : (\mathsf{SID}(\ell') = \mathsf{SID}(\ell) \neq \bot \wedge \mathsf{PID}(\ell) = \mathsf{ID}(\ell')$

6 : $\wedge \, \mathsf{ATT}(\ell') = \mathsf{ATT}(\ell))]$

7 :   **endforeach**

8 :   // Collisions among identifiers only between opposite partners

9 :   **foreach**

10 : $(\ell, \ell') \in \{(\ell, \ell') \mid \ell \neq \ell' \wedge \mathsf{ID}(\ell), \mathsf{ID}(\ell') \notin \mathsf{Corrupt} \wedge \mathsf{SID}(\ell) = \mathsf{SID}(\ell') \neq \bot\}$

11 :   **do**

12 : $p \leftarrow p \wedge [(\mathsf{ID}(\ell), \mathsf{ID}(\ell')) \in \mathcal{C} \times \mathcal{S} \cup \mathcal{S} \times \mathcal{C}]$

13 :   **endforeach**

14 :   **return** p

Fig. 6. Security predicate ImpResPred for impersonation resistance.

cannot be two honest cards with the same session identifiers. This is checked in the **foreach** loop in Line 9 in Fig. 6.

Note that, in the predicate ImpResPred, if the responding party accepts and outputs some session identifier, then the card must have already accepted before, i.e., we assume that the responder receives the last message. This ensures that there is always a card with the same identifier sid at this point, unless the aversary has managed to break security. This holds in our setting here as the card sends the attributes or acknowledges the storage of the session context.

Definition 1 (Impersonation Resistance). *An access system $\mathcal{AS}$ is impersonation resistant if for any efficient adversary $\mathcal{A}$ the following is negligible:*

$$\mathrm{Prob}\left[\, \mathit{ImpRes}_{\mathcal{A}}^{\mathcal{AS}}(n) = 1 \right] \approx 0.$$

Note that we let the adversary $\mathcal{A}$ decide when to stop the execution and to start evaluating the predicate. Hence, if it is advantageous and the adversary already detects a winning situation, it may end the execution immediately (instead of messing up the winning state by, say, corrupting another party). In our case this is easy to detect since all the data required to evaluate the predicate are known to the adversary. In general, if the predicate relies on some information unavailable to the adversary, then the adversary may just guess the point in time for such a state.

3.3 Privacy of Attributes

Privacy of attributes ensures that no adversary can learn the card's attributes (unless it is the responder and controls that party's long-term key). We use an indistinguishability-based approach here in which a privacy-adversary can, besides regular sessions, also initiate (multiple) executions on a random choice of one of two adversarially chosen attributes A_0, A_1.

The attack model is the same as for impersonation resistance. The only difference is that the adversary now also gets a challenge oracle CHALL, which is initialized with a secret bit $b \leftarrow \{0,1\}$. When called about identity id $\in C$ and two attributes A_0, A_1, the challenge oracle executes $\ell \leftarrow$ INIT(id, A_b) to initialize an execution with the card. It returns the session label ℓ to the adversary. From then on the adversary can communicate with the card's sessions via the SEND oracle for the corresponding label. The adversary eventually should predict the bit b.

To rule out trivial attacks, say, in which the adversary controls the corrupt responder, we require that the adversary has only asked the challenge oracle for identities of honest cards which refer to an honest partner. For this we check that for each query (id, A_0, A_1) to CHALL we neither have id $\in$ Corrupt nor PID(ℓ) $\in$ Corrupt, where a yet unset partner identifier PID(ℓ) $= \bot$ does not belong to Corrupt by definition.

We can now define privacy with the experiment in Fig. 7.

Definition 2 (Attribute-Privacy). *An attribute-based access system $\mathcal{AS}$ provides attribute-privacy private if for any efficient adversary $\mathcal{A}$ the following is negligibly close to $\frac{1}{2}$:*

$$\mathrm{Prob}\left[\mathsf{APriv}_{\mathcal{A}}^{\mathcal{AS}}(n) = 1 \right] \leq \tfrac{1}{2} + \mathsf{negl}(n).$$

Experiment $\mathsf{APriv}_{\mathcal{A}}^{\mathcal{AS}}(n)$

1 : $b \leftarrow \{0,1\}$

2 : **foreach** $i \in C \cup S$ **do**

3 :   **if** $i \in C$ **then** $(sk_i, pk_i) \leftarrow \mathsf{KG}_C(1^n)$ **fi**

4 :   **if** $i \in S$ **then** $(sk_i, pk_i) \leftarrow \mathsf{KG}_S(1^n)$ **fi**

5 : **endforeach**

6 : $pks \leftarrow \{(i, pk_i) \mid i \in C \cup S\}$

7 : $a \leftarrow \mathcal{A}^{\mathrm{INIT}(\cdot,\cdot),\mathrm{SEND}(\cdot,\cdot),\mathrm{CORRUPT}(\cdot),\mathrm{CHALL}(b,\cdots)}(1^n, pks)$

8 : // check for trivial attacks where card or responder corrupt

9 : $p \leftarrow \mathbf{true}$

10 : **foreach** ℓ returned by CHALL **do**

11 : $p \leftarrow p \wedge [\mathsf{ID}(\ell) \notin \mathsf{Corrupt} \wedge \mathsf{PID}(\ell) \notin \mathsf{Corrupt}]$

12 : **endforeach**

13 : **return** $p \wedge (a = b)$

Fig. 7. Attribute privacy experiment

4   On the Security of EAC with Secure Messaging

Before discussing our analyses let us motivate the setting by the general idea behind the security argument.

Outline. Our general proof strategy is roughly as follows. Dagdelen and Fischlin [16] have basically shown that the EAC protocol is a Bellare-Rogaway secure key exchange protocol. Assuming that secure messaging of the eID system, which follows ISO/IEC 9791-1 resp. ISO/IEC 10116, provides a secure channel for fresh keys, we can then apply the composition theorem of Brzuska et al. [13] to conclude that the combined protocol (where the channel keys are now determined by the EAC key exchange protocol) also provides a secure channel. In particular, it follows that the transmissions of the card's attributes via secure messaging can only be carried out by the corresponding party, and that any attack will lead the partner to reject. Let us elaborate on these steps in more detail.

Security of EAC. The result by Dagdelen and Fischlin [16] shows that EAC is a secure key exchange protocol in the Bellare-Rogaway sense. This means that EAC provides keys which are indistinguishable from random, even in presence of active adversaries.[1] In particular, and omitting some negligible terms for collisions among group elements and nonces, they show that the advantage of distinguishing actual keys from random is bounded by the terms to break the used MAC, signature and certification algorithms, to find second pre-images in the compression function, and to solve the Diffie-Hellman problem when given a decisional Diffie-Hellman oracle as help. All formal security notions of these primitives are given in Appendix A:

$$\mathbf{Adv}^{\mathrm{AKE}}_{\mathcal{A},\mathrm{EAC}}(n) \leq q_e \cdot \left(\mathbf{Adv}^{\mathrm{forge}}_{\mathcal{B}_1,\mathrm{MAC}}(n) + \mathbf{Adv}^{\mathrm{forge}}_{\mathcal{B}_2,\mathrm{Sig}}(n) + \mathbf{Adv}^{\mathrm{SecPre}}_{\mathcal{B}_3,\mathrm{Compr}}(n) \right)$$
$$+ \mathbf{Adv}^{\mathrm{forge}}_{\mathcal{B}_4,\mathrm{Cert}}(n) + 2q_e^2 \cdot \mathbf{Adv}^{\mathrm{GapDH}}_{\mathcal{B}_5,\mathrm{DH}}(n)$$

Here, q_e is the number of executions in the attack, and $\mathcal{B}_1, \ldots, \mathcal{B}_5$ are adversaries with a comparable run time as the attacker $\mathcal{A}$ on the EAC protocol. Since all advantages for the underlying primitives are assumed to be negligible, this shows security of the EAC protocol as an authenticated key exchange. The authors of [16] also discuss that security holds in case of a projection of the curve point onto the x-coordinate, making the compression function two-to-one.

Security of Secure Messaging. The proposed channel protocol is secure messaging [3], which either uses 3DES in CBC mode with $\mathrm{IV} = 0$ according to ISO/IEC 10116 for encryption, and in retail mode (MAC algorithm 3 with DES as block

---

[1] Dagdelen and Fischlin actually show a slight modification of EAC (with an independent authentication key) to be a BR-secure protocol; without this modification such a proof cannot go though. We also adopt this approach here, but as pointed out in [16] one can in principle use the strategy in [13,14] to lift this to a security for the original protocol, at the cost of a more complicated proof.

cipher) with IV = 0 according to ISO/IEC 9797-1 for authentication, with the data prepended by send sequence counter SSC which is incremented for each operation. The other option is to use AES in CBC mode according to ISO/IEC 10116 with IV = AES(K_{enc}, SSC) and to use AES in CMAC for authentication with 8 bytes of output according to SP 800-38B, where, again, the data is prepended by SSC before authentication.

In [24] Rogaway analyzes the encryption modes proposed in SP 800-38A resp. ISO/IEC 10116, including the CBC mode used in secure messaging with the IV = AES(K_{enc}, SSC) computed by applying the block cipher to the current send sequence counter SSC. Rogaway proposes an attack if the adversary has full control over the value SSC. The attack does not carry over to the setting used in secure messaging, where the encrypting party increments the value for each operation. This version can be actually shown to be secure [7]. Rogaway [24] confirms the authentication properties of the proposed MAC algorithms in ISO/IEC 9791-1 which are proposed here for secure messaging.

We thus assume that secure messaging provides a secure channel (in the sense of [13, Sect. 6.3] which in turn is based on the the notion of stateful authenticated encryption [20,23]). The experiment lets an adversary call a challenge oracle to enqueue one of two message blocks m_0, m_1 into the channel, the choice made according to a secret but then fixed bit b, and to dequeue arbitrary ciphertexts on the receiver's side. The adversary wins if it manages to predict b or to make the receiver accept a decryption of an out-of-order sent ciphertext. See Fig. 8. The advantage $\mathbf{Adv}_{\mathcal{A},\mathsf{Ch}}^{\mathrm{SecCh}}(n)$ of the adversary $\mathcal{A}$ is then defined to be the probability of predicting b beyond the pure guessing probability of $\frac{1}{2}$ (in the multi-instance setting).

Note that a secure channel in our scenario here comprises both confidentiality of the attributes, as well as authenticity. The latter suffices if the goal is to ensure that only the designated card can send the attributes, whereas the former also guarantees privacy of the attributes. If authentication suffices may be application dependent.

Secure Channel	Oracle SEND(m_0, m_1)	Oracle RCV(C)
$(k, \mathsf{st}_S, \mathsf{st}_R) \leftarrow \mathsf{KG}(n)$	$(C_0, \mathsf{st}'_{S,0}) \leftarrow \mathsf{Send}(k, m_0, \mathsf{st}_S)$	$(m, \mathsf{st}_R) \leftarrow \mathsf{Rcv}(k, C, \mathsf{st}_R)$
$b \leftarrow \{0,1\}$	$(C_1, \mathsf{st}'_{S,1}) \leftarrow \mathsf{Send}(k, m_1, \mathsf{st}_S)$	**if** $b = 1$ **and**
$\mathcal{Q} \leftarrow ()$	**if** $C_0, C_1 \neq \bot$ **then**	$\mathcal{Q}.\mathsf{dequeue}() \neq C$ **then**
$a \leftarrow \mathcal{A}^{\mathrm{SEND}(\cdots),\mathrm{RCV}(\cdots)}$	$\mathsf{st}_S \leftarrow \mathsf{st}'_{S,b}$	**return** m
return $a = b$	$\mathcal{Q}.\mathsf{enqueue}(C_b)$	**else**
	return C_b	**return** $\bot$
	else	**fi**
	return $\bot$	
	fi	

Fig. 8. Security Experiment of (single instance of) channel protocol (KG, Send, Rcv).

Compositional Security. Next we apply the compositional result in [13, Sect. 4] The theorem says that the combined protocol EAC; SM (where the channel keys for secure messaging in the multiple instances are determined by executing the EAC key exchange protocol first) also provides a secure channel, as if the keys have been chosen freshly. In particular we apply the composition theorem for so-called single-restricted games. This is a property which basically says that multiple concurrently running instances of a game correspond to several independent sessions, as in case of secure channels. For such games, it is shown that:

$$\mathbf{Adv}^{\mathrm{SecCh}}_{\mathcal{A},\mathrm{EAC;SM}}(n) \leq q_e \cdot \mathbf{Adv}^{\mathrm{AKE}}_{\mathcal{B}_1,\mathrm{EAC}}(n) + \mathbf{Adv}^{\mathrm{SecCh}}_{\mathcal{B}_2,\mathrm{SM}}(n).$$

Note that this also requires for EAC to provide *match-security*, a property about collision-freeness of session identifiers, and to have *public session matching*, the ability to determine partnered sessions from the public transcript. Neither property has been discussed in [16] but it is easy to show them to hold for EAC.

EAC and Impersonation Resistance. The EAC protocol not only provides a secure key exchange protocol but it also ensures impersonation resistance. This roughly means that, at the end of the EAC protocol, no adversary can make the responder accept a card, unless the card has been corrupted before or if the adversary merely relayed the communication between the card and the reader. Based on the results in [16] this has been proven formally in [22] for EAC with auxiliary data, when the system is viewed as a transaction system. For "empty" transaction data their protocol is identical to the EAC protocol here, including also the choice for session identifiers, and their security guarantee of session-definite unforgeability is stronger than the requirement of impersonation resistance here. (It has also been shown there that session identifiers collide with negligible probability only.)

More precisely, Morgner et al. [22] show that for any efficient adversary $\mathcal{A}$ (against their unforgeability notion and thus our impersonation resistance notion of the EAC protocol without attributes) there exists efficient adversaries $\mathcal{B}_1, \mathcal{B}_2, \mathcal{B}_3$ against the underlying cryptographic primitives for forging signatures on behalf of terminals, forging MACs on behalf of cards, and solving the computational Diffie-Hellman problem in the presence of a decisional DH oracle. Concretely, the probability of forging transaction resp. impersonating here is bounded from above by:

$$\mathrm{Prob}\left[\mathsf{ImpRes}^{\mathrm{EAC}-\mathcal{AS}}_{\mathcal{A}}(n) = 1\right] \leq \binom{s}{2} \cdot \left(2^{-n} + \frac{R}{q}\right) + S \cdot \mathbf{Adv}^{\mathrm{unf}}_{\mathcal{B}_1,\mathcal{SIG}}(n)$$
$$+ S \cdot \mathbf{Adv}^{\mathrm{unf}}_{\mathcal{B}_2,\mathcal{MAC}}(n) + C \cdot S \cdot \mathbf{Adv}^{\mathrm{GapDH}}_{\mathcal{B}_3,D_C}(n)$$

where it is assumed that Compr is a R-regular function, i.e., every image has exactly R pre-images, q is the group size specified by D_C, the adversary initiates at most s sessions, and there are at most C cards and S terminals.

5   Security of the Architectures

Here we discuss the cryptographic strength of the various settings of the access system. For the analysis we assume that the other channels between parties, e.g., connecting the controller with the management system, are strongly secure. This is modeled by disallowing the adversary to tamper with, or even read the data, sent over these secured channels. We first treat the cases of the integrated, distributed, and eID-service architecture. By the assumption about secure connection between the various parties, we can view the reader, controller, server and management as a single entity in these settings. Only the authentication-service architecture with the split cryptographic operations requires a special treatment.

5.1   The Integrated, Distributed and eID-Service Architectures

We give the security statements for the integrated architecture only. Recall that the integrated terminal architecture, for example, assumes all eID operations are carried out by the reader itself. After completion of the TA and CA phase, the reader gets the attributes of the card (where the communication is secured via the secure messaging), and forwards the attributes of the card to the management system for approval. The communication with the management system is secured via a TLS channel. Upon approval, the reader grants access. Analogously, if restoring a session, then the reader only accepts if the securely sent attributes are approved.

Theorem 1 (Impersonation Resistance). *The integrated terminal architecture provides an impersonation-resistant access system, such that for any efficient adversary $\mathcal{A}$ there exists efficient adversaries $\mathcal{B}_1, \mathcal{B}_2$ such that*

$$\text{Prob}\left[\textit{ImpRes}_{\mathcal{A}}^{AS}(n) = 1 \right] \leq \text{Prob}\left[\textit{ImpRes}_{\mathcal{B}_1}^{EAC-AS}(n) = 1 \right] + 2 \cdot \textit{Adv}_{\mathcal{B}_2, EAC; SM}^{SecCh}(n)$$

Moreover, adversaries $\mathcal{B}_1, \mathcal{B}_2$ have roughly the same running time $\mathcal{A}$ plus the time to carry out the other steps in the experiment. Note that since the terms on the right hand side are assumed to be negligible, as discussed in Sect. 4, it follows that the system is impersonation resistance.

Proof. We consider three cases: (a) either the adversary manages to create collisions in two honest card sessions or in two honest reader sessions; or (b) an honest reader accepts at the end of the EAC protocol but such that the identified card is neither corrupt and there is no genuine session of the card with the same session identifier; or (c) an honest reader accepts some encrypted and authenticated attributes in a secure-messaging protocol where this ciphertext has not been sent by an honest card.

The first two cases are covered by the impersonation resistance of the EAC protocol. It is straightforward to build an adversary $\mathcal{B}_1$ simulating the environment for $\mathcal{A}$ through its own attack and by adding the extra steps for the secure messaging. If $\mathcal{A}$ breaks the impersonation resistance of the combined protocol then $\mathcal{B}_1$ breaks the security of the EAC protocol. This in particular also implies that the continuously growing session identifiers in restored sessions stay distinct among card sessions as well as among responder sessions, i.e., a subsequent collisions cannot happen anymore.

It remains to argue that case (c) cannot occur. In order to violate the predicate in the impersonation experiment, an honest reader accepts a ciphertext C_i^* in some session with identifier sid $= (\mathrm{Compr}(epk_T), r_C, C_1, C_2, \ldots, C_{i-1})$ for previously sent ciphertexts $C_1, C_2, \ldots$ in the restored sessions before. Since we quantify over all adversaries we can assume that C_i^* is the first ciphertext which deviates from a session of an honest card, i.e., there exists a session of a card with sid $= (\mathrm{Compr}(epk_T), r_C, C_1, C_2, \ldots, C_{i-1})$ or already with sid $= (\mathrm{Compr}(epk_T), r_C, C_1, C_2, \ldots, C_i)$. But then we must have that C_i^* is new or that $C_i^* \neq C_i$, and yet C_i^* decrypts to some attribute which the reader accepts. This can be straightforwardly used in a reduction against the authenticity of the composed channel protocol such that the probability of this event is bounded by the security of the secure messaging channel.

More formally, construct algorithm $\mathcal{B}_2$ against the combined protocol EAC; SM from $\mathcal{A}$ as follows. Recall that in this combined protocol the keys for the channel are generated by the EAC protocol, such that this perfectly simulates $\mathcal{A}$'s environment up to this step. We also assume, by the above discussion, that session identifiers are unique between cards and responders, and that each honest responder has a unique partnered honest card.

For simulating the channel transmission of an honest card, algorithm $\mathcal{B}_2$ calls the SEND oracle for the pair (A, A) for the card's attribute A to get a (valid) ciphertext. For simulating the receipt of a ciphertext at the responder's side, for an honest responder, there are two cases. If the intended partner is a corrupt card, then we can assume that $\mathcal{B}_2$ already knows the shared key (via a reveal query at the end of the key exchange protocol) and can simply act as the original responder. Otherwise, algorithm $\mathcal{B}_2$ forwards the ciphertext to its RCV oracle. If this oracle returns a message $m \neq \bot$, then $\mathcal{B}_2$ immediately outputs 1. Else, $\mathcal{B}_2$ lets the responder in the simulation for $\mathcal{A}$ accept if and only if the ciphertext has been created by a partnered card before, complying with the "queue property" of the channel protocol.

If, at the end, $\mathcal{B}_2$ has not returned 1 yet, then it outputs a random guess. This completes the description of the perfect simulation (up to the point where an honest responder can correctly decrypt a new ciphertext sent through the channel protocol). If the above now happens in an actual attack, that C_i^* is new or that $C_i^* \neq C_i$ but the original responder would accept but we reject, then we would break the authenticity of the channel protoocl with the same probability. That is, we then have

$$\mathrm{Prob}\,[\text{case (c)}] \leq 2 \cdot \mathbf{Adv}_{\mathcal{B}_2, \mathsf{EAC;SM}}^{\mathrm{SecCh}}(n)$$

where the factor of 2 is due to the fact that we have $b = 1$ and can thus see an output by the RCV oracle with probability $\frac{1}{2}$ only.

Note that this argument about the channel is independent of whether restored sessions have been overwritten or not. □

Attribute privacy follows analogously, using again the fact that secure messaging provides a secure channel:

Theorem 2 (Privacy). *The integrated terminal architecture provides an attribute-private access system, such that for any efficient adversary $\mathcal{A}$ there exists an efficient adversary $\mathcal{B}$ such that*

$$\mathrm{Prob}\left[\mathsf{APriv}_{\mathcal{A}}^{AS}(n) = 1\right] \leq \tfrac{1}{2} + \boldsymbol{Adv}_{\mathcal{B},EAC;SM}^{SecCh}(n)$$

Proof. Note that the adversary $\mathcal{A}$ against privacy can only win in the experiment if it does not query the challenge oracle about a card identity such that the card or its partner is corrupt. This in particular means that the derived key for secure messaging must still be secure, and the adversary here can only distinguish the attributes if it breaks confidentiality of the channel protocol. This can again be formalized easily via a reduction to the corresponding game.

More formally, construct adversary $\mathcal{B}$ as in the previous theorem, running the combined protocol EAC; SM to simulate $\mathcal{A}$'s attack. For every call of $\mathcal{A}$ about attributes A_0, A_1 to the challenge oracle CHALL to start a new session in this attack, adversary $\mathcal{B}$ simply initiates a new session and stores A_0, A_1 for later use. If the card is later supposed to send its attributes in this session, then $\mathcal{B}$ calls its SEND oracle about A_0, A_1 to get a ciphertext. The (honest) responder of that ciphertext in the simulation simply accepts.

Eventually, if $\mathcal{A}$ outputs a bit b, then $\mathcal{B}$ copies this bit to its output and stops. Since the simulation is perfect, it follows that $\mathcal{A}$'s advantage is at most the one of $\mathcal{B}$. □

5.2   The Authentication-Service Architecture

In principle one can show the same results as for the other architectures to the case of the authentication-service scenario. Recall that there an authentication server signs the TA data forwarded by the controller, and the controller continues the execution with that signature. The other steps are as in the other cases.

Note that the signature and the (ephemeral) DH key in the EAC protocol serve different cryptographic purposes. The signature only binds the ephemeral key to the terminal's identity and prevents the adversary to inject its own key. The DH key is used to establish the session key and, as long as the adversary does not get to learn the ephemeral secret key, the adversary is not able to compute the joint DH key with the card. This has been discussed in [16] in the context of key-compromise impersonation (KCI) resistance.

For us this means that even corruption of the authentication service's signing key does not allow to complete the EAC protocol and to learn the channel keys, for sessions in which an honest reader picks the ephemeral key. In particular, knowledge of the signing key does not allow to break security of previously completed sessions (forward security). Formally, we can augment both attack model by granting the adversary another SigKey oracle which, when queried about a responder's identity, returns the party's secret signing key. The party may still act as an honest party in sessions, with the internal choices hidden from the adversary.

The conditions for impersonation resistance remain unchanged, except for giving the adversary access to the SigKey oracle. Since a responder party only completes a session (and accepts with a session identifier) if it executes the protocol steps itself, any such session in question uses an honestly chosen ephemeral key epk_T on the responder's side. Hence, the security of session keys for such honestly ephemeral keys argued in [22] still holds.[2]

For attribute privacy we need to change the non-triviality check in Line 11 of the experiment in Fig. 7. There, we checked for each card session ℓ returned by the challenge oracle that the card nor its intended partner is corrupt:

$$[\mathsf{ID}(\ell) \notin \mathsf{Corrupt} \land \mathsf{PID}(\ell) \notin \mathsf{Corrupt}]$$

Here, we need to check that the responder's party has contributed the ephemeral key honestly:

$$[\mathsf{ID}(\ell) \notin \mathsf{Corrupt} \land \exists \ell' \neq \ell : (\mathsf{SID}(\ell) = \mathsf{SID}(\ell) \neq \bot \land \mathsf{PID}(\ell) = \mathsf{ID}(\ell'))]$$

Given this, attribute privacy follows as before, because session keys are still fresh for such sessions.

6   Conclusion

The access system based on EAC with session restoring provides an impersonation resistant and attribute-hiding solution. Here, both security properties hold in a very strong sense, thwarting active adversaries with strong control over the network, and leaving the adversary essentially only trivial attacks from a cryptographic viewpoint. On top, the system is very similar to the existing EAC system and may thus be easy to implement on existing infrastructures for the German identity card (or the future eIDAS system).

Acknowledgments. We thank the anonymous reviewers of SSR 2016 for valuable comments.

A   Security Notions of Cryptographic Primitives

This part of the paper here is almost verbatim from the full version of [9].

---

[2] The proof relies on the unforgeability of signatures only to ensure that the adversary cannot inject its own ephemeral key, which is guaranteed by construction here.

Message Authentication Codes. A message authentication code $\mathcal{M}$ consists of three efficient algorithms (MKGen, MAC, MVf) where $\mathsf{MAC}(k, m)$ maps any key k generated by key generation algorithm MKGen and any message m to a MAC (resp. tag) T which is verifiable with the help of $\mathsf{MVf}(k, m, T)$ with binary output. Completeness demands again that for any valid key k and any message m the value $T \leftarrow \mathsf{MAC}(k, m)$ makes $\mathsf{MVf}(k, m, T)$ return 1.

We require that the message authentication code $\mathcal{M}$ is unforgeable under adaptively chosen-message attacks. That is, the adversary is granted oracle access to $\mathsf{MAC}(k, \cdot)$ and $\mathsf{MVf}(k, \cdot, \cdot)$ for random key k generated by MKGen and wins if it, at some point, makes a verification query (m, T) about a message m which has not been sent previously to MAC, and such that MVf returns 1 for this message. We denote by $\mathbf{Adv}_{\mathcal{M}}^{\mathrm{forge}}(t, q_m, q_v)$ a (bound on the) value ϵ for which no attacker in time t can win (making at most q_m MACs queries and q_v verification queries) with probability more than ϵ. For a concrete attacker $\mathcal{A}$ we write $\mathbf{Adv}_{\mathcal{A},\mathcal{M}}^{\mathrm{forge}}(n)$ to denote the fact that $\mathcal{A}$ attacks the scheme in the above sense (for security parameter n).

Signatures and Certificates. A signature scheme $\mathcal{S} = (\mathsf{SKGen}, \mathsf{Sig}, \mathsf{SVf})$ consists of efficient algorithms for creating key pairs (sk, pk), signing messages $s \leftarrow \mathsf{Sig}(sk, m)$, and verifying signatures, $d \leftarrow \mathsf{SVf}(pk, m, s)$ with $d \in \{0, 1\}$. It must be that for signatures created under valid key pairs SVf always returns 1 (correctness). Unforgeability says that no algorithm should be able to forge the signer's signature. That is, a signature scheme $\mathcal{S} = (\mathsf{SKGen}, \mathsf{Sig}, \mathsf{SVf})$ is (t, q_s, ϵ)-unforgeable if for any algorithm $\mathcal{A}$ running in time t the probability that $\mathcal{A}$ outputs a signature to a fresh message under a public key is $\mathbf{Adv}_{\mathcal{S}}^{\mathrm{forge}}(t, q_s)$ (which should be negligible small) while $\mathcal{A}$ has access (at most q_s times) to a singing oracle. As before, for a concrete attacker $\mathcal{A}$ we write $\mathbf{Adv}_{\mathcal{A},\mathcal{S}}^{\mathrm{forge}}(n)$ to denote the fact that $\mathcal{A}$ attacks the scheme in the above sense (for security parameter n).

We also assume a certification authority CA, modeled like the signature scheme through algorithms $\mathcal{CA} = (\mathsf{CKGen}, \mathsf{Certify}, \mathsf{CVf})$, but where we call the "signing" algorithm Certify. This is in order to indicate that certification may be done by other means than signatures. We assume that the keys $(sk_{\mathrm{CA}}, pk_{\mathrm{CA}})$ of the CA are generated at the outset and that pk_{CA} is distributed securely to all parties (including the adversary). We also often assume that the certified data is part of the certificate. We define unforgeability for a certification scheme $\mathcal{CA}$ analogously to signatures, and denote the advantage bound of outputting a certificate of a new value in time t after seeing q_c certificates by $\mathbf{Adv}_{\mathcal{CA}}^{\mathrm{forge}}(t, q_c)$. We assume that the certification authority only issues unique certificates in the sense that for distinct parties the certificates are also distinct; we besides assume that the authority checks whether the keys are well-formed group elements. For a concrete attacker $\mathcal{A}$ we again write $\mathbf{Adv}_{\mathcal{A},\mathcal{CA}}^{\mathrm{forge}}(n)$ to denote the fact that $\mathcal{A}$ attacks the scheme in the above sense (for security parameter n).

Second Preimage Resistance. We say that the compression function Compr is (t, ϵ)-second preimage resistant if the probability $\mathbf{Adv}_{\mathsf{Compr}}^{\mathrm{SecPre}}(t)$ of finding to a random ephemeral public key epk_T another key epk_T^* with the same compressed value is bounded by ϵ. For a concrete attacker $\mathcal{A}$ we again write $\mathbf{Adv}_{\text{Compr}}^{\text{SecPre}}(t)$ to denote the fact that $\mathcal{A}$ finds a second preimage in the above sense (for security parameter n).

Gap Diffie-Hellman Problem. We need the following gap Diffie-Hellman problem [4]. For a group $\mathcal{G}$ generated by g let $\text{DH}(X,Y)$ be the Diffie-Hellman value X^y for $y = \log_g Y$ (with g being an implicit parameter for the function). Then the gap Diffie-Hellman assumption says that solving the computational DH problem for (g^a, g^b), i.e., computing $\text{DH}(g^a, g^b)$ given only the random elements (g^a, g^b) and $\mathcal{G}, g$, is still hard, even when one has access to a decisional oracle $\text{DDH}(X,Y,Z)$ which returns 1 iff $\text{DH}(X,Y) = Z$, and 0 otherwise. We say that the GDH problem is $(t, q_{\text{DDH}}, \epsilon)$-hard if no algorithm can in time t compute the DH value with probability larger than ϵ, if making at most q_{DDH} queries. We let $\mathbf{Adv}_{\mathcal{G}}^{\text{GDH}}(t, q_{\text{DDH}})$ denote (a bound on) the value ϵ for which the GDH problem is (t, q_{DDH}, ϵ)-hard. For a concrete attacker $\mathcal{A}$ we write $\mathbf{Adv}_{\mathcal{A},\mathcal{G}}^{\text{GDH}}(n)$ to denote the fact that $\mathcal{A}$ attacks the problem in the above sense (for security parameter n).

References

1. Bundesamt für Sicherheit in der Informationstechnik (BSI): Advanced Security Mechanism for Machine Readable Travel Documents – Extended Access Control (EAC), Password Authenticated Connection Establishment (PACE), and Restricted Identification (RI). BSI-TR-03110, Version 2.0 (2008)
2. Bundesamt für Sicherheit in der Informationstechnik (BSI): Technical Guideline TR-03110-2: Advanced Security Mechanisms for Machine Readable Travel Documents and eIDAS Token, Part 2, Protocols for electronic IDentification, Authentication and trust Services (eIDAS). BSI-TR-03110, Version 2.20 (2015)
3. Bundesamt für Sicherheit in der Informationstechnik (BSI): Technical Guideline TR-03110-3: Advanced Security Mechanisms for Machine Readable Travel Documents and eIDAS Token, Part 3, Common Specifications. BSI-TR-03110, Version 2.20 (2015)
4. Boneh, D., Lynn, B., Shacham, H.: Short signatures from the weil pairing. In: Boyd, C. (ed.) ASIACRYPT 2001. LNCS, vol. 2248, pp. 514–532. Springer, Heidelberg (2001). doi:10.1007/3-540-45682-1_30
5. Morgner, F.: Transaktionsabsicherung mit der Online-Ausweisfunktion. Kryptographische Bindung von Transaktionsdaten an den Personalausweis. Presentation, CeBit 2014, March 2014
6. Bastian, P.: Physical Access Control Systems Using Asymmetric Cryptography, Master-Arbeit, Humboldt-Universität zu Berlin (2015)
7. Bellare, M., Anand Desai, E., Jokipii, P.R.: A concrete security treatment of symmetric encryption. In: FOCS, pp. 394–403. IEEE (1997)
8. Bellare, M., Rogaway, P.: Entity authentication and key distribution. In: Stinson, D.R. (ed.) CRYPTO 1993. LNCS, vol. 773, pp. 232–249. Springer, Heidelberg (1994). doi:10.1007/3-540-48329-2_21
9. Bender, J., Dagdelen, Ö., Fischlin, M., Kügler, D.: The PACE|AA protocol for machine readable travel documents, and its security. In: Keromytis, A.D. (ed.) FC 2012. LNCS, vol. 7397, pp. 344–358. Springer, Heidelberg (2012). doi:10.1007/978-3-642-32946-3_25

10. Bender, J., Dagdelen, Ö., Fischlin, M., Kügler, D.: Domain-specific pseudonymous signatures for the German identity card. In: Gollmann, D., Freiling, F.C. (eds.) ISC 2012. LNCS, vol. 7483, pp. 104–119. Springer, Heidelberg (2012). doi:10.1007/978-3-642-33383-5_7

11. Bender, J., Fischlin, M., Kügler, D.: Security analysis of the PACE key-agreement protocol. In: Samarati, P., Yung, M., Martinelli, F., Ardagna, C.A. (eds.) ISC 2009. LNCS, vol. 5735, pp. 33–48. Springer, Heidelberg (2009). doi:10.1007/978-3-642-04474-8_3

12. Bender, J., Fischlin, M., Kügler, D.: The PACE|CA protocol for machine readable travel documents. In: Bloem, R., Lipp, P. (eds.) INTRUST 2013. LNCS, vol. 8292, pp. 17–35. Springer, Heidelberg (2013). doi:10.1007/978-3-319-03491-1_2

13. Brzuska, C.: On the Foundations of Key Exchange. Dissertation, Technische Universität Darmstadt (2013). http://tuprints.ulb.tu-darmstadt.de/id/eprint/3414

14. Brzuska, C., Fischlin, M., Smart, N.P., Warinschi, B., Williams, S.C.: Less is more: relaxed yet composable security notions for key exchange. Int. J. Inf. Sec. 12(4), 267–297 (2013)

15. Coron, J.-S., Gouget, A., Icart, T., Paillier, P.: Supplemental access control (PACE v2): security analysis of PACE integrated mapping. In: Naccache, D. (ed.) Cryptography and Security: From Theory to Applications. LNCS, vol. 6805, pp. 207–232. Springer, Heidelberg (2012). doi:10.1007/978-3-642-28368-0_15

16. Dagdelen, Ö., Fischlin, M.: Security analysis of the extended access control protocol for machine readable travel documents. In: Burmester, M., Tsudik, G., Magliveras, S., Ilić, I. (eds.) ISC 2010. LNCS, vol. 6531, pp. 54–68. Springer, Heidelberg (2011). doi:10.1007/978-3-642-18178-8_6

17. Hanzlik, L., Kutylowski, M.: Restricted identification secure in the extended Canetti-Krawczyk model. J. UCS 21(3), 419–439 (2015)

18. Hanzlik, L., Krzywiecki, Ł., Kutyłowski, M.: Simplified PACE|AA protocol. In: Deng, R.H., Feng, T. (eds.) ISPEC 2013. LNCS, vol. 7863, pp. 218–232. Springer, Heidelberg (2013). doi:10.1007/978-3-642-38033-4_16

19. International Civil Aviation Organization: Doc 9303, Machine Readable Travel Documents, Part 11, Security Mechanisms for MRTDs, 7th edn. (2015)

20. Jager, T., Kohlar, F., Schäge, S., Schwenk, J.: On the security of TLS-DHE in the standard model. In: Safavi-Naini, R., Canetti, R. (eds.) CRYPTO 2012. LNCS, vol. 7417, pp. 273–293. Springer, Heidelberg (2012). doi:10.1007/978-3-642-32009-5_17

21. Kutyłowski, M., Krzywiecki, Ł., Kubiak, P., Koza, M.: Restricted identification scheme and Diffie-Hellman linking problem. In: Chen, L., Yung, M., Zhu, L. (eds.) INTRUST 2011. LNCS, vol. 7222, pp. 221–238. Springer, Heidelberg (2012). doi:10.1007/978-3-642-32298-3_15

22. Morgner, F., Bastian, P., Fischlin, M.: Securing transactions with the eIDAS protocols. In: Foresti, S., Lopez, J. (eds.) WISTP 2016. LNCS, vol. 9895, pp. 3–18. Springer, Heidelberg (2016). doi:10.1007/978-3-319-45931-8_1

23. Paterson, K.G., Ristenpart, T., Shrimpton, T.: Tag size Does matter: attacks and proofs for the TLS record protocol. In: Lee, D.H., Wang, X. (eds.) ASIACRYPT 2011. LNCS, vol. 7073, pp. 372–389. Springer, Heidelberg (2011). doi:10.1007/978-3-642-25385-0_20

24. Rogaway, P.: Evaluation of some blockcipher modes of operation. Cryptography Research and Evaluation Committees (CRYPTREC) for the Government of Japan, February 2011

Secure Multicast Group Management and Key Distribution in IEEE 802.21

Yoshikazu Hanatani[1]([✉]), Naoki Ogura[1], Yoshihiro Ohba[2],
Lidong Chen[3], and Subir Das[4]

[1] Toshiba Corporation, 1, Komukai Toshiba-cho,
Saiwai-ku, Kawasaki 212-8582, Japan
{yoshikazu.hanatani,naoki.ogura}@toshiba.co.jp
[2] Toshiba Electronics Asia Pte. Ltd., 20 Pasir Panjang Road,
#12-25/28 Mapletree Business City, Singapore 117439, Singapore
yoshihiro.ohba@toshiba.co.jp
[3] National Institute of Standards and Technology, 100 Bureau Dr.,
Gaithersburg, MD 20899-8930, USA
lily.chen@nist.gov
[4] Applied Communication Sciences, 150 Mount Airy Road,
Basking Ridge, NJ 7920, USA
sdas@appcomsci.com

Abstract. Controlling a large number of devices such as sensors and smart end points, is always a challenge where scalability and security are indispensable. This is even more important when it comes to periodic configuration updates to a large number of such devices belonging to one or more groups. One solution could be to take a group of devices as a unit of control and then manage them through a group communication mechanism. An obvious challenge to this approach is how to create such groups dynamically and manage them securely. Moreover, there need to be mechanisms in place by which members of the group can be removed and added dynamically. In this paper, we propose a technique that has been recently standardized in IEEE 802.21 (IEEE Std 802.21d™-2015) with the objective of providing a standard-based solution to the above challenges. The approach relies on Logical Key Hierarchy (LKH) based key distribution mechanism but optimizes the number of encryption and decryption by using "Complete Subtree". It leverages IEEE 802.21 framework, services, and protocol for communication and management, and provides a scalable and secure way to manage (e.g., add and remove) devices from one or more groups. We describe the group key distribution protocol in details and provide a security analysis of the scheme along with some performance results from a prototype implementation.

Keywords: Group communication · Group key and management · Multicast · Group Key Block (GKB) · Subtree · IEEE 802.21™

© Springer International Publishing AG 2016
L. Chen et al. (Eds.): SSR 2016, LNCS 10074, pp. 227–243, 2016.
DOI: 10.1007/978-3-319-49100-4_10

1 Introduction

In today's networked world, it is becoming more and more expensive when it comes to configuring and updating software to large number of remote sensors and smart devices. To alleviate the cost and scalability issues, operators and vendors perform these operations remotely, commonly known as remote device management. While remote configurations updates are very common and secure networking technologies are available, normally it happens via a remote server in which each device requires to connect the server. This process becomes bandwidth inefficient (n unicast connections) and time consuming when the configuration update of a group of devices involves transferring a large amount of data. On the contrary, if these updates can be performed via a secure group communication mechanism whereby the network entity can multicast or broadcast the messages to a group of devices, the process becomes more efficient and saves a great deal of time and network resources.

IEEE Std 802.21™-2008 [1] defines a media independent framework, services and signaling protocol that are standardized in IEEE while the transport of the signaling protocol over Internet Protocol (IP) is standardized by the Internet Engineering Task Force (IETF). The standard [1] addresses the handover optimization use case whereby the user experience of ongoing application flows can be improved significantly for mobile nodes (MNs) that are moving from one link layer access technology to another irrespective of whether the access network is managed by the same or different network operators. The framework provides a signaling protocol that can be transported natively over the link layer or over Internet Protocol (IP) using underlying unicast and multicast mechanisms. In subsequent years of Standards amendment process, IEEE 802.21 Working Group addressed other use cases and defined signaling protocol and services security along with a group management mechanism in [2, 3]. In particular, Standards published in [3] targeted the use case where a large number of groups of devices are required to be managed from a group manager that resides in an entity in the network. Therefore [3] is relevant to our discussion in which a network entity can multicast a message to a group of nodes (or devices) using IEEE 802.21 media independent protocol interface, and secure group key distribution mechanism to cryptographically protect these multicast messages. The amendment [3] not only adds the secure group communication mechanism but also allows network nodes to communicate handover messages and to perform other management operations such as failover, failback, and configuration updates to a group of devices that are part of the network. The standardized approach relies on Logical Key Hierarchy (LKH) based key distribution mechanism [4–6] and uses "Complete Subtree" to optimize the number of encryption and decryption.

In this paper, we first introduce IEEE Std 802.21d™-2015 [3] defined group key distribution protocol and then discuss how to use the complete subtree method to optimize the performance of group communication. Subsequently, we introduce specific methods to handle the issues in group key distribution for IEEE 802.21 applications. In addition, we also analyze security of the group key distribution protocol as specified in IEEE Std 802.21d-2015 [3].

The paper is organized as follows: Sect. 2 discusses the related work. Section 3 presents the preliminaries of group key distribution approach while Sect. 4 describes the Group Key Block (GKB). Section 5 describes the group key distribution scheme and Sect. 6 provides a formal model-based security analysis. Section 7 captures our initial prototype implementation results and Sect. 8 concludes the paper.

2 Related Work and Our Approach

Secure multicast-based communication has been an important research topic in cryptography and in communication security. Most of the research discusses theoretical boundaries on the message length (i.e., number of encryptions), storage (i.e., number of keys each member holds), and computations for each receiver [7]. Some of the research also discusses trace-and-revoke algorithm with an upper bound of coalitions, which is outside the scope of this paper.

In practical applications, the secure group communications have been handled through initial pairwise group key distribution to group members [8, 9]. The schemes in [8] allow group key distribution for rekeying. On the other hand, whenever new members join the group or some current members leave the group, the schemes defined in [9] have to use pairwise secure channels for key distribution.

Logical Key Hierarchy (LKH) has been introduced in [4–6] for group key update, assuming each group member has been provisioned with one fixed individual key or the individual keys are established using other methods. The LKH is represented as a tree while the individual keys are represented as leaves of the tree. The nodes above the leaf level represent the keys shared by different members represented as leaves which have a path to the node. Every time a member joins or leaves the group, the tree is updated.

The group key distribution scheme introduced in this paper uses a similar tree to represent the fixed keys that each group member holds. The group key is encrypted by a set of keys represented in the tree such that each member in the group owns a key to decrypt it, while the nodes not in the group do not have the proper decryption keys. Each time when a group member joins or leaves, a new group key is distributed using the proper keys for the new group. Intuitively, in a given group, if more group members shared the same key that is, their paths meet at the same node fewer encryptions are needed. In order to gain such efficiency, the scheme in this paper uses 'Complete Subtree'. The 'Complete Subtree' method is introduced in [10] to optimize the number of encryptions and decryptions for each group key distribution. These methods have not been adopted in the practical applications to the best of our knowledge.

In particular, the method in this paper uses a single key tree to distribute keys for different groups. For a given group, our method generally requires fewer key encryptions than LKH for the key distributor, which also means lower transmission burden. Let $L(>1)$ denote the number of leaf nodes of the key tree, $N(<L)$ denote the number of root nodes of complete subtrees covering all leaf nodes of the members of the group, and M denote the number of ancestor nodes of the N root nodes. In initial group key distribution, LKH requires at least L encryptions to distribute the group key (which is the key corresponding to the root node of the key tree in LKH) and other keys

to be used for key update. In group key update, LKH requires $(N + M)$ encryptions to update the group key for all group members excluding revoked members. In contrast, our method requires N encryptions of the group key for both initial group key distribution and group key update. Therefore, if we assume the same key tree size, our method always requires less number of encryptions than LKH. Our method allows to take advantage of complete subtrees when possible. That is, when the group members represented by the leaf nodes can be grouped to complete subtrees, the number of key encryptions can be further reduced.

For any group member m, our method requires a single decryption to obtain the group key, while for LKH, $(H - H_m + 1)$ decryptions are needed where H represents the height of the key tree and H_m represents the height of the complete subtree that covers the leaf node of member m. In the applications where each group member is a constrained device such as a sensor, our method has significant advantages.

On the other hand, it has not been clear how scalable complete subtree is and no specific algorithms have been proposed to identify the complete subtrees. The use of a media independent framework and a signaling protocol, which can be transported natively over Ethernet or IP using underlying unicast and multicast mechanisms, is another important aspect that has not been standardized or published earlier to the best of our knowledge.

While different security notions for group key agreement protocols have been introduced in [11–14], we define a variant of formal security model called Bresson and Manulis (BM) model [15] satisfying the similar security requirements. The BM model cannot be applied directly for our security proof because the group key distribution protocol specified in [3] does not provide perfect forward secrecy.

3   Preliminaries

In this section, we introduce some basic concepts used in group management and key distribution. The concepts of key tree and complete subtree are essential for the key distribution protocol that we discuss in Subsect. 3.1. When a group key is distributed, it is protected by a key wrapping mechanism. To authenticate the sender, the encrypted group key is digitally signed. The security notions and definitions of key wrapping and signatures are introduced in Subsects. 3.2 and 3.3, respectively.

3.1   Key Tree and Complete Subtree Method

In this paper, we assume there are a large set of devices $\mathcal{U} = \{U_1, U_2, ..., U_m\}$ in which each device is provisioned with a set of keys, called *device keys, DK_i*. In the group key distribution protocol, the key is distributed by a group manager (GM) to a subset of the devices $S = \{U_{i1}, U_{i2}, ..., U_{ik}\}$.

A key tree is a binary tree with depth n and it has t levels from the root to the leaves. Therefore, such a key tree has 2^n leaf nodes whereby each leaf node is a device and to represent all the devices $\{U_1, U_2, ..., U_m\}$, it requires $m \leq 2^n$. Figure 1 is an example of depth-3 tree. Each node (e.g., a leaf node, an inner node, or the root node) is coded with a binary string called *index* and a key. Assume the root node is on the top. The next level nodes have indices 0 and 1 from the left to the right. The corresponding keys are denoted k_0 and k_1. The next level nodes have indices 00, 01 as decedents of node 0 while 10 and 11 as decedents of node 1. The corresponding keys are denoted k_{00}, k_{01}, k_{10}, k_{11}. Nodes in every level are indexed this way until the level t. In the rest of this paper, we will denote the node with the index and the key (I_i, k_i). We simply call each key as a node key labeled with its index. For the leaf node, we also use the integer converted from its index as the leaf number which maps to a specific device.

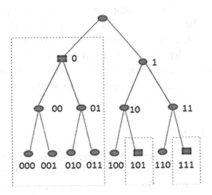

Fig. 1. A depth-3 key tree

For device U_j, the provisioned device keys consist of all the node keys from the leaf along the path to the root. In the example depicted in Fig. 1, a device represented by leaf "000" is provisioned with device keys $\{k(\text{root}), k_0, k_{00}, \text{and } k_{000}\}$.

In order to distribute a master group key to the devices in a specific group, the master group key mgk is protected with a set of keys in such a way that each device in the group must own a key in its device key set to recover the mgk, while for any device not in the group, it cannot recover the mgk. For a given group, there must be many different ways to protect the mgk. For example, in Fig. 1 consider a group represented by the leaf nodes 000, 001, 010, 011, 101, and 111. Notice that nodes 000 and 001 share the same key k_{00} and nodes 000, 001, 010, 011 all share the key k_0, then protection with the following key sets all satisfy the condition stated above.

a. $k_{000}, k_{001}, k_{010}, k_{011}, k_{101}, k_{111}$;
b. $k_{00}, k_{01}, k_{101}, k_{111}$;
c. k_0, k_{101}, k_{111}.

Obviously, key set c is more appealing because it calls the least number of the protection mechanisms and thus, generated the shortest of the ciphertext for broadcast. The concept of complete subtree is introduced to optimize the number of calls to the protection mechanisms. In this paper, the protection mechanisms can be a key wrapping algorithm or an encryption algorithm.

A complete (depth-l) subtree in a depth-t tree is a subtree with 2^l leaf nodes such that their indices have common prefix of t-l bits. For the tree in Fig. 1, nodes represented with indices 000 and 001 form a depth-1 complete subtree at root 00, while nodes represented with indices 000, 001, 010, and 011 form a depth-2 complete subtree at root 0. For a subset of the group, if it can form a complete subtree, using the key represented by the subtree root allows all the members to recover the protected group key. Therefore, identifying complete subtrees in a given group can optimize the computation and communication resources in group key distribution for that group.

It shall be noticed that a single leaf is a depth-0 complete subtree. In fact, the optimization is to find out the non-overlapping maximum complete subtrees, which can cover the whole group. The set of non-overlapping maximum complete subtrees is unique for a given group. For example, for the group with the leaf nodes 000, 001, 010, 011, 101, 111, the set of the non-overlapping maximum complete subtrees that covers all the members is a depth-2 complete subtree and two depth-0 complete subtrees. Standards published in [3] specifies a complete subtree algorithm to determine such set.

3.2   Key-Wrapping Scheme

After determining which keys to use through the complete subtrees, for the group key distribution, the key is protected by a key wrapping scheme. Key-wrapping scheme is a symmetric key encryption scheme for sending a group key. For group key distribution, IEEE Std 802.21d-2015 [3] supports two deterministic symmetric key schemes based on the Advanced Encryption Standard (AES), AES-key-wrapping-128 and AES-ECB-128. Here $x \leftarrow_R X$ means that x is an element chosen uniformly at random in a finite set X.

Definition 1. *Key-wrapping* $\mathcal{KW}$ *is a 3-tuple of algorithms* ($\mathsf{KeyGen}_{\mathcal{KW}}$, $\mathsf{Wrap}, \mathsf{Unwrap}$) *satisfying:*

- $\mathsf{KeyGen}_{\mathcal{KW}}$: *a probabilistic algorithm takes the security parameter* κ, *and returns* $K \in \{0,1\}^\kappa$,
- Wrap: *a deterministic algorithm takes* $K \in \{0,1\}^\kappa$ *and* $D \in \{0,1\}^l$, *and returns* $C \in \mathcal{C}$ *where* l *is a bit-length of key to be wrapped.*
- Unwrap: *a deterministic algorithm takes* $K \in \{0,1\}^\kappa$ *and* $C \in \mathcal{C}$, *and returns* $D \in \{0,1\}^l \cup \{\perp\}$,

where $\forall K \leftarrow \mathsf{KeyGen}_{\mathcal{KW}}(\kappa), \forall D \in \{0,1\}^l$: $\mathsf{Unwrap}(K, \mathsf{Wrap}(K,D)) = D$.

A basic security requirement for symmetric encryption scheme is the indistinguishability against chosen plaintext attack (IND-CPA), and it is well-known that no deterministic encryption schemes can satisfy the IND-CPA. On the other hand, for sending a random key, the following weaker security requirement is sufficient.

Definition 2 *(Indistinguishability against Random-Plaintext Attack). Let* $b \leftarrow_R \{0,1\}$ *and* $W \leftarrow \mathsf{KeyGen}_{\mathcal{KW}}(\kappa)$ *where* κ *is a security parameter. The RPA-advantage of* $\mathcal{A}$ *can send queries to oracles* Wrap_W *and* LR_W. *When the oracle* Wrap_W *receives a query,* Wrap_W *selects* $D \leftarrow_R \{0,1\}^l$, *and returns* $(D, \mathsf{Wrap}(W,D))$. *When the oracle*

LR_W receives a query, LR_W selects $D_0, D_1 \leftarrow_R \{0, 1\}^l$, and returns $(D_0, D_1,$ $\mathsf{Wrap}(W, D_b))$. The RPA-advantage of $\mathcal{A}$ is defined as

$$\mathsf{Adv}^{\mathrm{kw.rpa}}_{\mathcal{A}, \mathcal{KW}}(\kappa) = \Pr\left[\mathcal{A}^{\mathsf{Wrap}_W, \mathsf{LR}_w} \rightarrow 1 | b = 1\right] - \Pr\left[\mathcal{A}^{\mathsf{Wrap}_W, \mathsf{LR}_w} \rightarrow 1 | b = 0\right]$$

where $\mathcal{A}$ is a probabilistic polynomial-time algorithm that sends at most q queries to Wrap_W and at most 1 query to LR_W.

$\mathcal{KW}$ is IND-RPA secure if for all $\mathcal{A}$, $\mathsf{Adv}^{\mathrm{kw.rpa}}_{\mathcal{A}, \mathcal{KW}}(\kappa)$ is negligible.

Random-Plaintext attack is originally defined in [16]. In the original definition in [16], the adversary is not allowed to query the Wrap_W. According to a similar discussion in [16], we can show that an ECB (electronic code book) mode based on a random permutation with block length n is IND-RPA secure per Definition 2.

3.3 Signature Scheme

In order to authenticate a sender, IEEE Std 802.21d-2015 [3] supports one digital signature scheme, ECDSA (Elliptic Curve Digital Signature Algorithm). Here $x \leftarrow_R X$ means that x is an element chosen uniformly at random in a finite set X.

Definition 3. Signature Σ is a 3-tuple of algorithms $(\mathsf{KeyGen}_{\mathcal{KW}}, \mathsf{Sign}, \mathsf{Verif})$ satisfying:

- KeyGen_Σ: a probabilistic algorithm that takes the security parameter κ, and returns a pair of public key and secret key (pk, sk),
- Sign: a probabilistic algorithm takes sk and a message $m \in \{0, 1\}^*$, and returns σ,
- Verif: a deterministic algorithm takes pk, m, and σ, and returns 0 or 1,

where $\forall (pk, sk) \leftarrow \mathsf{KeyGen}_\Sigma(\kappa)$, $\forall m \in \{0, 1\}^*$: $\mathsf{Verif}(pk, m, \mathsf{Sign}(sk, m)) = 1$.

Definition 4 (Existential Unforgeability against Chosen Message Attacks). Let $\Sigma = (\mathsf{KeyGen}_\Sigma, \mathsf{Sign}, \mathsf{Verif})$ be a digital signature scheme, and $(pk, sk) \leftarrow \mathsf{KeyGen}_\Sigma(\kappa)$. When a signing oracle Sign_{sk} receives a query $m \in \{0, 1\}^*$, it returns $\sigma = \mathsf{Sign}(sk, m)$. The advantage of $\mathcal{A}$ is defined as

$$\mathsf{Adv}^{\mathrm{euf-cma}}_{\mathcal{A}, \Sigma}(\kappa) = \Pr[\mathcal{A}^{\mathsf{Sign}_{sk}}(pk) \rightarrow (m^*, \sigma^*) : \mathsf{Verif}(pk, m^*, \sigma^*) = 1 \wedge m^* \notin \mathcal{M}]$$

where $\mathcal{M}$ is the set of message queried to Sign_{sk} and $\mathcal{A}$ is a probabilistic polynomial-time algorithm who sends at most q_S queries to Sign_{sk}.

Σ is EUF-CMA secure if for all $\mathcal{A}$, $\mathsf{Adv}^{\mathrm{euf-cma}}_{\mathcal{A}, \Sigma}(\kappa)$ is negligible.

4   Group Key Block

Group Key Block (GKB) is a data format defined in IEEE Std 802.21d-2015 [3] for encoding a group key and other data associated with the group key. The following attributes are contained in a GKB:

- GroupKeyData: a list of octet strings, each of them contains the group key encrypted by using a distinct node key specified in 'CompleteSubtree'. Either AES_Key_Wrapping-128 or AES_ECB-128 is used for encrypting the group key.
- GroupIdentifier: an identifier of a group.
- CompleteSubtree: a list of node indices corresponding to root nodes of specific subtrees of the key management tree. See Sect. 4.1 for more details.
- SubgroupRange: a range of valid leaf identifiers in the 'CompleteSubtree'. A 'SubgroupRange' is used when a GKB is fragmented into multiple smaller pieces (see Sect. 4.2).
- VerifyGroupCode: a pre-known octet string encrypted by the group key. A 'VerifyGroupCode' is used for checking whether the decrypted group key is the same as the one generated by the GM. 'VerifyGroupCode' may be used when AES_ECB-128 is used for group key encryption (Note that AES_Key_Wrapping has a built-in key verification mechanism).

Digital signature is added to each message carrying a GKB using the signature scheme described in Sect. 3.3.

4.1   Encoding Complete Subtrees

IEEE Std 802.21d-2015 [3] defines three methods for encoding 'CompleteSubtree'. In this section, the default encoding method is explained. In the default encoding method, a list of the node indices is contained in the 'CompleteSubtree' where each node index in the key management tree represents the root node of a distinct subtree covering only leaf nodes corresponding to members of the group. A node index consists of a depth in the key management tree and a subindex that is unique within the depth. In 'Group-KeyData', i-th string contains the group key encrypted by the node key corresponding to the i-th node index in the 'CompleteSubtree'.

4.2   GKB Fragmentation

As described in Sect. 4.1, the size of CompleteSubtree in Method 1 is proportional to the number of subtrees encoded. Also, when a GKB is multicast and the number of recipient is large (e.g., thousands or more), it is difficult to reliably deliver the GKB to all recipients.

IEEE Std 802.21d-2015 [3] addresses this issue by defining a special fragmentation mechanism for fragmenting GKB. Unlike other general-purpose fragmentation mechanisms (e.g., IP fragmentation), a recipient of GKB does not have to receive all the fragments of a single complete GKB and reassemble into the original GKB data.

The recipient can instead determine whether it is a member of the group and can obtain the group key by receiving one GKB fragment that contains in 'SubgroupRange' attribute. Suppose a single complete GKB is fragmented into five GKB fragments with 'SubgroupRange' of each fragment set to (0,99), (100,199), (200,299), (300,399), and (400,499). A recipient whose leaf identifier is 250, when receiving the GKB fragment with 'SubgroupRange (200,299)', can determine whether it is a member of the group. Thus it can obtain the group key if it is a group member and can simply ignore other four GKB fragments.

5   Group Key Distribution Protocol

IEEE Std 802.21d-2015 [3] defines an architecture and a group key distribution protocol that a group manager (GM) can use to communicate to group members via a multicast transport. The group key distribution protocol uses the 'Complete Subtree' method with a deterministic symmetric key encryption scheme and a digital signature scheme. In this section, we introduce a simplified version of the group key distribution protocol using an option that is described in [3]. In this section we refer a group member to a user.

Provisioning
IEEE Std 802.21d-2015 [3] assumes that a group manager and each user has device keys, which are also called long-term keys. The secure provisioning method is not defined in the standard.

1. Let 2^n be the number of (potential) users managed by the group manager GM, and let $\mathcal{U}$ be a set of all users. GM generates a key tree T with depth n, and assigns (I_i, k_i) to each node in T where I_i is a node index represented as a binary string of length between 1 to n and $k_i \leftarrow \mathsf{KeyGen}_{\mathcal{CW}}(\kappa)$ is a node key where i corresponding to the node index I_i. For digital signature, GM generates $(pk, sk) \leftarrow \mathsf{KeyGen}_\Sigma(\kappa)$.
2. For all user U_i in $\mathcal{U}$, GM assigns each user U_i to a leaf node in T. Let $Path_{U_i}$ be a set of node indices of nodes from the leaf node which is assigned to U_i along the path to the root node. GM assigns $DK_i = \left\{ (I_j, k_j) \right\}_{I_j \in Path_{U_i}}$, to U_i as the long-term keys.
3. GM securely sends pk and DK_i to each of U_i.

Procedure of GM

1. Decide a set of group members, S, which is a target for group key distribution and a group identifier GI which identifies a group using the distributed group key.
2. Pick a current sequence number SN for GI.
3. Decide a destination group DG for the group key distribution message. GM is required to send the group key distribution message to all of its members S. For simplicity, we assume that DG includes S. A broadcast group BG including all users may be used as DG.
4. Select a master group key $\mathsf{mgk} \in \{0,1\}^l$ uniformly at random and select a security association identifier SAID which is an identifier of a group session key $\mathsf{gsk} = \mathsf{KDF}(\mathsf{mgk})$ where KDF is a key derivation function which is publicly shared.

5. Compute a list of indices CS from $\mathcal{U} \backslash S$ and T by 'Complete Subtree' method.
6. For all $I_i \in CS$, compute $c_i = \mathsf{Wrap}(k_i, \mathsf{mgk})$ where (I_i, k_i) is a node of T, and adds c_i to a group key data $GKD = GKD||c_i$.
7. Read a sequence number sq for the destination group DG.
8. Compute $\sigma = \mathsf{Sign}(sk, GI||SN||CS||GKD||\mathsf{SAID}||sq)$.
9. Send $(GI||SN||CS||GKD||\mathsf{SAID}||sq||\sigma)$ to DG.

Procedure of receiver U_i

1. Receive $(GI||SN||CS||GKD||\mathsf{SAID}||sq||\sigma)$.
2. Check sq whether the received message is not a replay attack. If the message with sq was already accepted, U_i stops the subsequent procedure.
3. If $\mathsf{Verif}(pk, GI||SN||CS||GKD||\mathsf{SAID}||sq, \sigma) \neq 1$, U_i stops the subsequent procedure.
4. If U_i has $(I_j, k_j) \in DK_i$ such that $I_j \in CS$,

   (a) compute $\mathsf{mgk} = \mathsf{Unwrap}(k, c_k)$ where $c_k \in GKD$ is the ciphertext corresponding with I_j,
   (b) compute the group session key $\mathsf{gsk} = \mathsf{KDF}(\mathsf{mgk})$, and record $(GI, SN, \mathsf{SAID}, \mathsf{gsk})$.

6 Security Analysis

6.1 Security Requirements

We define a formal security model based on the BM model [15]. Our security model modifies the definition of *freshness* from BM model by removing *perfect forward secrecy*. This is due to the reason that for IEEE 802.21 applications, reducing the number of multicast communication traffic is an important requirement.

Attack Model. Let an adversary $\mathcal{A}$ and the users (including the group manager GM) be probabilistic polynomial-time algorithms. In order to capture multiple sessions, each user U is modeled by an oracle Π_U^s for $s \in \mathbb{N}$. Every session is identified by a unique, publicly-known sid_U^s. Let pid_U^s be a partner id that contains the identities of participating users (including U), and $\mathcal{G}(\Pi_{U_j}^s) = \{\Pi_{U_j}^t$ where $U_j \in \mathsf{pid}_{U_i}^s$ and $\mathsf{sid}_{U_i}^s = \mathsf{sid}_{U_j}^t\}$. $\Pi_{U_i}^s$ and $\Pi_{U_j}^t$ are called partner if $\Pi_{U_j}^t \in \mathcal{G}(\Pi_{U_i}^s)$ and $\Pi_{U_i}^s \in \mathcal{G}(\Pi_{U_j}^t)$. $\mathcal{A}$ learns each message to be sent, and it can prevent sending or modifying the message. We assume that receivers always receive the original message sent by the sender, even if $\mathcal{A}$ blocks or modifies it.

$\mathcal{A}$ issues following queries.

– *Initialize(S)*: For each user in the set S, a new oracle Π_U^s is initialized and the resulting session id sid is given to $\mathcal{A}$.
– *Invoke*(sid, S'): It assumes that sid is a valid session id and S' is a set of initialized oracles ($S' \subset S$ where S led to the construction of sid). In response, for each $U \in S'$, the oracle Π_U^s turns into the processing stage. If Π_U^s is an initiator of the protocol, Π_U^s outputs the first protocol message.

- *Send*(Π_U^s, m): The message m is sent to Π_U^s. In response, $\mathcal{A}$ receives a processing result of m based on the protocol. The response may be empty, if m is incorrect.
- *Corrupt*(U): In response, $\mathcal{A}$ obtains the long-term key of U, LL_U.
- *AddUser*(U, Λ): In response, a new user U with a long-term key is added to $\mathcal{U}$ where Λ contains the registration information and the long-term key. If the protocol prohibits U from selecting the long-term key, the long-term key in Λ is empty, and in response $\mathcal{A}$ additionally receives U's long-term key.
- *RevealState*(Π_U^s): In response, $\mathcal{A}$ obtains ephemeral secrets stored in $state_U^s$.
- *RevealKey*(Π_U^s): In response, $\mathcal{A}$ obtains the group session key k_U^s (only if Π_U^s has already accepted).

We say U is corrupted if LL_U is known to $\mathcal{A}$, either via *Corrupt*(U) or *AddUser*(U, Λ); if no such queries have been asked then U is honest.

Definition 5. *(Oracle Freshness) In a session* sid *of P, an oracle Π_U^s has accepted is fresh if all of the following holds:*

1. *no $U' \in \mathsf{pid}_U^s$ has been added by $\mathcal{A}$ via corresponding AddUser query,*
2. *no $U' \in \mathsf{pid}_U^s$ has been corrupted via corresponding Corrupt query,*
3. *neither Π_U^s nor any of its partners is asked for a query RevealState until Π_U^s and its partners accept,*
4. *neither Π_U^s nor any of its partners is asked for a query RevealKey after having accepted*

In the original definition in [2], the condition 2. is "*no $U' \in \mathsf{pid}_U^s$ is asked for a query Corrupt prior to a query of the form* Send($\Pi_{U_j}^t, m$) *with $U_j \in \mathsf{pid}_U^s$ until Π_U^s and its partners accept*". It means that Π_U^s is *fresh* even if $U' \in \mathsf{pid}_U^s$ who is a participant of a future session is corrupted, i.e., it represents *perfect forward secrecy*.

In order to provide a formal security proof of our protocol without *perfect forward secrecy*, we modify condition 2 for the weaken $\mathcal{A}$ as descried in Definition 5.

Definition 6 *(Authenticated Key Exchange (AKE) security). Let P be a group key distribution protocol. Let $b \leftarrow_R \{0, 1\}$ and $\mathcal{A}_{AKE}$ be an adversary against AKE security of P. The attack game* $\mathsf{Game}_{\mathcal{A}_{AKE}, P}^{ake-b}$ *is defined as follows.*

1. *$\mathcal{A}_{AKE}$ interacts with each oracle using the queries defined in Sect. 6.1.*
2. *$\mathcal{A}_{AKE}$ sends Test query to Π_U^s in arbitrary timing. Π_U^s returns k_U^s if $b = 0$, else U returns a key k_r chosen from the key space uniformly at random.*
3. *$\mathcal{A}_{AKE}$ continues to interact with each oracles using the queries defined in Sect. 6.1.*
4. *$\mathcal{A}_{AKE}$ outputs $b' \in \{0, 1\}$ and stops.*

Let Fr *be an event that Π_U^s who receives Test query is still Fresh when $\mathcal{A}_{AKE}$ has been stopped. The advantage of $\mathcal{A}_{AKE}$ is defined as follows:*

$$\mathsf{Adv}^{\text{ake}-b}_{\mathcal{A}_{AKE},P}(\kappa) = \left| \Pr\left[\mathsf{Game}^{\text{ake}-b}_{\mathcal{A}_{AKE},P}(\kappa) = \mathsf{b} \ \wedge \mathsf{Fr}\right] - \frac{1}{2} \right|.$$

We say that a protocol P *is AKE secure if for all probabilistic polynomial-time adversary* $\mathcal{A}_{AKE}$, $\mathsf{Adv}^{\text{ake}-b}_{\mathcal{A}_{AKE},P}(\kappa)$ *is negligible.*

6.2   Security Proof

Theorem 1. *If* Σ *satisfies EUF-CMA security and* $\mathcal{KW}$ *satisfies IND-RPA security, the protocol* P *described in Sect. 5 satisfies AKE-security in Definition 6, and*

$$\mathsf{Adv}^{\text{gk}-b}_{\mathcal{A}_{AKE},P}(\kappa) \le \frac{(2N-1) \cdot n_s \cdot n_g^*}{2} \cdot \mathsf{Adv}^{\text{kw.rpa}}_{A,\mathcal{KW}}(\kappa) + \mathsf{Adv}^{\text{euf}-cma}_{A,\Sigma}(\kappa)$$

where N *is the maximum number of users,* n_g^* *is the number of ciphertexts containing within GKD in* $\Pi^s_{U^*}$ *who is the receiver of Test query, and* n_s *is the maximum number of sessions.*

Proof of Theorem 1. The security proof is given by the game hopping technique [17]. Let W_i be an event that $b = b'$ and Π^s_U who receives Test query is *fresh* at the end of Game i.

Game 0: The original attack game of AKE security. Due to Definition 6,

$$\mathsf{Adv}^{\text{gk}-b}_{\mathcal{A}_{AKE},P}(\kappa) = |\Pr[W_0] - 1/2|. \tag{1}$$

Game 1: Let L_{GM} be a list of messages issued by GM. In Game 1, each Π^s_U ignores *Send* (Π^s_U, m) if $m \notin L_{GM}$, and other operations are the same as Game 0.

In the protocol P, the protocol message without the valid signature of GM is dropped by the receivers. The behavior of Π^s_U may be different between Game 0 and Game 1, if and only if $\mathcal{A}_{AKE}$ succeeds the existential forgery of Σ. We assume Σ is EUF-CMA secure, then

$$|\Pr[W_0] - \Pr[W_1]| \le \mathsf{Adv}^{\text{euf}-cma}_{A,\Sigma}(\kappa). \tag{2}$$

Game 2: Let L_U be a list of messages received by the user U. In Game 2, Π^s_U ignores *Send* (Π^s_U, m) if $m \in L_U$, and other operations are the same as Game 1.

The message of P contains the sequence number sq, and each receiver does not accept the same sequence number. The number of *Send* queries is at most polynomial times in κ since $\mathcal{A}$ is a polynomial-time algorithm. If the space of sq is exponentially large in κ, the behaviors of Π^s_U in Game 1 and Game 2 are the same, then

$$\Pr[S_2] = \Pr[S_1]. \tag{3}$$

Game 3: GM tries to guess a session s^* that $\mathcal{A}_{AKE}$ sends *Test* query and (I^*, k^*) used in s^*. If it finds that the guess is failed, Game 3 is aborted, and GM decides b' which is the output of Game 3 instead of $\mathcal{A}_{AKE}$. Game 3 is the same as Game 2 excluding following operations;

- After the *Provisioning* phase, GM randomly selects a session $s^* \in \{1, \ldots, n_s\}$ and a node in the key management tree T which has N leaf nodes[1], for guessing the session s^* and the node key k^* used in s^*. Let *Hit* be an event that GM succeeds the guess[2].
- When it finds *Hit* does not occur, Game 3 is aborted and GM decides $b' \leftarrow_R \{0, 1\}$ instead of $\mathcal{A}_{AKE}$.

When *Hit* occurs, Game 3 and Game 2 are the same. When *Hit* does not occur, W_3 occurs at random since GM selects $b' \leftarrow_R \{0, 1\}$.

$$\begin{aligned}
\Pr[W_3] &= \Pr[W_3 \wedge Hit] + \Pr[W_3 \wedge \neg Hit] \\
&= \Pr[Hit]\Pr[W_3|Hit] + \Pr[\neg Hit]\Pr[W_3|\neg Hit] \\
&\geq \frac{1}{(2N-1)n_s}\Pr[W_2] + \frac{1}{2} - \frac{1}{2(2N-1)n_s}
\end{aligned} \tag{4}$$

where N is the maximum number of users, n_s is the maximum number of the sessions.

Game 4: In order to estimate $|\Pr[W_3] - 1/2|$, we consider the following hybrid game.

In order to replace the reply of *Test* query with C where $(D_0, D_1, C) \leftarrow \text{LR}_W$, a node key k^* is replaced by W using an Wrap_W oracle. Game 4 is the same as Game 3 excluding the following operations;

- For a session s excluding s^*, when the group manager Π^s_{GM} needs a ciphertext with k^* for generating a group key data GKD, Π^s_{GM} accesses Wrap_W oracle and it receives (D, C). D is regarded as a master group key mgk distributed in s, GKD is generated by C and D with other node keys excluding k^* in T, e.g., $\text{Wrap}(k_{i_1}, D), \ldots, \text{Wrap}\left(k_{i_{k-1}}, D\right), C, \text{Wrap}\left(k_{i_{k-1}}, D\right), \ldots, \text{Wrap}\left(k_{k_{n_k}}, D\right)$ where n_k is the number of ciphertext contained in GKD.
- For the session s^*, the group manager $\Pi^{s^*}_{GM}$ sends a query to LR_W and receives (D_0, D_1, C^*). D_0 is regarded as a master group key mgk distributed in s^*, and D_1 is regarded as a random key. Let GKD^* be a group key data for s^*. GKD^* is generated by C^*, D_0, and D_1 with other node keys excluding k^* in T, e.g.,

---

[1] The complete binary tree T with N leaf nodes has $(2N\text{-}1)$ nodes.

[2] If the guess is correct, i.e., *Hit* occurs, no U^* assigned (I^*, dk^*) is corrupted at the end of Game 3 since Π^*_U who receives Test query must be *fresh*.

$$\mathrm{Wrap}(k_{i_1}, D_0), \ldots, \mathrm{Wrap}\left(k_{i_{j-1}}, D_0\right), C^*, \mathrm{Wrap}\left(k_{i_{j+1}}, D_1\right), \ldots, \mathrm{Wrap}\left(k_{i_{n_g^*}}, D_1\right)$$

where n_g^* is the number of ciphertext contained in GKD^*

- When $\Pi_{U_j}^{s^*}$ receives Test query, it returns a group session key $\mathrm{KDF}(D_0)$.

Let H_j be a hybrid game that $GKD^* = \mathrm{Wrap}(k_{i_1}, D_0), \ldots, \mathrm{Wrap}\left(k_{i_{j-1}}, D_0\right)$, $\mathrm{Wrap}(k_{i_j}, D_0), \mathrm{Wrap}\left(k_{i_{j+1}}, D_1\right), \ldots, \mathrm{Wrap}\left(k_{i_{n_g^*}}, D_1\right)$. Let b_r be the bit of *IND-RPA* game. If $b_r = 0$, Game 4 is the same as H_{j+1} since $C^* = \mathrm{Wrap}(W, D_0)$. If $b_r = 1$, Game 4 is the same as H_j since $C^* = \mathrm{Wrap}(W, D_1)$. Let E_i be an event that occurs if $\mathcal{A}_{\mathrm{AKE}}$ outputs 1 in H_i, then $|\Pr[E_{i-1}] - \Pr[E_i]| \leq \mathrm{Adv}_{A,\mathcal{KW}}^{\mathrm{kw.rpa}}(\kappa)$ holds. By the hybrid argument, we have

$$\left|\Pr[E_0] - \Pr\left[E_{n_g^*}\right]\right| = \sum_{i=1}^{n_{g^*}} |\Pr[E_{i-1}] - \Pr[E_i]| \leq n_g^* \cdot \mathrm{Adv}_{A,\mathcal{KW}}^{\mathrm{kw.rpa}}(\kappa).$$

Accordingly, H_0 is the same as Game 3 when $b = 1$, and $H_{n_g^*}$ is the same as Game 3 when $b = 0$;

$$
\begin{aligned}
\Pr[W_3] - 1/2 &= |\Pr[\mathcal{A}_{AKE} \rightarrow 1 \,\mathrm{in\ Game\ 3} \wedge b = 1] + \Pr[\mathcal{A}_{AKE} \rightarrow 0 \,\mathrm{in\ Game\ 3} \wedge b = 0] - 1/2| \\
&= \frac{1}{2} |\Pr[\mathcal{A}_{AKE} \rightarrow 1 \,\mathrm{in\ Game\ 3}|b = 1] + (1 - \Pr[\mathcal{A}_{AKE} \rightarrow 1 \,\mathrm{in\ Game\ 3}|b = 0]) - 1| \\
&= \frac{1}{2} \left|\Pr[E_0] - \Pr\left[E_{n_g^*}\right]\right|.
\end{aligned}
$$

$$(5)$$

According to Eqs. (1), (2), (3), (4), and (5),

$$
\begin{aligned}
\mathrm{Adv}_{\mathcal{A}_{AKE}, P}^{\mathrm{gk}-b}(\kappa) &= \left|\Pr[W_0] - \frac{1}{2}\right| \\
&= \left|\Pr[W_1] + |\Pr[W_1] - \Pr[W_0]| - \frac{1}{2}\right| \leq \left|\Pr[W_1] + \mathrm{Adv}_{A,\Sigma}^{\mathrm{euf}-cma}(\kappa) - \frac{1}{2}\right| \\
&= \left|\Pr[W_2] + \mathrm{Adv}_{A,\Sigma}^{\mathrm{euf}-cma}(\kappa) - \frac{1}{2}\right| \\
&= \left|(2N - 1) \cdot n_s \left(\Pr[W_3] - \frac{1}{2}\right) + \mathrm{Adv}_{A,\Sigma}^{\mathrm{euf}-cma}(\kappa)\right| \\
&\leq \frac{(2N - 1) \cdot n_s \cdot n_g^*}{2} \cdot \mathrm{Adv}_{A,\mathcal{KW}}^{\mathrm{kw.rpa}}(\kappa) + \mathrm{Adv}_{A,\Sigma}^{\mathrm{euf}-cma}(\kappa).
\end{aligned}
$$

7 Prototyping

We implemented the group key distribution protocol as described in Sect. 5 and measured the processing time of group manager (GM) and receivers. In real systems, the receivers may have memory constraints. For such system, the code footprint size is also important. Therefore, we also measure the footprint size of the receivers. Table 1 shows the benchmark of the computing machine used for GM and receivers[3].

Table 1. Computing machine specification

	GM	Receivers
CPU	Core i5-4310 M, 2.7 GHz	ARM11176JZF-S, 700 MHz
RAM	4 GB	512 MB
OS	Ubuntu 14.04.4	Raspbian

We considered the number of receivers are 1024, with threshold of fragmentation as 32. Table 2 shows processing time that GM takes to generate the protocol messages and the receiver takes to process them. During processing cycle, signing time and verification time of ECDSA are dominant, when ECDSA is attached to each messages. Table 3 shows the size of the protocol messages. The processing time and message size depend on the selection of group members.

Table 2. Processing times

	GM		Receiver	
	Average [msec]	Max [msec]	Average [msec]	Max [msec]
Best case	4.71	4.74	265.15	303.59
Worst case	83.80	85.01	4253.91	4276.05

In a best case scenario, *GroupKeyData* contains only one ciphertext and hence GM sends only one message. In worst case scenario, GM sends 512 ciphertexts, where GM issues 16 messages with *GroupKeyData* which contains 32 ciphertexts (given the threshold of fragmentation is 32). In our implementation, when the receiver receives a message, it first verifies an ECDSA signature in the message. Therefore, in worst case scenario, receiver verifies 16 messages and hence the processing time increases. On the decryption side though the receiver needs to decrypt only one message that carries the Complete Subtree covering the receiver in order to extract the group key, and other 15 messages can be ignored after verification. So even in worst case, there is a significant advantage in terms of overall processing time.

---

[3] Disclaimer: Any mention of commercial products or organizations is for informational purposes only; it is not intended to imply recommendation or endorsement by the National Institute of Standards and Technology (NIST), nor is it intended to imply that the products identified are necessarily the best available for the purpose.

Table 3. Protocol message size

	Message size[bytes]
Best case	272
Worst case	18 336

Table 4 shows foot print size of the receivers.

Table 4. Footprint size of Receivers

	Size [Byte]
heap	55 264
stack	12 200
text	172 257
data	1 268
bss	119 900
Total	360 889

We measured the memory usage occupied on the virtual memory space. The *text* segment corresponds to the code size. The *data* and *bss* segments include pre-defined variables (*data* has initialized data, while *bss* is uninitialized). The *stack* area is used for storing temporal variables on the program that is executed. The *heap* area is managed by malloc()-like functions. Each size of *text*, *data*, and *b*ss segments are fixed in every program execution. These values are measured by the size of the command. In this early prototype implementation, we focus on reducing the heap size for memory management simplification. The maximum sizes of *stack* or *heap* areas are measured by valgrind[TM] [18].

8   Conclusion

We introduced a secure multicast-based group key management and key distribution protocol that is recently standardized in IEEE 802.21. Although it is based on the concept of logical key hierarchy, a method has been specified on how the 'Complete Subtree' can be used to optimize the number of encryptions for each group key distribution. A data format called 'Group Key Block' has been used for encoding the 'Complete Subtree' and other data associated with it. To support the practical applications, the standard assumes an architecture whereby a group manager is responsible for distributing the group key. The group key distribution protocol uses a deterministic symmetric key wrapping scheme and a digital signature scheme. A formal security analysis and corresponding proof have been performed based on Bresson and Manulis model. While additional work is required, an early prototype implementation results with 1024 nodes and tree depth of seven (7) show that the scheme is realizable in memory constrained devices. It provides an easy way to securely add and remove the group members.

References

1. IEEE Standard for Local and Metropolitan Area Networks- Part 21: Media independent handover services- IEEE Std 802.21™-2008, January 2009
2. IEEE Standard for Local and Metropolitan Area Networks- Part 21: Media independent handover; amendment 1: security extensions to media independent handover services and protocol, IEEE Std 802.21a™-2012, May 2012
3. IEEE Standard for Local and Metropolitan Area Networks- Part 21: Media independent handover; amendment 4: multicast group management, IEEE Std 802.21d™-2015, July 2015
4. Wallner, D., Harder, E., Agee, R.: Key management for multicast: issues and architectures request for comments 2627, June 1999
5. Wong, C.K., Gouda, M., Lam, S.S.: Secure group communications using key graphs. IEEE/ACM Trans. Netw. **8**(1), 16–30 (2000)
6. ISO/IEC 11770-5 Information Technology – Security techniques - key management – Part 5: Group key management (2011)
7. Fiat, A., Naor, M.: Broadcast encryption. In: Stinson, D.R. (ed.) CRYPTO 1993. LNCS, vol. 773, pp. 480–491. Springer, Heidelberg (1994). doi:10.1007/3-540-48329-2_40
8. Weis, B., Rowles, S., Hardjono, T.: The group domain of interpretation IETF, Request for comments 6407, October 2011
9. IEEE Standard for Information Technology—Telecommunications and information exchange between systems—Local and metropolitan area networks—Specific requirements Part 11: Wireless LAN Medium Access Control (MAC) and Physical Layer (PHY) Specifications (2015)
10. Naor, D., Naor, M., Lotspiech, J.: Revocation and tracing schemes for stateless receivers. In: Kilian, J. (ed.) CRYPTO 2001. LNCS, vol. 2139, pp. 41–62. Springer, Heidelberg (2001). doi:10.1007/3-540-44647-8_3
11. Diffie, W., van Oorschot, P.C., Wiener, M.J.: Authentication and authenticated key exchanges. Des. Codes Cryptogr. **2**(2), 107–125 (1992)
12. Burmester, M.: On the risk of opening distributed keys. In: Desmedt, Y.G. (ed.) CRYPTO 1994. LNCS, vol. 839, pp. 308–317. Springer, Heidelberg (1994). doi:10.1007/3-540-48658-5_29
13. Kim, Y., Perrig, A., Tsudik, G.: Simple and fault-tolerant key agreement for dynamic collaborative groups. In: CCS 2000, Proceedings of the 7th ACM Conference on Computer and Communications Security, Athens, Greece, 1–4 November 2000, pp. 235–244 (2000)
14. Günther, C.G.: An identity-based key-exchange protocol. In: Quisquater, J.-J., Vandewalle, J. (eds.) EUROCRYPT 1989. LNCS, vol. 434, pp. 29–37. Springer, Heidelberg (1990). doi:10.1007/3-540-46885-4_5
15. Brecher, T., Bresson, E., Manulis, M.: Fully robust tree-diffie-hellman group key exchange. In: Proceedings of Cryptology and Network Security, 8th International Conference, CANS 2009, Kanazawa, Japan, 12–14 December 2009, pp. 478–497 (2009)
16. Gennaro, R., Halevi, S.: More on key wrapping. In: Jacobson, M.J., Rijmen, V., Safavi-Naini, R. (eds.) SAC 2009. LNCS, vol. 5867, pp. 53–70. Springer, Heidelberg (2009). doi:10.1007/978-3-642-05445-7_4
17. Shoup, V.: Sequences of games: a tool for taming complexity in security proofs. IACR Cryptology ePrint Archive, p. 332 (2004)
18. Valgrind. http://valgrind.org/

State Management for Hash-Based Signatures

David McGrew[1]([✉]), Panos Kampanakis[1], Scott Fluhrer[1],
Stefan-Lukas Gazdag[2], Denis Butin[3], and Johannes Buchmann[3]

[1] Cisco Systems, San Jose, USA
{mcgrew,pkampana,sfluhrer}@cisco.com
[2] genua GmbH, Munich, Germany
stefan-lukas_gazdag@genua.eu
[3] TU Darmstadt, Darmstadt, Germany
{dbutin,buchmann}@cdc.informatik.tu-darmstadt.de

Abstract. The unavoidable transition to post-quantum cryptography requires dependable quantum-safe digital signature schemes. Hash-based signatures are well-understood and promising candidates, and the object of current standardization efforts. In the scope of this standardization process, the most commonly raised concern is statefulness, due to the use of one-time signature schemes. While the theory of hash-based signatures is mature, a discussion of the system security issues arising from the concrete management of their state has been lacking. In this paper, we analyze state management in N-time hash-based signature schemes, considering both security and performance, and categorize the security issues that can occur due to state synchronization failures. We describe a state reservation and nonvolatile storage, and show that it can be naturally realized in a hierarchical signature scheme. To protect against unintentional copying of the private key state, we consider a hybrid stateless/stateful scheme, which provides a graceful security degradation in the face of unintentional copying, at the cost of increased signature size. Compared to a completely stateless scheme, the hybrid approach realizes the essential benefits, with smaller signatures and faster signing.

Keywords: Post-quantum cryptography · Hash-based signatures · Statefulness · System integration

1   Introduction

Security protocols routinely rely on digital signatures for authentication. Common examples are code signing for software updates, server authentication for TLS, and S/MIME for secure email. The most common cryptographic schemes for digital signatures (RSA [26], DSA [8], and ECDSA [17]) are all susceptible to quantum computer cryptanalysis using Shor's algorithm [28]. While the concrete realization of quantum computers still is an object of ongoing research, substantial efforts in this area are ongoing [23,27].

Independently of the actual realization of quantum computing, governmental and standardization organizations are encouraging the transition to post-quantum cryptography, i.e. cryptographic schemes not known to be vulnerable

© Springer International Publishing AG 2016
L. Chen et al. (Eds.): SSR 2016, LNCS 10074, pp. 244–260, 2016.
DOI: 10.1007/978-3-319-49100-4_11

Table 1. Signature sizes (in KB) of hash-based signature schemes (128-bit security level, 2^{60} messages).

	Stateful		Stateless
	LMS	XMSS^{MT}	SPHINCS
Signature size (KB)	5	15 | 28	41

to quantum computer attacks. Notably, the NSA recently announced its transition from the Suite B set of cryptographic algorithms towards post-quantum cryptography [16]. Standardization efforts are also underway, for instance by NIST [6] and ETSI [9]. As more stakeholders are required to heed official recommendations, the deployment of post-quantum cryptography becomes inevitable.

Fortunately, post-quantum cryptographic schemes exist, and some are already well-understood. In particular, hash-based signatures have been thoroughly analyzed [2,3,7,13,19,22] and are currently undergoing standardization [14,21].

Motivation. One major obstacle to the widespread use of hash-based signatures is the fact that the signing algorithm is stateful. That is, with each message being signed, the private key must change. There are stateless hash-based signature schemes [1,12] that address state concerns, but their signature sizes are significantly higher. Table 1 shows the signature size of two stateful schemes (LMS [21], XMSS^{MT} [15]) and stateless SPHINCS [1] for parameters that lead to 2^{60} signed messages and a security level of 128-bits. For LMS we are considering LMS_SHA256_N32_H10 with LMOTS_SHA256_N32_W16 with a supertree height of $l = 6$. For XMSS, we use XMSSMT_SHA2-256_M32_W16_H60_D6 and XMSSMT_SHA2-256_M32_W16_H60_D12 with $n = 32$ respectively. For SPHINCS, the parameters $h = 60$, $d = 12$, $w = 16$ and $n = 32$ are considered. It is clear that stateless SPHINCS has significantly larger signatures, which could make it impractical in some scenarios. The public key size of the stateful schemes are in the range of 70 B. The SPHINCS public key is in the 1000 B range.

In a stateful scheme, when a private key is long-lived, it must be stored in nonvolatile memory, and the version of the private key in memory must continuously be synchronized with that in volatile memory (e.g. Random Access Memory, or RAM). State synchronization is especially important because it is critical to the security of the system; if two distinct messages are signed with the same private key, then an attacker can use those signatures to construct a forgery. Thus, after signing one message, the signer must update the state so the same key is not reused. Key synchronization also requires a time delay between signatures that can lead to a significant performance penalty.

In this paper, we consider the design of N-time signature schemes and the system engineering considerations needed to ensure that they avoid the problems outlined above. To the best of our knowledge, no work addressing state management strategies for stateful hash-based signatures exists so far. We describe a simple state management scheme for hierarchical signature schemes that minimizes synchronization delay and reduces the chance of synchronization failure. It works by storing only the root (or topmost) level(s) of the signature hierarchy in nonvolatile storage, and having the remaining levels exist only in volatile memory. However, this scheme does not address the cloning problem, which occurs when a system, e.g. a virtual machine may be copied and reveal sensitive cryptographic data; to address that point, we then consider a hybrid scheme: a hierarchical signature scheme in which the root level consists of a stateless N-time scheme, while the other levels are stateful.

Outline. The remainder of this paper is organized as follows. We recall one-time signature schemes as well as N-time and hierarchical signature schemes, and establish some notation (Sect. 2). We then review the security and performance issues with stateful signature schemes, notably the impact of volatile and nonvolatile cloning (Sect. 3). Next, we cover the basics of synchronization between volatile and nonvolatile storage (Sect. 4), including possible mitigation for caching mechanisms, illustrated with concrete examples. We proceed by describing a strategy for loosening the coupling between those data stores by having the signer 'reserve' the state needed to sign multiple messages (Sect. 5). We show that hierarchical signature schemes naturally support this state reservation strategy, in a way that benefits security and performance. These techniques provide the best possible security for stateful signature schemes, but they do not address scenarios in which a private key may be unintentionally cloned. To address those cases, we outline a hybrid approach, in which the root level scheme of a hierarchical scheme is stateless — ensuring inadvertent nonvolatile cloning does not compromise the whole structure — but the lower levels are stateful (Sect. 6). We then offer our conclusions and sketch future work (Sect. 7).

2   Stateful Hash-Based Signature Schemes

One-time Signature Schemes. Hash-based signatures use one-time signature schemes as a fundamental building block. One-time signature schemes, unlike most other signature schemes, require only a secure cryptographic hash function and no other hardness assumption (about a number-theoretic problem) and are not known to be vulnerable to Shor's algorithm. *Secure* here refers to either collision resistance or mere second-preimage resistance, depending on the specific one-time signature used. Common examples of one-time signature schemes are the seminal one by Lamport [19], the Winternitz scheme [7], and its recent variant W-OTS$^+$ [13]. In one-time signatures, the private key is usually randomly generated and the public key is a function of the private key, involving the underlying hash function. Advanced one-time signature schemes feature a parameter enabling a time/memory trade-off, e.g. the Winternitz parameter. These schemes are inadequate on their own in practice, since each one-time private key can only be used to securely sign a single message.

N-time Signature Schemes. Stateful N-time signature schemes, introduced by Merkle [22] and often improved since (e.g. [2,3,20]), are built out of one-time signature schemes. They make one-time signatures practical by combining $N = 2^H$ of them in a single structure — a complete binary tree of height H. Let $\varUpsilon_N = (K, S, V)$ denote an N-time signature scheme that consists of a key generation algorithm K, a signing algorithm S, and a signature validation algorithm V. The private key $\varPsi$ for the N-time scheme $\varUpsilon_N$ consists of the set of N private keys of the underlying one-time scheme. An integer counter has to keep track of the advancement of the key, as with each signature generation another one-time private key has to be used. A simple way to reduce the size of that N-time key is to instead define it to be a short string, and then use a cryptographically secure pseudorandom function to generate the keys of the underlying one-time scheme [22]. Formally speaking, this strategy changes the algorithms K and S by creating an additional preprocessing step. The private state is thus reduced down to the short private key and the integer counter, simplifying state management somewhat through a reduction in scale. Nonetheless, the correct management of the counter across multiple invocations of S is critical to security, as any one-time private key must not be used twice.

Hierarchical Signatures. A *hierarchical signature scheme* is an N-time signature scheme that uses other hash-based signatures in its construction. Let $\varGamma = (\varUpsilon_{N_0}, \varUpsilon_{N_1}, \ldots, \varUpsilon_{N_{l-1}})$ denote a hierarchical signature scheme with l levels. The public key Z for $\varGamma$ is the output of K_0 (that is, the key generation algorithm of the top level). The private key for $\varGamma$ consists of the private keys of each level: $\varPsi_0, \varPsi_1, \ldots, \varPsi_{l-1}$. A signature for $\varGamma$ consists of the public keys $Z_1, \ldots, Z_{l-1}$ of levels 1 through $l - 1$, along with the signatures $Y_0(Z_1), Y_1(Z_2), \ldots, Y_{l-2}(Z_{l-1})$ of the ith level's public key by the $(i - 1)^{th}$ level private key, and the signature $Y_{l-1}(M)$ of the message M with the private key of the last level. If the signature scheme $\varUpsilon_{N_i}$ at the ith level of $\varGamma$ can sign N_i signatures, then $\varGamma$ is an N-time signature scheme with $N = \prod_{i=0}^{l-1} N_i$. Hierarchical signatures allow for shorter signing time of a message M by a N_{l-1}-time (instead of $\prod_{i=0}^{l-1} N_i$-time) signature while offering a higher total number ($\prod_{i=0}^{l-1} N_i$) of signed messages. Concrete examples of hierarchical hash-based signatures include XMSS^{MT} [15], a scheme by Leighton and Micali [20] and SPHINCS [1]. XMSS^{MT} and SPHINCS define parameter d as the number of layers in the hierarchical structure. Additionally, the LMS [21] specification describes a hierarchical hash-based signature variant based on Leighton and Micali's scheme.

3   State Synchronization Security Risks

We identified several distinct issues with stateful signature schemes, which we consider here. Ensuring the correct synchronization of the private key between a storage unit and the execution unit requires a carefully engineered system. In most cases, the synchronization cost is likely to add to the time required for signature generation. We call this additional latency the *synchronization delay*.

We say that a *synchronization failure* occurs if the private key or counter in nonvolatile storage fails to advance at or before the time that the private key in RAM advances. This could be caused by the crash of an application or an operating system, by a power outage, by the corruption of the nonvolatile state, or by a software bug. Another issue with statefulness is the *cloning problem*: the situation arising when a private key is copied and then used without coordination by two or more execution units. This can for instance happen through Virtual Machine (VM) image cloning, or by the restoration of a key file to a previous state from a backup system. Cloning will cause multiple signatures to be generated from the same system state, thus undermining security. The most important issue is *nonvolatile cloning*, as outlined above. A related but distinct problem is that of *volatile cloning*, which is the copying of a private key from volatile memory, as discussed below.

In a well-designed stateful signature system, synchronization failure can be avoided, but also synchronization delay will greatly impact performance. Nonvolatile cloning may not be a consideration on a system that is dedicated to signature generation, but it is a significant risk on general-purpose software systems.

Volatile Cloning in VM Environments. There is a low risk of volatile cloning, except in VM environments. Most contemporary VM environments (e.g. VMware Virtual Center, Oracle Virtual Box, KVM or Xen) support live cloning. This is usually achieved by first capturing a system snapshot. Such environments introduce several other risks for cryptography and security protocols. Pseudorandom number generators are at risk, since their state can be cloned, too. The exact risk to pseudorandom number generation depends on the method of entropy collection (possibly causing state divergence), but the risk is great enough that volatile cloning should be avoided. Generally speaking, values that may only be used once are at risk from live VM cloning. In addition to random numbers, this includes "initialization vectors, counters for encryption, seeds for digital signatures, and one-time passwords" [10]. Issues with such primitives can result in catastrophic failures for classic (pre-quantum) digital signature schemes such as DSA, and even on the level of security protocols such as TLS [25]. These vulnerabilities relate to random number generators caching randomness far in advance. Many other systems are at risk from live virtual machine cloning, including the S/KEY one-time password system and the TCP protocol [11], for which initial sequence numbers could be reused for hijacking. Volatile cloning therefore appears problematic to such an extent that the vulnerability of hash-based signature to this scenario is by no means a special case.

In our view, stateful hash-based signature techniques can be safely implemented in some scenarios, such as dedicated cryptographic hardware, which can then benefit from their smaller signatures and signing times. On the other hand, there is also a need for techniques that are secure even when nonvolatile cloning occurs, for use in general purpose software environments. The hybrid approach of Sect. 6 addresses the latter need.

4 State Synchronization Considerations

State synchronization can be delayed by caching, or interfered with by other processes on the used system. Of course, it is neither possible nor reasonable to avoid caching and therefore the resulting delay completely. Multiple levels of caches coexist on typical systems, both in hardware and software, helping the system to function quickly and properly, by making frequently used data easily accessible. Nevertheless, partially mitigating measures can be applied by forcing cache flushing, or by deactivating it. As dealing with the state synchronization is highly dependent on several factors like the used operating system or hardware specifics, no universal approach exists. In the following, we present diverse options to cope with state synchronization.

The access to nonvolatile storage deserves more detailed consideration as the essential operation in our case is storing the new key state held in the main or volatile memory on that nonvolatile storage (as shown in Fig. 1). To minimize I/O operations e.g. on hard disks for frequently used or written data, caches provide recently used or repeatedly accessed data based on prior operations. So data supposed to be written to the disk may stay in the cache rather than being written to the actual disk memory. Hard disks and other nonvolatile storage devices often feature a (disk) cache that holds the data before actually writing to disk. Most modern operating systems offer a page cache which behaves similarly to the memory caches of hard disks but remains in the main memory of the system. Usually data that is read or written for the first time is held in the page cache which gets synchronized to the disk or disk cache in fixed intervals, by exceeding thresholds e.g. a limit for non-synchronized data or due to system calls. Data sometimes can be swapped between both caches. In most cases the use of those caches is transparent and therefore unknown to applications running in userspace. In matters of key state synchronization, a write-through is ideal. In such a scenario using stateful schemes it is desirable to use state-of-the-art techniques to overwrite the sections of the main memory with random values if they hold cryptographic data that is not needed after writing to disk. Mechanisms that come with the operating system (and may be applied automatically) should be preferred over self-made implementations which need special attention i.e. regarding compiler optimizations.

In terms of file I/O, on POSIX environments, the O_SYNC flag (for the open() system call) will cause invocations of the write() system call to block the calling process until the data has been written to the underlying hardware. Equivalent flags (e.g. FILE_FLAG_WRITE_THROUGH for CreateFile() on Win32 API) exist on other platforms. Modern Linux systems offer writeback or flusher threads (formerly pdflush) for the page cache that may be optimized. Synchronization may be triggered manually by the sync or fsync system calls. However, if hardware has its own memory cache, it must be separately dealt with using an operating system- or device-specific tool such as hdparm to flush the on-drive cache, or to deactivate write caching for that drive. The secure way to ensure that the data was written is to read it again and compare it to what was expected, which requires the data to be written to disk without cache interruption and would add to the synchronization delay.

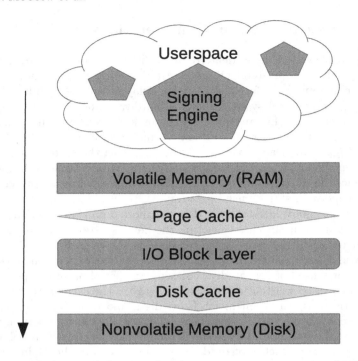

Fig. 1. A simplified view of the data flow from signing engine to nonvolatile storage, via cache layers.

4.1 Overhead for Hash-Based Signatures

The synchronization latency introduced earlier depends on the chosen hash-based signature scheme and its implementation. A typical example following the specification of XMSS [14] merely requires updating the leaf index in the secret key, a 4-byte value; or an 8-byte value for $XMSS^{MT}$. This assumes that all data including the one-time keys and all nodes are stored in the global secret key. The LMS [21] specification also requires updating a 16 or 32-byte random private key value. Of course, generating 16 or 32-byte values can be avoided by generating them from a seed and index with a pseudorandom number generator (PRNG), which would reduce the state update of a few byte long index.

A PRNG is often used to help generating the one-time signature (OTS) keys [5]. That way one is able to reduce the size of the scheme's secret key by storing only a part of it and rebuilding the necessary information on the fly. A sequence of 2^h seeds is computed from a single initial seed, iteratively (Fig. 2). In that case, the one-time key pairs (2^h in total) are not all stored in the overall secret key but are generated successively instead. This generation

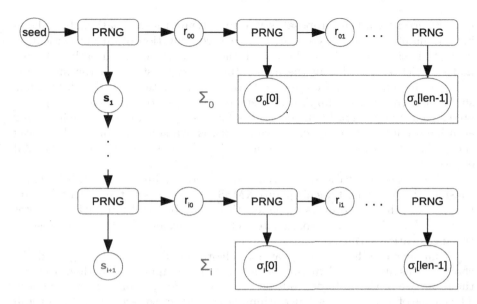

Fig. 2. Iterative generation of successive PRNG seeds (s_i) from an initial one (seed), and OTS signing key generation. The OTS signing keys are $\Sigma_i = \sigma_i[0] \ldots \sigma_i[len-1], i \leq 2^h$, where len is the number of n-byte string elements in a W-OTS$^+$ secret key, public key, and signature. As part of the state synchronization, after the generation of the ith OTS signing key, the next seed s_{i+1} (in red) must be stored (Color figure online).

takes place twice: for the generation of the overall public key and for signing[1]. The very basic data to be synchronized are the index and the succeeding seed. This would be just 36 bytes with $n = 32$ and XMSS or 72 bytes with $n = 64$ and XMSS^{MT}.

The total size of the state data to be updated then depends on the used parameters and implementation choices. In particular, different methods to update the authentication path[2] involve the storage of different elements (e.g. nodes for the next authentication path or precomputed nodes) as part of the state.

We now consider this case where a PRNG is used. When nodes are computed on the fly like this, an important concern is the worst case running time. Without precomputation, the large variation in node computing time (depending on how many already known nodes can be reused) would lead to unbalanced node computations and unacceptable delays in signing speed. By precomputation, modern

---

[1] This allows for forward-secure constructions if used with the right schemes, e.g. special instantiations of XMSS using a forward-secure PRNG as shown by [2]. That way an attacker may get access to the secret key on a system but is not able to forge signatures using previous keys. A hash-based secret key is then to be seen just as secure as any other signing key that an attacker gets access to.

[2] The authentication path is the sequence of tree nodes that a verifier needs to reconstruct the path to reach the root of the tree from a leaf.

tree traversal algorithm proposals strive to mitigate these variations by balancing the number of leaves computed in each computation of an authentication path [4]. Besides the index and the seed, the next authentication path and some nodes, which are needed in the near future, must be stored in the meantime (while some older nodes may be deleted). As more data has to be written one should also consider the impact of interrupts to the storing procedure. A generated signature must not be handed out before a new state, in this case including additional data by tree traversal algorithms, is available in storage. That way the old key state does not get compromised in case of an outage or other harmful events.

To give a sense of the size of the state to be synchronized in this case, we consider the following typical (plain) XMSS parameter set: tree height $h = 16$, message length $m = 32$ bytes, node length $n = 32$ bytes, Winternitz parameter $w = 16^3$. For LMS [21], the parameter set are equivalent. They are provided in the specification's Table 1.

A number of different tree traversal algorithms exist (e.g. [4,18]), and the choice of this algorithm defines the exact node precomputation method. In turn, the total size of the state depends on the chosen node precomputation method. The choice of a tree traversal algorithm does not affect the security of the overall signature scheme, but has a massive impact on performance. As an example, consider the BDS tree traversal algorithm [4]. We assume the value $K = 2$ for the BDS parameter. The state of the BDS algorithm comprises the current authentication path, an array of nodes used for the efficient computation of left authentication nodes, a single right authentication node, tail nodes on the stack and nodes for the treehash algorithm. Buchmann, Dahmen and Schneider showed [4] that the total space requirement of this algorithm depends only on the height of the tree and the size of the nodes: it is bounded by $(3.5h - 4)n$ bytes for that algorithm, i.e. 1664 bytes for our chosen concrete parameter set, which have to be written to the nonvolatile storage in addition. The algorithm computes $\frac{h-1}{2}$ leaves and $\frac{h-3}{2}$ inner nodes on average for each authentication path.

Storing therefore adds to each signing operation by several milliseconds, but using the techniques introduced in the following section helps reducing the need for storing each update of the key.

5   A State Reservation Strategy

When an N-time signature system's private key is read from nonvolatile storage into RAM, it can use a *state reservation* approach by writing back into storage the private key that is u signatures ahead of the current signature. In this way, the execution unit reserves the next u signatures for use, and avoids the need to write the updated private key u times into nonvolatile storage.

---

[3] Recall that the Winternitz parameter is used as a trade-off setting for the underlying one-time signature scheme.

We formalize this idea by introducing a new *reserve* operation $R : [0, N] \rightarrow \{0,1\}^K$, which takes as input the number of private keys to reserve for use, and returns their values after it has updated the nonvolatile storage. We define an N-*time signature system with reservation* as an N-time system $\Upsilon = (K, R, S, V)$ in which the signing algorithm cannot directly access any private key information, and must first call the reserve function to obtain that key. For example, to sign the next X messages with $X \leq N$ the signer will receive X one-time signature keys from the reserve function R (or i.e. a key that may be advanced for up to X signatures, depending on the implementation). These keys are not sequentially synchronized in nonvolatile storage. They are delivered to the signing function only after the key state of the last key in the reservation is synchronized by R. If the signer crashes while it is using the X keys to sign the messages, the remaining keys in the reservation will not be used, which reduces the maximum number of signed messages, but there is no change of key reuse since the key state has already been updated in nonvolatile storage.

Given any N-time signature system, it is easy to define a signature system with reserve by introducing the appropriate function and a counter. Multiple signing engines can be accommodated by calling the reserve function to obtain a distinct private key range for each signing engine. The key still is a critical resource with this approach, but access to it is accelerated, as an engine calling the reserve function does not have to wait for another engine or process to finish signing first.

The reserve strategy minimizes the number of write operations to nonvolatile storage, which significantly reduces synchronization delay. The larger the interval u is, the less storage overhead is necessary. It also incurs a small penalty. Interrupting the update process of the reserve function is not a problem, as the key may not be written to nonvolatile storage but also will not be handed to a signing engine. However, any interruption of the signing process — including a crash, a graceful shutdown or the signing process simply not using all the signatures available — will reduce the number of messages that can be signed by the long-term key.

To offer an optimal coverage on diverse keys for addressing different use cases, for example with keys using different parameter sets or to provide backup keys if the current key's compromised somehow, a key provider tool may be used, holding a key pool $P = (\Psi_0, \Psi_1, \ldots, \Psi_{p-1})$ where p is the number of different keys. Each private key Ψ can be accessed via a reserve function.

Even though a reservation function introduces extra processing to generates a series of keys, key generation is less costly than signing. When decoupled from signing, a reservation function does not introduce a performance high risk factor. Several ways to improve the performance of N-time signature schemes in practice exist. As mentioned above, one common strategy is to generate the one-time signature key pairs by using a PRNG, instead of creating each key pair randomly following a uniform distribution. That way a seed s is used to feed the PRNG, which returns output for the key generation as well as the successor seed s'. In this case the nature of N-time signature schemes can be used in favor of more security. Instead of creating all one-time signature key pairs using one initial seed that is employed iteratively by the PRNG, one may reseed the PRNG for every fixed interval u and limit the reserve function to a maximum limit of u signatures per call of the function by an engine. That way a signing engine receives several signing keys, but cannot get any information about the remainder of the long-term key. One then has to consider the compatibility with the used tree traversal algorithm and call that one correctly. As mentioned above, a tree traversal algorithm may precalculate further nodes to allow for a balanced average signing time. If using different seeds, a tree traversal algorithm used by the signing engine must be compatible with that behavior. To simplify implementation and streamline operation, the interval u should be a divisor of the number of leafs of a (bottom-layer) subtree so subtree boundaries are not crossed. The reserve function does have access to all secret key information and therefore has no problem updating the secret key using several seeds.

Another way to improve security is to introduce volatile and nonvolatile levels within the signature scheme Υ. This approach is detailed next.

5.1   Volatile and Nonvolatile Levels

A hierarchical signature scheme very naturally supports a reserve operation of all $r = N_{l-1}$ signatures associated with level $l - 1$. We formalize this notion in this section with the idea of a *volatile level*. In a hierarchical signature system, the first $k \leq l$ levels can be maintained in nonvolatile storage, while the remaining $l - k$ levels can be volatile (Fig. 3).

Without essential loss of generality, we consider a signature chain with exactly two levels[4]; Υ_0 is nonvolatile, and Υ_1 is volatile. The overall scheme is an $N_0 N_1$ time signature scheme that naturally supports a reserve of exactly $r = N_1$. The only time that Υ_0 needs to sign is when the reserve operation is invoked and when Υ_1 is exhausted (that is, it has produced all N_1 of its signatures). Each invocation of the reserve operation invokes the top level signing algorithm and the bottom level key generation algorithm. The key generation process may take a long time, but the system could generate bottom-level private keys in advance of when they are needed, and bring them into Υ at that time.

When a bottom level public/private key pair is generated, any public data (such as the components of a Merkle hash tree) can be cached in nonvolatile storage without raising any security issues. Furthermore, a private key could be kept in nonvolatile storage for some period of time pending its use in a volatile level, as long as it is erased from nonvolatile storage before it is used. That is to say, the private key of a volatile level may be temporarily stored in nonvolatile memory between the time that it is generated and the time that it is linked into Υ by signing its public key with the top level. We emphasize, however, that all private keys at the volatile level must not be synchronized with nonvolatile storage. A system that uses this *volatile key precomputation* strategy

---

[4] Note that either of these two levels could themselves be hierarchical signature schemes.

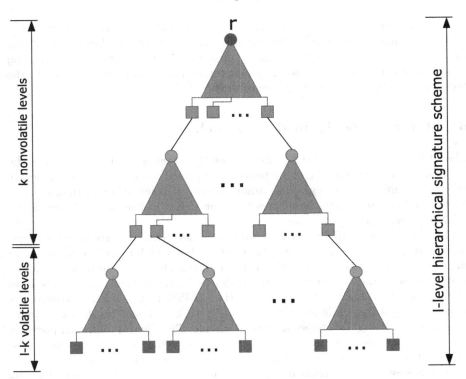

Fig. 3. Combined volatile/nonvolatile hierarchical signature scheme with $l = 3$ and $k = 2$. r is the multitree root, i.e. the public key of the entire scheme. Each subtree can be a stateful $N - time$ signature scheme like XMSS or LMS.

must carefully avoid synchronization issues that might cause a cached private key to be used in multiple levels.

A hierarchical signature scheme with a volatile bottom level enforces the reservation property; since the private key of the volatile level is not synchronized in nonvolatile storage, it avoids synchronization problems. Of course, the root level must be nonvolatile, but it only rarely performs signing, and thus rarely changes its state. This is a benefit because synchronization delay is no longer an issue, and there is less chance of a synchronization problem (in the reasonable model that problems occur when there is a crash or power outage during a write operation).

We conjecture that a nonvolatile level with 2^{20} signatures is sufficient to provide security in general-purpose software environments, since that number of keys can be used to sign once per hour for over a century, or once per second for nearly two years. This is enough time to allow for almost all types of system failures to be detected and corrected. Even 2^{16} signatures may be sufficient if a signature is associated with an hourly re-initialization, considering that it is enough to last for seven years.

However, the reservation strategy and hierarchical signature schemes do not address the nonvolatile cloning problem. If a root level private key is copied and then used by multiple execution units, an attacker could forge a signature on a bottom level public key, and thus perpetrate N_{l-1} forgeries. This limits the scenarios in which signature scheme could be used.

6   Stateless and Hybrid Approaches

The SPHINCS hash-based signature scheme [1] is stateless, and thus avoids the synchronization delay and cloning problems outlined above. It can sign a nearly arbitrary number of messages, but unfortunately, it is less efficient than stateful hash-based signatures; its signatures are over 40 KB in length, and they take a relatively long time to generate.

Ideally, we would like to have a signature scheme that has the shorter signatures and quicker signing of a stateful method, but which has the advantages of the stateless methods. A reasonable compromise is the following hybrid scheme: a hierarchical signature scheme with a stateless N_0-time scheme at the root level of Υ, while the other levels are stateful (i.e. XMSS, LMS). Such a structure is shown in Fig. 4 (which is similar to Fig. 3) with $k = 1$ and the top tree (nonvolatile level) being a stateless signature scheme. This hybrid approach provides security against nonvolatile cloning, because it does not require any state synchronization at the root level. It also avoids synchronization delay.

A stateless N-time signature scheme can sign up to N signatures at a certain security level. If more than N signatures are generated, its security will degrade, but this degradation can be graceful. The Hash to Obtain Random Subset (HORS) scheme [24] is a good example of this type of system. Each distinct message that is signed reveals a small subset of the private state, i.e. a few-time signature scheme is used instead of a one-time signature scheme as a cornerstone of the system. In order to perpetrate a forgery, an attacker would need to collect the private state that is revealed from many different signatures. HORS is further improved by HORST which is used in SPHINCS.

The hybrid approach described above can bring worthwhile advantages, because it can make use of a stateless signature scheme that can sign only a limited number of signatures, e.g. 64K or 1M. It does not entirely eliminate all of the issues surrounding state management. Even with a stateless N-time signature scheme, there is still a need to limit the number of signatures created with the scheme, and the enforcement of that limit might require some state synchronization. Of course, this need to restrict the number of signatures is fundamental to *any* N-time signature scheme. However, there may be some natural bounds on the number of signatures that a system could create with a nonvolatile private key. If those signatures are associated with the initialization of an application or an operating system, for example, then even if a restart or reboot occurs every hour, it would take seven years to reach $N = 2^{16}$ root-level signatures and over a century to reach $N = 2^{20}$ signatures. In a backup scenario, either of those root level schemes would be adequate, since the restoration of an operating system

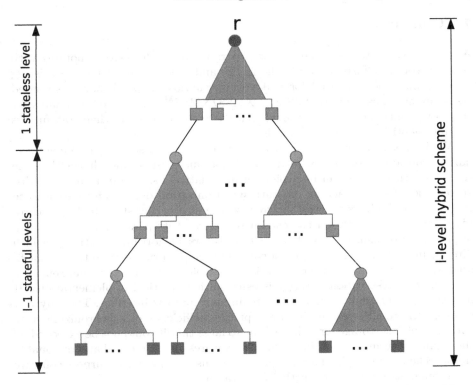

Fig. 4. A hybrid approach combining a stateless signature scheme like HORST [1] at the root level and stateful schemes like LMS and XMSS at the lower levels.

or application from backup does not change the number of execution units. In a VM scenario, however, each cloning would produce multiple execution units; we do not recommend the hybrid approach for the volatile part of the hybrid structure for such environments. As discussed earlier (Sect. 3), there are several other security issues with the cloning of VMs, so it is not clear how important this limitation is in practice.

If volatile private keys are cached in nonvolatile storage, it is essential to make sure that they are not cloned. For instance, it is acceptable to have the private key stored in swap memory (assuming that there are adequate security protections in place), but it is not acceptable to cache those keys in a file that might be cloned in a VM or backed up.

In practice, with a hybrid scheme, if one never performs more than N restarts (for some reasonable N), all issues with state management are eliminated. One would regenerate the volatile state after every reboot (and generate a signature of that volatile state based on the stateless scheme); one would then generate signatures based on the volatile state. If the volatile signature scheme is designed to be able to generate enough signatures, one can avoid regenerating that state until the next reboot.

7   Conclusions

As the transition to post-quantum cryptography moves forward — notably with standardization efforts at NIST, the IETF, and other organizations — existing schemes must be evaluated for real-world scenarios. In particular, hash-based signature schemes such as LMS and XMSS/XMSS^{MT} are good candidates for the post-quantum era, with minimal security requirements, but their statefulness is often mentioned when adoption is discussed.

We have taken a closer look at concrete cloning and state management scenarios, considered examples with typical parameter sets, and shown that the security-critical issues can be avoided using relatively simple measures. We discussed the effects of caching on state synchronization delays, and measures to mitigate these effects. It was shown how the size of the state to be synchronized depends not only on the chosen scheme and its parameters, but also on implementation choices — such as the tree traversal algorithm selection — which directly impact performance. A trade-off between performance and the (quantifiable) risk of slower state synchronization is therefore available to signing engines.

The state reservation strategy is essential for practical implementations. It makes sense to formalize this fact by defining it into the interface. The only way to avoid the reserve scheme is to accept the inefficiency of synchronizing state with nonvolatile storage, or to have N be so large that it could not be exceeded by the signing systems in use. Hierarchical signatures are a practical and reasonably simple scheme. The hybrid approach could be useful in general-purpose software environments, and deserves further exploration.

Currently specifications of hash-based signature schemes do not allow reserve parameters to be set. Since the reserve operation is not scheme-dependent, it can be specified generically. To offer an optimal granularity of reserve parameter choices for end users, feedback from stakeholders on this matter would be beneficial. Since hash-based signature schemes normally already require a large number of parameters to be set, additional complexity may impede usability.

While the statefulness of hash-based signature schemes must be carefully managed, it can be seen that a number of trade-offs are available to accelerate state synchronization if need be. This flexibility underscores the need to select parameters according to use case constraints, instead of always simply opting for maximal speed. We consider a detailed analysis of use case requirements for widespread security protocols relying on digital signatures as the next step in this direction. This study of use case requirements would pave the way for the standardization of state management strategies for typical applications.

References

1. Bernstein, D.J., Hopwood, D., Hülsing, A., Lange, T., Niederhagen, R., Papachristodoulou, L., Schneider, M., Schwabe, P., Wilcox-O'Hearn, Z.: SPHINCS: practical stateless hash-based signatures. In: Oswald, E., Fischlin, M. (eds.) EUROCRYPT 2015. LNCS, vol. 9056, pp. 368–397. Springer, Heidelberg (2015). doi:10.1007/978-3-662-46800-5_15

2. Buchmann, J., Dahmen, E., Hülsing, A.: XMSS - a practical forward secure signature scheme based on minimal security assumptions. In: Yang, B.-Y. (ed.) PQCrypto 2011. LNCS, vol. 7071, pp. 117–129. Springer, Heidelberg (2011). doi:10.1007/978-3-642-25405-5_8
3. Buchmann, J., Dahmen, E., Klintsevich, E., Okeya, K., Vuillaume, C.: Merkle signatures with virtually unlimited signature capacity. In: Katz, J., Yung, M. (eds.) ACNS 2007. LNCS, vol. 4521, pp. 31–45. Springer, Heidelberg (2007). doi:10.1007/978-3-540-72738-5_3
4. Buchmann, J., Dahmen, E., Schneider, M.: Merkle tree traversal revisited. In: Buchmann, J., Ding, J. (eds.) PQCrypto 2008. LNCS, vol. 5299, pp. 63–78. Springer, Heidelberg (2008). doi:10.1007/978-3-540-88403-3_5
5. Buchmann, J., García, L.C.C., Dahmen, E., Döring, M., Klintsevich, E.: CMSS – an improved Merkle signature scheme. In: Barua, R., Lange, T. (eds.) INDOCRYPT 2006. LNCS, vol. 4329, pp. 349–363. Springer, Heidelberg (2006). doi:10.1007/11941378_25
6. Chen, L., Jordan, S., Liu, Y.K., Moody, D., Peralta, R., Perlner, R., Smith-Tone, D.: Report on Post-quantum cryptography (NISTIR 8105 Draft) (2016). http://csrc.nist.gov/publications/drafts/nistir-8105/nistir_8105_draft.pdf. Accessed 06 June 2016
7. Dods, C., Smart, N.P., Stam, M.: Hash based digital signature schemes. In: Smart, N.P. (ed.) Cryptography and Coding 2005. LNCS, vol. 3796, pp. 96–115. Springer, Heidelberg (2005). doi:10.1007/11586821_8
8. ElGamal, T.: A public key cryptosystem and a signature scheme based on discrete logarithms. In: Blakley, G.R., Chaum, D. (eds.) CRYPTO 1984. LNCS, vol. 196, pp. 10–18. Springer, Heidelberg (1985). doi:10.1007/3-540-39568-7_2
9. ETSI: White paper no. 8: quantum safe cryptography and security. an introduction, benefits, enablers and challenges (2015). http://www.etsi.org/images/files/ETSIWhitePapers/QuantumSafeWhitepaper.pdf. Accessed 06 June 2016
10. Everspaugh, A.C., Bose, B.: Virtual Machine Reset-Atomicity in Xen. Technical report, University of Wisconsin-Madison (2013). http://pages.cs.wisc.edu/~ace/reset-atomic/reset-paper.pdf. Accessed 06 June 2016
11. Garfinkel, T., Rosenblum, M.: When virtual is harder than real: security challenges in virtual machine based computing environments. In: Proceedings of HotOS 2005: 10th Workshop on Hot Topics in Operating Systems. USENIX Association (2005)
12. Goldreich, O.: Foundations of Cryptography. Basic Applications, vol. 2. Cambridge University Press, Cambridge (2004)
13. Hülsing, A.: W-OTS+ – shorter signatures for hash-based signature schemes. In: Youssef, A., Nitaj, A., Hassanien, A.E. (eds.) AFRICACRYPT 2013. LNCS, vol. 7918, pp. 173–188. Springer, Heidelberg (2013). doi:10.1007/978-3-642-38553-7_10
14. Hülsing, A., Butin, D., Gazdag, S., Mohaisen, A.: XMSS: Extended hash-based signatures (2016). https://datatracker.ietf.org/doc/draft-irtf-cfrg-xmss-hash-based-signatures/. Internet-Draft. Accessed 06 June 2016
15. Hülsing, A., Rausch, L., Buchmann, J.: Optimal parameters for $XMSS^{MT}$. In: Cuzzocrea, A., Kittl, C., Simos, D.E., Weippl, E., Xu, L. (eds.) CD-ARES 2013. LNCS, vol. 8128, pp. 194–208. Springer, Heidelberg (2013). doi:10.1007/978-3-642-40588-4_14
16. Information assurance directorate at the National Security Agency: commercial national security algorithm suite (2015). https://www.iad.gov/iad/programs/iad-initiatives/cnsa-suite.cfm. Accessed 06 June 2016
17. Johnson, D., Menezes, A., Vanstone, S.: The elliptic curve digital signature algorithm (ECDSA). Int. J. Inf. Secur. 1(1), 36–63 (2001)

18. Knecht, M., Meier, W., Nicola, C.U.: A space- and time-efficient implementation of the Merkle tree traversal algorithm. CoRR abs/1409.4081 (2014)
19. Lamport, L.: Constructing digital signatures from a one way function. Technical report, SRI International Computer Science Laboratory (1979). http:// research.microsoft.com/en-us/um/people/lamport/pubs/dig-sig.pdf. Accessed 06 June 2016
20. Leighton, T., Micali, S.: Large provably fast and secure digital signature schemes from secure hash functions. U.S. Patent 5,432,852 (1995)
21. McGrew, D., Curcio, M.: Hash-based signatures (2016). https://datatracker.ietf. org/doc/draft-mcgrew-hash-sigs/. Internet-Draft. Accessed 06 June 2016
22. Merkle, R.C.: A certified digital signature. In: Brassard, G. (ed.) CRYPTO 1989. LNCS, vol. 435, pp. 218–238. Springer, Heidelberg (1990). doi:10.1007/ 0-387-34805-0_21
23. Monz, T., Nigg, D., Martinez, E.A., Brandl, M.F., Schindler, P., Rines, R., Wang, S.X., Chuang, I.L., Blatt, R.: Realization of a scalable Shor algorithm. Science 351(6277), 1068–1070 (2016)
24. Reyzin, L., Reyzin, N.: Better than BiBa: short one-time signatures with fast signing and verifying. In: Batten, L., Seberry, J. (eds.) ACISP 2002. LNCS, vol. 2384, pp. 144–153. Springer, Heidelberg (2002). doi:10.1007/3-540-45450-0_11
25. Ristenpart, T., Yilek, S.: When good randomness goes bad: virtual machine reset vulnerabilities and hedging deployed cryptography. In: Proceedings of the Network and Distributed System Security Symposium (NDSS). The Internet Society (2010)
26. Rivest, R., Shamir, A., Adleman, L.: A method for obtaining digital signatures and public-key cryptosystems. Commun. ACM 21, 120–126 (1978)
27. Saeedi, K., Simmons, S., Salvail, J.Z., Dluhy, P., Riemann, H., Abrosimov, N.V., Becker, P., Pohl, H.J., Morton, J.J.L., Thewalt, M.L.W.: Room-temperature quantum bit storage exceeding 39 min using ionized donors in silicon-28. Science 342(6160), 830–833 (2013)
28. Shor, P.W.: Polynomial-time algorithms for prime factorization and discrete logarithms on a quantum computer. SIAM J. Comput. 26(5), 1484–1509 (1997)

Analysis of a Proposed Hash-Based Signature Standard

Jonathan Katz[✉]

Department of Computer Science, University of Maryland, College Park, USA
jkatz@cs.umd.edu

Abstract. We analyze the concrete security of a hash-based signature scheme described in a recent series of Internet Drafts by McGrew and Curcio. We show that an original version of their proposal achieves only a "loose" security bound, but that the latest version can be proven to have tighter security in the random-oracle model.

1 Introduction

There has been growing interest in standardizing "post-quantum" public-key cryptosystems, i.e., schemes that are not based on the hardness of factoring or computing discrete logarithms, but are instead based on other problems that are not known (or believed) to be solvable in polynomial time by a quantum computer. In the context of digital signatures, where it is known that one-way functions suffice to construct secure schemes [7,11–14] (see [5]), a number of proposals based on cryptographic hash functions have been suggested recently for standardization [1,4,10].

We analyze the security of a signature scheme described in two successive versions of an Internet Draft by McGrew and Curcio [9,10]. Both versions of their proposal construct a (stateful, many-time) signature scheme by instantiating Merkle's tree-based approach [11,12] with an underlying one-time signature scheme based on work of Lamport, Diffie, Winternitz, and Merkle [7,11,12]. We provide a *concrete-security analysis* of their proposals in the *multi-user setting* [3,6], where we explicitly model an adversary who simultaneously attacks multiple users running independent instances of the scheme, and who succeeds if it is able to forge a signature with respect to any one of those users.[1] In the

---

Work performed under a consultancy agreement with University Technical Services, Inc. on behalf of the National Security Agency. Portions of this work were also supported by a gift from the Cisco University Research Program Fund, a corporate advised fund of Silicon Valley Community Foundation.

[1] It is easy to see that if no attack (subject to some time bound T) targeting a single user can succeed with probability better than ϵ, then no attack (subject to roughly the same time bound) can succeed in attacking one out of N independent users of that scheme with probability better than $N \cdot \epsilon$. But we are interested in settings where N is large and we do not want to lose the factor of N in the security bound.

L. Chen et al. (Eds.): SSR 2016, LNCS 10074, pp. 261–273, 2016.
DOI: 10.1007/978-3-319-49100-4_12

context of the McGrew-Curcio drafts, a single instance of the tree-based (many-time) signature scheme is itself composed of multiple instances of an underlying one-time signature scheme, and so obtaining a tight security reduction for the many-time signature scheme—*even in the single-user setting*—inherently requires tight security for the underlying one-time signature scheme in the *multi-user setting*.

As noted above, we study two versions of the McGrew-Curcio draft. We show that the many-time signature scheme in version 02 of their proposal [9] does not have a tight security reduction (even in the single-user setting), because the underlying one-time signature scheme used is not tightly secure in the multi-user setting. Fortunately, we show that the many-time signature scheme in version 04 of their proposal [10], which incorporates modifications first suggested by Leighton and Micali [8], *is* tightly secure—even in the multi-user setting—if the underlying hash function is modeled as a random oracle.

Note that we restrict ourselves to an analysis of the one-time signature scheme and the many-time signature scheme described in Sects. 4, 5 of the McGrew-Curcio draft, respectively. We leave an analysis of their hierarchical signature scheme (proposed in Sect. 6 of their draft) for future work.

1.1 Organization of the Paper

As explained above, both versions of the McGrew-Curcio proposal construct a (stateful, many-time) tree-based signature scheme based on an underlying one-time signature scheme. In both cases, concrete security of the tree-based scheme—even in the single-user setting—depends on the concrete security of the underlying one-time signature scheme in the multi-user setting.

In Sect. 2, we look at the one-time signature scheme used in version 02 of the McGrew-Curcio draft [9]. After describing the scheme, we show that it is *not* tightly secure in the multi-user setting. This implies that the tree-based signature scheme of that draft is not tightly secure, even in the single-user setting.

We look at the most recent version of the McGrew-Curcio draft (version 04) in Sect. 3. We begin by focusing on the underlying one-time signature scheme used there, showing that it *does* have a tight security reduction in the multi-user setting if the hash functions used are modeled as random oracles. Building on this analysis, we then study the tree-based scheme proposed in that version of their draft, proving that it is tightly secure in the multi-user setting as well.

1.2 Related Work

There are several other works proposing candidate tree-based signature schemes, and analyzing their (concrete) security based on various assumptions about the underlying hash function(s) [1,2,4]. It is not the goal of this work to propose a new scheme, or to weigh the pros and cons of the various competing proposals; our aim is simply to provide a concrete analysis of the tree-based scheme described in the McGrew-Curcio draft.

2   Version 02 of the McGrew-Curcio Draft

As noted earlier, we focus in this section on the one-time signature scheme from version 02 of the McGrew-Curcio draft, and show that it does not have tight security in the multi-user setting. Because of the way the many-time signature scheme in version 02 of their draft is constructed from the one-time signature scheme, our result implies that their many-time scheme does not have a tight security proof even in the single-user setting.

2.1   Description of the One-Time Signature Scheme

We begin by describing the one-time signature scheme, called the *LDWM scheme*, contained in version 02 of the internet draft by McGrew and Curcio [9]. Let $H : \{0,1\}^* \rightarrow \{0,1\}^{8n}$ and $F : \{0,1\}^{8m} \rightarrow \{0,1\}^{8m}$ be cryptographic hash functions. Let F^i, for integer $i \geq 1$, denote i-fold iterated application of F, and let F^0 denote the identity function. Fix $w \in \{1,2,4,8\}$ as a parameter of the scheme, and set $e \overset{\text{def}}{=} 2^w - 1$. Set $u \overset{\text{def}}{=} 8n/w$; note that outputs of H can be viewed as a sequence of u integers, each exactly w bits long. Set $v \overset{\text{def}}{=} \lceil \lfloor \log u \cdot (2^w - 1) + 1 \rfloor / w \rceil$, and define a function $\mathsf{checksum} : (\{0,1\}^w)^u \rightarrow \{0,1\}^{wv}$ as follows:

$$\mathsf{checksum}(h_0, \ldots, h_{u-1}) \overset{\text{def}}{=} \sum_{i=0}^{u-1} (2^w - 1 - h_i),$$

where each $h_i \in \{0,1\}^w$ is viewed as an integer in the range $\{0, \ldots, 2^w - 1\}$ and the result is written as an integer using exactly wv bits. Set $p \overset{\text{def}}{=} u + v$.

Define a one-time signature scheme as follows:

Key generation

1. Choose p uniform values $x_0, \ldots, x_{p-1} \in \{0,1\}^{8m}$.
2. For $i = 0$ to $p - 1$, compute $y_i := F^e(x_i)$.
3. Compute $pk := H(y_0, \ldots, y_{p-1})$.

The public key is pk, and the private key is $x_0, \ldots, x_{p-1}$.

Signing

To sign a message $M \in \{0,1\}^*$ using private key $x_0, \ldots, x_{p-1}$ do:

1. Compute $h := H(M)$ and $c := \mathsf{checksum}(h)$. Set $V := h\|c$, and parse V as a sequence of w-bit integers $V_0, \ldots, V_{p-1}$.
2. For $i = 0, \ldots, p - 1$, compute $\sigma_i := F^{V_i}(x_i)$.
3. Return the signature $\sigma_0, \ldots, \sigma_{p-1}$.

Verifying

To verify a signature $\sigma_0, \ldots, \sigma_{p-1}$ on a message $M \in \{0,1\}^*$ with respect to the public key pk do:

1. Compute $h := H(M)$ and $c := \mathsf{checksum}(h)$. Set $V := h\|c$, and parse V as a sequence of w-bit integers $V_0, \ldots, V_{p-1}$.

2. For $i = 0, \ldots, p - 1$, compute $y_i := F^{e-V_i}(\sigma_i)$.
3. Return 1 if and only if $pk = H(y_0, \ldots, y_{p-1})$.

2.2 Security Analysis

We are interested in understanding the concrete security of the one-time signature scheme described above, as a function of the total number q of H- and F-evaluations performed by an attacker. (Thus, we will effectively be treating H and F as independent random oracles.) We sketch two approaches that may be used to attempt a signature forgery in the multi-user setting. In each case, for simplicity, we assume all signers use the same value for w.

First approach. Assume N instances of the LDWM scheme are run, either by the same signer or by multiple signers. Recall that the ith public key pk^i has the form

$$pk^i = H(y_0^i, \ldots, y_{p-1}^i).$$

Consider computing the Q values $y_0^* := F^e(x_0^*), \ldots, y_{Q-1}^* := F^e(x_{Q-1}^*)$, for distinct x_i^*, and evaluating H on all (ordered) length-p lists of the y_i^*. (There are $q \stackrel{\text{def}}{=} Q!/(Q - p)!$ such lists. Note that $eQ \ll q$ for practical settings of the parameters, so the overall work is dominated by the q evaluations of H.) If any of the resulting hashes is equal to some pk^i, then it becomes trivial to forge arbitrary signatures with respect to that public key. The probability that this occurs is roughly $qN \cdot 2^{-8n}$.

Second approach. A similar issue as above arises because F is used in all instances of the scheme. As above, let pk^i (for $1 \le i \le N$) denote the ith public key, and assume a signature with respect to each public key has been released so that, in particular, values $y_0^i, \ldots, y_{p-1}^i$ with $pk^i = H(y_0^i, \ldots, y_{p-1}^i)$ are known for all i. Consider evaluating F^e on q/e random inputs, looking for an input x such that $F^e(x) = y_j^i$ for some i, j. If such an x is found, a forgery becomes possible with high probability.[2] The probability that such an x is found is roughly $(q/e) \cdot pN \cdot 2^{-8m}$. (Small variants of this approach, having slightly better parameters, are also possible.)

We thus see that in the multi-user setting, security of the LDWM scheme can be no better than $O(qN \cdot (2^{-8n} + 2^{-8m}))$, and so in particular degrades linearly in the number of users N.

3   Version 04 of the McGrew-Curcio Draft

In analyzing the most recent version of the McGrew-Curcio proposal, we begin by showing that their underlying one-time signature scheme has tight security in the multi-user setting. We then build on this to prove tight security for the (tree-based, stateful, many-time) signature scheme they propose.

---

[2] A precise calculation depends on the messages that have already been signed.

3.1 Description of the LM-OTS Scheme

We begin with a description of the *LM-OTS scheme* [10], the underlying one-time signature scheme used. Let $H : \{0,1\}^* \rightarrow \{0,1\}^{8n}$ be a cryptographic hash function. Fix $w \in \{1,2,4,8\}$ as a parameter of the scheme, and set $e \stackrel{\text{def}}{=} 2^w - 1$. Set $u \stackrel{\text{def}}{=} 8n/w$; note that the output of H can be viewed as a sequence of u integers, each w bits long. Set $v \stackrel{\text{def}}{=} \lceil \lfloor \log u \cdot (2^w - 1) + 1 \rfloor / w \rceil$, and $p \stackrel{\text{def}}{=} u + v$. Define a function checksum : $(\{0,1\}^w)^u \rightarrow \{0,1\}^{wv}$ as follows:

$$\text{checksum}(h_0, \ldots, h_{u-1}) \stackrel{\text{def}}{=} \sum_{i=0}^{u-1} (2^w - 1 - h_i),$$

where each $h_i \in \{0,1\}^w$ is viewed as an integer in the range $\{0, \ldots, 2^w - 1\}$ and the result is expressed as an integer using exactly wv bits.[3] For integers i, b with $0 \leq i < 2^{8b}$, we let $[i]_b$ denote the b-byte representation of i. For a string s and integer $j \geq 0$, set $H_s^0(x; j) \stackrel{\text{def}}{=} x$. For integers $k \geq 1, j \geq 0$, define

$$H_s^k(x; j) \stackrel{\text{def}}{=} H\left(H_s^{k-1}(x; j), s, [j + k - 1]_1, \text{0x00}\right).$$

The LM-OTS scheme is defined as follows:

Key-generation algorithm Gen

Key generation takes as input id $= (I, q)$, where I is a 31-byte *identifier* and q is a 4-byte *diversification factor*.[4] The steps of the algorithm are:

1. Choose p uniform values $x_0, \ldots, x_{p-1} \in \{0,1\}^{8n}$.
2. For $i = 0$ to $p - 1$, compute $y_i := H_{\text{id},[i]_2}^e(x_i; 0)$.
3. Compute $pk := H(\text{id}, y_0, \ldots, y_{p-1}, \text{0x01})$.

The public key is pk, and the private key is $sk = (x_0, \ldots, x_{p-1})$.

Signing algorithm Sign

Signing takes as input a private key $sk = (x_0, \ldots, x_{p-1})$ and message $M \in \{0,1\}^*$ as usual, as well as id $= (I, q)$ as above. It does:

1. Choose uniform $C \in \{0,1\}^{8n}$.
2. Compute $Q := H(M, C, \text{id}, \text{0x02})$ and $c := \text{checksum}(Q)$. Set $V := Q \| c$, and parse V as a sequence of w-bit integers $V_0, \ldots, V_{p-1}$.
3. For $i = 0, \ldots, p - 1$, compute $\sigma_i := H_{\text{id},[i]_2}^{V_i}(x_i; 0)$.
4. Return the signature $\sigma = (C, q, \sigma_0, \ldots, \sigma_{p-1})$.

Verification algorithm Vrfy

Verification takes as input a message $M \in \{0,1\}^*$ and a signature $(C, q, \sigma_0, \ldots, \sigma_{p-1})$ as usual, as well as I as above. It sets id $:= (I, q)$ and does:

---

[3] In [10] the result is expressed as a 16-bit integer, but only the top wv bits are used.
[4] The purpose of I and q will become clear later, when we describe the many-time scheme based on LM-OTS.

1. Compute $Q := H(M, C, \mathsf{id}, \mathsf{0x02})$ and $c := \mathsf{checksum}(Q)$. Set $V := Q \| c$, and parse V as a sequence of w-bit integers $V_0, \ldots, V_{p-1}$.
2. For $i = 0, \ldots, p - 1$, compute $y_i := H^{e-V_i}_{\mathsf{id}, [i]_2}(\sigma_i; V_i)$.
3. Output $H(\mathsf{id}, y_0, \ldots, y_{p-1}, \mathsf{0x01})$.

We note that, in contrast to the usual convention, Vrfy outputs a string rather than a bit and does not take a public key as input. A signature σ on some message M is valid relative to some fixed public key pk if the output of Vrfy is equal to pk. One can verify that correctness holds in the following sense: for any I, q, any (pk, sk) output by $\mathsf{Gen}(I, q)$, and any message M, we have

$$\mathsf{Vrfy}(M, \mathsf{Sign}(sk, M, I, q), I) = pk.$$

3.2   Security of the LM-OTS Scheme

We adapt the standard notion of security for one-time signature schemes (see [5]) to the multi-user setting, where multiple (independent) instances of the scheme are run and the attacker is considered successful if it generates a signature forgery with respect to any of those instances. We also explicitly handle the values I, q used as additional input to the various algorithms of the scheme.

  If values $\mathsf{id} = (I, q)$ are used for key generation in some instance of the scheme, we refer to id as the *identifier* for that instance. Let N be an upper bound on the number of instances overall. We assume[5] some fixed set $\{\mathsf{id}^i = (I^i, q^i)\}_{i=1}^N$ of identifiers, where $\mathsf{id}^i \neq \mathsf{id}^j$ for $i \neq j$.

  We are interested in bounding the attacker's success probability in the following experiment. (We explicitly incorporate choice of the random oracle H into the experiment.)

1. A random function $H : \{0, 1\}^* \rightarrow \{0, 1\}^{8n}$ is chosen.
2. For $i = 1, \ldots, N$, the key-generation algorithm is run using identifier id^i to obtain (pk^i, sk^i). The attacker is given $(\mathsf{id}^1, pk^1), \ldots, (\mathsf{id}^N, pk^N)$.
3. The attacker is given oracle access to H, plus a signing oracle $\mathsf{Sign}(\cdot, \cdot)$ such that $\mathsf{Sign}(i, M)$ returns $\mathsf{Sign}(sk^i, M, \mathsf{id}^i)$. For each i, the attacker may make at most one query $\mathsf{Sign}(i, \star)$. Without loss of generality we assume the attacker makes exactly one signing query $\mathsf{Sign}(i, M^i)$ for each value of i. We also assume that when the attacker is given a signature, it is additionally given the answers to all the H-queries needed to verify that signature.
3. The attacker outputs (i, M, σ) with $M \neq M^i$. The attacker succeeds if σ is a valid signature on M for the ith instance, i.e., if $\mathsf{Vrfy}(M, \sigma, I^i) = pk^i$. Without loss of generality we assume the attacker has previously made (or has been given the answers to) all the H-queries needed to run the verification algorithm on these inputs.

---

[5] These identifiers could be chosen adaptively by the attacker (subject to being distinct) without any significant change to the proof in the following section, but for simplicity we treat them as fixed in advance. When LM-OTS is subsequently used in the many-time signature scheme, the identifiers will be fixed in advance.

Instantiating the security experiment above with the algorithms of the LM-OTS scheme, and performing some syntactic changes that do not change the probability space, we obtain the following experiment (we use $\|$ for string concatenation when using commas would cause confusion):

1. Initialize an empty set H. (H will contain defined query/answer pairs for the function H. That is, if $(x, y) \in H$ then $H(x) = y$.)
2. For $i = 1, \dots, N$, do:
   (a) For $j = 0, \dots, p - 1$, choose uniform $x_{j,0}^i \in \{0, 1\}^{8n}$.
   (b) For $j = 0, \dots, p - 1$ and $k = 0, \dots, e - 1$, choose uniform $x_{j,k+1}^i \in \{0, 1\}^{8n}$ and add $\left(x_{j,k}^i \parallel \mathsf{id}^i \parallel [j]_2 \parallel [k]_1 \parallel \mathsf{0x00},\ x_{j,k+1}^i \right)$ to H. Define $y_j^i := x_{j,e}^i$.
   (c) Choose uniform $pk^i \in \{0, 1\}^{8n}$. Add $(\mathsf{id}^i \| y_0^i \| \cdots \| y_{p-1}^i \| \mathsf{0x01},\ pk^i)$ to H.
   (d) Choose uniform $C^i \in \{0, 1\}^{8n}$ and $Q^i \in \{0, 1\}^{8n}$.
   (e) Give (id^i, pk^i) to the attacker.
3. When the attacker makes a query $H(x)$, answer it as follows:
   (a) If there is an entry $(x, y) \in H$ for some y, then return y.
   (b) Otherwise, choose uniform $y \in \{0, 1\}^{8n}$, return y to the attacker, and store (x, y) in H.
4. When the attacker makes a query $\mathsf{Sign}(i, M^i)$, answer it as follows:
   (a) If there is an entry $(M^i \| C^i \| \mathsf{id}^i \| \mathsf{0x02},\ Q) \in H$ for some Q, then redefine $Q^i := Q$. Store $(M^i \| C^i \| \mathsf{id}^i \| \mathsf{0x02},\ Q^i)$ in H.
   (b) Let $c^i := \mathsf{checksum}(Q^i)$, and set $V^i := Q^i \| c^i$. Parse V^i as a sequence of w-bit integers $V_0^i, \dots, V_{p-1}^i$.
   (c) Return the signature $(C^i, x_{0, V_0^i}^i, \dots, x_{p-1, V_{p-1}^i}^i)$.
5. The attacker outputs (i, M, σ) with $M \neq M^i$. The attacker succeeds if $\mathsf{Vrfy}(M, \sigma, I^i) = pk^i$.

Note we assume that all instances of the scheme use the same value e; however, one can check that the proof can be suitably modified if this is not the case.

We define the following events in the above experiment:

- $\mathsf{Coll}_{1,i}$ is the event that the attacker queries $H(I^i, q, y_0, \dots, y_{p-1}, \mathsf{0x01})$ with $(q, y_0, \dots, y_{p-1}) \neq (q^i, y_0^i, \dots, y_{p-1}^i)$, and receives the response pk^i.
- $\mathsf{Coll}_{2,i}$ is the event the attacker queries $H(\star, C^i, \mathsf{id}^i, \mathsf{0x02})$ before making the query $\mathsf{Sign}(i, \star)$.
- $\mathsf{Coll}_{2,i}^*$ is the event that either $\mathsf{Coll}_{2,i}$ occurs, or either of the following occur: (1) before making the query $\mathsf{Sign}(i, \star)$, the attacker queries $H(\star, \star, \mathsf{id}^i, \mathsf{0x02})$ and receives the response Q^i, or (2) after making the query $\mathsf{Sign}(i, M^i)$, the attacker queries $H(M, \star, \mathsf{id}^i, \mathsf{0x02})$ with $M \neq M^i$, and receives the response Q^i.
- $\mathsf{Coll}_{3,i,j,k}$ is the event that the attacker queries $H(x_{j,k}^i, \mathsf{id}^i, [j]_2, [k]_1, \mathsf{0x00})$ either before making the query $\mathsf{Sign}(i, \star)$, or after making the query $\mathsf{Sign}(i, \star)$ but with $k < V_j^i$.
- $\mathsf{Coll}_{3,i,j,k}^*$ is the event that either $\mathsf{Coll}_{3,i,j,k}$ occurs, or that the attacker queries $H(x, \mathsf{id}^i, [j]_2, [k]_1, \mathsf{0x00})$ with $x \neq x_{j,k}^i$, and receives the response $x_{j,k+1}^i$.

We first observe that the probability of forgery can be upper-bounded by the probability that one of the above events occurs.

Lemma 1. *If the attacker succeeds, then either* $\mathsf{Coll}_{1,i}$ *or* $\mathsf{Coll}_{2,i}^*$ *occur for some* $i \in \{1, \ldots, N\}$, *or else* $\mathsf{Coll}_{i,j,k}^*$ *occurs for some* $i \in \{1, \ldots, N\}, j \in \{0, \ldots, p-1\}$, *and* $k \in \{0, \ldots, e-1\}$.

Proof. Say the attacker outputs (i, M, σ) with $M \neq M^i$ and σ a valid signature on M with respect to I^i, pk^i. By assumption, all the H-queries needed to verify σ on M with respect to I^i, pk^i are defined when the attacker outputs (i, M, σ). Parse σ as $(C, q, \sigma_0, \ldots, \sigma_{p-1})$ and set $\mathsf{id} = (I^i, q)$. Define $Q = H(M, C, \mathsf{id}, 0\mathsf{x}02)$ and $c = \mathsf{checksum}(Q)$, and let $V_0, \ldots, V_{p-1} = Q\|c$ and $y_j = H_{\mathsf{id}, [j]_2}^{e-V_j}(\sigma_j; V_j)$ be the values computed by running the verification algorithm on M, σ, and I^i. Since the attacker succeeds, $H(\mathsf{id}, y_0, \ldots, y_{p-1}, 0\mathsf{x}01) = pk^i$.

We show that if $\mathsf{Coll}_{1,i}$ and $\mathsf{Coll}_{2,i}^*$ have not occurred (where i is the instance of the attacker's forgery), then $\mathsf{Coll}_{i,j,k}^*$ must have occurred for some j, k. If $\mathsf{Coll}_{1,i}$ has not occurred, we must have $(q, y_0, \ldots, y_{p-1}) = (q^i, y_0^i, \ldots, y_{p-1}^i)$ and so $\mathsf{id} = \mathsf{id}^i$. If $\mathsf{Coll}_{2,i}^*$ (and hence $\mathsf{Coll}_{2,i}$) has not occurred, the value of Q^i was not changed in step 4(a) of the experiment, and $Q \neq Q^i$. By construction of $\mathsf{checksum}$, we must therefore have $V_j < V_j^i$ for some j. But then one can verify by inspection that $\mathsf{Coll}_{3,i,j,k}^*$ must have occurred for some k.

Thus, to bound the success probability of the attacker it suffices to bound the probabilities of the above events.

Lemma 2. *For all* i, $\Pr[\mathsf{Coll}_{1,i}] \leq q_{1,i} \cdot 2^{-8n}$, *where* $q_{1,i}$ *is the number of H-queries of the form* $H(I^i, \star, \star, \ldots, \star, 0\mathsf{x}01)$.

Proof. Any H-query $H(I^i, q, y_0, \ldots, y_{p-1}, 0\mathsf{x}01)$ for which $(q, y_0, \ldots, y_{p-1}) \neq (q^i, y_0^i, \ldots, y_{p-1}^i)$ returns a uniform value in $\{0, 1\}^{8n}$ that is independent of pk^i. The lemma follows.

Lemma 3. *For all* i, $\Pr[\mathsf{Coll}_{2,i}] \leq q_{2,i} \cdot 2^{-8n}$, *where* $q_{2,i}$ *is the number of H-queries of the form* $H(\star, \star, \mathsf{id}^i, 0\mathsf{x}02)$.

Proof. C^i is a uniform $8n$-bit string, and the attacker has no information about C^i until it queries $\mathsf{Sign}(i, \star)$. The lemma follows.

Lemma 4. *For all* i, $\Pr[\mathsf{Coll}_{2,i}^*] \leq 2q_{2,i} \cdot 2^{-8n}$, *where* $q_{2,i}$ *is as in the previous lemma.*

Proof. We have $\Pr[\mathsf{Coll}_{2,i}^*] \leq \Pr[\mathsf{Coll}_{2,i}] + \Pr[\mathsf{Coll}_{2,i}^* \mid \neg \mathsf{Coll}_{2,i}]$. The previous lemma provides an upper bound on the first term. As for the second term, when $\mathsf{Coll}_{2,i}$ does not occur, the value of Q^i does not change in step 4(a) of the experiment. Each time the attacker queries $H(\star, \star, \mathsf{id}^i, 0\mathsf{x}02)$ before making the query $\mathsf{Sign}(i, \star)$, or queries $H(M, \star, \mathsf{id}^i, 0\mathsf{x}02)$ with $M \neq M^i$ after the query $\mathsf{Sign}(i, M^i)$, the value returned is uniform in $\{0, 1\}^{8n}$ and independent of Q^i.

Lemma 5. *For all* i, j, k,

$$\Pr\left[\mathsf{Coll}_{3,i,j,k} \mid \bigwedge_{\ell=0}^{k-1} \neg\mathsf{Coll}^*_{3,i,j,\ell}\right] \leq \frac{q_{3,i,j,k}}{2^{8n} - q_{3,i,j,k-1}},$$

where $q_{3,i,j,k}$ *for* $k \geq 0$ *is the number of the attacker's* H-*queries of the form* $H(\star, \mathrm{id}^i, [j]_2, [k]_1, \mathtt{0x00})$, *and* $q_{3,i,j,-1} \stackrel{\mathrm{def}}{=} 0$.

Proof. As long as $\mathsf{Coll}^*_{3,i,j,k-1}$ has not occurred, the attacker's information about the uniform value $x^i_{j,k}$ (assuming $k < V^i_j$ in case the attacker has already made the query $\mathsf{Sign}(i, M^i)$) is limited to the fact that $x^i_{j,k}$ was not the result of one of the attacker's previous queries of the form $H(\star, \mathrm{id}^i, [j]_2, [k-1]_1, \mathtt{0x00})$. The lemma follows.

Lemma 6. *For all* i, j, k,

$$\Pr\left[\mathsf{Coll}^*_{3,i,j,k} \mid \bigwedge_{\ell=0}^{k-1} \neg\mathsf{Coll}^*_{3,i,j,\ell}\right] \leq \frac{q_{3,i,j,k}}{2^{8n} - q_{3,i,j,k-1}} + \frac{q_{3,i,j,k}}{2^{8n}},$$

where $q_{3,i,j,k}$ *is as in the previous lemma.*

Proof. We have

$$\Pr\left[\mathsf{Coll}^*_{3,i,j,k} \mid \bigwedge_{\ell=0}^{k-1} \neg\mathsf{Coll}^*_{3,i,j,\ell}\right]$$
$$\leq \Pr\left[\mathsf{Coll}_{3,i,j,k} \mid \bigwedge_{\ell=0}^{k-1} \neg\mathsf{Coll}^*_{3,i,j,\ell}\right]$$
$$+ \Pr\left[\mathsf{Coll}^*_{3,i,j,k} \mid \bigwedge_{\ell=0}^{k-1} \neg\mathsf{Coll}^*_{3,i,j,\ell} \bigwedge \neg\mathsf{Coll}_{3,i,j,k}\right].$$

The previous lemma provides an upper bound on the first term. As for the second term, note that when $\mathsf{Coll}_{3,i,j,k}$ does not occur then whenever the attacker queries $H(\star, \mathrm{id}^i, [j]_2, [k]_1, \mathtt{0x00})$, the value returned is uniform in $\{0,1\}^{8n}$ and independent of $x^i_{j,k+1}$. The lemma follows.

Lemma 7. *For all* i, j, $\Pr\left[\bigvee_{k=0}^{e-1} \mathsf{Coll}^*_{3,i,j,k}\right] \leq 3 \cdot \sum_{k=0}^{e-1} q_{3,i,j,k} \cdot 2^{-8n}$, *where* $q_{3,i,j,k}$ *is as in the previous lemma.*

Proof. Let $q^* \stackrel{\mathrm{def}}{=} \sum_{k=0}^{e-1} q_{3,i,j,k}$, and note that the lemma is trivially true when $q^* \geq 2^{8n}/2$. Otherwise, we have

$$\Pr\left[\bigvee_{k=0}^{e-1} \mathsf{Coll}^*_{3,i,j,k}\right] \leq \sum_{k=0}^{e-1} \Pr\left[\mathsf{Coll}^*_{3,i,j,k} \mid \bigwedge_{\ell=0}^{k-1} \neg\mathsf{Coll}^*_{3,i,j,\ell}\right]$$
$$\leq \sum_{k=0}^{e-1} \frac{q_{3,i,j,k}}{2^{8n} - q_{3,i,j,k-1}} + \sum_{k=0}^{e-1} q_{3,i,j,k} \cdot 2^{-8n},$$

using the previous lemma. Since $q_{3,i,j,k-1} \leq q^*$, when $q^* < 2^{8n}/2$ each term in the first summation is upper-bounded by $2q_{3,i,j,k} \cdot 2^{-8n}$. This proves the lemma.

Putting everything together, we have:

Theorem 1. *For any adversary attacking any number of instances of the LM-OTS scheme and making at most q hash queries of the form $H(\star, \ldots, \star, n)$ with $n \in \{0x00, 0x01, 0x02\}$, the probability that the adversary forges a signature with respect to any of the instances is at most $3q \cdot 2^{-8n}$.*

Proof. Let N denote the number of instances of the scheme. Using Lemma 1 and a union bound, the probability with which the adversary forges a signature is at most

$$\sum_{i=1}^{N} \Pr[\mathsf{Coll}_{1,i}] + \sum_{i=1}^{N} \Pr[\mathsf{Coll}_{2,i}^*] + \sum_{i=1}^{N} \sum_{j=0}^{p-1} \Pr\left[\bigvee_{k=1}^{e-1} \mathsf{Coll}_{3,i,j,k}^*\right].$$

Using Lemmas 2, 4 and 7, the above is at most

$$\sum_{i=1}^{N} q_{1,i} \cdot 2^{-8n} + 2 \cdot \sum_{i=1}^{N} q_{2,i} \cdot 2^{-8n} + 3 \cdot \sum_{i=1}^{N} \sum_{j=0}^{p-1} \sum_{k=0}^{e-1} q_{3,i,j,k} \cdot 2^{-8n}$$

$$\leq 3 \cdot \left(\sum_{i=1}^{N} q_{1,i} + \sum_{i=1}^{N} q_{2,i} + \sum_{i=1}^{N} \sum_{j=0}^{p-1} \sum_{k=0}^{e-1} q_{3,i,j,k}\right) \cdot 2^{-8n}.$$

Each of the adversary's H-queries of the stated form increases the value of at most one of $q_{1,i}, q_{2,i}$, or $q_{3,i,j,k}$ and so the sum in the parentheses is at most q. This proves the theorem. ∎

3.3   The LMS Scheme

An instance of the LMS scheme is defined by computing a Merkle tree of height h using 2^h LM-OTS public keys at the leaves. We give a formal definition now.

<u>Key-generation algorithm Gen'</u>

Key generation takes as input a 31-byte *identifier* I and a parameter h. Set $N = 2^h - 1$. The algorithm proceeds as follows:

1. For $q = 0, \ldots, N$, compute $(pk^q, sk^q) \leftarrow \mathsf{Gen}(I, q)$.
2. For $r = 2^h, \ldots, 2^{h+1} - 1$, set $T[r] := H(pk^{r-2^h}, I, [r]_4, 0x03)$.
3. For $r = 2^h - 1, \ldots, 1$, set $T[r] := H(T[2r], T[2r+1], I, [r]_4, 0x04)$.

The public key is $pk = (h, I, T[1])$, and the private key is $sk = (0, sk^0, \ldots, sk^N)$.

<u>Signing algorithm Sign'</u>

Signing takes as input a private key $(q, sk^0, \ldots, sk^N)$ and a message $M \in \{0, 1\}^*$ as usual, as well as I as above. It sets $\mathsf{id} = (I, q)$ and does:

1. Compute $\sigma := \mathsf{Sign}(sk^q, M, \mathsf{id})$.
2. Also compute $p_0, \ldots, p_{h-1}$, the siblings of the nodes on the path from leaf q to the root in the Merkle tree.
3. Return the signature $\Sigma = (\sigma, p_0, \ldots, p_{h-1})$.

After generating a signature, the value of q is incremented. (Signing is stateful.) If $q = 2^h$ the key is erased, and no more signatures can be issued.

Verification algorithm Vrfy′
Verification takes as input a public key (h, I, T), a message $M \in \{0, 1\}^*$, and a signature $\Sigma = (\sigma, p_0, \ldots, p_{h-1})$. It does:

1. Compute $pk := \mathsf{Vrfy}(M, \sigma, I)$.
2. Extract value q from σ. Compute $T[q + 2^h] := H(pk, I, [q + 2^h]_4, \mathtt{0x03})$.
3. Using $p_0, \ldots, p_{h-1}$, compute a value $T[1]$. Return 1 if and only if $T[1] = T$.

3.4 Security of the LMS Scheme

Security of the LMS scheme can be proven generically based on any one-time signature scheme and any second preimage-resistant hash function. However, since the hash function H was modeled as a random oracle in our analysis of the LM-OTS scheme, we continue to model it as a random oracle here. Note also that although the same function H is used both to compute the Merkle tree and in the underlying one-time signature scheme, the fact that domain separation is used means that we can cleanly separate these two usages.

Here, we are interested in the attacker's success probability in the following experiment:

1. A random function $H : \{0, 1\}^* \rightarrow \{0, 1\}^{8n}$ is chosen.
2. The key-generation algorithm for the LMS scheme is run using I and h to obtain (pk, sk). The attacker is given pk.
3. The attacker is given oracle access to H, plus a stateful signing oracle $\mathsf{Sign}'(\cdot)$ such that $\mathsf{Sign}'(M)$ returns $\mathsf{Sign}'(sk, M, I)$ and updates the private key.
   We assume that when the attacker is given a signature, it is additionally given the answers to all the H-queries needed to verify that signature.
4. The attacker outputs (M, Σ), where M was not previously submitted to its signing oracle. The attacker succeeds if Σ is a valid signature on M, i.e., if $\mathsf{Vrfy}'(pk, M, \Sigma) = 1$. Without loss of generality we assume the attacker has previously made (or has been given the answers to) all the H-queries needed to run the verification algorithm on these inputs.

We remark that we consider the single-user setting for simplicity, but one can verify that security does not degrade in the multi-user setting as long as each instance uses a distinct value of I.

Considering an execution of the above experiment, let $pk^0, \ldots, pk^{2^h - 1}$ be the LM-OTS public keys at the leaves, and let $T[r]$ denote the intermediate values computed during the course of key generation. Denote the components of the signature output by the attacker by $\Sigma = (\sigma, p_0, \ldots, p_{h-1})$. (We may assume Σ has this form, since otherwise the signature will surely be invalid. In particular, we may assume without loss of generality that Σ consists of a value σ in the format of an LM-OTS signature and h values $p_0, \ldots, p_{h-1}$.) Let q be the value contained in σ, and let pk be the value computed during verification of Σ on M.

Let Forge_1 be the event that attacker succeeds and $pk = pk^q$, and let Forge_2 be the event that the attacker succeeds but $pk \neq pk^q$.

We have

Lemma 8. $\Pr[\mathsf{Forge}_1] \leq 3q_1 \cdot 2^{-8n}$, where q_1 is the number of H-queries of the form $H(\star, \ldots, \star, n)$ with $n \in \{\mathtt{0x00}, \mathtt{0x01}, \mathtt{0x02}\}$.

Proof. Let $\mathcal{A}$ be an adversary attacking the LMS scheme; we construct an attacker $\mathcal{A}'$ attacking the LM-OTS scheme.

Fix some I, h, and let $\mathsf{id}^q = (I, q)$ for $q = 0, \ldots, 2^h - 1$. Attacker $\mathcal{A}'$ is given public keys $pk^0, \ldots, pk^{2^h-1}$ and does as follows:

1. Compute $T[1]$ from $pk^0, \ldots, pk^{2^h-1}$ as in algorithm Gen'. Give public key $pk = (h, I, T[1])$ to $\mathcal{A}$.
2. When $\mathcal{A}$ requests the ith signature on a message M^i (for $i = 0, \ldots, 2^h - 1$), attacker $\mathcal{A}'$ queries $\mathsf{Sign}(i, M)$ to obtain σ. It then computes $p_0, \ldots, p_{h-1}$ as in algorithm Sign', and returns the signature $(\sigma, p_0, \ldots, p_{h-1})$ to $\mathcal{A}$.
3. $\mathcal{A}'$ answers H-queries of $\mathcal{A}$ by forwarding them to its own H-oracle.
4. When $\mathcal{A}$ outputs a forgery $(M, \Sigma = (\sigma, p_0, \ldots, p_{h-1}))$, adversary $\mathcal{A}'$ extracts the value q contained in σ and outputs (q, M, σ).

Observe that $\mathcal{A}'$ succeeds if Forge_1 occurs. Moreover, although $\mathcal{A}'$ may make H-queries in addition to those made by $\mathcal{A}$ (to compute $T[1]$), all those queries are of the form $H(\star, \ldots, \star, n)$ with $n \in \{\mathtt{0x03}, \mathtt{0x04}\}$; the number of H-queries of the form $H(\star, \ldots, \star, n)$ with $n \in \{\mathtt{0x00}, \mathtt{0x01}, \mathtt{0x02}\}$ is exactly the same as the number made by $\mathcal{A}$. Theorem 1 thus implies the claim.

We turn to bounding Forge_2. For some fixed I, h, define the following events:

- Coll_r, for $r = 2^h, \ldots, 2^{h+1} - 1$, is the event that the attacker makes a query of the form $H(pk, I, [r]_4, \mathtt{0x03})$ with $pk \neq pk^{r-2^h}$ and receives the response $T[r]$.
- Coll_r, for $r = 1, \ldots, 2^h - 1$, is the event that the attacker makes a query of the form $H(T, T', I, [r]_4, \mathtt{0x04})$ with $(T, T') \neq (T[2r], T[2r+1])$ and receives the response $T[r]$.

Lemma 9. $\Pr[\mathsf{Forge}_2] \leq q' \cdot 2^{-8n}$, where q' is the number of H-queries of the form $H(\star, \ldots, \star, n)$ with $n \in \{\mathtt{0x03}, \mathtt{0x04}\}$.

Proof. If Forge_2 occurs then Coll_r occurs for some r. It is also easy to see that $\Pr[\mathsf{Coll}_r] \leq q_r \cdot 2^{-8n}$, where q_r is the number of H-queries of the form $H(\star, I, [r]_4, \star)$. Since each of the adversary's queries of the stated form increases the value of at most one q_r, the claim follows.

Theorem 2. For any adversary attacking the LMS scheme and making at most q hash queries, the probability the adversary forges a signature is at most $3q \cdot 2^{-8n}$.

Proof. The attacker forges a signature with probability $\Pr[\mathsf{Forge}_1] + \Pr[\mathsf{Forge}_2]$. By Lemmas 8 and 9, this is bounded by $3q_1 \cdot 2^{-8n} + q' \cdot 2^{-8n}$, where q_1, q' are as in those claims. Since each H-query by the attacker increases the value of at most one of q_1 or q', the claimed bound follows.

Acknowledgments. I thank Laurie E. Law and Jerome A. Solinas for their encouragement and suggestions, as well as for bringing the Leighton-Micali patent [8] to my attention.

References

1. Bernstein, D.J., et al.: SPHINCS: practical stateless hash-based signatures. In: Oswald, E., Fischlin, M. (eds.) EUROCRYPT 2015, Part I. LNCS, vol. 9056, pp. 368–397. Springer, Heidelberg (2015). doi:10.1007/978-3-662-46800-5_15
2. Buchmann, J., Dahmen, E., Szydlo, M.: Hash-based digital signature schemes. In: Bernstein, D.J., Buchmann, J., Dahmen, E. (eds.) Post-Quantum Cryptography, pp. 35–93. Springer, Heidelberg (2009)
3. Galbraith, S.D., Malone-Lee, J., Smart, N.: Public-key signatures in the multi-user setting. Inf. Process. Lett. **83**(5), 263–266 (2002)
4. Hülsing, A., Butin, D., Gazdag, S., Mohaisen, A.: XMSS: extended hash-based signatures. Internet Draft draft-irtf-cfrg-xmss-hash-based-signatures-06, 6 July 2016. http://datatracker.ietf.org
5. Katz, J., Lindell, Y.: Introduction to Modern Cryptography, 2nd edn. Chapman & Hall/CRC Press, New York (2014)
6. Kiltz, E., Masny, D., Pan, J.: Optimal security proofs for signatures from identification schemes. In: Robshaw, M., Katz, J. (eds.) CRYPTO 2016, Part II. LNCS, vol. 9815, pp. 33–61. Springer, Heidelberg (2016). doi:10.1007/978-3-662-53008-5_2
7. Lamport, L.: Constructing digital signatures from a one-way function. Tehcnical Report SRI-CSL-98, SRI Intl. Computer Science Laboratory (1979)
8. Leighton, F.T., Micali, S.: Large provably fast and secure digital signature schemes based on secure hash functions. U.S. Patent 5,432,852, 11 July 1995
9. McGrew, D., Curcio, M.: Hash-based signatures. Internet Draft draft-mcgrew-hash-sigs-02, 4 July 2014. https://datatracker.ietf.org/doc/draft-mcgrew-hash-sigs/02
10. McGrew, D., Curcio, M.: Hash-based signatures. Internet Draft draft-mcgrew-hash-sigs-04, 21 March 2016. https://datatracker.ietf.org/doc/draft-mcgrew-hash-sigs
11. Merkle, R.C.: Secrecy, authentication, and public-key systems. Ph.D. Thesis, Stanford University (1979)
12. Merkle, R.C.: A certified digital signature. In: Brassard, G. (ed.) CRYPTO 1989. LNCS, vol. 435, pp. 218–238. Springer, Heidelberg (1990). doi:10.1007/0-387-34805-0_21
13. Naor, M., Yung, M.: Universal one-way hash functions and their cryptographic applications. In: Proceedings of 21st Annual Symposium on Theory of Computing (STOC), pp. 33–44. ACM (1989)
14. Rompel, J.: One-way functions are necessary and sufficient for secure signatures. In: Proceedings of 22nd Annual ACM Symposium on Theory of Computing (STOC), pp. 387–394. ACM (1990)

Author Index

Printed in the United States
by Bookmasters

Printed in the United States
By Bookmasters